FOUR GEORGIAN AND PRE-REVOLUTIONARY PLAYS

Also edited by David Thomas and published by St. Martin's Press

SIX RESTORATION AND FRENCH NEOCLASSIC PLAYS

PHEDRA, THE MISER, TARTUFFE, ALL FOR LOVE,
THE COUNTRY WIFE, LOVE FOR LOVE

Four Georgian and Pre-Revolutionary Plays

The Rivals

She Stoops to Conquer

The Marriage of Figaro

Emilia Galotti

Introduced and Edited by

DAVID THOMAS
Professor of Theatre Studies, University of Warwick

St. Martin's Press
New York

FOUR GEORGIAN AND PRE-REVOLUTIONARY PLAYS

For information, address:

St. Martin's Press, Scholarly and Reference Division, 175 Fifth Avenue, New York, N.Y. 10010

First published in the United States of America in 1998

This book is printed on paper suitable for recycling and made from fully managed and sustained forest sources.

Printed in Malaysia

ISBN 0–312–21398–0 clothbound
ISBN 0–312–21399–9 paperback

Library of Congress Cataloging-in-Publication Data
Four Georgian and pre-revolutionary plays / introduced and edited by David Thomas.
p. cm.
Includes bibliographical references.
Contents: 1. The rivals — 2. She stoops to conquer — 3. The marriage of Figaro — 4. Emilia Galotti.
ISBN 0–312–21398–0 (cloth : alk. paper). — ISBN 0–312–21399–9 (pbk. : alk. paper)
1. Drama—18th century—History and criticism. 2. Drama—18th century. I. Thomas, David, 1942–
PN1841.F68 1998
822'.508—dc21 98–10702
CIP

Contents

List of Illustrations

(*Reproduced from the author's collection*)

Acknowledgements

In preparing this volume, I have had invaluable help from staff in the Reading Room of the British Library, and the University Libraries of Warwick and Bristol. I should also like to record my thanks to the University of Warwick for generous research leave and for making a grant to cover some of the costs involved in preparing this volume for publication. In that context I would like to thank Kate Brennan for helping to key in the play texts for this volume. My thanks are also due to Professor W. D. Howarth, Emeritus Professor of French at the University of Bristol, and Honorary Professor at the University of Warwick, for his helpful comments on my introduction to *The Marriage of Figaro*. As ever, the staff at Macmillan Press have given their unstinting help and support in bringing this volume to publication. I am particularly indebted to my commissioning editors, Margaret Bartley and Belinda Holdsworth. I would also like to thank Valery Rose and Nick Allen for their attention to detail in copy-editing and setting the text. On a more personal note, I would like to thank Coucou Lyall for her warm and untiring support.

General Introduction

England: The Cultural and Political Context

After a century of rebellion and civil discord, provoked by power struggles between a succession of Stuart monarchs and parliament, the eighteenth century brought relative peace and stability to English society. Following the death of Queen Anne in 1714, the Protestant succession was guaranteed, in accordance with the Act of Settlement of 1701, by inviting George I (great-grandson of James I and Elector of Hanover) to be king of England. Speaking no English and with little interest in his new kingdom, George I was content to leave the government of the country to the group of powerful Whig grandees who had engineered his accession to the throne. This permitted the development of a system of government by cabinet, consisting of senior members of the dominant party in the House of Commons, presided over by a chairman or prime minister. Policy decisions for most of the eighteenth century were therefore shaped by elected politicians, including powerful prime ministers, such as Walpole and Pitt, and by rivalry between the political parties (the Tories and the Whigs), rather than by a destructive and damaging struggle for supremacy between king and parliament.

In contrast to continental Europe, where middle-class aspirations remained largely thwarted by various forms of absolute rule, the power and wealth of England's middle classes had grown steadily since the Glorious Revolution of 1688, when the Catholic monarch James II had been ousted from the throne by his own daughter Mary and her Protestant husband, William of Orange. Throughout the eighteenth century, international trade and commerce (including the lucrative slave trade), as well as new opportunities for personal investment, brought increased potential for advancement to large numbers of people throughout the kingdom. Traditional class barriers still existed, but education and enterprise enabled talented individuals to achieve a degree of social mobility that was unthinkable elsewhere in Europe. Although there was much grinding poverty, with all the brutality and suffering that followed from it, there was also the possibility of gracious living for those who knew how to benefit from an enterprise culture. The growing wealth of the middle classes brought with it opportunities for local craftsmen and artisans of all kinds, as well as architects and builders. The style of furniture, interior decoration and architecture that developed during the Georgian era represents a norm of functional elegance which still inspires the work of modern designers and architects. It was an age that likewise saw an unprecedented blossoming in the worlds of the arts and letters.[1]

These are some of the positive achievements for which the reigns of George I, II and III are remembered. But the Georgian era was also an age of remarkable hypocrisy. The middle classes prided themselves on their Protestant and even Puritan values, which led them to demand the banishing of all crudity and obscenity from theatres and places of public entertainment. Meanwhile, many were content to make their fortunes from the slave trade and others engaged in commerce with the kind of rapaciousness satirised in John Gay's *Beggar's Opera*. The same people who expected plays and novels to offer sentimental character drawing and plot lines were content to ignore the poverty and degradation confronting them, on a daily basis, in their towns and cities. Underneath the veneer of polite manners, gentility and sentimental attitudes in literature, there was a hard streak of selfishness and brutality just below the surface of Georgian society. It was this that Sheridan was to reflect so brilliantly in his icy masterpiece, *The School for Scandal*.

The eighteenth century began and ended with major wars: the war of the Spanish succession in the first decade and the Napoleonic wars in the last. The only trace of these momentous events in the plays of the period is a fleeting reference to some of Marlborough's victories in Farquhar's play *The Recruiting Officer* (1706). By the 1770s, the effects of the direct censorship imposed by the Lord Chamberlain's office and the indirect censorship exercised by the theatre managers of Drury Lane and Covent Garden ensured that contemporary playwrights avoided any subject matter that might give the least offence. In the 1770s when Sheridan and Goldsmith

1. See John Brewer, *The Pleasures of the Imagination: English Culture in the Eighteenth Century* (London: Harper Collins, 1997).

wrote their major plays, England was at war in North America, losing its American colonies in the war of independence; France was in turmoil and was later to find itself in the throes of revolution (1789). There is no hint of this in the work of Goldsmith and Sheridan. Both men wrote for a society that was more interested in looking inwards at its own concerns than in looking outwards to a wider world.

France: The Cultural and Political Context

Politics in France during the eighteenth century was dominated by the legacy of Louis XIV. When he died in 1715 he bequeathed to his five-year-old successor a highly centralised state which he had ruled with a rod of iron. He had moulded France into a powerful nation by the sheer force of his own personality. In reality, however, he had not resolved the conflict between king and nobles; he had merely succeeded in taming them for the duration of his reign. Nor had he managed to reform the judiciary or France's antiquated system of taxation. He left behind him an essentially unstable structure which depended for its success far too much on the skills and personality of the ruler.

After the death of Louis XIV, two kings ruled France in the eighteenth century. Louis XV, following the regency of Philip of Orleans, reigned from 1723 to 1774, and his grandson, Louis XVI, reigned from 1774 until his execution during the reign of terror in 1792. Both were weak and indecisive. This opened the way for greedy and fractious nobles, who had last flexed their muscles during the Fronde in the 1650s, to regain some of the power they had sacrificed to Louis XIV. Versailles had been exploited by Louis XIV to impoverish the nobility with expensive dress codes and to fetter them with the iron bands of court ritual and etiquette. The two kings who ruled after him found the position reversed. It was now the nobility who exploited the intrigue and formal etiquette of the court to ensure that royal policies, especially any attempt at political reform, were invariably thwarted. Individuals approaching the king, or ministers appointed by the king, found themselves facing hostile groups of high-born nobles who fought for their privileges, and against any reform, with great ferocity.[1] Even the local *parlements*

1. This process is reflected in some detail in Patrice Leconte's film *Ridicule* (1996).

which administered justice were controlled by greedy and corrupt nobles. Throughout the century, the two kings fought repeated but fruitless battles against these *parlements*.

The most significant social change of the century occurred unnoticed by royalty or aristocracy: arguably they were too self-engrossed to notice. This was the growing importance of what was called the third estate: the middle class of enterprising lawyers, minor civil servants, financiers, small landowners and intellectuals who ran the towns and cities of the nation, raised loans for the nation's wars, and wrote the artistic and cultural masterpieces of the age. It was this same class who had spearheaded the English revolution, the Civil War, in the 1640s. In England, they finally achieved the recognition and the constitutional monarchy they desired in 1688. In France, throughout the eighteenth century, their political and social ambitions were constantly thwarted.

As a typical representative of the upper middle class, the story of Beaumarchais's life sums up the frustrations and limitations suffered by men of his class on an almost daily basis. When Figaro utters his astonishing critique of the nobility in his final-act soliloquy, he is essentially expressing the resentment felt by the whole third estate in France. Beaumarchais was only allowed to express this critique in public in 1784 because powerful groups of nobles, including the king's brother, saw him as a useful tool to be exploited in their own campaigns against royal authority. Four years later, in 1788, aristocratic and ecclesiastic members of the recalled *parlements* and the States General made the same assumption that they could exploit the views of the minority third estate representatives to further their essentially aristocratic rebellion against the king's authority. They miscalculated badly. In much the same way that Beaumarchais refused to be used as a mere tool of the nobility, the enterprising representatives of the third estate refused to be exploited by nobles and priests in the meeting of the States General in June 1788. They insisted on their representation being doubled and then renamed the States General the National Assembly. In the following month, the Bastille was stormed and revolution began.

The lawyers, landowners and officials who belonged to the National Assembly found, as did Beaumarchais, that they had unleashed forces in the revolution which they could not always control. The impoverished members of the mob in Paris and in other provincial cities were the necessary shock troops of the revolution. Occasionally, their behaviour got out of hand and even the enterprising members of the third estate found themselves threatened. However, by the mid-1790s the mob was suppressed (having gained nothing), the aristocracy had been either executed or forced into exile, and the members of the third estate emerged as the true victors of the revolution they had unleashed.

It is fascinating how many of these tensions emerge from Beaumarchais's play *Le Mariage de Figaro*. Beaumarchais was in many ways a typical representative of the third estate or upper middle classes who invariably found his progress in life either threatened or thwarted by the snobbery, the intrigues, the arrogance and the corruption of the nobility and the system of justice they administered. In *Figaro*, underneath the superficial gaiety, Beaumarchais's own frustration (and those of his class) are given frank and effective expression.

Germany: The Cultural and Political Context

The history of Germany in the eighteenth century is very different from that of England and France. For a start, Germany was not a nation state and would not become one until 1871. Since the Middle Ages, Germany had been a sprawling collection of large and small principalities, duchies and free cities held together within a federation known grandly as the Holy Roman Empire. The emperor who ruled over this federation was elected by the most important princes within the federation: hence the title given them of Elector or (in German) Kurfürst. In both England and France, the daily lives of citizens and peasants were affected by the legislative decisions of the central authority: an elected government in England and an absolute monarch in France. In Germany the whole structure of government was different. The distant figure-head of the emperor might pursue grand alliances and engage in international politics, but the day-to-day reality of life for the citizens in their various principalities was controlled by their immediate ruler.

Tensions between an absolute monarch and increasingly ambitious members of the middle classes led to civil war in England in the 1640s and to revolution in France in 1789. Such tensions were diluted through fragmentation in Germany. In the first half of the seventeenth century, the German-speaking lands had been ravaged by thirty years of warfare fought between the largely Catholic forces of the south and the Protestant forces of the north, allied with King Gustavus Adolphus of Sweden. The Peace of Westphalia of 1648, which brought these long years of conflict to an end, only served to confirm the essentially fragmented structure of government within Germany. The princes within the federation of the Holy Roman Empire were given even greater power than before, extending now to the choice of religious confession for their particular state: Protestant or Catholic. After the many years of religious conflict and pointless slaughter, ordinary citizens were content to accept the absolute authority of their particular ruler if this brought them peace and stability.

The quality of government in Germany's principalities and free cities varied enormously. The larger states were governed by an efficient and able bureaucracy (answerable to the ruler). They were also able to fund a large standing army, which made them forces to be reckoned with. Throughout the eighteenth century, the state of Prussia saw a steady growth in its power and importance, which increased dramatically after it triumphed in a seven-year war against its neighbouring state of Saxony. Most principalities were untroubled by any such conflicts right up until the time of the French Revolution. In all principalities, however, there was an enormous feudal gulf between members of the aristocracy and the middle classes, who provided the lawyers, many of the administrators, the tutors, the financiers and the creative artists of the period. Members of the middle classes might be permitted to contribute to the work of the bureaucracy which governed a principality, but they had no political power at all.

Germany's various princes and dukes exercised absolute authority over their subjects. For the most part, they were benevolent autocrats. Viewing their neighbours as competitors, they were keen to govern prosperous states and keen to show their prowess in cultural political terms by building fine palaces, theatres and opera houses for themselves. Initially the culture they aspired to emulate was French; their role model was Louis XIV. Even in the Prussian court at Berlin, French was the official court language. Until the mid-eighteenth century, German was regarded as the inferior tongue of uneducated peasants. Thus it was that German princes brought French actors and Italian singers into their courts. It was not until the latter half of the eighteenth century that they began to offer patronage to German men of letters, including Lessing, Schiller and Goethe, all of whom enjoyed the support of a noble patron.

Similar cultural priorities were to be found amongst the middle classes. In the first part of the eighteenth century, it was French culture that was taken seriously. There were no German plays, no serious German actors (only poor strolling players), and no permanent playhouses in German towns and cities. Lessing was to play a significant role, not only as Germany's first great man of letters, but also in helping to launch the first permanent theatre company in Hamburg in the 1760s.

Most of Germany's states were governed effectively and reasonably. Inevitably, however, there were examples of unenlightened rule. The structure of absolute power all too easily invites abuse. This was something that worried Germany's new men of letters. Both Lessing in his play *Emilia Galotti* and Schiller in *Love and Intrigue* show how the exercise of absolute authority can corrupt to the point where it leads to murder. Both of them also show an unbridgeable gulf – socially, emotionally and sexually – between the aristocracy and the middle classes. It is significant, however, that Lessing's play could be given its first performance at the court of his patron, the Duke of Brunswick, to celebrate the Duchess's birthday. This suggests that his play was intended and viewed by his contemporaries, not as a revolutionary piece in the manner of *Le Mariage de Figaro*, but as a thoughtful piece exploring a difficult issue, namely a young prince's inability to cope with the awesome responsibility of absolute power.

The response to Lessing's play and the calm, thoughtful way in which it was written may help to explain why Germany, unlike England or France, did not experience the political upheaval of revolution. There was dissatisfaction in the middle classes at the way absolute authority was wielded by the various princes and dukes in Germany, but it was not uniformly experienced, and there was no central authority against which to rebel. Devolution brought with it many different forms of frustration, but it also brought a kind of stability.

The Plays

The plays chosen for this volume were all written in the 1770s and represent outstanding achievements in the dramatic literature of their respective countries. Stylistically, they all look back to earlier periods and make use of well-established structural or character archetypes. But they also articulate the values and concerns of their age and their society. All four plays are concerned with the theme of sex and class, but the contrasting treatment of this theme is a reflection of the profoundly different social and political realities of life in England, France and Germany at the time.

In the plays of Sheridan and Goldsmith, the issue of sex and class is treated with gentle and essentially good-natured humour. For Lydia Languish, for instance, a love affair across class boundaries is a question of romantic caprice. She wants to elope with a handsome young man from a lower social class so that she can forfeit her fortune and immerse herself, not in the real world of poverty, but in its make-believe image. For her it is no more than a game. Fortunately, her young lover, Captain Absolute (masquerading as Ensign Beverley), is blessed with enough sound common sense to realise only too well the social and financial advantages of a life underpinned by private wealth, namely property, an estate and above all the freedom to live a life where real choices can be made. In *The Rivals*, issues of caste, family and inherited wealth still play their part. Sir Anthony, for instance, expects his son to accept his father's choice of a bride without demur. But his view is shown to be hopelessly old-fashioned (much as in Congreve's play *Love for Love* where the figure of Sir Sampson is mocked for his authoritarian view of fatherhood). In place of his outmoded view, we have the level-headed approach of his son, Jack: a young man who does his best to reconcile love and reason. He may be in love with Lydia, but he is not blind to her faults. He humours her in her desire to play the rich girl wishing to be poor, but his overriding aim is to get her to marry him. For this he needs sharp wits and a great deal of patience. In contrast to him, his friend Falkland is too irrational to recognise a good woman even when he has already won her commitment. For Sheridan's characters, class does matter. There is a huge gulf between poverty and wealth, but it is not the most important obstacle in affairs of the heart. Destructive games, of the kind Falkland plays, or romantic games, of which Lydia is fond, are both viewed as serious obstacles to human happiness and fulfilment. What is needed above all, when young people feel sexually attracted to each other, is sound common sense.

Goldsmith seems to view class as more of a psychological construct than a tangible reality. Tony Lumpkin, for instance, is a squire's son. But, like his late father, Tony prefers alehouse companions and buxom country wenches to folk of his own class, notably his family. The play shows us the reality of class distinctions and class snobbery. Parents of good stock are keen to find socially appropriate marriage partners for their children. Young men from good families might consider sleeping with a barmaid, but would not normally consider marrying one. Nevertheless, in the figure of Marlow, Goldsmith shows us that class prejudices are the product of social and psychological conditioning. Confronted by Kate Hardcastle as a woman of his own class, Marlow is terrified of her respectability. Confronted by Kate as a barmaid, Marlow is sexually roused. Confronted by Kate as a poor relative, Marlow is emotionally roused. Kate is the same person, simply playing different roles. It is Marlow who invests those roles with social and psychological value. In *She Stoops to Conquer*, Goldsmith probes very convincingly beneath the supposed reality of class and shows it to be no more than a figment of the imagination. For some characters in the play, class is an important issue; for others, it is not. What matters most is the ability to respond openly and honestly to others of whatever social class. In this play, as in Sheridan's, the issue of sex and class gives rise to laughter rather than anger, and laughter that is essentially good natured.

In Beaumarchais's *Le Mariage de Figaro*, the situation is very different. In this play, class divisions are not a mere psychological construct, they are based on harsh realities. Here there is an unbridgeable gulf between the arrogance and selfishness of the aristocracy and the gentler, kinder world of their servants. Count Almaviva could never envisage marrying a serving girl, quite apart from the fact that he is already married to an attractive, but much neglected partner. This does not prevent him, however, from exploiting his social and political status to obtain sexual favours from those he governs. Beaumarchais shows Almaviva's attempt to interfere with the sexual autonomy of his servants to be a corrupt abuse of power. Confronted by the Count's remorseless and repeated attempts to sleep with his bride, Figaro uses the only weapon at his disposal: his quick wits. In the end, however, it is feminine adroitness and solidarity that wins out. Suzanne and the Countess together devise their own effective way of humiliating the Count in public. Their liberal alliance prefigures what was to happen in the coming political revolution in France. Underneath the laughter, Beaumarchais has written a challenging play where the issue of sex and class is shown to be at the very heart of the political debate.

In Lessing's Germany, the abuse of absolute authority is an important issue, but it is not such a burning political issue as in

France. Nevertheless, the divisions between the classes in Germany are as concrete and as important as they are in France. There is a yawning chasm between the aristocracy and those of lesser social rank. Based on a classical model, Lessing's play approaches the problem of sex and class in a more abstract manner than Beaumarchais. What would happen if a prince were to fall in love with a girl from the middle class? Lessing shows us the likely outcome. He might be tempted to use his authority to obtain control over her, effectively to make her his prisoner. While he could never marry her, he might try to prevent her from marrying anyone else. Here too the attempt to use political power to interfere with a subject's sexual and emotional autonomy is viewed with great distaste. However, the play lacks the immediacy of Beaumarchais's attack on the aristocracy. Lessing's play, unlike Beaumarchais's, is not intended to show what does happen but what might happen. Absolute power has temptations built into its fabric, and these can easily be triggered where sexual and emotional responses cut across class and caste boundaries.

The contrasting treatments of the issue of sex and class tell us a great deal about the respective societies for which these four plays were written. In England, for instance, there were real class divisions. But the enterprising middle classes had long since fought and won their battle against the kind of authoritarian regimes that were still the norm in France and Germany. In England there was far greater social mobility than in Continental Europe. There was also very little trace of the frustration of France's third estate which was eventually to explode in bloody revolution. The image we are given of English middle-class society in the plays of Sheridan and Goldsmith is essentially of a country at ease with itself. The problems shown in the plays are more a cause for laughter than anger. In Beaumarchais's play the deceptively light-hearted tone of the piece masks the very real anger and frustration that underpins its whole conception. The play clearly prefigures the revolution that is about to engulf French society and sweep away a stagnating and corrupt absolutist system, based exclusively on aristocratic privilege and royal prerogative. In Germany, there are worries about absolute authority, but these are more abstract than real. The system of government is so diverse and so fragmented that little of the frustration felt by the middle classes in France is to be found in German literature. In Lessing's play, his audience is made very aware of the dangers inherent in a system that gives absolute authority to an immature ruler. However, the problem is seen as a philosophical issue rather than a matter requiring direct political action. This accurately reflects the views of Germany's middle classes who, for the sake of order and stability, continued to show their willingness to tolerate authoritarian government throughout the whole of the nineteenth century.

A Note on Eighteenth-century Theatre in England, France and Germany

Throughout the eighteenth century in England, no formal censorship was applied to literature, journalism and the fine arts. Nor were there laws of libel offering the kind of protection to individuals expected today. This explains the extraordinary ferocity to be found in many eighteenth-century cartoons, lampooning public and even royal personages, along with the outspoken comments to be found in journals and newspapers. For a brief period during the 1720s and early 1730s, it seemed as if the theatre might be set to achieve the same independence from censorship and legal control. London saw an unprecedented blossoming of small fringe theatres, and writers such as Gay and Fielding emerged to satisfy a growing popular demand for topical political satires. Eventually the prime minister, Walpole, grew tired of finding himself and his fellow Whigs subjected to every kind of satirical attack on the London stage. In 1737 he decided to take action and did so with characteristic ruthlessness. Biding his time, he waited until the end of the parliamentary session, when many Members of Parliament had already left for their vacation, and introduced draconian new controls over the theatre by way of an amendment to a vagrancy law passed in 1714. In future public performances throughout the kingdom were to be restricted to the patent houses in Drury Lane, Covent Garden and the King's Theatre in the Haymarket. All plays acted for 'hire, gain or reward' were to be submitted to the Lord Chamberlain's office for approval at least fourteen days before the intended performance. Anyone contravening these provisions would be subject to a severe fine and would lose any licence for performance they may previously have obtained. There was little opposition to the new bill in the House of Commons; in the House of Lords only Lord Chesterfield spoke eloquently against it. It received the royal assent on 21 June 1737.

In London, the Licensing Act had immediate and far-reaching

effects. The various uncontrolled and outspoken fringe theatres were soon forced to close their doors and any attempts to build new playhouses were firmly resisted by the patent holders. The monopoly enjoyed by the patent holders at Drury Lane and Covent Garden made it very difficult for aspiring young playwrights to have their work accepted for perfomance. The managers of the two patent theatres preferred to revive tried and tested favourites from earlier periods. This explains why the great actors of the eighteenth century, such as Garrick, Kemble and Macklin, are remembered primarily for their performances in plays by Shakespeare. Popular entertainment was catered for in comedy or pantomime afterpieces.

In the provinces, the provisions of the Licensing Act were widely ignored by local justices as long as visiting theatre troupes played in temporary or converted locations. By the middle of the century, however, new permanent playhouses were constructed in a number of provincial cities, which meant that individuals could and did bring prosecutions against the theatre owners under the terms of the Licensing Act.[1] However, there was growing pressure from provincial audiences for more theatrical performances, not less. From the late 1760s, the problem was resolved by a series of parliamentary Enabling Acts designed to give letters patent to individual playhouses already constructed in provincial cities. Edinburgh was the first to acquire its 'Theatre Royal' with an Enabling Act passed in 1767, Bath followed in 1768, and similar patents were granted to theatres throughout the kingdom over the next few decades. In contrast, the situation in London remained unaltered until the Theatres Act of 1843 permitted the construction of new theatre buildings. The censorship provisions contained in Walpole's Licensing Act of 1737 were re-enacted by the 1843 legislation and were not finally repealed until the Theatres Act of 1968. For over two hundred years, Walpole's censorship provisions imposed severe restrictions upon the dialogue and subject matter that might be used by English playwrights in their work. Arguably, this was a disproportionately heavy price to pay for a few impudent political satires written by Gay and Fielding.

The production of *Le Mariage de Figaro* at the Comédie-Française in 1784 caused widespread astonishment. Unaware of the support Beaumarchais had enjoyed amongst powerful and rebellious nobles,

1. See David Thomas (ed.), *Theatre in Europe: A Documentary History. Restoration and Georgian England 1660–1788* (Cambridge: Cambridge University Press, 1989) p. 222.

audiences and critics alike were amazed that the play had been sanctioned for public performance. Throughout the eighteenth century, the Bourbon dynasty had kept tight control over the theatres in Paris. With some justice, the theatre was viewed as a potentially dangerous and subversive place. The only regular companies licensed for performance in Paris were the Comédie-Française, the Italian Players and the Opéra. Direct control over the Comédie-Française and the Italian Players was exercised by MM les Premiers Gentilshommes de la Chambre du Roi, who operated under the overall control of the Office of Menus Plaisirs du Roi. The players in these companies were all answerable to the Office of the Menus Plaisirs: they received a royal pension, but otherwise organised their company finances on a sharing basis. Their company structure was democratic, with no single player in overall control. Although the patent companies were subject to strict royal control, they enjoyed a number of privileges, including pensions and monopoly performance rights.

The Comédie-Française went through a long period of declining popularity from the death of Louis XIV until 1750. New forms of entertainment offered by the Italians and the fairground theatres were proving very attractive to Paris audiences. However, from 1750 until the outbreak of revolution, the theatre began to recover its former popularity. In particular, the production of *Le Mariage de Figaro* in 1784 was an enormous public success, enjoying the longest run of packed performances ever seen in the history of the company. Throughout the early part of the century, members of the audience were permitted to pay for expensive seats on the stage. This privilege was eventually abolished in 1759, much to the chagrin of the wealthy young men of fashion. Another significant feature of the playhouse, the standing pit, was also finally abolished in 1782 with the move to a new theatre building. This produced a noticeable calming effect on audiences. The outbreak of revolution led to a rapid proliferation of new theatre companies and playhouses in Paris, which in turn had a catastrophic effect on the box office takings of the patent houses.

After the silencing of the Italian players in 1697, fairground theatres began to mount improvised pieces to cater for the tastes of the audience who had patronised the Italian players. Initially they were tolerated as long as they did not perform straight plays or any other form of entertainment in direct competition with the officially licensed companies. But when the Italians returned to Paris in 1716, and especially after they were made an official troupe with royal subsidy in 1723, there were constant legal battles between the fairground theatres and the patent companies. The fairground theatres attempted to keep a step ahead by developing new forms of entertainment, including pantomime and comic opera. But as new forms grew into popular and established genres, they were sometimes annexed by the patent companies. For instance, the enormous popularity of comic opera in the fairground theatres of the 1750s led to the Italian players asking for the exclusive rights to perform *opéra comique*. This they were granted in 1762. Undaunted, the fairground companies opened boulevard theatres in the Boulevard du Temple during the 1760s where they presented a repertoire based on pantomime and melodrama.

In the provinces at the beginning of the century, small itinerant troupes were unlicensed but normally operated under the protection of an aristocratic patron. Later in the century, patents were granted by the King's Intendant or Governor in each province for the building of playhouses and the formation of permanent companies in France's major cities. This led to the construction of a veritable spate of new theatre buildings from the 1760s. All plays performed in public in Paris and the provinces were subject to strict police censorship, although this was less rigorously applied in the provinces. The object of this tight system of playhouse licences combined with strict censorship was to ensure that the theatre remained firmly under royal control. Any breaches in the system of control led to immediate royal intervention. Beaumarchais, for instance, found himself confined to prison, albeit briefly, for daring to comment on the difficulties he had faced in bringing *Le Mariage de Figaro* to performance. More drastic punishment was meted out to the Italian players in 1697 by Louis XIV for daring to make disparaging comments about his mistress, Mme de Maintenon, in one of their improvised performances. They were exiled from France and were not allowed back into the country until 1716, during the regency of Philip of Orleans. Faced with such threats of arbitrary silencing, imprisonment or banishment, it is not surprising that most playwrights and actors during the eighteenth century were content to obey the rules and to do their best to avoid offending their royal masters.

In contrast to England and France, there were no permanent playhouses in German cities at the beginning of the eighteenth century. Throughout the seventeenth century and the early part of the eighteenth century, travelling troupes of players (including English players) had visited German towns and cities and had given occasional command performances at aristocratic courts. Most of these entertainments were primitive and distinctly earthy in flavour. It was not until the late 1720s that any attempt was made to introduce a more demanding repertoire by a touring company. This occurred when the troupe of players belonging to Caroline Neuber began to collaborate with a distinguished academic writer, Johann Christoph Gottsched. In 1730 Gottsched wrote his *Critical Poetics for Germans* (*Versuch einer critischen Dichtkunst vor die Deutschen*) in which he roundly condemned Baroque extravagance in literature and theatrical forms such as opera and robust farce. Instead he commended French classicism as a model to be followed by German writers. His ideas had a profound influence on Caroline Neuber, whose troupe began to present performances of French classical plays as well as Gottsched's own piece *The Dying Cato*, adapted mainly from Addison's play *Cato*.

As the century progressed, troupes of French and Italian players gave command performances at court theatres throughout Germany. However, it was not until 1753 that the first purpose-built theatre was constructed for public performance in Germany. This building was erected in Königsberg, East Prussia, by Konrad Ackermann. In the following decade, Ackermann constructed a second purpose-built theatre in Hamburg in 1765. It was in this playhouse that the first German National Theatre company began performing in 1767, having engaged Lessing as their dramaturgical advisor. The enterprise lasted for only two years. However, the example set by the Hamburg theatre company, and the impact of Lessing's *Hamburg Dramaturgy*, led to the rapid formation of further companies in purpose-built theatres all over Germany. By 1774 there were some fourteen companies playing in both courts and towns.

Two court theatres had a particularly strong impact on the development of German theatrical traditions. The first, formed at Mannheim in 1777, took over the title of National Theatre. Mannheim's National Theatre company was directed by Baron von Dalberg, who held regular committee meetings with staff to discuss the running of the company and questions of acting style. Dalberg's company acquired a reputation for distinguished ensemble work and were even prepared to mount productions of controversial plays, including the young Schiller's pre-Romantic dramas, beginning with *Die Räuber* (*The Robbers*) in 1782. The second court theatre that was to have a significant impact on German theatre traditions was in Weimar. A new theatre was built there in 1780 to replace an older building that had burnt down. The writer Goethe was appointed director of the theatre in 1791. His interest in verse drama, visual composition and precise rules for actors ushered in a new form of neoclassicism in the theatre. Goethe's reputation as a writer ensured that his theatrical work at Weimar attracted widespread attention.

In general, most German theatres by the end of the century were presenting the same mixture of light comedy and melodrama that was popular in the French theatre. Any censorship exercised in German theatres normally depended on the attitude of the particular court authorities. However, in Prussia, which was the largest and most powerful state, control over censorship was given to the police authorities with effect from 1810. (These censorship provisions were not finally abolished until the start of the Weimar Republic in Germany after the end of the First World War.) By the end of the eighteenth century, German theatre had grown from nothing to fifty theatre companies housed in permanent buildings in the various large and small states as well as the free cities. This was a remarkable achievement, in which artistic endeavour and cultural politics were inextricably intertwined. A mixture of civic and aristocratic pride ensured that every major city or major court wished to be seen as a centre for artistic excellence. Theatres and opera houses provided a visible and tangible expression of this desire. This same tradition has continued in modern Germany, where funding for the arts is provided, not by the federal government, but by the various Länder who all wish to be seen as centres for artistic excellence and achievement.

A Note on the Texts

The text of *The Rivals* is taken mainly from Sheridan's third corrected edition of the play, published in 1776, with some further small corrections in respect of punctuation from the fourth and fifth editions of 1785 and 1791. The Preface is taken from the first edition; it was omitted from all later editions. The text of *She Stoops to Conquer* is taken from the first edition. I have retained the original spelling and punctuation of the first editions, though a number of silent editorial changes have been made. Obvious typographical errors have been corrected on the basis of later editions; the modern spelling of the letter 's' has been used throughout. All stage directions have been placed between square brackets, and conventions of punctuation and syntax within the brackets have been silently standardised. I have made no attempt to list variant readings in later editions in footnotes. Generally, footnotes have been kept to a minimum so that the text may be read without constant editorial interruption.

The same general editorial principles have been applied to the translations of plays by Lessing and Beaumarchais. The translated text of Lessing's *Emilia Galotti* is an accurate and close rendering of the original. However, Holcroft makes it clear in his preface that his version of *Le Mariage de Figaro* is an adaptation, based on a memorised version of the original Paris production. When he visited Paris to obtain a copy of the play late in 1784, he found that publication of an authorised version had been delayed as Beaumarchais was experiencing problems with the censors. A pirated edition of the play, based on a memorised version of the original Paris production, was published in Amsterdam in 1785; but this also appeared too late in print for Holcroft to use. Instead, he drew on yet another memorised version of the original Paris production. In Holcroft's adaptation, prepared from this memorised version, longer speeches are broken up and there are more exchanges of dialogue between characters. The strict order in which topics are dealt with is also altered. Some cuts are made, though surprisingly few, given the length of the original (Holcroft suggests further cuts that may be made in performance). Far more detailed stage directions are included than in Beaumarchais's authorised text. If the printed stage directions are based on what actually happened in the Paris production of 1784, they are likely to provide a real clue as to how the play was interpreted by the original cast. One thing that comes over far more strongly than in the authorised text is the depth of feeling the Countess has for Chérubin. (By 1784 Beaumarchais had begun work on his final play in the Figaro trilogy, *La mère coupable*, which revolves around the Countess's later adultery with Chérubin.) Some references in the authorised text are omitted, for instance, the Countess contemplating entering a convent in Act II; the Count finding himself unable to understand why he has become so entangled with Suzanne; and Figaro's 'God damn' speech, which is transposed to comments on a jingling purse and the phrase 'S'il vous plait'. One significant section omitted altogether (as it was in the Paris production) is Marceline's tirade against men in Act III. In Act V, Figaro's long monologue is broken up by making the initial section a dialogue between Figaro and the Doctor. Additional lines are added to Figaro's monologue that seem to have more in common with Beaumarchais's original manuscript version of the play than the text that was finally approved for publication. In particular, there is outspoken criticism of the behaviour of the Count and the aristocracy in general and there are also pointed references to economic affairs and to censorship. Finally, the vaudeville with which the play closes in the authorised text is omitted. Despite these various changes and cuts, Holcroft's adaptation was faithful to the spirit of the original and provided a lively version of the play that was suited to English tastes. The puzzle with which it leaves us is this: did Holcroft's French collaborator have access to an early manuscript version of the play which Beaumarchais had to alter before meeting the demands of the censors, or were some of the lines included in Holcroft's version ever spoken by the actor playing Figaro in an actual performance of the play in Paris? If they were, it may help to explain the sense of astonishment on the part of Beaumarchais's contemporaries that permission was ever given for his play to be performed in public.

The editions of the plays consulted may be found at the following locations in the British Library:

Text	*British Library Press Mark*
R. B. Sheridan, *The Rivals*	
First edition (London: John Wilkie, 1775)	[C.71.e.3]
Third edition (London: John Wilkie, 1776)	[1342.o.13]
Fourth edition (London: G. Wilkie, 1785)	[1508/645]
Fifth edition (London: G. & T. Wilkie, 1791)	[11777.e.65]
Oliver Goldsmith, *She Stoops to Conquer*	
First edition (London: F. Newbery, 1773)	[643.i.8 (3)]
Second edition (London: F. Newbery, 1773)	[1486.c.18]
Third edition (London: F. Newbery, 1773)	[1578/8099]
Caron de Beaumarchais, *The Marriage of Figaro*, from the French by Thomas Holcroft	
(London: G. G. J. Robinson, 1785)	[11777.g.9]
G. E. Lessing, *Emilia Galotti*, trans. Benjamin Thompson	
(London: Vernor & Hood, 1800)	[1506/65]

A number of modern scholarly editions of the plays by Sheridan and Goldsmith have been consulted. These include:

The Dramatic Works of Richard Brinsley Sheridan, vol. 1, ed. Cecil Price (Oxford: Clarendon Press, 1973).
The Collected Works of Oliver Goldsmith, vol. 5, ed. Arthur Friedman (Oxford: Clarendon Press, 1966).

A number of modern translations and adaptations of Beaumarchais are in print, but at present there are no scholarly editions available of his plays in translation. There are no easily available modern translations of Lessing's play.

The Rivals

Richard Sheridan

INTRODUCTION

Sheridan was born in Dublin in 1751. His father, Thomas Sheridan, was at the time the manager of the Smock Alley Theatre in Dublin. After a serious riot in the theatre in 1754, Thomas relinquished control of the theatre and moved for two years to London, working as an actor under John Rich's management at Covent Garden. He returned to Dublin in 1756 and attempted once more to manage the Smock Alley Theatre, but this time he faced the prospect of ruinous competition from a new theatre built by the actor Spranger Barry. Once again, he was forced to return to London. Thomas Sheridan was one of those individuals who seem destined to be in the wrong place at the wrong time. Apart from his skills as an actor (and he was once considered a potential rival to Garrick), he also had talents as an educational theorist and a compiler of dictionaries. None of these enterprises met with sufficient acclaim to ensure a stable livelihood. Thomas aspired to the status of a gentleman, but all he managed was to accumulate sufficient debts to oblige him to flee from his creditors to France with his wife in 1764.

For most of this turbulent period, the young Richard Sheridan was forced to live apart from his parents. Initially, he was left with relatives in Dublin. Later, when the family fled to France, he was sent to board at Harrow and to fend for himself during the vacations. In contrast, the eldest son Charles was allowed to accompany his parents wherever they lived. It takes little imagination to see how this must have rankled. For most of his childhood, young Sheridan felt neglected and passed over. Not surprisingly, he turned into something of a rebel, a wild and impetuous lad, given to practical jokes and tricks, who found it easier to laugh at life than face up to the sadness he felt deep within him. The same is true of so many of the characters he was to create a decade later in his best-known comedies.

Having survived the vicissitudes of a less than happy childhood, Sheridan was denied the possibility of studying at university because of his father's precarious financial position. Instead, he was obliged to rejoin his family and help to run the household when his father returned from France in 1770 and moved to Bath with the aim of setting up an Academy of Oratory. (His mother had died in France in 1766.) These next few years in Bath were to be decisive for Sheridan's future career. They not only furnished him with a wealth of autobiographical material on which to draw in his first play, *The Rivals*, but they also provided him with a rich gallery of character types of the kind he grew accustomed to meeting and observing in Bath's elegant assembly rooms and in the many public squares and parades.

Bath had developed by the 1770s into a fashionable spa town for the rich and the indolent. Its splendid new buildings, including the Circus and the Royal Crescent, designed by John Wood the Younger, were the envy of England. Its theatre in Orchard Street, opened in 1750, frequently attracted star actors from London, and it was the first provincial theatre in England to be granted a royal patent in 1768. Its Pump Room and recently completed New Assembly Rooms provided the setting for expensive entertainments as well as everyday social intercourse. Concerts, balls and gaming, regulated by strict rules of conduct established by Beau Nash, ensured an unbroken round of pleasurable activities for those with the leisure and the money to enjoy them. This was the clientele on which Thomas Sheridan set his sights in moving to Bath; his Academy of Oratory was aimed at wealthy patrons. In order to advertise his undertaking, he organised a series of so-called 'Attic Entertainments', or programmes of oratory and music. In these he collaborated with Thomas Linley, who was one of the leading musicians in Bath at the time. Linley's sixteen-year-old daughter, Elizabeth, often took part in these entertainments. Her voice was much admired, as indeed was her beauty. Predictably perhaps, young Richard Sheridan was soon infatuated with her, as was his brother Charles. But they were only two of her many admirers.

Richard Sheridan's love affair with Elizabeth, which blossomed over the three years 1770–1773 and culminated in their marriage in April 1773, provided the raw material for *The Rivals*. Theirs was a romantic tale, with moments of high drama and near farce. It involved challenges and duels, elopement and flight, followed by parental anger and forced separation. Differences in social class and financial status were at the heart of the problem. Thomas Sheridan viewed himself as a gentleman; Linley was socially his inferior. It was therefore unthinkable that one of his sons should marry beneath himself into Linley's family. Linley, however, was determined to improve his status in society, using the skills and talents he and his family possessed. (And to signal his social aspirations, he moved into one of the first houses completed in the Royal Crescent in 1771.) Because of her outstanding musical skills, his daughter Elizabeth was a particularly valuable asset. He was only willing to part with her if a potential husband was wealthy enough to make a generous marriage settlement.[1] Clearly, from Linley's point of view, Sheridan was quite unacceptable as a husband, given his lack of wealth.

To begin with, Sheridan had not communicated his feelings to Elizabeth or anyone else for that matter. Although ebullient and headstrong by nature, he could also be silent and calculating when it suited his purpose. Elizabeth was surrounded by potential suitors, including some who posed a real threat to her safety. One such was Captain Charles Matthews. Although recently married to secure himself a comfortable living, he pursued Elizabeth with every kind of emotional blackmail. He threatened either to commit suicide or to blacken her character in public. The upshot was that she was driven to a state of desperation by his constant harassment and even contemplated suicide. It was at this point that Sheridan offered his good offices as a friend who would be prepared to accompany her on a clandestine journey from Bath to find security and peace of mind in a French convent. The idea was of course totally impractical, but it gave the young Sheridan a chance to prove his devotion and affection for Elizabeth. A post-chaise was hired, a chaperon engaged, and the young couple set off from the Royal Crescent while Linley was engaged at a public concert. They even made it to France,

1. Thomas Linley did make one unsuccessful attempt to marry Elizabeth off to a wealthy, elderly suitor called Walter Long. The story of this affair was used by the writer Samuel Foote as the basis for his play *The Maid of Bath*, performed at the Little Theatre in the Haymarket in 1771. See Madeleine Bingham, *Sheridan: The Track of a Comet* (London: George Allen & Unwin, 1972) p. 61.

though by then Elizabeth was too ill to spend more than a few days in a convent.

Inevitably their friendship blossomed into romance. While in France, it is even rumoured that they underwent a form of secret marriage ceremony with the help of a Catholic priest, though this could be no more than a symbolic gesture as they were both still minors. As soon as Linley discovered his daughter's whereabouts, he travelled across the Channel to fetch her home. Sheridan, meanwhile, returned to Bath to find that Matthews had in his absence published a statement in a local newspaper branding him a liar and a scoundrel. Although Matthews had wisely taken refuge in London, Sheridan now set off in hot pursuit. Like his father, he regarded himself with some passion as a gentleman and this was an insult not to be tolerated. Matthews was tracked down late at night and forced to rise from his bed. He refused stubbornly to publish an apology, which meant that a duel was the only way to settle the issue. Eventually a sword-fight was arranged, during which Matthews was forced to beg for his life. Sheridan extracted the apology he wanted and set off for Bath to publish it.

Had the matter rested there, Sheridan might have enjoyed some genuine favour with both friends and family. After all, he had behaved like a true gentleman, the family honour was vindicated, and his conduct towards a young lady in distress had been without blemish. Matthews, in contrast, found himself treated like a leper in polite society. One of his new acquaintances in Wales, Mr Barnett, urged him to fight a second duel, fulfilling in the process much the same role as Sir Lucius O'Trigger in *The Rivals*. A challenge was duly issued and the contestants rode to Kingsdown above Bath.

On this occasion, their duel degenerated into an uncontrolled brawl, with Matthews eventually sitting astride Sheridan, his sword broken, stabbing at his rival's neck with what remained of the blade and the hilt. Eventually, the seconds intervened to stop Matthews butchering his defenceless rival. Matthews fled to France, and Sheridan was driven back to Bath for emergency treatment of his various wounds. The romantic aura of the elopement and the first duel in London had now become tainted. Parental wrath was not slow to follow. Thomas Sheridan had been absent in Dublin while the elopement and first duel had taken place. But now he was back in Bath and determined to put an end to his son's troublesome romance. Young Sheridan was banished to Essex to study for the bar and strictly forbidden even to write to the young Miss Linley. It is not difficult to see how Thomas Sheridan provided the perfect model for the father figure, Sir Anthony Absolute in *The Rivals*. However, unlike Sir Anthony, Thomas Sheridan refused for some years to be reconciled to his son, after Richard had managed to marry his beloved Elizabeth.

The Rivals

In *The Rivals*, Sheridan took the living flesh of his own thoughts, experiences and disappointments, and transformed them into a high comedy of manners in which disaster is miraculously averted through the sudden shifts of his carefully contrived plot. In real life, Sheridan almost bled to death after his duel; in *The Rivals*, the duel is averted. In real life, Sheridan's father obdurately refused to be reconciled with his son until long after the successful performance of *The Rivals*; in the play, Sir Anthony easily forgives his son his various acts of deception and affectionately regards him as a chip off the old block. Sheridan's is not a world in which morality or reason have the upper hand. The world is chaos. People seem impelled to say and do foolish things without knowing why. This is particularly true of Faulkland who seems driven to torment his beloved Julia with senseless doubts and scruples; it is equally true of Acres and Jack Absolute who both find themselves manoeuvred into an absurd situation where they are to fight a duel for no good reason. Love seems perilously close to foolish self-indulgence; self-deception and vapid ignorance seem all pervasive. And yet there is an endearing warmth in his character drawing that reconciles us to the stupidity and folly of the individuals concerned. Above all there is the artist's own supreme control over events through the mechanism of his plot, which ensures that in art, if not in life, it is the writer who has the last laugh.

The hallmark of Sheridan's comedy is his artistic control over experiences that are potentially damaging and destructive. (And this is as true of his later masterpiece *The School for Scandal* as it is of *The Rivals*.) Any production of his plays has to keep this effect of light and shade in a delicately poised balance. If the serious subtext is neglected, what is left is no more than an idle romp. If the folly and even cruelty of some of the characters' behaviour is unduly emphasised, what remains is a world of savage dark farce in which the happy endings of the plays seem strangely out of place. In production, the through-line of the plot needs to be taken seriously.

For it is there one finds Sheridan's artistic triumph over the dark comedy of life.

Although the characters are ultimately subservient to the plot, thoughout the play there are distinct tensions between plot and character drawing, which merit more detailed investigation. A young army officer called Captain Jack Absolute has come to Bath to pay his court to a society heiress called Lydia Languish. She, for her part, is determined not to marry a man of her own class and be made a mere 'Smithfield bargain', as she puts it. On the face of it, such a motive might not seem unreasonable, but in fact Lydia is a romantic dreamer who plays with the notion of elopement and economic hardship without the first idea of what these might entail. Jack Absolute therefore pretends to be a mere ensign by the name of Beverley, in order to gratify her romantic caprice. Meanwhile, Lydia's aunt, Mrs Malaprop, guards her jealously from the attentions of unsuitable lovers and is quite opposed to the notion of her marrying an infantry officer of low rank. Jack's father, Sir Anthony Absolute, arrives on the scene and causes total consternation to his son by demanding that he marry a girl of his father's choice, without even knowing who this might be. Jack of course refuses, much to the fury of his father.

Even more complications follow, however, when Jack discovers that his father intends him to marry Lydia. If he obeys his father, he will disappoint Lydia's romantic dreams. If he disobeys his father, he will lose Lydia anyway. Faced by this choice, he must needs risk disappointing Lydia rather than lose her by defying his father's wishes. Initially, he still attempts to manage a meeting with Mrs Malaprop as Captain Absolute while at the same time pretending to Lydia that he is Ensign Beverley; eventually, however, his deception is revealed and Lydia is petulantly obdurate in her refusal to listen to his excuses. The play on mistaken identities is pure farce, but it underlines a serious point about the nature of identity. Sheridan sees it as not immutable and fixed, but mercurial and changing and ultimately dependent upon one's interaction with others. Yet people are given social labels by others in a way that can blight their happiness and their lives. When Lydia discovers Jack Absolute's real identity, she refuses to have him; he no longer fits her romantic social image of him. It is only through the shifts and turns of the plot that bring her lover face to face with death in the shape of Sir Lucius O'Trigger, a foolish and pugnacious Irishman, that Lydia finally changes her mind and resolves to have her man despite his wealth.

While Jack and Lydia establish for us the social nature of identity, Jack's friend Faulkland and his beloved Julia set out the parameters of psychological identity. Faulkland has an idealised image of his beloved, against which he always measures her in reality. The result is that whatever she does, she is in the wrong because she can never live up to her image. He quarrels with her when he learns that she has danced and sung in society during his absence from her. He also puts her faith in him to a ridiculous test by pretending he must flee the country, only to find that she is more than willing to flee with him. But she is outraged by his behaviour when he reveals that he was only testing her constancy. By failing to accept her as she is in reality, he risks losing her altogether. Indeed, she too, like Lydia, is only reconciled with her lover through the same twists of the plot that bind the other pair. And in her case, the shift is even more tenuously motivated. After Jack Absolute is prevented from duelling by the arrival of his father (the shock of the threatened duel makes Lydia declare her love), Julia observes Faulkland standing unhappy and dejected and she melts. There is no rhyme nor reason to it, merely the hope that her love will be strong enough to withstand his jealousy and fits of self doubt. Even Sir Lucius, the fighting fool who seems intent on engineering duels between others as well as fighting his own, finds the plot has things to teach him. He thought he was writing love letters to Lydia. But the maid delivered them to Mrs Malaprop who has responded in kind. At the end of the play he is denied his duel and his love, but, through the momentum of the plot, generously gives up both for the satisfaction of seeing others happy. A whole series of catastrophes is avoided but only through the plot. The patterns of social and psychological interaction that Sheridan has shown in the play all have the seeds of disaster built into them. The pairs of lovers, the father and son, aunt and niece, respond to each other in ways that are potentially destructive. But the plot conquers all. Ultimately this is not a play about the triumph of love over life, but the triumph of art over life.

For the actors there are delightful character parts to fill out and embroider. The most famous is naturally Mrs Malaprop who never seems able to match any word to its meaning and who has a correspondingly dislocated vision of her own importance. Sheridan may well have borrowed the idea for the character from Congreve's *Way of the World*, where Lady Wishfort shows a similar antagonism towards her niece's love life and a corresponding inability to cope with the complexities of real emotions expressed in real words. But

Sheridan has transformed Congreve's quite realistically conceived old widow into a full-blown travesty. Mrs Malaprop is much larger than life and her foibles need to be filled out by comic character acting of great vigour and assurance.

Hers is not the only part requiring such character acting. Sir Anthony is another. Here too one can find a model in Congreve: Sir Sampson in *Love for Love,* who treats his son Valentine in much the same manner as does Sir Anthony. Once again, however, we find Sheridan aiming at an exaggerated effect that is closer to travesty than is the case with Congreve's more realistically fleshed out, although admittedly satiric portrait of an authoritarian father figure. In Congreve, the follies of characters like Lady Wishfort and Sir Sampson are ultimately deflected by the prudent stratagems of other characters. In Sheridan, it is only the artifice of his plot that prevents such characters exercising total and totally destructive control over their charges, even though their foibles and faults are gross and excessive.

Throughout the whole play, one can detect echoes of Sheridan's own recent experiences as a young man in Bath. He takes the stuff and substance of these experiences (his quarrels with his father, his elopement with and courtship of Elizabeth, his duel with Matthews) and weaves his memories into an artistic pattern that smoothes away all the rough edges and creates a sense of harmony and completeness that life simply does not exhibit. Sheridan was pre-eminently a comic dramatist who knew intuitively how to mould and shape his own experiences in life, particularly those experiences that had caused him pain, stress and disappointment, into an artistic mould that would give delight. In that sense his plays are an assertion of human dignity and value in the face of some of life's absurdities. We may be foolish and fragile creatures, but at least in our art we can rise above our folly through the creative perceptions of the artist. Sheridan's is a comic universe that constantly threatens to explode into chaotic fragments, but somehow he holds it all together with a vivacious and fast-moving plot. And even his most stupid characters have an attractive side to them. Although life played him cruel tricks, some of which he reflects in his play, he was well able as an artist to rise above such experiences and to present his audiences with a gallery of entertaining figures, all of whom are drawn from an ultimately warm and benign perspective. Sheridan knew only too well that life could be a disappointment and a cheat, but in his art he could give to life what it sometimes lacked, namely an affectionate and endearing warmth.

When Sheridan wrote *The Rivals*, he was a young married man of twenty-three who had never before written anything for the theatre, even though he came from an actor-manager's family. His objectives in writing his first comedy were to find an entrée into London society and a means of supporting his young wife. His wife's musical talents could easily have supported both of them, but Sheridan took the view that a gentleman should not permit his wife to sing in public for hire, gain or reward. Luckily for him, he succeeded beyond his wildest dreams as a fledgeling playwright.

By the 1770s it was notoriously difficult to place a new play with one of London's two patent theatres at Drury Lane and Covent Garden. The rival managers of the two theatres (Garrick at Drury Lane and Harris at Covent Garden) were conservative and cautious in their choice of repertoire, preferring well-tried successes to uncertain experiments. Sheridan was, however, undaunted by this hurdle. His skill in character drawing, his intuitive feel for comic dialogue, along with a robust plot that was based on his own colourful life, must have seemed a reasonable gamble to Harris at Covent Garden. It was a gamble that almost failed. The first night was a disaster. Not only was the play too long, but the character of Sir Lucius O'Trigger was deemed to be too offensively drawn.[1]

Having listened carefully to his first-night critics, Sheridan withdrew the play following the second performance, in order to rework it. After ten days of feverish activity (he always operated best under pressure) the play was returned to the repertoire in its revised form, and with a new actor playing O'Trigger. The town was well pleased with Sheridan's labours. What had been a near disaster was turned into a sparkling triumph. The play ran for fourteen performances (instead of the usual four or five) and netted several hundred pounds for its young author. Successfully launched on his new-found career as a playwright, Sheridan did not rest on his laurels. By May 1775, he had completed a light-hearted afterpiece called *St Patrick's Day*, which was well received. By November, he went on to complete a music drama called *The Duenna*, collaborating very effectively with his father-in-law, Thomas Linley, who provided the musical settings, and took charge of the Covent Garden orchestra for the production. This proved to be an outstanding

1. Sheridan admits his errors with disarming candour in his Preface to the published edition.

artistic and commercial success, running for seventy-five performances at Covent Garden, and establishing Sheridan beyond any doubt as the leading playwright of the age.

Within a year, Garrick, who was retiring from his lengthy and distinguished career as leading actor and manager of Drury Lane, offered his half share in the theatre to Richard Sheridan and his partners, Thomas Linley and Dr James Ford. Garrick was obviously sufficiently impressed by Sheridan's year of triumph at Covent Garden to assume that he would bring the same energy and commitment to the role of theatre manager as he had already shown in his work as a playwright. Initially his hopes seemed well founded. Confronted by this astonishing challenge for one so young, Sheridan set about the task of managing Drury Lane with real flair and vigour. He also had a pressing financial reason for wishing to succeed. Linley and Ford were sufficiently wealthy to put up front the money required of them; Sheridan had to borrow extensively. This may explain why so many of his early memoranda to the staff at Drury Lane exhort them to be thrifty and not to overlook even the smallest of economies.[1]

Having rapidly settled into the task of managing the theatre, Sheridan found the time to adapt Vanbrugh's *The Relapse* for performance at Drury Lane in February 1777, calling it *A Trip to Scarborough*. It enjoyed only a modest initial success, but for Sheridan it was an important preparation for his next play, *The School for Scandal*. Planned over a lengthy period, the play was written in feverish haste (with legendary tales of Act 4 delivered sheet by sheet to the prompter in the space of a single day).[2] At its première on 8 May 1777, *The School for Scandal* was greeted with huge waves of applause. Its success was so outstanding that an oil painting was commissioned to depict the famous screen scene in Act 4; the same scene was also depicted in a popular engraving.[3]

Sheridan was now well and truly launched on his meteoric career; it seemed as if nothing could hold him back. But like his father, he had a natural genius for squandering the rich opportunities that came his way. In the next few years, he wrote only two

1. See Katharine Worth, *Sheridan and Goldsmith* (London: Macmillan, 1992) p. 28.
2. Ibid., p. 29.
3. This engraving, showing the actors on stage, playing to a full and appreciative auditorium, is one of the very few extant illustrations of a comedy in performance on the Restoration and Georgian stage. The painting and engraving are reproduced in David Thomas (ed.), *Theatre in Europe: A Documentary History. Restoration and Georgian England 1660–1788* (Cambridge: Cambridge University Press, 1989) p. 338.

further works for the theatre: a lightweight afterpiece called *The Camp* in October 1778, and a popular burlesque called *The Critic* in October 1779. By now Sheridan was far more interested in London's glittering social life than in furthering his career as playwright and theatre manger. He was also pursuing the notion of a career in politics. For him the theatre had never been more than a means to an end. Now that the end had been achieved, namely his steady advancement in society, it was time to move on.

Sheridan was elected Member of Parliament for Stafford in 1780 and was to serve as an MP until 1812. Only at the beginning of his parliamentary career did he hold any form of minor government office. To his contemporaries in the Commons, he was best known as a fine orator and an inveterate plotter. His one outstanding moment of glory came in 1788 when the Commons debated whether Warren Hastings, the Governor-General of India, should be impeached. Sheridan mounted a savage attack on Hastings and on Britain's colonial exploitation of India in a speech that lasted five hours and which ensured his involvement in the actual trial. Despite this and other moments of oratorical triumph, Sheridan's political career was characterised by disappointed ambition. By the time he finally lost his seat in 1812, his various backers and followers had all deserted him. His last few years were full of poverty and loneliness.

His personal life was no more successful. After all the energy he had expended to make young Elizabeth Linley his wife, he soon neglected her for others in London's fashionable salons. Over the years, their relationship deteriorated steadily. When she died in 1792, she had just given birth to a daughter, possibly fathered by another man. After her death, Sheridan was consumed by remorse for his betrayal and neglect of a woman he had once so passionately adored. He poured out his feelings in some moving verses, but all too soon he closed his mind to his sufferings and continued to live much as before.[1] Within three years of Elizabeth's death, Sheridan married again; his bride was a much younger women called Esther Ogle, daughter of the Dean of Winchester. This marriage proved even less happy than his first. By now, Sheridan was drinking heavily and was totally incapable of facing the various financial and emotional problems that confronted him. For her part, his young wife had neither the patience nor the experience to offer him the support he needed. Inevitably, they drifted apart.

1. See Bingham, *Sheridan*, pp. 280–9.

Throughout his career as an MP Sheridan remained the manager of Drury Lane. For him it was primarily a means of mortgaging his debts and providing much needed pocket money. He took little day-to-day interest in the affairs of the theatre and was ill at ease with the actors.[1] However, even here there were odd bursts of energy, notably when he masterminded the demolition of Wren's old Drury Lane and the building of a much larger new theatre, designed by Henry Holland: the whole project took from 1791 to 1794. Some years later, in 1799, Sheridan even wrote another piece for the new Drury Lane, a melodrama called *Pizarro,* adapted from the work of the German writer Kotzebue. The play enjoyed enormous popular success; once again Sheridan showed himself finely in tune with the sensibilities of his audience. But the debts were mounting, and actors often remained unpaid. When the new Drury Lane theatre burnt to the ground in 1809, Sheridan found himself barred from any further involvement in the management. That was the harsh precondition insisted upon by those funding the rebuilding.

The story of Sheridan's life is a tale of wasted genius and missed opportunity. In his mid-twenties he had everything a young man might wish for: a glittering career as playwright and manager of one the great theatres in the world; a beautiful and musically gifted wife; loyal and talented supporters. All of this he threw away because he aspired to the life of a gentleman in London's glittering but ultimately superficial social whirl. Arguably the sadness and neglect he had experienced in his youth had so scarred him that he was incapable of committing himself fully to those who loved him as an adult. At least he left a few great plays to posterity in which remarkably he overcame all of life's defeats; his comedies were carefully crafted celebrations of art triumphing over life. Such is the enduring power of art that we remember him for these and not for the disaster that his own life became.

1. See Bingham, *Sheridan,* pp. 343–4.

The Rivals

A

COMEDY

As it is ACTED at the

Theatre-Royal in Covent-Garden

LONDON:
Printed for JOHN WILKIE, No. 71, St. Paul's Church-Yard

M DCCLXXV.

Preface[1]

A PREFACE to a Play seems generally to be considered as a kind of Closet-prologue, in which – if his Piece has been successful – the Author solicits that indulgence from the Reader which he had before experienced from the Audience: But as the scope and immediate object of a Play is to please a mixed assembly in *Representation* (whose judgment in the Theatre at least is decisive) its degree of reputation is usually as determined as public, before it can be prepared for the cooler tribunal of the Study. Thus any farther solicitude on the part of the Writer becomes unnecessary at least, if not an intrusion: and if the Piece has been condemned in the Performance, I fear an Address to the Closet,[2] like an Appeal to Posterity, is constantly regarded as the procrastination of a suit,[3] from a consciousness of the weakness of the cause. From these considerations, the following Comedy would certainly have been submitted to the Reader, without any further introduction than what it had in the Representation, but that its success has probably been founded on a circumstance which the Author is informed has not before attended a theatrical trial, and which consequently ought not to pass unnoticed.

I need scarcely add, that the circumstance alluded to, was the withdrawing of the Piece, to remove those imperfections in the first Representation which were too obvious to escape reprehension, and too numerous to admit of a hasty correction. There are few writers, I believe, who, even in the fullest consciousness of error, do not wish to palliate the faults which they acknowledge; and, however trifling the performance, to second their confession of its deficiencies, by whatever plea seems least disgraceful to their ability. In the present instance, it cannot be said to amount either to candour or modesty in me, to acknowledge an extreme inexperience and want of judgment on matters, in which, without guidance from practice, or spur from success, a young man should scarcely boast of being an adept. If it be said, that under such disadvantages no one should attempt to write a play – I must beg leave to dissent from the position, while the first point of experience that I have gained on the subject is, a knowledge of the candour and judgment with which an impartial Public distinguishes between the errors of inexperience and incapacity, and the indulgence which it shews even to a disposition to remedy the defects of either.

It were unnecessary to enter into any farther extenuation of what was thought exceptionable in this Play, but that it has been said, that the Managers should have prevented some of the defects before its appearance to the Public – and in particular the uncommon length of the piece as

1. The Preface was printed in the first edition of the play, but omitted from subsequent editions.
2. A private room where a play might be read.
3. Lawsuit.

represented the first night. – It were an ill return for the most liberal and gentlemanly conduct on their side, to suffer any censure to rest where none was deserved. Hurry in writing has long been exploded as an excuse for an Author; – however, in the dramatic line, it may happen, that both an Author and a Manager may wish to fill a chasm in the entertainment of the Public with a hastiness not altogether culpable. The season was advanced when I first put the play into Mr. Harris's hands:[1] – it was at that time at least double the length of any acting comedy. – I profited by his judgment and experience in the curtailing of it – 'till, I believe, his feeling for the vanity of a young Author got the better of his desire for correctness, and he left many excrescences remaining, because he had assisted in pruning so many more. Hence, though I was not uninformed that the Acts were still too long, I flatter'd myself that, after the first trial, I might with safer judgment proceed to remove what should appear to have been most dissatisfactory. – Many other errors there were, which might in part have arisen from my being by no means conversant with plays in general, either in reading or at the theatre. – Yet I own that, in one respect, I did not regret my ignorance: for as my first wish in attempting a Play was to avoid every appearance of plagiary, I thought I should stand a better chance of effecting this from being in a walk which I had not frequented, and where consequently the progress of invention was less likely to be interrupted by starts of recollection: for on subjects on which the mind has been much informed, invention is slow of exerting itself. – Faded ideas float in the fancy like half-forgotten dreams; and the imagination in its fullest enjoyment becomes suspicious of its offspring, and doubts whether it has created or adopted.

With regard to some particular passages which on the First Night's Representation seemed generally disliked, I confess, that if I felt any emotion of surprise at the disapprobation, it was not that they were disapproved of, but that I had not before perceived that they deserved it. As some part of the attack on the Piece was begun too early to pass for the sentence of *Judgment*, which is ever tardy in condemning, it has been suggested to me, that much of the disapprobation must have arisen from virulence of Malice, rather than severity of Criticism: But as I was more apprehensive of there being just grounds to excite the latter than conscious of having deserved the former, I continue not to believe that probable, which I am sure must have been unprovoked. However, if it was so, and I could even mark the quarter from whence it came, it would be ungenerous to retort; for no passion suffers more than malice from disappointment. For my own part, I see no reason why the author of a play should not regard a First Night's Audience, as a candid and judicious friend attending, in behalf of the Public, at his last Rehearsal. If he can dispense with flattery, he is sure at least of sincerity, and even though the annotation be rude, he may rely upon the justness of the comment. Considered in this light, that Audience,

1. The manager of Covent Garden.

whose *fiat* is essential to the Poet's claim, whether his object be Fame or Profit, has surely a right to expect some deference to its opinion, from principles of Politeness at least, if not from Gratitude.

As for the little puny Critics, who scatter their peevish strictures in private circles, and scribble at every Author who has the eminence of being unconnected with them, as they are usually spleen-swoln from a vain idea of increasing their consequence, there will always be found a petulance and illiberality in their remarks, which should place them as far beneath the notice of a gentleman, as their original dulness had sunk them from the level of the most unsuccessful Author.

It is not without pleasure that I catch at an opportunity of justifying myself from the charge of intending any national reflection in the character of Sir *Lucius O'Trigger*. If any Gentlemen opposed the Piece from that idea, I thank them sincerely for their opposition; and if the condemnation of this Comedy (however misconceived the provocation) could have added one spark to the decaying flame of national attachment to the country supposed to be reflected on, I should have been happy in its fate; and might with truth have boasted, that it had done more real service in its failure, than the successful morality of a thousand stage-novels will ever effect.

It is usual, I believe, to thank the Performers in a new Play, for the exertion of their several abilities. But where (as in this instance) their merit has been so striking and uncontroverted, as to call for the warmest and truest applause from a number of judicious Audiences, the Poet's after-praise comes like the feeble acclamation of a child to close the shouts of a multitude. The conduct, however, of the Principals in a Theatre cannot be so apparent to the Public. – I think it therefore but justice to declare, that from this Theatre (the only one I can speak of from experience) those Writers who wish to try the Dramatic Line, will meet with that candour and liberal attention, which are generally allowed to be better calculated to lead genius into excellence, than either the precepts of judgment, or the guidance of experience.

THE AUTHOR

Prologues

Prologue[1]

Spoken by MR. WOODWARD and MR. QUICK.

[*Enter* SERJEANT AT LAW, *and* ATTORNEY *following, and giving a Paper.*]

SERJEANT: What's here – a vile cramp hand! I cannot see
Without my spectacles.
ATTORNEY: He means his fee. Nay, Mr. Serjeant, good Sir, try again.
[*Gives money.*]
SERJEANT: The scrawl improves [*more*] O come, 'tis pretty plain.
Hey! how's this? – *Dibble*![2] – sure it cannot be!
A Poet's Brief! A Poet and a Fee!
ATTORNEY: Yea Sir! – tho' *you* without Reward, I know,
Would gladly plead the muses cause –
SERJEANT: So – So!
ATTORNEY: And if the Fee offends – your wrath should fall
On me –
SERJEANT: Dear *Dibble* no offence at all –
ATTORNEY: Some Sons of Phœbus[3] – in the Courts we meet,
SERJEANT: And fifty Sons of Phœbus in the Fleet![4]
ATTORNEY: Nor pleads he worse, who with a decent sprig
Of Bays – adorns his legal waste of wig.
SERJEANT: Full-bottom'd Heroes thus, on signs, unfurl
A leaf of laurel – in a grove of curl!
Yet tell your Client, that, in adverse days,
This Wig is warmer than a bush of Bays.[5]
ATTORNEY: Do you then, Sir, my Client's place supply,
Profuse of robe, and prodigal of tye –
Do you, with all those blushing pow'rs of face,
And wonted bashful hesitating grace,
Rise in the Court, and flourish on the Case. [*Exit.*]
SERJEANT: For practice then suppose – this Brief will shew it, –
Me, Serjeant *Woodward*, – Counsel for the Poet.
Us'd to the ground – I know 'tis hard to deal
With this dread *Court*, from whence there's *no appeal*;
No *Tricking* here, to blunt the edge of *Law*,

1. This is the revised version of the Prologue printed in the third and subsequent editions.
2. The attorney's name.
3. Poets.
4. The debtor's prison.
5. The laurel wreath of success.

Or, damn'd in *Equity* – escape by *Flaw*:
But *Judgment* given – *your Sentence* must remain;
– No *Writ of Error* lies – to *Drury-lane*!
Yet when so kind you seem – 'tis past dispute
We gain some favour, if not *Costs of Suit*.
No spleen is here! I see no hoarded fury;
– I think I never fac'd a milder Jury!
Sad else our plight! – where frowns are transportation,
A hiss the gallows, – and a groan, damnation!
But such the public candour, without fear
My Client waves all *right of challenge* here.
No Newsman from *our* Session is dismiss'd,
Nor Wit nor Critic *we* scratch off the list;
His faults can never hurt another's ease,
His crime at worst – a *bad attempt* to please:
Thus, all respecting, he appeals to all,
And by the general voice will *stand* or *fall*.

Prologue[1]

Spoken on the Tenth Night, by MRS. BULKLEY.

Granted our Cause, our suit and trial o'er,
The worthy Serjeant need appear no more:
In pleasing I a different Client chuse,
He serv'd the Poet, – I would serve the Muse:
Like him, I'll try to merit your applause,
A female counsel in a female's cause.
– Look on this form,[2] – where Humour quaint and fly,
Dimples the cheek, and points the beaming eye;
Where gay Invention seems to boast its wiles
In amorous hint, and half-triumphant smiles;
While her light masks or covers Satire's strokes,
All hides the conscious blush, her wit provokes.
– Look on her well – does she seem form'd to teach?
Shou'd you *expect* to hear this lady – preach?
Is grey experience suited to her youth?
Do solemn sentiments become that mouth?
Bid her be grave, those lips should rebel prove
To every theme that slanders mirth or love.
– Yet thus adorn'd with every graceful art
To charm the fancy and yet reach the heart –
Must we displace her? And instead advance

1. This tenth night prologue was not included in the first edition.
2. 'Pointing to the Figure of Comedy', at the base of the proscenium arch. The statue of Tragedy was on the other side of the stage.

The Goddess of the woeful countenance –
The sentimental Muse! – Her emblems view,
The Pilgrim's Progress, and a sprig of rue!
View her – too chaste to look like flesh and blood –
Primly portray'd on emblematic wood!
There fix'd in usurpation shou'd she stand,
She'll snatch the dagger from her sister's hand:
And having made her votaries *weep a flood*
Good Heav'n! she'll end her Comedies in blood –
Bid *Harry Woodward* [1] break poor *Dunstall's* crown!
Imprison *Quick* – and knock *Ned Shuter* down;
While sad *Barsanti* – weeping o'er the scene,
Shall stab herself – or poison Mrs. *Green*. –
– Such dire encroachments to prevent in time,
Demands the Critic's voice – the Poet's rhyme.
Can our light scenes add strength to Holy laws!
Such puny patronage but hurts the cause:
Fair Virtue scorns our feeble aid to ask;
And moral Truth disdains the trickster's mask.
For here their fav'rite stands,[2] whose brow – severe
And sad – claims Youth's respect, and Pity's tear;
Who – when oppress'd by foes her worth creates –
Can point a poignard at the Guilt she hates.

Dramatis Personæ

SIR ANTHONY ABSOLUTE,	*Mr Shuter*
CAPT. ABSOLUTE,	*Mr. Woodward*
FAULKLAND,	*Mr. Lewes.*
ACRES,	*Mr. Quick.*
SIR LUCIUS O'TRIGGER,	*Mr. Clinch.*
FAG,	*Mr Lee-Lewes.*
DAVID,	*Mr. Dunstall.*
COACHMAN,	*Mr. Fearon.*
MRS. MALAPROP,	*Mrs. Green.*
LYDIA LANGUISH,	*Miss Barsanti.*
JULIA,	*Mrs. Bulkley.*
LUCY,	*Mrs. Lessingham.*

MAID, BOY, SERVANTS &c.

1. These were all players in the first performance of *The Rivals.*
2. 'Pointing to Tragedy'.

SCENE, *Bath.*
Time of Action, within One Day.

Act I, Scene I

[A STREET *in* Bath.
COACHMAN *crosses the stage. – Enter* FAG, *looking after him.*]

FAG: What! – Thomas! – Sure 'tis he? – What! – Thomas! – Thomas!

COACHMAN: Hey! – Odd's[1] life! – Mr. Fag! – give us your hand, my old fellow-servant.

FAG: Excuse my glove, Thomas: – I'm dev'lish glad to see you, my lad: why, my prince of charioteers, you look as hearty! – but who the deuce thought of seeing you in Bath!

COACHMAN: Sure, Master, Madam Julia, Harry, Mrs. Kate, and the postillion be all come!

FAG: Indeed!

COACHMAN: Aye! Master thought another fit of the gout was coming to make him a visit: – so he'd a mind to gi't the slip, and whip we were all off at an hour's warning.

FAG: Aye, aye! hasty in every thing, or it would not be Sir Anthony Absolute!

COACHMAN: But tell us, Mr. Fag, how does young Master? Odd! Sir Anthony will stare to see the Captain here!

FAG: I do not serve Capt. Absolute now. –

COACHMAN: Why sure!

FAG: At present I am employ'd by Ensign Beverley.

COACHMAN: I doubt, Mr. Fag, you ha'n't changed for the better.

FAG: I have not changed, Thomas.

COACHMAN: No! why didn't you say you had left young Master?

FAG: No – Well, honest Thomas, I must puzzle you no farther: – briefly then – Capt. Absolute and Ensign Beverley are one and the same person.

COACHMAN: The devil they are!

FAG: So it is indeed, Thomas; and the *Ensign* half of my master being on guard at present – the *Captain* has nothing to do with me.

COACHMAN: So, so! – what, this is some freak, I warrant! – Do, tell us, Mr. Fag, the meaning o't – you know I ha' trusted you.

FAG: You'll be secret, Thomas.

COACHMAN: As a coach-horse.

FAG: Why then the cause of all this is – LOVE, – Love, Thomas, who (as you may get read to you) has been a masquerader ever since the days of Jupiter.

COACHMAN: Aye, aye; – I guessed there was a lady in the case: but pray, why

1. God's.

does your Master pass only for *Ensign*? – now if he had shamm'd *General* indeed –

FAG: Ah! Thomas, there lies the mystery o' the matter. – Hark'ee, Thomas, my Master is in love with a lady of a very singular taste: a lady who likes him better as a *half-pay Ensign* than if she knew he was son and heir to Sir Anthony Absolute, a baronet with three thousand a-year!

COACHMAN: That is an odd taste indeed! – but has she got the stuff, Mr. Fag; is she rich, hey?

FAG: Rich! – why, I believe she owns half the stocks! – Z—ds! Thomas, she could pay the national debt as easily as I could my washer woman! – She has a lap-dog that eats out of gold, – she feeds her parrot with small pearls, – and all her thread-papers are made of bank-notes!

COACHMAN: Bravo! – faith! – Odd! I warrant she has a set of thousands at least: – but does she draw kindly with the Captain?

FAG: As fond as pigeons.

COACHMAN: May one hear her name?

FAG: Miss Lydia Languish – But there is an old tough aunt in the way; – though by the bye – she has never seen my Master – for he got acquainted with Miss while on a visit in Gloucestershire.

COACHMAN: Well – I wish they were once harness'd together in matrimony. – But pray, Mr. Fag, what kind of a place is this Bath? – I ha' heard a deal of it – here's a mort[1] o'merry-making – hey?

FAG: Pretty well, Thomas, pretty well – 'tis a good lounge; in the morning we go to the pump-room (though neither my Master nor I drink the waters); after breakfast we saunter on the parades or play a game at billiards; at night we dance: but d—n the place, I'm tired of it: their regular hours stupify me – not a fiddle nor a card after eleven![2] – however Mr. Faulkland's gentleman and I keep it up a little in private parties; – I'll introduce you there, Thomas – you'll like him much.

COACHMAN: Sure I know Mr. Du-Peigne – you know his Master is to marry Madam Julia.

FAG: I had forgot. – But Thomas, you must polish a little – indeed you must: – here now this wig! – what the devil do you do with a *wig*, Thomas? – none of the London whips of any degree of Ton wear *wigs* now.

COACHMAN: More's the pity! more's the pity, I say. – Odd's life! when I heard how the lawyers and doctors had took to their own hair, I thought how 'twould go next: – Odd rabbit it! when the fashion had got foot on the Bar, I guess'd 'twould mount to the Box! – but 'tis all out of character, believe me, Mr. Fag: and look'ee, I'll never gi' up mine – the lawyers and doctors may do as they will.

FAG: Well, Thomas, we'll not quarrel about that.

COACHMAN: Why, bless you, the gentlemen of they professions ben't all of a

1. A great amount.
2. Regular hours and strict rules of conduct were enforced in Bath by Beau Nash.

mind – for in our village now tho'ff[1] *Jack Gauge* the *exciseman*, has ta'en to his carrots,[2] there's little Dick the farrier swears he'll never forsake his *bob*, tho' all the college should appear with their own heads!

FAG: Indeed! well said Dick! but hold – mark! mark! Thomas.

COACHMAN: Zooks! 'tis the Captain – Is that the lady with him?

FAG: No! no! that is Madam Lucy – my Master's mistress's maid. – They lodge at that house – but I must after him to tell him the news.

COACHMAN: Odd! he's giving her money! – well, Mr. Fag –

FAG: Good bye, Thomas. – I have an appointment in Gyde's Porch[3] this evening at eight; meet me there, and we'll make a little party.

[*Exeunt severally.*]

Act I, Scene II

[*A Dressing-room in* MRS. MALAPROP's *Lodgings.*
LYDIA *sitting on a sopha with a book in her hand.* – LUCY, *as just returned from a message.*]

LUCY: Indeed, Ma'am, I travers'd half the town in search of it: – I don't believe there's a circulating library in Bath I ha'n't been at.

LYDIA: And could not you get *The Reward of Constancy?*

LUCY: No, indeed, Ma'am.

LYDIA: Nor *The Fatal Connection?*

LUCY: No, indeed, Ma'am.

LYDIA: Nor *The Mistakes of the Heart?*

LUCY: Ma'am, as ill-luck would have it, Mr. Bull said Miss Sukey Saunter had just fetch'd it away.

LYDIA: Heigh-ho! – Did you inquire for *The Delicate Distress?* –

LUCY: – Or *The Memoirs of Lady Woodford*? Yes indeed, Ma'am. – I ask'd every where for it; and I might have brought it from Mr. Frederick's,[4] but Lady Slattern Lounger, who had just sent it home, had so soiled and dog's-ear'd it, it wa'n't fit for a christian to read.

LYDIA: Heigh-ho! – Yes, I always know when Lady Slattern has been before me. – She has a most observing thumb; and I believe cherishes her nails for the convenience of making marginal notes. – Well, child, what *have* you brought me?

LUCY: Oh! here Ma'am.

[*Taking books from under her cloke, and from her pockets.*]

This is *The Gordian Knot*, – and this *Peregrine Pickle*. Here are *The Tears of*

1. Though.
2. Ginger hair.
3. Gyde kept the Lower Assembly Rooms in Bath.
4. A Bath bookseller.

Sensibility and *Humphry Clinker*. This is *The Memoirs of a Lady of Quality, written by herself*, – and here the second volume of *The Sentimental Journey*.

LYDIA: Heigh-ho! – What are those books by the glass?

LUCY: The great one is only *The whole Duty of Man* – where I press a few blonds[1] , Ma'am.

LYDIA: Very well – give me the *sal volatile*.[2]

LUCY: Is it in a blue cover, Ma'am?

LYDIA: My smelling-bottle, you simpleton!

LUCY: O, the drops! – here Ma'am.

LYDIA: Hold! – here's some one coming – quick, see who it is. – [*Exit* LUCY.] Surely I heard my cousin Julia's voice!

[*Re-enter* LUCY.]

LUCY: Lud! Ma'am, here is Miss Melville.

LYDIA: Is it possible! –

[*Enter* JULIA.]

LYDIA: My dearest Julia, how delighted am I! – [*Embrace*.] How unexpected was this happiness!

JULIA: True, Lydia – and our pleasure is the greater; – but what has been the matter? – you were denied to me at first!

LYDIA: Ah! Julia, I have a thousand things to tell you! – but first inform me, what has conjur'd you to Bath? – Is Sir Anthony here?

JULIA: He is – we are arrived within this hour – and I suppose he will be here to wait on Mrs. Malaprop as soon as he is dress'd.

LYDIA: Then before we are interrupted, let me impart to you some of my distress! – I know your gentle nature will sympathize with me, tho' your prudence may condemn me! – My letters have inform'd you of my whole connexion with Beverley; – but I have lost him, Julia! – my aunt has discover'd our intercourse by a note she intercepted, and has confin'd me ever since! – Yet, would you believe it? she has fallen absolutely in love with a tall Irish baronet she met one night since we have been here, at Lady Macshuffle's rout.[3]

JULIA: You jest, Lydia!

LYDIA: No, upon my word. – She really carries on a kind of correspondence with him, under a feigned name though, till she chuses to be known to him; – but it is a *Delia* or a *Celia*, I assure you.

JULIA: Then, surely, she is now more indulgent to her niece.

LYDIA: Quite the contrary. Since she has discovered her own frailty, she is

1. Blonds or blondes were pieces of lace.
2. Smelling salts.
3. Party.

become more suspicious of mine. Then I must inform you of another plague! – That odious Acres is to be in Bath to-day; so that I protest I shall be teased out of all spirits!

JULIA: Come, come, Lydia, hope the best. – Sir Anthony shall use his interest with Mrs. Malaprop.

LYDIA: But you have not heard the worst. Unfortunately I had quarrell'd with my poor Beverley, just before my aunt made the discovery, and I have not seen him since, to make it up.

JULIA: What was his offence?

LYDIA: Nothing at all! – But, I don't know how it was, as often as we had been together, we had never had a quarrel! – And, somehow I was afraid he would never give me an opportunity. – So, last Thursday, I wrote a letter to myself, to inform myself that Beverley was at that time paying his addresses to another woman. – I sign'd it *your Friend unknown*, shew'd it to Beverley, charg'd him with his falsehood, put myself in a violent passion, and vow'd I'd never see him more.

JULIA: And you let him depart so, and have not seen him since?

LYDIA: 'Twas the next day my aunt found the matter out. I intended only to have teased him three days and a half, and now I've lost him for ever.

JULIA: If he is as deserving and sincere as you have represented him to me, he will never give you up so. Yet consider, Lydia, you tell me he is but an ensign, and you have thirty thousand pounds!

LYDIA: But you know I lose most of my fortune, if I marry without my aunt's consent, till of age; and that is what I have determin'd to do, ever since I know the penalty. – Nor could I love the man, who would wish to wait a day for the alternative.

JULIA: Nay, this is caprice!

LYDIA: What, does Julia tax me with caprice? – I thought her lover Faulkland had enured her to it.

JULIA: I do not love even *his* faults.

LYDIA: But a-propos – you have sent to him, I suppose?

JULIA: Not yet, upon my word – nor has he the least idea of my being in Bath. – Sir Anthony's resolution was so sudden, I could not inform him of it.

LYDIA: Well, Julia, you are your own mistress (though under the protection of Sir Anthony), yet have you, for this long year, been a slave to the caprice, whim, the jealousy of this ungrateful Faulkland, who will ever delay assuming the right of a husband, while you suffer him to be equally imperious as a lover.

JULIA: Nay, you are wrong entirely. – We were contracted before my father's death. – *That*, and some consequent embarrassments, have delay'd what I know to be my Faulkland's most ardent wish. – He is too generous to trifle on such a point. – And for his character, you wrong him there too. – No, Lydia, he is too proud, too noble to be jealous; if he is captious, 'tis without dissembling; if fretful, without rudeness. – Unus'd to the fopperies of love, he is negligent of the little duties expected from a lover – but being unhackney'd in the passion, his affection is ardent and sincere; and as it engrosses his whole soul, he expects every thought and emotion of his mistress to move in unison with his. – Yet, though his pride calls for this full return – his humility makes him undervalue those qualities in him, which would entitle him to it; and not feeling why he should be lov'd to the degree he wishes, he still suspects that he is not lov'd enough: – This temper, I must own has cost me many unhappy hours; but I have learn'd to think myself his debtor, for those imperfections which arise from the ardour of his attachment.

LYDIA: Well, I cannot blame you for defending him. – But tell me candidly, Julia, had he never sav'd your life, do you think you should have been attach'd to him as you are? – Believe me, the rude blast that overset your boat was a prosperous gale of love to him.

JULIA: Gratitude may have strengthened my attachment to Mr. Faulkland, but I lov'd him before he had preserv'd me; yet surely that alone were an obligation sufficient.

LYDIA: Obligation! – Why a water-spaniel would have done as much. – Well, I should never think of giving my heart to a man because he could swim!

JULIA: Come, Lydia, you are too inconsiderate.

LYDIA: Nay, I do but jest. – What's here?

[*Enter* LUCY *in a hurry.*]

LUCY: O Ma'am, here is Sir Anthony Absolute just come home with your aunt.

LYDIA: They'll not come here. – Lucy do you watch. [*Exit* LUCY.]

JULIA: Yet I must go. – Sir Anthony does not know I am here, and if we meet, he'll detain me, to shew me the town. – I'll take another opportunity of paying my respects to Mrs. Malaprop, when she shall treat me, as long as she chooses, with her select words so ingeniously *misapplied*, without being *mispronounced*.

[*Re-enter* LUCY.]

LUCY: O Lud! Ma'am, they are both coming up stairs.

LYDIA: Well, I'll not detain you, Coz. – Adieu, my dear Julia, I'm sure you are in haste to send to Faulkland. – There – through my room you'll find another stair-case.

JULIA: Adieu. – [*Embrace.*] [*Exit* JULIA.]

LYDIA: Here, my dear Lucy, hide these books. – Quick, quick. – Fling *Peregrine Pickle* under the toilet[1] – throw *Roderick Random* into the closet[2]

1. Dressing-table.
2. Cupboard.

– put *The Innocent Adultery* into *The Whole Duty of Man* – thrust *Lord Aimworth* under the sofa – cram *Ovid*[1] behind the bolster – there – put *the Man of Feeling* into your pocket – so, so, now lay *Mrs. Chapone*[2] in sight, and leave Fordyce's *Sermons* open on the table.

LUCY: O burn it, Ma'am, the hair-dresser has torn away as far as *Proper Pride*.

LYDIA: Never mind – open at *Sobriety*. – Fling me *Lord Chesterfield's Letters*. – Now for 'em.

[*Enter* MRS. MALAPROP *and* SIR ANTHONY ABSOLUTE.]

MRS. MALAPROP: There, Sir Anthony, there sits the deliberate Simpleton, who wants to disgrace her family, and lavish herself on a fellow not worth a shilling!

LYDIA: Madam, I thought you once –

MRS. MALAPROP: You thought, Miss! – I don't know any business you have to think at all – thought does not become a young woman. But the point we would request of you is, that you will promise to forget this fellow – to illiterate[3] him, I say, quite from your memory.

LYDIA: Ah! Madam! our memories are independent of our wills. – It is not so easy to forget.

MRS. MALAPROP: But I say it is, Miss; there is nothing on earth so easy as to *forget*, if a person chooses to set about it. – I'm sure I have as much forgot your poor dear uncle as if he had never existed – and I thought it my duty so to do; and let me tell you, Lydia, these violent memories don't become a young woman.

SIR ANTHONY: Why sure she won't pretend to remember what she's order'd not! – aye, this comes of her reading!

LYDIA: What crime, Madam, have I committed to be treated thus?

MRS. MALAPROP: Now don't attempt to extirpate[4] yourself from the matter; you know I have proof controvertible[5] of it. – But tell me, will you promise to do as you're bid? – Will you take a husband of your friend's choosing?

LYDIA: Madam, I must tell you plainly, that had I no preference for any one else, the choice you have made would be my aversion.

MRS. MALAPROP: What business have you, Miss, with *preference* and *aversion*? They don't become a young woman; and you ought to know, that as both always wear off, 'tis safest in matrimony to begin with a little *aversion*. I am sure I hated your poor dear uncle before marriage as if he'd been a black-a-moor – and yet, Miss, you are sensible what a wife I made! – and when it pleas'd Heav'n to release me from him, 'tis unknown what tears

1. Presumably Ovid's *Art of Love*.
2. *Letters on the Improvement of the Mind*.
3. Obliterate.
4. Extricate.
5. Incontrovertible.

I shed! – But suppose we were going to give you another choice, will you promise us to give up this Beverley?

LYDIA: Could I belie my thoughts so far, as to give that promise, my actions would certainly as far belie my words.

MRS. MALAPROP: Take yourself to your room. – You are fit company for nothing but your own ill-humours.

LYDIA: Willingly, Ma'am – I cannot change for the worse. [*Exit* LYDIA.]

MRS. MALAPROP: There's a little intricate[1] hussy for you!

SIR ANTHONY: It is not to be wonder'd at Ma'am – all this is the natural consequence of teaching girls to read. – Had I a thousand daughters, by Heavens! I'd as soon have them taught the black-art as their alphabet!

MRS. MALAPROP: Nay, nay, Sir Anthony, you are an absolute misanthropy.[2]

SIR ANTHONY: In my way hither, Mrs. Malaprop, I observed your niece's maid coming forth from a circulating library! – She had a book in each hand – they were half-bound volumes, with marbled covers! – From that moment I guess'd how full of duty I should see her mistress!

MRS. MALAPROP: Those are vile places, indeed!

SIR ANTHONY: Madam, a circulating library in a town is, as an ever-green tree of diabolical knowledge! – It blossoms through the year! – And depend on it, Mrs. Malaprop, that they who are so fond of handling the leaves, will long for the fruit at last.

MRS. MALAPROP: Fie, fie, Sir Anthony, you surely speak laconically![3]

SIR ANTHONY: Why, Mrs. Malaprop, in moderation, now, what would you have a woman know?

MRS. MALAPROP: Observe me, Sir Anthony. – I would by no means wish a daughter of mine to be a progeny[4] of learning; I don't think so much learning becomes a young woman; for instance – I would never let her meddle with Greek, or Hebrew, or Algebra, or Simony,[5] or Fluxions,[6] or Paradoxes,[7] or such inflammatory branches of learning – neither would it be necessary for her to handle any of your mathematical, astronomical, diabolical instruments; – But, Sir Anthony, I would send her, at nine years old, to a boarding-school, in order to learn a little ingenuity and artifice. – Then, Sir, she should have a supercilious[8] knowledge in accounts; – and as she grew up, I would have her instructed in geometry,[9] that she might know something of the contagious[10] countries; – but above all, Sir

1. Probably 'ingrate'.
2. Misanthrope.
3. Ironically.
4. Prodigy.
5. Possibly 'cyclometry'.
6. Newtonian calculus.
7. Possibly 'parallaxes', a term used in astronomy.
8. Superficial.
9. Geography.
10. Contiguous.

Anthony, she should be mistress of orthodoxy, that she might not mis-spell, and mis-pronounce words so shamefully as girls usually do; and likewise that she might reprehend[1] the true meaning of what she is saying. – This, Sir Anthony, is what I would have a woman know; – and I don't think there is a superstitious[2] article in it.

SIR ANTHONY: Well, well, Mrs. Malaprop, I will dispute the point no further with you; though I must confess, that you are a truly moderate and polite arguer, for almost every third word you say is on my side of the question. – But, Mrs. Malaprop, to the more important point in debate, – you say, you have no objection to my proposal.

MRS. MALAPROP: None, I assure you. – I am under no positive engagement with Mr. Acres, and as Lydia is so obstinate against him, perhaps your son may have better success.

SIR ANTHONY: Well, Madam, I will write for the boy directly. – He knows not a syllable of this yet, though I have for some time had the proposal in my head. He is at present with his regiment.

MRS. MALAPROP: We have never seen your son, Sir Anthony; but I hope no objection on his side.

SIR ANTHONY: Objection! – let him object if he dare! – No, no, Mrs. Malaprop, Jack knows that the least demur puts me in a frenzy directly. – My process was always very simple – in their younger days, 'twas 'Jack, do this'; – if he demur'd – I knock'd him down – and if he grumbled at that – I always sent him out of the room.

MRS. MALAPROP: Aye, and the properest way, o' my conscience! – nothing is so conciliating[3] to young people as severity. – Well, Sir Anthony, I shall give Mr. Acres his discharge, and prepare Lydia to receive your son's invocations; – and I hope you will represent *her* to the Captain as an object not altogether illegible.[4]

SIR ANTHONY: Madam, I will handle the subject prudently. – Well, I must leave you – and let me beg you, Mrs. Malaprop, to enforce this matter roundly to the girl; – take my advice – keep a tight hand – if she rejects this proposal – clap her under lock and key: – and if you were just to let the servants forget to bring her dinner for three or four days, you can't conceive how she'd come about! [*Exit Sir* ANTHONY.]

MRS. MALAPROP: Well, at any rate I shall be glad to get her from under my intuition.[5] – She has somehow discovered my partiality for Sir Lucius O'Trigger – sure, Lucy can't have betray'd me! – No, the girl is such a simpleton, I should have made her confess it. – Lucy! – Lucy! – [*calls*] Had she been one of your artificial ones, I should never have trusted her.

1. Apprehend.
2. Superfluous.
3. Pleasing.
4. Ineligible.
5. Tuition.

[*Enter* LUCY.]

LUCY: Did you call, Ma'am?

MRS. MALAPROP: Yes, girl – Did you see Sir Lucius while you was out?

LUCY: No, indeed, Ma'am, not a glimpse of him.

MRS. MALAPROP: You are sure, Lucy, that you never mention'd –

LUCY: O Gemini! I'd sooner cut my tongue out.

MRS. MALAPROP: Well, don't let your simplicity be impos'd on.

LUCY: No. Ma'am.

MRS. MALAPROP: So, come to me presently, and I'll give you another letter to Sir Lucius; – but mind Lucy – if ever you betray what you are entrusted with – (unless it be other people's secrets to me) you forfeit my malevolence[1] for ever: – and your being a simpleton shall be no excuse for your locality.[2] [*Exit* MRS. MALAPROP.]

LUCY: Ha! ha! ha! – So, my dear *simplicity*, let me give you a little respite – [*altering her manner*] – let girls in my station be as fond as they please of appearing expert, and knowing in their trusts; – commend me to a mask of *silliness*, and a pair of sharp eyes for my own interest under it! – Let me see to what account I have turn'd my *simplicity* lately – [*looks at a paper*]

For *abetting Miss Lydia Languish in a design of running away with an Ensign! – in money – sundry times – twelve pound twelve – gowns, five – hats, ruffles, caps, &. &. – numberless! – From the said Ensign, within this last month, six guineas and a half.* – About a quarter's pay! – Item, *from Mrs. Malaprop, for betraying the young people to her* – when I found matters were likely to be discovered – *two guineas, and a black paduasoy.*[3] – Item, *from Mr. Acres, for carrying divers letters* – which I never deliver'd – *two guineas, and a pair of buckles.* – Item, *from Sir Lucius O'Trigger – three crowns – two gold pocket-pieces – and a silver snuff-box!* – Well done, *simplicity!* – yet I was forced to make my Hibernian believe, that he was corresponding, not with the *Aunt*, but with the *Niece*: for, though not over rich, I found he had too much pride and delicacy to sacrifice the feelings of a gentleman to the necessities of his fortune. [*Exit.*]

Act II, Scene I

[*Captain* ABSOLUTE'S *Lodgings.*
Captain ABSOLUTE *and* FAG.]

FAG: Sir, while I was there, Sir Anthony came in: I told him, you had sent me to inquire after his health, and to know if he was at leisure to see you.

1. Benevolence.
2. Loquacity.
3. A gown of heavy corded silk.

ABSOLUTE: And what did he say, on hearing I was at Bath?

FAG: Sir, in my life I never saw an elderly gentleman more astonished! He started back two or three paces, rapt out a dozen interjectoral oaths, and asked, what the devil had brought you here!

ABSOLUTE: Well, Sir, and what did you say?

FAG: O, I lied, Sir – I forget the precise lie, but you may depend on't; he got no truth from me. Yet, with submission, for fear of blunders in future, I should be glad to fix what *has* brought us to Bath: in order that we may lie a little consistently. – Sir Anthony's servants were curious, Sir, very curious indeed.

ABSOLUTE: You have said nothing to them – ?

FAG: O, not a word, Sir – not a word. – Mr. Thomas, indeed, the coachman (whom I take to be the discreetest of whips) –

ABSOLUTE: S'death! – you rascal! you have not trusted him!

FAG: O, *no,* Sir – no – no – not a syllable, upon my veracity! – He was, indeed, a little inquisitive; but I was sly, Sir – devilish sly! – My Master (said I) honest Thomas (you know, Sir, one says *honest* to one's inferiors) is come to Bath to *recruit* – Yes, Sir – I said, *to recruit* – and whether for men, money, or constitution, you know, Sir, is nothing to him, nor any one else.

ABSOLUTE: Well – *recruit* will do – let it be so –

FAG: O, Sir, recruit will do surprisingly – indeed, to give the thing an air, I told Thomas, that your Honour had already inlisted, five disbanded chairmen, seven minority waiters, and thirteen billiard markers.

ABSOLUTE: You blockhead, never say more than is necessary.

FAG: I beg pardon, Sir – I beg pardon – But with submission, a lie is nothing unless one supports it. – Sir, whenever I draw on my invention for a good current lie, I always forge *indorsements*, as well as the bill.

ABSOLUTE: Well, take care you don't hurt your credit, by offering too much security. – Is Mr. Faulkland returned?

FAG: He is above, Sir, changing his dress.

ABSOLUTE: Can you tell whether he has been informed of Sir Anthony's and Miss Melville's arrival?

FAG: I fancy not, Sir; he has seen no one since he came in, but his gentleman, who was with him at Bristol. – I think, Sir, I hear Mr. Faulkland coming down –

ABSOLUTE: Go, tell him I am here.

FAG: Yes, Sir – [*going*] I beg pardon, Sir, but should Sir Anthony call, you will do me the favour to remember, that we are *recruiting*, if you please.

ABSOLUTE: Well, well.

FAG: And in tenderness to my character, if your Honour could bring in the chairmen and waiters, I shall esteem it as an obligation; – for though I never scruple a lie to serve my Master, yet it *hurts* one's conscience, to be found out. [*Exit.*]

ABSOLUTE: Now for my whimsical friend – if he does not know that his mistress is here, I'll tease him a little before I tell him –

[*Enter* FAULKLAND.]

Faulkland, you're welcome to Bath again; you are punctual in your return.

FAULKLAND: Yes; I had nothing to detain me, when I had finished the business I went on. Well, what news since I left you? How stand matters between you and Lydia?

ABSOLUTE: Faith, much as they were; I have not seen her since our quarrel, however I expect to be recalled every hour.

FAULKLAND: Why don't you persuade her to go off with you at once?

ABSOLUTE: What, and lose two thirds of her fortune? You forget that my friend. – No, no, I could have brought her to that long ago.

FAULKLAND: Nay then, you trifle too long – if you are sure of *her*, propose to the aunt *in your own character*, and write to Sir Anthony for his consent.

ABSOLUTE: Softly, softly, for though I am convinced my little Lydia would elope with me as Ensign Beverley, yet am I by no means certain that she would take me with the impediment of our friend's consent, a regular humdrum wedding, and the reversion of a good fortune on my side; no, no, I must prepare her gradually for the discovery, and make myself necessary to her, before I risk it. – Well, but Faulkland, you'll dine with us to-day at the Hotel?

FAULKLAND: Indeed I cannot: I am not in spirits to be of such a party.

ABSOLUTE: By Heavens! I shall forswear your company. You are the most teasing, captious, incorrigible lover! – Do love like a man.

FAULKLAND: I own I am unfit for company.

ABSOLUTE: Am not *I* a lover; aye, and a romantic one too? Yet do I carry every where with me such a confounded farago of doubts, fears, hopes, wishes, and all the flimsy furniture of a country Miss's brain!

FAULKLAND: Ah! Jack, your heart and soul are not, like mine, fixed immutably on one only object. – You throw for a large stake, but losing – you could stake, and throw again: – but I have set my sum of happiness on this cast, and not to succeed, were to be stript of all.

ABSOLUTE: But for Heaven's sake! what grounds for apprehension can your whimsical brain conjure up at present?

FAULKLAND: What grounds for apprehension did you say? Heavens! are there not a thousand! I fear for her spirits – her health – her life. – My absence may fret her; her anxiety for my return, her fears for me, may oppress her gentle temper. And for her health – does not every hour bring me cause to be alarmed? If it rains, some shower may even then have chilled her delicate frame! – If the wind be keen, some rude blast may have affected her! The heat of noon, the dews of the evening, may endanger the life of her, for whom only I value mine. O! Jack, when delicate and feeling souls are separated, there is not a feature in the sky, not a movement of the elements; not an aspiration of the breeze, but hints some cause for a lover's apprehension!

ABSOLUTE: Aye, but we may choose whether we will take the hint or not. –

Well then, Faulkland, if you were convinced that Julia were well and in spirits, you would be entirely content.

FAULKLAND: I should be happy beyond measure – I am anxious only for that.

ABSOLUTE: Then to cure your anxiety at once – Miss Melville is in perfect health, and is at this moment in Bath.

FAULKLAND: Nay Jack – don't trifle with me.

ABSOLUTE: She is arrived here with my father within this hour.

FAULKLAND: Can you be serious?

ABSOLUTE: I thought you knew Sir Anthony better than to be surprised at a sudden whim of this kind. – Seriously then, it is as I tell you – upon my honour.

FAULKLAND: My dear friend! – Hollo, Du-Peigne! my hat – my dear Jack – *now nothing on earth can give me a moment's uneasiness.*

[*Enter* FAG.]

FAG: Sir, Mr. Acres just arrived is below.

ABSOLUTE: Stay, Faulkland, this Acres lives within a mile of Sir Anthony, and he shall tell you how your mistress has been ever since you left her. – Fag, shew the gentleman up. [*Exit* FAG.]

FAULKLAND: What, is he much acquainted in the family?

ABSOLUTE: O, very intimate: I insist on your not going: besides, his character will divert you.

FAULKLAND: Well, I should like to ask him a few questions.

ABSOLUTE: He is likewise a rival of mine – that is of my *other self's*, for he does not think his friend Capt. Absolute ever saw the lady in question; – and it is ridiculous enough to hear him complain to me of *one Beverley*, a concealed sculking rival, who –

FAULKLAND: Hush! – He's here.

[*Enter* ACRES.]

ACRES: Hah! my dear friend, noble captain, and honest Jack, how do'st thou? just arrived faith, as you see. – Sir, your humble servant. Warm work on the roads Jack – Odds whips and wheels, I've travelled like a Comet, with a tail of dust all the way as long as the Mall.

ABSOLUTE: Ah! Bob, you are indeed an excentric Planet, but we know your attraction hither – give me leave to introduce Mr. Faulkland to you; Mr Faulkland, Mr. Acres.

ACRES: Sir, I am most heartily glad to see you: Sir, I solicit your connections. – Hey Jack – what this is Mr. Faulkland, who –

ABSOLUTE: Aye, Bob, Miss Melville's Mr. Faulkland.

ACRES: Od'so! she and your father can be but just arrived before me – I suppose you have seen them. – Ah! Mr. Faulkland, you are indeed a happy man.

FAULKLAND: I have not seen Miss Melville yet, Sir – I hope she enjoyed full health and spirits in Devonshire?

ACRES: Never knew her better in my life, Sir, – never better. – Odd's Blushes and Blooms! she has been as healthy as the German Spa.

FAULKLAND: Indeed! – I did hear that she had been a little indisposed.

ACRES: False, false, Sir – only said to vex you: quite the reverse I assure you.

FAULKLAND: There, Jack, you see she has the advantage of me; I had almost fretted myself ill.

ABSOLUTE: Now are you angry with your mistress for not having been sick.

FAULKLAND: No, no, you misunderstand me: – yet surely a little trifling indisposition is not an unnatural consequence of absence from those we love. – Now confess – isn't there something unkind in this violent, robust, unfeeling health?

ABSOLUTE: O, it was very unkind of her to be well in your absence to be sure!

ACRES: Good apartments, Jack.

FAULKLAND: Well, Sir, but you were saying that Miss Melville has been so *exceedingly* well – what then she has been merry and gay I suppose? – Always in spirits – hey?

ACRES: Merry, Odds Crickets! she has been the bell and spirit of the company wherever she has been – so lively and entertaining! so full of wit and humour!

FAULKLAND: There, Jack, there. – O, by my soul! there is an innate levity in woman, that nothing can overcome. – What! happy and I away!

ABSOLUTE: Have done: how foolish this is! just now you were only apprehensive for your mistress's *spirits*.

FAULKLAND: Why, Jack, have I been the joy and spirit of the company?

ABSOLUTE: No indeed, you have not.

FAULKLAND: Have I been lively and entertaining?

ABSOLUTE: O, upon my word, I acquit you.

FAULKLAND: Have I been full of wit and humour?

ABSOLUTE: No, faith, to do you justice, you have been confoundedly stupid indeed.

ACRES: What's the matter with the gentleman?

ABSOLUTE: He is only expressing his great satisfaction at hearing that Julia has been so well and happy – that's all – hey, Faulkland?

FAULKLAND: Oh! I am rejoiced to hear it – yes, yes, she has a *happy* disposition!

ACRES: That she has indeed – then she is so accomplished – so sweet a voice – so expert at her Harpsichord – such a mistress of flat and sharp, squallante, rumblante, and quiverante! – there was this time month – Odds Minnums and Crotchets! how she did chirup at Mrs. Piano's Concert.

FAULKLAND: There again, what say you to this? you see she has been all mirth and song – not a thought of me!

ABSOLUTE: Pho! man, is not music the food of love?

FAULKLAND: Well, well, it may be so. – Pray Mr. – what's his d – d name? – Do you remember what songs Miss Melville sung?

ACRES: Not I, indeed.

ABSOLUTE: Stay now, they were some pretty, melancholy, purling stream airs, I warrant; perhaps you may recollect: – did she sing – '*When absent from my soul's delight*?'

ACRES: No, that wa'n't it.

ABSOLUTE: Or – '*Go, gentle Gales!*' – '*Go, gentle Gales!*'[1] [*sings*]

ACRES: O no! nothing like it. – Odds! now I recollect one of them – '*My heart's my own, my will is free.*'[2] [*sings*]

FAULKLAND: Fool! fool that I am! to fix all my happiness on such a trifler! S'death! to make herself the pipe and ballad-monger of a circle! to sooth her light heart with catches and glees! – What can you say to this, Sir?

ABSOLUTE: Why, that I should be glad to hear my mistress had been so merry, *Sir*.

FAULKLAND: Nay, nay, nay – I am not sorry that she has been happy – no, no, I am glad of that – I would not have had her sad or sick – yet surely a sympathetic heart would have shewn itself even in the choice of a song – she might have been temperately healthy, and somehow, plaintively gay; – but she has been dancing too, I doubt not!

ACRES: What does the gentleman say about dancing?

ABSOLUTE: He says the lady we speak of dances as well as she sings.

ACRES: Aye truly, does she – there was at our last race-ball –

FAULKLAND: Hell and the devil! – There! there! I – told you so! I told you so! Oh! she thrives in my absence! – Dancing! – but her whole feelings have been in opposition with mine! – I have been anxious, silent, pensive, sedentary – my days have been hours of care, my nights of watchfulness. – She has been all Health! Spirit! Laugh! Song! Dance! – Oh! d—n'd, d—n'd levity!

ABSOLUTE: For Heaven's sake! Faulkland, don't expose yourself so. – Suppose she has danced, what then? – does not the ceremony of society often oblige –

FAULKLAND: Well, well, I'll contain myself – perhaps, as you say – for form sake. – What, Mr. Acres, you were praising Miss Melville's manner of dancing a *minuet* – hey?

ACRES: O I dare insure her for that – but what I was going to speak of was her *country dancing*: – Odds swimmings! she has such an air with her! –

FAULKLAND: Now disappointment on her! – defend this, Absolute, why don't you defend this? – Country-dances! jiggs, and reels! am I to blame now? A Minuet I could have forgiven – I should not have minded that – I say I should not have regarded a Minuet – but *Country-dances*! z—ds!

1. The lyrics of both songs are full of lush sentimentality. Reproduced in Price (ed.), *The Dramatic Works of Richard Brinsley Sheridan*, p. 93.
2. The lyrics of this song embody a forthright assertion of independence. Reproduced in ibid., p. 93.

had she made one in a *Cotillon* – I believe I could have forgiven even that – but to be monkey-led for a night! – to run the gauntlet thro' a string of amorous palming[1] puppies! – to shew paces like a managed filly![2] – O Jack, there never can be but *one* man in the world, whom a truly modest and delicate woman ought to pair with in a *Country-dance*; and even then, the rest of the couples should be her great uncles and aunts!

ABSOLUTE: Aye, to be sure! – grand-fathers and grand-mothers!

FAULKLAND: If there be but one vicious mind in the Set, 'twill spread like a contagion – the action of their pulse beats to the lascivious movement of the jigg – their quivering, warm-breath'd sighs impregnate the very air – the atmosphere becomes electrical to love, and each amorous spark darts thro' every link of the chain! – I must leave you – I own I am somewhat flurried – and that confounded looby has perceived it. [*Going.*]

ABSOLUTE: Nay, but stay Faulkland, and thank Mr. Acres for his good news.

FAULKLAND: D—n his news! [*Exit* FAULKLAND.]

ABSOLUTE: Ha! ha! ha! poor Faulkland five minutes since – 'nothing on earth could give him a moment's uneasiness!'

ACRES: The gentleman wa'n't angry at my praising his mistress, was he?

ABSOLUTE: A little jealous, I believe, Bob.

ACRES: You don't say so? Ha! ha! jealous of me – that's a good joke.

ABSOLUTE: There's nothing strange in that, Bob: let me tell you, that sprightly grace and insinuating manner of yours will do some mischief among the girls here.

ACRES: Ah! you joke – ha! ha! mischief – ha! ha! but you know I am not my own property, my dear Lydia, has forestalled me. – She could never abide me in the country, because I used to dress so badly – but odds frogs and tambours! I shan't take matters so here – now ancient Madam[3] has no voice in it – I'll make my old clothes know who's master – I shall straitway cashier the hunting-frock – and render my leather breeches incapable – My hair has been in training some time.

ABSOLUTE: Indeed!

ACRES: Aye – and tho'ff the side-curls are a little restive, my hind-part takes to it very kindly.

ABSOLUTE: O, you'll polish, I doubt not.

ACRES: Absolutely I propose so – then if I can find out this Ensign Beverley, odds triggers and flints! I'll make him know the difference o't.

ABSOLUTE: Spoke like a man – but pray, Bob, I observe you have got an odd kind of a new method of swearing –

ACRES: Ha! ha! you've taken notice of it – 'tis genteel, isn't it – I didn't invent it myself though; but a commander in our militia – a great scholar, I assure you – says that there is no meaning in the common oaths, and that

1. Stroking with palms.
2. Manège exercises, as if she were a horse.
3. His mother.

nothing but their antiquity makes them respectable; – because, he says, the ancients would never stick to an oath or two, but would say By Jove! or by Bacchus! or by Mars! or by Venus! or by Pallas! according to the sentiment – so that to swear with propriety, says my little Major, the 'oath should be an echo to the sense'; and this we call the *oath referential*, or *sentimental swearing* – ha! ha! ha! 'tis genteel, isn't it?

ABSOLUTE: Very genteel, and very new indeed – and I dare say will supplant all other figures of imprecation.

ACRES: Aye, aye, the best terms will grow obsolete – D—ns have had their day.

[*Enter* FAG.]

FAG: Sir, there is a gentleman below, desires to see you – shall I shew him into the parlour?

ABSOLUTE: Aye – you may.

ACRES: Well, I must be gone –

ABSOLUTE: Stay; who is it, Fag?

FAG: Your father, Sir.

ABSOLUTE: You puppy, why didn't you shew him up directly? [*Exit* FAG.]

ACRES: You have business with Sir Anthony. – I expect a message from Mrs. Malaprop at my lodgings – I have sent also to my dear friend Sir Lucius O'Trigger. – Adieu, Jack, we must meet at night, when you shall give me a dozen bumpers[1] to little Lydia.

ABSOLUTE: That I will with all my heart. [*Exit* ACRES.]
Now for a parental lecture – I hope he has heard nothing of the business that has brought me here. – I wish the gout had held him fast in Devonshire, with all my soul!

[*Enter* SIR ANTHONY.]

ABSOLUTE: Sir, I am delighted to see you here; and looking so well! – your sudden arrival at Bath made me apprehensive for your health.

SIR ANTHONY: Very apprehensive, I dare say, Jack. – What, you are recruiting here, hey?

ABSOLUTE: Yes, Sir, I am on duty.

SIR ANTHONY: Well, Jack, I am glad to see you, tho' I did not expect it, for I was going to write to you on a little matter of business. – Jack, I have been considering that I grow old and infirm, and shall probably not trouble you long.

ABSOLUTE: Pardon me, Sir, I never saw you look more strong and hearty; and I pray frequently that you may continue so.

SIR ANTHONY: I hope your prayers may be heard with all my heart. Well then, Jack, I have been considering that I am so strong and hearty, I may continue to plague you a long time. – Now, Jack, I am sensible that the

1. Toasts.

income of your commission, and what I have hitherto allowed you, is but a small pittance for a lad of your spirit.

ABSOLUTE: Sir, you are very good.

SIR ANTHONY: And it is my wish, while yet I live, to have my Boy make some figure in the world. – I have resolved, therefore, to fix you at once in a noble independence.

ABSOLUTE: Sir, your kindness overpowers me – such generosity makes the gratitude of reason more lively than the sensations even of filial affection.

SIR ANTHONY: I am glad you are so sensible of my attention – and you shall be master of a large estate in a few weeks.

ABSOLUTE: Let my future life, Sir, speak my gratitude: I cannot express the sense I have of your munificence. – Yet, Sir, I presume you would not wish me to quit the army?

SIR ANTHONY: O, that shall be as your wife chooses.

ABSOLUTE: My wife, Sir!

SIR ANTHONY: Aye, aye, settle that between you – settle that between you.

ABSOLUTE: A *wife*, Sir, did you say?

SIR ANTHONY: Aye, a wife – why; did not I mention her before?

ABSOLUTE: Not a word of her, Sir.

SIR ANTHONY: Odd so! – I mustn't forget *her* tho'. – Yes, Jack, the independence I was talking of is by marriage – the fortune is saddled with a wife – but I suppose that makes no difference.

ABSOLUTE: Sir! Sir! – you amaze me!

SIR ANTHONY: Why, what the d—l's the matter with the fool? Just now you were all gratitude and duty.

ABSOLUTE: I was, Sir, – you talked to me of independence and a fortune, but not a word of a wife.

SIR ANTHONY: Why – what difference does that make? Odd's life, Sir! if you have the estate, you must take it with the live stock on it, as it stands.

ABSOLUTE: If my happiness is to be the price, I must beg leave to decline the purchase. – Pray, Sir, who is the lady?

SIR ANTHONY: What's that to you, Sir? – Come, give me your promise to love, and to marry her directly.

ABSOLUTE: Sure, Sir, this is not very reasonable, to summon my affections for a lady I know nothing of !

SIR ANTHONY: I am sure, Sir, 'tis more unreasonable in you to *object* to a lady you know nothing of.

ABSOLUTE: Then, Sir, I must tell you plainly, that my inclinations are fix'd on another – my heart is engaged to an Angel.

SIR ANTHONY: Then prey let it send an excuse. – It is very sorry – but *business* prevents its waiting on her.

ABSOLUTE: But my vows are pledged to her.

SIR ANTHONY: Let her foreclose, Jack; let her foreclose; they are not worth redeeming: besides, you have the Angel's vows in exchange, I suppose; so there can be no loss there.

ABSOLUTE: You must excuse me, Sir, if I tell you, once for all, that in this point I cannot obey you.

SIR ANTHONY: Hark'ee Jack; – I have heard you for some time with patience – I have been cool, – quite cool; – but take care – you know I am compliance itself – when I am not thwarted; – no one more easily led – when I have my own way; – but don't put me in a phrenzy.

ABSOLUTE: Sir, I must repeat it – in this I cannot obey you.

SIR ANTHONY: Now, d—n me! if ever I call you *Jack* again while I live!

ABSOLUTE: Nay, Sir, but hear me.

SIR ANTHONY: Sir, I won't hear a word – not a word! not one word! so give me your promise by a nod – and I'll tell you what, Jack – I mean, you Dog – if you don't, by –

ABSOLUTE: What, Sir, promise to link myself to some mass of ugliness! to –

SIR ANTHONY: Z—ds! sirrah! the lady shall be as ugly as I choose; she shall have a hump on each shoulder; she shall be as crooked as the Crescent;[1] her one eye shall roll like the Bull's in Cox's musæum[2] – she shall have a skin like a mummy, and the beard of a Jew – she shall be all this, sirrah! – yet I'll make you ogle her all day, and sit up all night to write sonnets on her beauty.

ABSOLUTE: This is reason and moderation indeed!

SIR ANTHONY: None of your sneering, puppy! no grinning, jackanapes![3]

ABSOLUTE: Indeed, Sir, I never was in a worse humour for mirth in my life.

SIR ANTHONY: 'Tis false, Sir! I know you are laughing in your sleeve: I know you'll grin when I am gone, sirrah!

ABSOLUTE: Sir, I hope I know my duty better.

SIR ANTHONY: None of your passion, Sir! none of your violence! if you please. – It won't do with me, I promise you.

ABSOLUTE: Indeed, Sir, I never was cooler in my life.

SIR ANTHONY: 'Tis a confounded lie! – I know you are in a passion in your heart; I know you are, you hypocritical young dog! but it won't do.

ABSOLUTE: Nay, Sir, upon my word.

SIR ANTHONY: So you will fly out! can't you be cool, like me? What the devil good can *Passion* do! – *Passion* is of no service, you impudent, insolent, over-bearing Reprobate! – There you sneer again! – don't provoke me! – but you rely upon the mildness of my temper – you do, you Dog! you play upon the meekness of my disposition! Yet take care – the patience of a saint may be overcome at last! – but mark! I give you six hours and a half to consider of this: if you then agree, without any condition, to do every thing on earth that I choose, why – confound you! I may in time forgive you – If not, z—ds! don't enter the same hemisphere with me! don't dare to breathe the same air, or use the same light with me; but get

1. The Royal Crescent in Bath.
2. James Cox exhibited his collection of mechanical toys in Spring Gardens.
3. Monkey.

an atmosphere and a sun of your own! I'll strip you of your commission; I'll lodge a five-and-threepence[1] in the hands of trustees, and you shall live on the interest. – I'll disown you, I'll disinherit you, I'll unget you! and – d—n me, if ever I call you Jack again. [*Exit* SIR ANTHONY.]

[ABSOLUTE, *solus*.]

ABSOLUTE: Mild, gentle, considerate father – I kiss your hands. – What a tender method of giving his opinion in these matters Sir Anthony has! I dare not trust him with the truth. – I wonder what old, wealthy Hag it is that he wants to bestow on me! – yet he married himself for love! and was in his youth a bold Intriguer, and a gay Companion!

[*Enter* FAG.]

FAG: Assuredly, Sir, our Father is wrath to a degree; he comes down stairs eight or ten steps at a time – muttering, growling, and thumping the bannisters all the way: I, and the Cook's dog, stand bowing at the door – rap! he gives me a stroke on the head with his cane; bids me carry that to my master, then kicking the poor Turnspit into the area, d—ns us all, for a puppy triumvirate! – Upon my credit, Sir, were I in your place, and found my father such very bad company, I should certainly drop his acquaintance.

ABSOLUTE: Cease your impertinence, Sir, at present. – Did you come in for nothing more? – Stand out of the way! [*Pushes him aside, and Exit.*]

[FAG, *solus*.]

FAG: Soh! sir Anthony trims[2] my Master; He is afraid to reply to his Father – then vents his spleen on poor Fag! – When one is vexed by one person, to revenge one's self on another, who happens to come in the way – is the vilest injustice! Ah! it shews the worst temper – the basest –

[*Enter* ERRAND-BOY.]

BOY: Mr. Fag! Mr. Fag! your Master calls you.

FAG: Well, you little, dirty puppy, you need not baul so! – The meanest disposition! the –

BOY: Quick, quick, Mr. Fag.

FAG: *Quick, quick*, you impudent Jackanapes! am I to be commanded by you too? you little, impertinent, insolent, kitchen-bred –

[*Exit, kicking and beating him.*]

1. A quarter of a guinea.
2. Scolds.

Act II, Scene II

[*The* North Parade.
Enter LUCY.]

LUCY: So – I shall have another Rival to add to my mistress's list – Captain Absolute. – However, I shall not enter his name till my purse has received notice in form. Poor Acres is dismissed! – Well, I have done him a last friendly office, in letting him know that Beverley was here before him. – Sir Lucius is generally more punctual, when he expects to hear from his *dear Dalia*, as he calls her: – I wonder he's not here! – I have a little scruple of conscience from this deceit; tho' I should not be paid so well, if my hero knew that *Delia* was near fifty, and her own mistress.

[*Enter* SIR LUCIUS O'TRIGGER.]

SIR LUCIUS: Hah! my little embassadress – upon my conscience I have been looking for you; I have been on the South Parade this half-hour.

LUCY: [*Speaking simply*] O gemini! and I have been waiting for your worship here on the North.

SIR LUCIUS: Faith! – may be, that was the reason we did not meet; and it is very comical too, how you could go out and I not see you – for I was only taking a nap at the Parade-Coffee-house, and I chose the *window* on purpose that I might not miss you.

LUCY: My stars! Now I'd wager a six-pence I went by while you were asleep.

SIR LUCIUS: Sure enough it must have been so – and I never dreamt it was so late, till I waked. Well, but my little girl, have you got nothing for me?

LUCY: Yes, but I have: – I've got a letter for you in my pocket.

SIR LUCIUS: O faith! I guessed you weren't come empty-handed – well – let me see what the dear creature says.

LUCY: There, Sir Lucius. [*Gives him a letter.*]

SIR LUCIUS: [*Reads*] *'Sir – there is often a sudden incentive*[1] *impulse in love, that has a greater induction*[2] *than years of domestic combination: such was the commotion*[3] *I felt at the first superfluous*[4] *view of Sir Lucius O'Trigger.'* Very pretty, upon my word. *'Female punctuation*[5] *forbids me to say more; yet let me add, that it will give me joy infallible*[6] *to find Sir Lucius worthy the last criterion of my affections. –* DELIA.' Upon my conscience! Lucy, your lady is a great mistress of language. – Faith, she's quite the queen of the dictionary! – for the devil a word dare refuse coming at her call – tho' one would think it was quite out of hearing.

1. Inventive.
2. Inducement.
3. Emotion.
4. Superficial.
5. Punctiliousness.
6. Ineffable.

LUCY: Aye, Sir, a lady of her experience.

SIR LUCIUS: Experience! what, at seventeen?

LUCY: O true, Sir – but then she reads so – my stars! how she will read off-hand![1]

SIR LUCIUS: Faith, she must be very deep read to write this way – tho' she is rather an arbitrary writer too – for there are a great many poor words pressed into service of this note, that would get their *habeas corpus*[2] from any court in Christendom.

LUCY: Ah! Sir Lucius, if you were to hear how she talks of you!

SIR LUCIUS: O tell her, I'll make her the best husband in the world, and Lady O'Trigger into the bargain! – But we must get the old gentle-woman's consent – and do every thing fairly.

LUCY: Nay, Sir Lucius, I thought you wa'n't rich enough to be so nice!

SIR LUCIUS: Upon my word, young woman, you have hit it: – I am so poor that I can't afford to do a dirty action. – If I did not want money, I'd steal your mistress and her fortune with a great deal of pleasure. – However, my pretty girl, [*gives her money*] here's a little something to buy you a ribband; and meet me in the evening, and I'll give you an answer to this. So, hussy, take a kiss before-hand, to put you in mind. [*Kisses her.*]

LUCY: O lud! Sir Lucius – I never seed such a gemman! My lady won't like you if you're so impudent.

SIR LUCIUS: Faith she will, Lucy – that same – pho! what's the name of it? – *Modesty!* – is a quality in a lover more praised by the women than liked; so, if your mistress asks you whether Sir Lucius ever gave you a kiss, tell her *fifty* – my dear.

LUCY: What, would you have me tell her a lie?

SIR LUCIUS: Ah then, you baggage! I'll make it a truth presently.

LUCY: For shame now; here is some one coming.

SIR LUCIUS: O faith, I'll quiet your conscience!

[*Sees* FAG. – *Exit, humming a Tune.*]

[*Enter* FAG.]

FAG: So, so, Ma'am. I humbly beg pardon.

LUCY: O lud! – now, Mr. Fag – you flurry one so.

FAG: Come, come, Lucy, here's no one bye – so a little less simplicity, with a grain or two more sincerity, if you please. – You play false with us, Madam. – I saw you give the Baronet a letter. – My Master shall know this – and if he don't call him out – I will.

LUCY: Ha! ha! ha! you gentlemen's gentlemen are so hasty. – That letter was from Mrs. Malaprop, simpleton. – She is taken with Sir Lucius's address.[3]

1. Straight off.
2. Release.
3. Behaviour.

FAG: How! what tastes some people have! – Why I suppose I have walked by her window an hundred times. – But what says our young lady? Any message to my master?

LUCY: Sad news! Mr. Fag. – A worse Rival than Acres! – Sir Anthony Absolute has proposed his son.

FAG: What, Captain Absolute!

LUCY: Even so. – I overheard it all.

FAG: Ha! ha! ha! – very good, faith. – Goodbye, Lucy, I must away with this news.

LUCY: Well – you may laugh – but it is true, I assure you. [*Going.*] But – Mr. Fag – tell your master not to be cast down by this.

FAG: O, he'll be so disconsolate!

LUCY: And charge him not to think of quarrelling with young Absolute.

FAG: Never fear! – never fear!

LUCY: Be sure – bid him keep up his spirits.

FAG: We will – we will. [*Exeunt severally.*]

Act III, Scene I

[*The* North Parade.
Enter ABSOLUTE.]

ABSOLUTE: 'Tis just as Fag told me, indeed. – Whimsical enough, faith! My Father wants to *force* me to marry the very girl I am plotting to run away with! – He must not know of my connection with her yet a-while. – He has too summary a method of proceeding in these matters. – However, I'll read my recantation instantly. – My conversion is something sudden, indeed – but I can assure him it is very *sincere*. – So, so – here he comes. – He looks plaguy gruff. [*Steps aside.*]

[*Enter* SIR ANTHONY.]

SIR ANTHONY: No – I'll die sooner than forgive him. – *Die*, did I say? I'll live these fifty years to plague him. – At our last meeting, his impudence had almost put me out of temper. – An obstinate, passionate, self-willed boy! – Who can he take after? This is my return for getting[1] him before all his brothers and sisters! – for putting him, at twelve years old, into a marching regiment, and allowing him fifty pounds a year, beside his pay ever since! – But I have done with him; – he's any body's son for me. – I never will see him more, – never – never – never – never.

1. Begetting.

ABSOLUTE: Now for a penitential face.

SIR ANTHONY: Fellow, get out of my way.

ABSOLUTE: Sir, you see a penitent before you.

SIR ANTHONY: I see an impudent scoundrel before me.

ABSOLUTE: A sincere penitent. – I am come, Sir, to acknowledge my error, and to submit entirely to your will.

SIR ANTHONY: What's that?

ABSOLUTE: I have been revolving, and reflecting, and considering on your past goodness, and kindness, and condescension to me.

SIR ANTHONY: Well, Sir?

ABSOLUTE: I have been likewise weighing and balancing what you were pleased to mention concerning duty, and obedience, and authority.

SIR ANTHONY: Well, Puppy?

ABSOLUTE: Why then, Sir, the result of my reflections is – a resolution to sacrifice every inclination of my own to your satisfaction.

SIR ANTHONY: Why now, you talk sense – absolute sense – I never heard any thing more sensible in my life. – Confound you; you shall be *Jack* again.

ABSOLUTE: I am happy in the appellation.

SIR ANTHONY: Why, then, Jack, my dear Jack, I will now inform you – who the lady really is. – Nothing but your passion and violence, you silly fellow, prevented my telling you at first. Prepare, Jack, for wonder and rapture – prepare. – What think you of Miss Lydia Languish?

ABSOLUTE: Languish! What, the Languishes of Worcestershire?

SIR ANTHONY: Worcestershire! No. Did you never meet Mrs. Malaprop and her Niece, Miss Languish, who came into our country just before you were last ordered to your regiment?

ABSOLUTE: Malaprop! Languish! I don't remember ever to have heard the names before. Yet, stay – I think I do recollect something. – *Languish*! *Languish*! She squints, don't she? – A little, red-haired girl ?

SIR ANTHONY: Squints? – A red-haired girl! – Z—ds, no.

ABSOLUTE: Then I must have forgot; it can't be the same person.

SIR ANTHONY: Jack! Jack! what think you of blooming, love-breathing seventeen?

ABSOLUTE: As to that, Sir, I am quite indifferent. – If I can please you in the matter, 'tis all I desire.

SIR ANTHONY: Nay, but Jack, such eyes! such eyes! so innocently wild! so bashfully irresolute! Not a glance but speaks and kindles some thought of love! Then, Jack, her cheeks! her cheeks, Jack! so deeply blushing at the insinuations of her tell-tale eyes! Then, Jack, her lips! – O Jack, lips smiling at their own discretion; and if not smiling, more sweetly pouting; more lovely in sullenness!

ABSOLUTE: That's she indeed. – Well done, old gentleman! [*Aside.*]

SIR ANTHONY: Then, Jack, her neck. – O Jack! Jack!

ABSOLUTE: And which is to be mine, Sir, the Niece or the Aunt?

SIR ANTHONY: Why, you unfeeling, insensible Puppy, I despise you. When I was of your age, such a description would have made me fly like a rocket! The *Aunt*, indeed! – Odds life! when I ran away with your mother, I would not have touched any thing old or ugly to gain an empire.

ABSOLUTE: Not to please your father, Sir?

SIR ANTHONY: To please my father! – Z—ds! not to please – O my father! – Oddso! – yes – yes! if my father indeed had desired – that's quite another matter. – Tho' he wa'n't the indulgent father that I am, Jack.

ABSOLUTE: I dare say not, Sir.

SIR ANTHONY: But, Jack, you are not sorry to find your mistress is so beautiful.

ABSOLUTE: Sir, I repeat it; if I please you in this affair, 'tis all I desire. Not that I think a woman the worse for being handsome; but, Sir, if you please to recollect, you before hinted something about a hump or two, one eye, and a few more graces of that kind – now, without being very nice,[1] I own I should rather chuse a wife of mine to have the usual number of limbs, and a limited quantity of back: and tho' *one* eye may be very agreeable, yet as the prejudice has always run in favour of *two*, I would not wish to affect a singularity in that article.

SIR ANTHONY: What a phlegmatic sot it is! Why, sirrah, you're an anchorite! – a vile insensible stock. – You a soldier! – you're a walking block, fit only to dust the company's regimentals on! – Odds life! I've a great mind to marry the girl myself!

ABSOLUTE: I am entirely at your disposal, Sir; if you should think of addressing Miss Languish yourself, I suppose you would have me marry the *Aunt*; or if you should change your mind, and take the old lady – 'tis the same to me – I'll marry the *Niece*.

SIR ANTHONY: Upon my word, Jack, thou'rt either a very great hypocrite, or – but, come, I know your indifference on such a subject must be all a lie – I'm sure it must – come, now – d—n your demure face! – come, confess, Jack – you have been lying – ha'n't you? You have been playing the hypocrite, hey – I'll never forgive you, if you ha'n't been lying and playing the hypocrite.

ABSOLUTE: I'm sorry, Sir, that the respect and duty which I bear to you should be so mistaken.

SIR ANTHONY: Hang your respect and duty! But, come along with me, I'll write a note to Mrs. Malaprop, and you shall visit the lady directly. Her eyes shall be the Promethian torch to you – come along, I'll never forgive you, if you don't come back, stark mad with rapture and impatience – if you don't, egad, I'll marry the girl myself! [*Exeunt.*]

1. Hard to please.

Act III, Scene II

[JULIA's *Dressing-room.*
FAULKLAND, *solus.*]

FAULKLAND: They told me Julia would return directly; I wonder she is not yet come! – How mean does this captious, unsatisfied temper of mine appear to my cooler judgment! Yet I know not that I indulge it in any other point: – but on this one subject, and to this one subject, whom I think I love beyond my life, I am ever ungenerously fretful, and madly capricious! – I am conscious of it – yet I cannot correct myself! What tender, honest joy sparkled in her eyes when we met! – How delicate was the warmth of her expressions! – I was ashamed to appear less happy – though I had come resolved to wear a face of coolness and upbraiding. Sir Anthony's presence prevented my proposed expostulations: – yet I must be satisfied that she has not been so *very* happy in my absence. – She is coming! – Yes! – I know the nimbleness of her tread, when she thinks her impatient Faulkland counts the moments of her stay.

[*Enter* JULIA.]

JULIA: I had not hop'd to see you again so soon.

FAULKLAND: Could I, Julia, be contented with my first welcome – restrained as we were by the presence of a third person?

JULIA: O Faulkland, when your kindness can make me thus happy, let me not think that I discovered something of coldness in your first salutation.

FAULKLAND: 'Twas but your fancy, Julia. – I *was* rejoiced to see you – to see you in such health – Sure I had no cause for coldness?

JULIA: Nay then, I see you have taken something ill. – You must not conceal from me what it is.

FAULKLAND: Well then – shall I own to you that my joy at hearing of your health and arrival here, by your neighbour Acres, was somewhat damped, by his dwelling much on the high spirits you had enjoyed in Devonshire – on your mirth – your singing – dancing, and I know not what! – For such is my temper, Julia, that I should regard every mirthful moment in your absence as a treason to constancy: – The mutual tear that steals down the cheek of parting lovers is a compact, that no smile shall live there till they meet again.

JULIA: Must I never cease to tax my Faulkland with this teasing minute caprice? – Can the idle reports of a silly boor weigh in your breast against my tried affection?

FAULKLAND: They have no weight with me, Julia: no, no – I am happy if you have been so – yet only say, that you did not sing with *mirth* – say that you *thought* of Faulkland in the dance.

JULIA: I never can be happy, in your absence. – If I wear a countenance of content, it is to shew that my mind holds no doubt of my Faulkland's truth. – If I seem'd sad – it were to make malice triumph; and say, that I had fixed my heart on one, who left me to lament his roving, and my own credulity. – Believe me, Faulkland, I mean not to upbraid you, when I say, that I have often dressed sorrow in smiles, lest my friends should guess whose unkindness had caused my tears.

FAULKLAND: You were ever all goodness to me. – O, I am a brute, when I but admit a doubt of your true constancy.

JULIA: If ever, without such cause from you, as I will not suppose possible, you find my affections veering but a point,[1] may I become a proverbial scoff for levity, and base ingratitude.

FAULKLAND: Ah! Julia, that *last* word is grating to me. I would I had no title to your *gratitude!* Search your heart, Julia; perhaps what you have mistaken for Love, is but the warm effusion of a too thankful heart!

JULIA: For what quality must I love you?

FAULKLAND: For no quality! To regard me for any quality of mind or understanding, were only to *esteem* me. And for person – I have often wish'd myself deformed, to be convinced that I owed no obligation *there* for any part of your affection.

JULIA: Where Nature has bestowed a shew of nice attention in the features of a man, he should laugh at it, as misplaced. I have seen men, who in *this* vain article perhaps might rank above you; but my heart has never asked my eyes if it were so or not.

FAULKLAND: Now this is not well from *you,* Julia – I despise person[2] in a man – Yet if you lov'd me as I wish, though I were an Æthiop, you'd think none so fair.

JULIA: I see you are determined to be unkind. – The *contract* which my poor father bound us in gives you more than a lover's privilege.

FAULKLAND: Again, Julia, you raise ideas that feed and justify my doubts. – I would not have been more free – no – I am proud of my restraint. – Yet – yet – perhaps your high respect alone for this solemn compact has fettered your inclinations, which else had made a worthier choice. – How shall I be sure, had you remained unbound in thought and promise, that I should still have been the object of your persevering love?

JULIA: Then try me now. – Let us be free as strangers as to what is past: – *my* heart will not feel more liberty!

FAULKLAND: There now! so hasty, Julia! so anxious to be free! – If your love for me were fixed and ardent, you would not loose your hold, even tho' I wish'd it!

JULIA: O, you torture me to the heart! – I cannot bear it.

FAULKLAND: I do not mean to distress you. – If I lov'd you less, I should never give you an uneasy moment. – But hear me. – All my fretful doubts

1. A compass point.
2. Good looks.

arise from this – Women are not used to weigh, and separate the motives of their affections: – the cold dictates of prudence, gratitude, or filial duty, may sometimes be mistaken for the pleadings of the heart. – I would not boast – yet let me say, that I have neither age, person, or character, to found dislike on; – my fortune such as few ladies could be charged with *indiscretion* in the match. – O Julia! when *Love* receives such countenance from *Prudence*, nice minds will be suspicious of its *birth*.

JULIA: I know not whither your insinuations would tend: – But as they seem pressing to insult me – I will spare you the regret of having done so. – I have given you no cause for this! [*Exit in Tears*.]

FAULKLAND: In Tears! stay, Julia: stay but for a moment. – The door is fastened! – Julia! – my soul – but for one moment: – I hear her sobbing! – 'Sdeath! what a brute am I to use her thus! Yet stay. – Aye – she is coming now: – how little resolution there is in woman! – how a few soft words can turn them! – No, faith! – she is *not* coming either. – Why, Julia – my love – say but that you forgive me – come but to tell me that – now, this is being *too* resentful: – stay! she *is* coming too – I thought she would – no *steadiness* in any thing! her going away must have been a mere trick then – she sha'n't see that I was hurt by it. – I'll affect indifference – [*hums a tune: then listens*] – No – Z—ds! she's *not* coming! – nor don't intend it, I suppose. – This is not *steadiness*, but *obstinacy*! Yet I deserve it. – What, after so long an absence, to quarrel with her tenderness! – 'twas barbarous and unmanly! – I should be ashamed to see her now. – I'll wait till her just resentment is abated – and when I distress her so again, may I lose her for ever! and be linked instead to some antique virago,[1] whose knawing passions, and long-hoarded spleen, shall make me curse my folly half the day, and all the night! [*Exit*.]

Act III, Scene III

[MRS. MALAPROP's *Lodgings*.
MRS. MALAPROP, *with a letter in her hand, and Captain* ABSOLUTE.]

MRS. MALAPROP: Your being Sir Anthony's son, Captain, would itself be a sufficient accommodation;[2] – but from the ingenuity[3] of your appearance, I am convinced you deserve the character here given of you.

ABSOLUTE: Permit me to say, Madam, that as I never yet have had the pleasure of seeing Miss Languish, my principal inducement in this affair at present is the honour of being allied to Mrs. Malaprop; of whose

1. Shrew.
2. Recommendation.
3. Ingenuousness.

intellectual accomplishments, elegant manners, and unaffected learning no tongue is silent.

MRS. MALAPROP: Sir, you do me infinite honour! – I beg, Captain, you'll be seated. – [*Sit*] – Ah! few gentlemen, now a days, know how to value the ineffectual[1] qualities in a woman! few think how a little knowledge becomes a gentlewoman! Men have no sense now but for the worthless flower of beauty!

ABSOLUTE: It is but too true indeed, Ma'am; – yet I fear our ladies should share the blame – they think our admiration of *beauty* so great, that *knowledge* in *them* would be superfluous. Thus, like garden-trees, they seldom shew fruit, till time has robb'd them of the more specious blossom. – Few, like Mrs. Malaprop and the Orange-tree, are rich in both at once!

MRS. MALAPROP: Sir – you overpower me with good-breeding. – He is the very Pine-apple[2] of politeness! You are not ignorant, Captain, that this giddy girl has somehow contrived to fix her affections on a beggarly, strolling,[3] eves-dropping Ensign, whom none of us have seen, and nobody knows any thing of.

ABSOLUTE: O, I have heard the silly affair before. – I'm not at all prejudiced against her on *that* account.

MRS. MALAPROP: You are very good, and very considerate, Captain. – I am sure I have done every thing in my power since I exploded[4] the affair! long ago I laid my positive conjunctions[5] on her never to think on the fellow again; – I have since laid Sir Anthony's preposition[6] before her; – but I'm sorry to say she seems resolved to decline every particle that I enjoin her.

ABSOLUTE: It must be very distressing indeed, Ma'am.

MRS. MALAPROP: Oh! it gives me the hydrostatics[7] to such a degree! – I thought she had persisted[8] from corresponding with him; but behold this very day, I have interceded[9] another letter from the fellow! I believe I have it in my pocket.

ABSOLUTE: O the devil! my last note. [*Aside.*]

MRS. MALAPROP: Aye, here it is.

ABSOLUTE: Aye, my note indeed! O the little traitress Lucy. [*Aside.*]

MRS. MALAPROP: There, perhaps you may know the writing.

[*Gives him the letter.*]

1. Intellectual.
2. Pinnacle.
3. Wandering.
4. Exposed.
5. Injunctions.
6. Proposition.
7. Hysterics.
8. Desisted.
9. Intercepted.

ABSOLUTE: I think I have seen the hand before – yes, I *certainly must* have seen this hand before: –

MRS. MALAPROP: Nay, but read it, Captain.

ABSOLUTE: [*Reads*] *'My soul's idol, my ador'd Lydia !'* – Very tender indeed!

MRS. MALAPROP: Tender! aye, and prophane too, o' my conscience!

ABSOLUTE: *'I am excessively alarmed at the intelligence you send me, the more so as my new rival'* –

MRS. MALAPROP: That's – *you*, Sir.

ABSOLUTE: *'has universally the character of being an accomplished gentleman, and a man of honour.'* – Well, that's handsome enough.

MRS. MALAPROP: O, the fellow had some design in writing so –

ABSOLUTE: That he had, I'll answer for him, Ma'am.

MRS. MALAPROP: But go on, Sir – you'll see presently.

ABSOLUTE: *'As for the old weather-beaten she-dragon who guards you,'* – Who can he mean by that?

MRS. MALAPROP: *Me*, Sir – *me* – he means *me* there – what do you think now – but go on a little further.

ABSOLUTE: Impudent scoundrel! – *'it shall go hard but I will elude her vigilance, as I am told that the same ridiculous vanity, which makes her dress up her coarse features, and deck her dull chat with hard words which she don't understand'* –

MRS. MALAPROP: There, Sir! an attack upon my language! what do you think of that? – an aspersion upon my parts of speech! was ever such a brute! Sure if I reprehend[1] any thing in this world, it is the use of my oracular[2] tongue, and a nice derangement of epitaphs![3]

ABSOLUTE: He deserves to be hang'd and quartered! let me see – *'same ridiculous vanity'* –

MRS. MALAPROP: You need not read it again, Sir.

ABSOLUTE: I beg pardon, Ma'am *'does also lay her open to the grossest deceptions from flattery and pretended admiration'* – an impudent coxcomb! *'so that I have a scheme to see you shortly with the old Harridan's consent, and even to make her a go between in our interviews.'* – Was ever such assurance.

MRS. MALAPROP: Did you ever hear any thing like it? – he'll elude my vigilance, will he? – yes, yes! ha! ha! he's very likely to enter these doors! – we'll try who can plot best!

ABSOLUTE: So we will Ma'am – so we will. – Ha! ha! ha! a conceited puppy, ha! ha! ha! – Well, but Mrs. Malaprop, as the girl seems so infatuated by this fellow, suppose you were to wink at her corresponding with him for a little time – let her even plot an elopement with him – then do you connive at her escape – while I, just in the nick, will have the fellow laid by the heels, and fairly contrive to carry her off in his stead.

1. Comprehend.
2. Vernacular.
3. Precise arrangement of epithets.

MRS. MALAPROP: I am delighted with the scheme, never was any thing better perpetrated!

ABSOLUTE: But, pray, could not I see the lady for a few minutes now? – I should like to try her temper a little.

MRS. MALAPROP: Why, I don't know – I doubt she is not prepared for a visit of this kind. – There is a decorum in these matters.

ABSOLUTE: O Lord! she won't mind *me* – only tell her Beverley –

MRS. MALAPROP: Sir! –

ABSOLUTE: Gently, good tongue. [*Aside.*]

MRS. MALAPROP: What did you say of Beverley?

ABSOLUTE: O, I was going to propose that you should tell her, by way of jest, that it was Beverley who was below – she'd come down fast enough then – ha! ha! ha!

MRS. MALAPROP:'Twould be a trick she well-deserves – besides you know the fellow tells her he'll get my consent to see her – ha! ha! – Let him if he can, I say again. – Lydia, come down here! [*Calling.*] – He'll make me a *go-between in their interviews*! – ha! ha! ha! Come down, I say, Lydia! – I don't wonder at your laughing, ha! ha! ha! his impudence is truly ridiculous.

ABSOLUTE: 'Tis very ridiculous, upon my soul, Ma'am, ha! ha! ha!

MRS. MALAPROP: The little hussy won't hear. – Well, I'll go and tell her at once who it is – she shall know that Capt. Absolute is come to wait on her. – And I'll make her behave as becomes a young woman.

ABSOLUTE: As you please, Ma'am.

MRS. MALAPROP: For the present, Captain, your servant – Ah! you've not done laughing yet, I see – *elude my vigilance*! yes, yes, ha! ha! ha! [*Exit.*]

ABSOLUTE: Ha! ha! ha! one would think now that I might throw off all disguise at once, and seize my prize with security – but such is Lydia's caprice, that to undeceive were probably to lose her. – I'll see whether she knows me.

[*Walks aside, and seems engaged in looking at the pictures.*]

[*Enter* LYDIA.]

LYDIA: What a scene am I now to go thro'! surely nothing can be more dreadful than to be obliged to listen to the loathsome addresses of a stranger to one's heart. – I have heard of girls persecuted as I am, who have appealed in behalf of their favoured lover to the generosity of his rival: suppose I were to try it – there stands the hated rival – an officer too! – but O how unlike my Beverley! – I wonder he don't begin – truly he seems a very negligent wooer! – quite at his ease, upon my word! I'll speak first – Mr. Absolute.

ABSOLUTE: Madam. [*Turns round.*]

LYDIA: O Heav'ns! Beverley!

ABSOLUTE: Hush! – hush, my life! – softly! be not surprised!

LYDIA: I am so astonished! and so terrified! and so overjoy'd! – for Heavn's sake! how came you here?

ABSOLUTE: Briefly – I have deceived your Aunt – I was informed that my new rival was to visit here this evening, and contriving to have him kept away, have passed myself on *her* for Capt. Absolute.

LYDIA: O, charming! – And she really takes you for young Absolute?

ABSOLUTE: O, she's convinced of it.

LYDIA: Ha! ha! ha! I can't forbear laughing to think how her sagacity is over-reached!

ABSOLUTE: But we trifle with our precious moments – such another opportunity may not occur – then let me now conjure my kind, my condescending angel, to fix the time when I may rescue her from undeserved persecution, and with a licensed warmth plead for my reward.

LYDIA: Will you then, Beverley, consent to forfeit that portion of my paltry wealth? – that burthen on the wings of love?

ABSOLUTE: O come to me – rich only thus – in loveliness – Bring no portion to me but thy love – 'twill be generous in you, Lydia – for well you know, it is the only dower your poor Beverley can repay.

LYDIA: How persuasive are his words! – how charming will poverty be with him!

ABSOLUTE: Ah! my soul, what a life will we then live? Love shall be our idol and support! we will worship him with a monastic strictness; abjuring all worldly toys, to center every thought and action there. – Proud of calamity, we will enjoy the wreck of wealth; while the surrounding gloom of adversity shall make the flame of our pure love show doubly bright. – By Heav'ns! I would fling all goods of fortune from me with a prodigal hand to enjoy the scene where I might clasp my Lydia to my bosom, and say, the world affords no smile to me – but here – [*Embracing her.*]

If she holds out now the devil is in it! [*Aside.*]

LYDIA: Now could I fly with him to the Antipodes! but my persecution is not yet come to a crisis.

[*Enter* MRS. MALAPROP, *listening.*]

MRS. MALAPROP: I'm impatient to know how the little huzzy deports herself [*Aside.*]

ABSOLUTE: So pensive, Lydia! – is then your warmth abated?

MRS. MALAPROP: *Warmth abated*! – so! – she has been in a passion, I suppose.

LYDIA: No – nor ever can while I have life.

MRS. MALAPROP: An ill-temper'd little devil! – She'll be *in a passion all her life* – will she?

LYDIA: Think not the idle threats of my ridiculous aunt can ever have any weight with me.

MRS. MALAPROP: Very dutiful, upon my word!

LYDIA: Let her choice be *Capt. Absolute*, but Beverley is mine.

MRS. MALAPROP: I am astonished at her assurance! – *to his face – this is to his face*!

ABSOLUTE: Thus then let me enforce my suit. [*Kneeling*.]

MRS. MALAPROP: Aye – poor young man! – down on his knees entreating for pity! – I can contain no longer. – Why, thou vixen! – I have overheard you.

ABSOLUTE: O confound her vigilance! [*Aside*]

MRS. MALAPROP: Capt. Absolute – I know not how to apologize for her shocking rudeness.

ABSOLUTE: So – all's safe, I find. [*Aside*]
I have hopes, Madam, that time will bring the young lady –

MRS. MALAPROP: O, there's nothing to be hoped for from her! she's as headstrong as an allegory[1] on the banks of Nile.

LYDIA: Nay, Madam, what do you charge me with now?

MRS. MALAPROP: Why, thou unblushing rebel – didn't you tell this gentleman to his face that you loved another better? – didn't you say you never would be his?

LYDIA: No, Madam – I did not.

MRS. MALAPROP: Good Heav'ns! what assurance! – Lydia, Lydia, you ought to know that lying don't become a young woman! – Didn't you boast that Beverley – that stroller Beverley, possessed your heart? – Tell me that, I say.

LYDIA: 'Tis true, Ma'am, and none but Beverley –

MRS. MALAPROP: Hold; – hold Assurance! – you shall not be so rude.

ABSOLUTE: Nay, pray Mrs. Malaprop, don't stop the young lady's speech: – she's very welcome to talk thus – it does not hurt *me* in the least, I assure you.

MRS. MALAPROP: You are *too* good, Captain – *too* amiably patient – but come with me, Miss – let us see you again soon, Captain – remember what we have fixed.

ABSOLUTE: I shall, Ma'am.

MRS. MALAPROP: Come, take a graceful leave of the gentleman.

LYDIA: May every blessing wait on my Beverley, my lov'd Bev –

MRS. MALAPROP: Huzzy! I'll choak the word in your throat! – come along – come along. [*Exeunt severally*.]

[BEVERLEY *kissing his hand to* LYDIA – MRS. MALAPROP *stopping her from speaking*.]

1. Alligator.

Act III, Scene IV

[ACRES's *Lodgings.*
ACRES *and* DAVID.
ACRES *as just dress'd.*]

ACRES: Indeed, David – do you think I become it so?[1]

DAVID: You are quite another creature, believe me Master, by the Mass! an' we've any luck we shall see the Devon monkeyrony,[2] in all the print-shops in Bath!

ACRES: Dress *does* make a difference, David.

DAVID: 'Tis all in all, I think – difference! why, an' you were to go now to Clod-Hall, I am certain the old lady wouldn't know you: Master Butler wouldn't believe his own eyes, and Mrs. Pickle would cry, 'Lard presarve me!' our dairy-maid would come giggling to the door, and I warrant Dolly Tester, your Honour's favourite, would blush like my waistcoat. – Oons! I'll hold a gallon,[3] there an't a dog in the house but would bark, and I question whether *Phillis* would wag a hair of her tail!

ACRES: Aye, David, there's nothing like *polishing*.

DAVID: So I says of your Honour's boots; but the boy never heeds me!

ACRES: But, David, has Mr. De-la-Grace been here? I must rub up my balancing, and chasing, and boring.[4]

DAVID: I'll call again, Sir.

ACRES: Do – and see if there are any letters for me at the post-office.

DAVID: I will. – By the Mass, I can't help looking at your head! – if I hadn't been by at the cooking, I wish I may die if I should have known the dish again myself! [*Exit.*]

[ACRES *comes forward, practising a dancing step.*]

ACRES: Sink, slide – coupee – [5] Confound the first inventors of cotillons! say I – they are as bad as algebra to us country gentlemen – I can walk a Minuet easy enough when I'm forced! – and I have been accounted a good stick in a Country-dance. – Odd's jigs and tabors! – I never valued your cross-over to couple – figure in – right and left – [6] and I'd foot it with e'er a captain in the county! – but these outlandish heathen Allemandes and Cotillons are quite beyond me! – I shall never prosper at 'em, that's sure – mine are true-born English legs – they don't understand their curst French lingo! – their *Pas* this, and *Pas* that, and *Pas* t'other! –

1. It suits me.
2. A macaroni or fop.
3. Bet a gallon.
4. Dance movements.
5. More dance movements.
6. Country dance movements.

d—n me, my feet don't like to be called Paws! no, 'tis certain I have most Antigallican[1] Toes!

[*Enter* SERVANT.]

SERV: Here is Sir Lucius O'Trigger to wait on you, Sir.
ACRES: Shew him in.

[*Enter* SIR LUCIUS.]

SIR LUCIUS: Mr. Acres, I am delighted to embrace you.
ACRES: My dear Sir Lucius, I kiss your hands.
SIR LUCIUS: Pray, my friend, what has brought you so suddenly to Bath?
ACRES: Faith! I have followed Cupid's Jack-a-Lantern, and find myself in a quagmire at last. – In short, I have been very ill-used, Sir Lucius. – I don't choose to mention names, but look on me as a very ill-used gentleman.
SIR LUCIUS: Pray, what is the case ? – I ask no names.
ACRES: Mark me, Sir Lucius, I fall as deep as need be in love with a young lady – her friends take my part – I follow her to Bath – send word of my arrival; and receive answer, that the lady is to be otherwise disposed of. – This, Sir Lucius, I call being ill-used.
SIR LUCIUS: Very ill, upon my conscience – Pray, can you divine the cause of it?
ACRES: Why, there's the matter: she has another lover, one *Beverley*, who, I am told, is now in Bath. – Odds slanders and lies! he must be at the bottom of it.
SIR LUCIUS: A rival in the case, is there? – and you think he has supplanted you unfairly.
ACRES: *Unfairly*! – to be sure he has. – He never could have done it fairly.
SIR LUCIUS: Then sure you know what is to be done!
ACRES: Not I, upon my soul!
SIR LUCIUS: We wear no swords here,[2] but you understand me.
ACRES: What! fight him!
SIR LUCIUS: Aye, to be sure: what can I mean else?
ACRES: But he has given me no provocation.
SIR LUCIUS: Now, I think he has given you the greatest provocation in the world. – Can a man commit a more heinous offence against another than to fall in love with the same woman? O, by my soul, it is the most unpardonable breach of friendship!
ACRES: Breach of *friendship*! Aye, aye; but I have no acquaintance with this man. I never saw him in my life.
SIR LUCIUS: That's no argument at all – he has the less right then to take such a liberty.
ACRES: 'Gad that's true – I grow full of anger, Sir Lucius! – I fire apace! Odds

1. Anti-French
2. Beau Nash had forbidden the wearing of swords in Bath.

hilts and blades! I find a man may have a deal of valour in him, and not know it! But couldn't I contrive to have a little right of my side ?

SIR LUCIUS: What the d—l signifies *right*, when your *honour* is concerned? Do you think *Achilles*, or my little *Alexander the Great* ever inquired where the right lay? No, by my soul, they drew their broad-swords, and left the lazy sons of peace to settle the justice of it.

ACRES: Your words are a grenadier's march to my heart! I believe courage must be catching! – I certainly do feel a kind of valour rising as it were – a kind of courage, as I may say – Odds flints, pans, and triggers! I'll challenge him directly.

SIR LUCIUS: Ah, my little friend! if we had *Blunderbuss-Hall* here – I could shew you a range of ancestry, in the O'Trigger line, that would furnish the new room;[1] every one of whom had killed his man! – For though the mansion-house and dirty acres have slipt through my fingers, I thank Heav'n our honour, and the family pictures, are as fresh as ever.

ACRES: O Sir Lucius! I have had ancestors too! every man of 'em colonel or captain in the militia! – Odds balls and barrels! say no more – I'm brac'd for it – The thunder of your words has soured the milk of human kindness in my breast! – z—ds! as the man in the play says, 'I could do such deeds!'[2]

SIR LUCIUS: Come, come, there must be no passion at all in the case – these things should always be done civilly.

ACRES: I must be in a passion, Sir Lucius – I must be in a rage – Dear Sir Lucius let me be in a rage, if you love me. – Come, here's pen and paper. [*Sits down to write.*] I would the ink were red! – Indite, I say, indite! – How shall I begin? Odds bullets and blades! I'll write a good *bold hand*, however.

SIR LUCIUS: Pray compose yourself.

ACRES: Come – now shall I begin with an oath? Do, Sir Lucius, let me begin with a damme.

SIR LUCIUS: Pho! pho! do the thing *decently*, and like a Christian. Begin now, – *'Sir'* –

ACRES: That's too civil by half.

SIR LUCIUS: *'To prevent the confusion that might arise.'*

ACRES: Well –

SIR LUCIUS: *'From our both addressing the same lady.'*

ACRES: Aye – there's the reason – *'same lady'* – Well –

SIR LUCIUS: *'I shall expect the honour of your company'* –

ACRES: Z—ds! I'm not asking him to dinner.

SIR LUCIUS: Pray be easy.

ACRES: Well then, 'honour of your company'

SIR LUCIUS: *'To settle our pretensions.'*

1. The Upper or New Assembly Rooms.
2. A misquotation from *King Lear*, II, iv.

ACRES: Well.

SIR LUCIUS: Let me see, aye, *King's Mead-fields* will do. – *'In King's Mead-fields.'*

ACRES: So that's done. – Well, I'll fold it up presently; my own crest – a hand and dagger shall be the seal.

SIR LUCIUS: You see now this little explanation will put a stop at once to all confusion or misunderstanding that might arise between you.

ACRES: Aye, we fight to prevent any misunderstanding.

SIR LUCIUS: Now, I'll leave you to fix your own time. – take my advice, and you'll decide it this evening if you can; then let the worst come of it, 'twill be off your mind to-morrow.

ACRES: Very true.

SIR LUCIUS: So I shall see nothing more of you, unless it be by letter, till the evening. – I would do myself the honour to carry your message; but, to tell you a secret, I believe I shall have just such another affair on my own hands. There is a gay captain here, who put a jest on me lately, at the expence of my country, and I only want to fall in with the gentleman, to call him out.

ACRES: By my valour, I should like to see you fight first! Odds life! I should like to see you kill him, if it was only to get a little lesson.

SIR LUCIUS: I shall be very proud of instructing you. – Well for the present – but remember now, when you meet your antagonist, do every thing in a mild and agreeable manner. Let your courage be as keen, but at the same time as polished as your sword. [*Exeunt severally.*]

Act IV, Scene I

[ACRES's *Lodgings.*
ACRES *and* DAVID.]

DAVID: Then, by the Mass, Sir! I would do no such thing – ne'er a Sir Lucius O'Trigger in the kingdom should make me fight, when I wa'n't so minded. Oons! what will the old lady say, when she hears o't!

ACRES: Ah! David, if you had heard Sir Lucius! – Odds sparks and flames! he would have rous'd your valour.

DAVID: Not he, indeed. I hates such bloodthirsty cormorants. Look'ee, Master, if you'd wanted a bout at boxing, quarter-staff, or short-staff, I should never be the man to bid you cry off: But for your curst sharps, and snaps,[1] I never knew any good come of 'em.

ACRES: But my *honour*, David, my *honour*! I must be very careful of my honour.

DAVID: Aye, by the Mass! and I would be very careful of it; and I think in return my *honour* couldn't do less than to be very careful of *me*.

1. Small duelling swords and pistols.

ACRES: Odds blades! David, no gentleman will ever risk the loss of his honour!

DAVID: I say then, it would be but civil in *honour* never to risk the loss of a *gentleman*. – Lookee, Master, this *honour* seems to me to be a marvellous false friend; aye, truly, a very courtier-like servant. – Put the case, I was a gentleman (which, thank God, no one can say of me); well – my honour makes me quarrel with another gentleman of my acquaintance. – So – we fight. (Pleasant enough that) Boh! – I kill him (the more's my luck.) Now, pray who gets the profit of it? – Why, my *honour*. – But put the case that he kills me! – by the Mass! I go to the worms, and my honour whips over to my enemy!

ACRES: No, David – in that case! – Odds crowns and laurels! your honour follows you to the grave.

DAVID: Now, that's just the place where I could make a shift to do without it.

ACRES: Z—ds, David! you're a coward! – It doesn't become my valour to listen to you. – What, shall I disgrace my ancestors? Think of that, David – think what it would be to disgrace my ancestors!

DAVID: Under favour, the surest way of not disgracing them, is to keep as long as you can out of their company. Look'ee now, Master, to go to them in such haste – with an ounce of lead in your brains – I should think might as well be let alone. Our ancestors are very good kind of folks; but they are the last people I should choose to have a visiting acquaintance with.

ACRES: But David, now, you don't think there is such very, very, *very* great danger, hey? – Odds life! people often fight without any mischief done!

DAVID: By the Mass, I think 'tis ten to one against you! – Oons! here to meet some lion-headed fellow, I warrant, with his d—n'd double-barrell'd swords, and cut and thrust pistols! Lord bless us! it makes me tremble to think o't! – Those be such desperate bloody-minded weapons! Well, I never could abide 'em! – from a child I never could fancy 'em! – I suppose there a'n't so merciless a beast in the world as your loaded pistol!

ACRES: Z—ds! I *won't* be afraid – Odds fire and fury! you shan't make me afraid. – Here is the challenge, and I have sent for my dear friend Jack Absolute to carry it for me.

DAVID: Aye, I'the name of mischief, let *him* be the messenger. – For my part, I wouldn't lend a hand to it for the best horse in your stable. By the Mass! it don't look like another letter! – It is, as I may say, a designing and malicious-looking letter! – and I warrant smells of gunpowder like a soldier's pouch! – Oons! I wouldn't swear it mayn't go off!

ACRES: Out, you poltroon! – you han't the valour of a grass-hopper.

DAVID: Well, I say no more – 'twill be sad news, to be sure, at Clod-Hall! – but I ha'done. – How Phyllis will howl when she hears of it! – Aye, poor bitch, she little thinks what shooting her Master's going after! – And I warrant old Crop, who has carried your honour, field and road, these ten years, will curse the hour he was born. [*Whimpering*.]

ACRES: It won't do, David – I am determined to fight – so get along, you Coward, while I'm in the mind.

[*Enter* SERVANT.]

SERVANT: Captain Absolute, Sir.

ACRES: O! shew him up. [*Exit* SERVANT.]

DAVID: Well, Heaven send we be all alive this time to-morrow.

ACRES: What's that! – Don't provoke me, David!

DAVID: Good bye, Master. [*Whimpering*.]

ACRES: Get along, you cowardly, dastardly, croaking raven. [*Exit* DAVID.]

[*Enter* ABSOLUTE.]

ABSOLUTE: What's the matter, Bob?

ACRES: A vile, sheep-hearted blockhead – If I hadn't the valour of St. George and the dragon to boot –

ABSOLUTE: But what did you want with me, Bob?

ACRES: O! – There – [*Gives him the challenge*.]

ABSOLUTE: '*To Ensign Beverley*.' So – what's going on now! [*Aside*.] Well, what's this?

ACRES: A challenge!

ABSOLUTE: Indeed! – Why, you won't fight him; will you Bob?

ACRES: 'Egad but I will, Jack. – Sir Lucius has wrought me to it. He has left me full of rage – and I'll fight this evening, that so much good passion mayn't be wasted.

ABSOLUTE: But what have I to do with this?

ACRES: Why, as I think you know something of this fellow, I want you to find him out for me, and give him this mortal *defiance*.

ABSOLUTE: Well, give it to me, and trust me he gets it.

ACRES: Thank you, my dear friend, my dear Jack; but it is giving you a great deal of trouble.

ABSOLUTE: Not in the least – I beg you won't mention it. – No trouble in the world, I assure you.

ACRES: You are very kind. – What it is to have a friend! – You couldn't be my second – could you, Jack?

ABSOLUTE: Why no, Bob – not in *this* affair – it would not be quite so proper.

ACRES: Well then I must get my friend Sir Lucius. I shall have your good wishes, however, Jack.

ABSOLUTE: Whenever he meets you, believe me.

[*Enter* SERVANT.]

SERVANT: Sir Anthony Absolute is below, inquiring for the Captain.

ABSOLUTE: I'll come instantly. – Well, my little hero, success attend you. [*Going.*]

ACRES: Stay – stay, Jack. – If Beverley should ask you what kind of a man your friend Acres is, do tell him I am a devil of a fellow – will you, Jack?

ABSOLUTE: To be sure I shall. – I'll say you are a determined dog – hey, Bob!

ACRES: Aye, do, do – and if that frightens him, 'egad perhaps he mayn't come. So tell him I generally kill a man a week; will you, Jack!

ABSOLUTE: I will, I will; I'll say you are call'd in the country *'Fighting Bob!'*

ACRES: Right, right – 'tis all to prevent mischief; for I don't want to take his life if I clear my honour.

ABSOLUTE: No! – that's very kind of you.

ACRES: Why, you don't wish me to kill him – do you, Jack?

ABSOLUTE: No, upon my soul, I do not. – But a devil of a fellow, hey? [*Going.*]

ACRES: True, true – but stay – stay, Jack – you may add that you never saw me in such a rage before – a most devouring rage!

ABSOLUTE: I will, I will.

ACRES: Remember, Jack – a determined dog!

ABSOLUTE: Aye, aye, *'Fighting Bob!'* [*Exeunt severally.*]

Act IV, Scene II

[MRS. MALAPROP*'s Lodgings.*
MRS. MALAPROP *and* LYDIA.]

MRS. MALAPROP: Why, thou perverse one! – tell me what you can object to him? – Isn't he a handsome man? – tell me that. – A genteel man? a pretty figure of a man?

LYDIA: She little thinks whom she is praising [*aside*] – So is Beverley, Ma'am.

MRS. MALAPROP: No caparisons,[1] Miss, if you please! – Caparisons don't become a young woman. – No! Captain Absolute is indeed a fine gentleman!

LYDIA: Aye, the Captain Absolute *you* have seen. [*Aside.*]

MRS. MALAPROP: Then he's *so* well bred; – *so* full of alacrity, and adulation![2] – and has *so much* to say for himself: – in such good language too! His physiognomy[3] so grammatical! – Then his presence is so noble! I protest, when I saw him, I thought of what Hamlet says in the Play: – 'Hesperian curls! – the front of *Job* himself ! – an eye, like *March,* to – threaten at

1. Comparisons.
2. Admiration.
3. Phraseology.

command! – a Station, like Harry Mercury, new –'[1] Something about kissing – on a hill – however, the similitude struck me directly.

LYDIA: How enraged she'll be presently when she discovers her mistake! [*Aside.*]

[*Enter* SERVANT.]

SERVANT: Sir Anthony, and Captain Absolute are below Ma'am.

MRS. MALAPROP: Shew them up here. [*Exit* SERVANT.] Now, Lydia, I insist on you behaving as becomes a young woman. Shew your good breeding at least, though you have forgot your duty.

LYDIA: Madam, I have told you my resolution; – I shall not only give him no encouragement, but I won't even speak to, or look at him. [*Flings herself into a chair, with her face from the door.*]

[*Enter* SIR ANTHONY *and* ABSOLUTE.]

SIR ANTHONY: Here we are, Mrs. Malaprop; come to mitigate the frowns of unrelenting beauty – and difficulty enough I had to bring this fellow. – I don't know what's the matter; but if I hadn't held him by force, he'd have given me the slip.

MRS. MALAPROP: You have infinite trouble, Sir Anthony, in the affair. – I am ashamed for the cause! Lydia, Lydia, rise I beseech you! – pay your respects! [*Aside to her.*]

SIR ANTHONY: I hope, Madam, that Miss Languish has reflected on the worth of this gentleman, and the regard due to her Aunt's choice, and *my* alliance. – Now, Jack, speak to her! [*Aside to him.*]

ABSOLUTE: What the d – l shall I do! – [*Aside*] – You see, Sir, she won't even look at me, whilst you are here. – I knew she wouldn't! – I told you so – Let me intreat you, Sir, to leave us together! [*Absolute seems to expostulate with his Father.*]

LYDIA: [*Aside.*] I wonder I ha'n't heard my Aunt exclaim yet! sure she can't have look'd at him! – perhaps their regimentals[2] are alike, and she is something blind.

SIR ANTHONY: I say, Sir, I won't stir a foot yet.

MRS. MALAPROP: I am sorry to say, Sir Anthony, that my affluence[3] over my Niece is very small. – Turn round Lydia, I blush for you! [*Aside to her.*]

SIR ANTHONY: May I not flatter myself that Miss Languish will assign what cause of dislike she can have to my son! – Why don't you begin, Jack? – Speak, you puppy – speak! [*Aside to him.*]

MRS. MALAPROP: It is impossible, Sir Anthony, she can have any. – She will not *say* she has. – Answer, hussy! why don't you answer? [*Aside to her.*]

SIR ANTHONY: Then, Madam, I trust that a childish and hasty predilection

1. Hamlet's description of his father, III, iv.
2. Uniforms.
3. Influence.

will be no bar to Jack's happiness. – Z—ds! sirrah! why don't you speak? [*Aside to him.*]

LYDIA: [*Aside.*] I think my lover seems as little inclined to conversation as myself. – How strangely blind my Aunt must be!

ABSOLUTE: Hem! hem! – Madam – hem! [*Absolute attempts to speak, then returns to Sir Anthony*] – Faith! Sir, I am so confounded! – and so – so – confused! – I told you I should be so, Sir, – I knew it. – The – the – tremor of my passion, entirely takes away my presence of mind.

SIR ANTHONY: But it don't take away your voice, fool, does it? – Go up, and speak to her directly!

[*Absolute makes signs to Mrs. Malaprop to leave them together.*]

MRS. MALAPROP: Sir Anthony, shall we leave them together? – Ah! you stubborn, little vixen! [*Aside to her.*]

SIR ANTHONY: Not yet, Ma'am, not yet! – what the d—l are you at ? unlock your jaws, sirrah, or – [*Aside to him.*] [*Absolute draws near Lydia.*]

ABSOLUTE: Now Heav'n send she may be too sullen to look round! – I must disguise my voice – [*Aside*] – [*Speaks in a low hoarse tone.*]
– Will not Miss Languish lend an ear to the mild accents of true love? – Will not –

SIR ANTHONY: What the d—l ails the fellow? – Why don't you speak out? – not stand croaking like a frog in a quinsey![1]

ABSOLUTE: The – the – excess of my awe, and my – my – my modesty, quite choak me!

SIR ANTHONY: Ah! your *modesty* again! – I'll tell you what, Jack; if you don't speak out directly, and glibly too, I shall be in such a rage! – Mrs. Malaprop, I wish the lady would favour us with something more than a side-front!

[MRS. MALAPROP *seems to chide Lydia.*]

ABSOLUTE: So ! – all will out I see [*Goes up to Lydia, speaks softly.*]
Be not surprised, my Lydia, suppress all surprise at present.

LYDIA: [*Aside*] Heav'ns! 'tis Beverley's voice! – Sure he can't have impos'd on Sir Anthony too! – [*Looks round by degrees, then starts up.*]
Is this possible! – my Beverley! – how can this be? – my Beverley?

ABSOLUTE: Ah! 'tis all over. [*Aside.*]

SIR ANTHONY: Beverley! – the devil – Beverley! – What can the girl mean? – This is my son, Jack Absolute!

MRS. MALAPROP: For shame, hussy! for shame! – your head runs so on that fellow, that you have him always in your eyes! – beg Captain Absolute's pardon directly.

LYDIA: I see no Captain Absolute, but my lov'd Beverley!

SIR ANTHONY: Z—ds! the girl's mad! – her brain's turn'd by reading!

MRS. MALAPROP: O' my conscience, I believe so! – what do you mean by

1. With a sore throat.

Beverley, hussy? – You saw Captain Absolute before to-day; there he is – your husband that shall be.

LYDIA: With all my soul, Ma'am – when I refuse my Beverley –

SIR ANTHONY: O! she's as mad as Bedlam! – or has this fellow been playing us a rogue's trick! – Come here, sirrah! who the d—l are you?

ABSOLUTE: Faith, Sir, I am not quite clear myself; but I'll endeavour to recollect.

SIR ANTHONY: Are you my son, or not? – answer for your mother, you dog, if you won't for me.

MRS. MALAPROP: Aye, Sir, who are you? O mercy! I begin to suspect! –

ABSOLUTE: Ye Powers of Impudence befriend me! [*aside*] Sir Anthony, most assuredly I am your wife's son; and that I sincerely believe myself to be *yours* also, I hope my duty has always shewn. – Mrs. Malaprop, I am your most respectful admirer – and shall be proud to add affectionate nephew. – I need not tell my Lydia, that she sees her faithful *Beverley*, who, knowing the singular generosity of her temper, assum'd that name, and a station, which has proved a test of the most disinterested love, which he now hopes to enjoy in a more elevated character.

LYDIA: So! – there will be no elopement after all! [*sullenly*.]

SIR ANTHONY: Upon my soul, Jack, thou art a very impudent fellow! to do you justice, I think I never saw a piece of more consummate assurance!

ABSOLUTE: O, you flatter me, Sir – you compliment – 'tis my *modesty* you know, Sir – my *modesty* that has stood in my way.

SIR ANTHONY: Well, I am glad you are not the dull, insensible varlet you pretended to be, however! – I'm glad you have made a fool of your father, you dog – I am. – So this was your *penitence*, your *duty*, and *obedience*! – I thought it was d—n'd sudden! – *You never heard their names before*, not you! – *What, Languishes of Worcestershire*, hey? – *if you could please me in the affair, 'twas all you desired*! – Ah! you dissembling villain! – What! [*pointing, to* LYDIA] *she squints, don't she*? – *a little red-hair'd girl*! – hey? – Why, you hypocritical young rascal – I wonder you a'n't asham'd to hold up your head!

ABSOLUTE: 'Tis with difficulty, Sir – I *am* confus'd – very much confus'd, as you must perceive.

MRS. MALAPROP: O Lud! Sir Anthony! – a new light breaks in upon me! – hey! how! what! Captain, did *you* write the letters then? – What! – am I to thank *you* for the elegant compilation[1] of '*an old weather-beaten she-dragon*' – hey? – O mercy! – was it *you* that reflected on my parts of speech?

ABSOLUTE: Dear Sir! my modesty will be overpowered at last, if you don't assist me. – I shall certainly not be able to stand it!

SIR ANTHONY: Come, come, Mrs. Malaprop, we must forget and forgive; – odds' life! matters have taken so clever a turn all of a sudden, that I could

1. Appellation.

find in my heart, to be so good-humour'd! and so gallant! – hey! Mrs. Malaprop!

MRS. MALAPROP: Well, Sir Anthony, since *you* desire it, we will not anticipate[1] the past; – so mind young people – our retrospection[2] will now be all to the future.

SIR ANTHONY: Come, we must leave them together; Mrs. Malaprop, they long to fly into each other's arms, I warrant! – Jack – is'n't the *cheek* as I said, hey? – and the eye, you rogue! – and the lip – hey? Come, Mrs. Malaprop, we'll not disturb their tenderness – theirs is the time of life for happiness! – *'Youth's the season made for joy'* – [*sings*][3] – hey! – Odds'life! I'm in such spirits, – I don't know what I couldn't do! – Permit me, Ma'am – [*gives his hand to* MRS. MALAPROP.] [*sings*] Tol-de-rol – 'gad I should like a little fooling myself – Tol-de-rol! de-rol!

[*Exit singing, and handing*[4] MRS. MALAPROP.]

[*Lydia sits sullenly in her chair.*]

ABSOLUTE: So much thought bodes me no good [*aside*] – So grave, Lydia!

LYDIA: Sir!

ABSOLUTE: So! – egad! I thought as much! – that d—n'd monosyllable has froze me! [*aside*] – What, Lydia, now that we are as happy in our *friends consent*, as in our *mutual vows* –

LYDIA: *Friends consent*, indeed! [*peevishly*]

ABSOLUTE: Come, come, we must lay aside some of our romance – a little *wealth* and *comfort* may be endur'd after all. And for your fortune, the lawyers shall make such settlements as –

LYDIA: *Lawyers*! I *hate* lawyers!

ABSOLUTE: Nay then, we will not wait for their lingering forms, but instantly procure the licence, and –

LYDIA: The *licence*! – I *hate* licence!

ABSOLUTE: O my Love! *be* not so unkind! – thus let me intreat – [*Kneeling.*]

LYDIA: Pshaw! – what signifies kneeling, when you know I *must* have you?

ABSOLUTE: [*Rising*] Nay, Madam, there shall be no constraint upon your inclinations, I promise you. – If I have lost your heart, – I resign the rest. – 'Gad, I must try what a little *spirit* will do. [*Aside.*]

LYDIA: [*Rising*] Then, Sir, let me tell you, the interest you had there was acquired by a mean, unmanly imposition, and deserves the punishment of fraud. – What, you have been treating *me* like a *child*! – humouring my romance! and laughing, I suppose, at your success!

ABSOLUTE: You wrong me, Lydia, you wrong me – only hear –

LYDIA: So, while *I* fondly imagined we were deceiving my relations, and flatter'd myself that I should outwit and incense them all – behold! my

1. Elaborate on.
2. Attention
3. A song from *The Beggar's Opera*, II, iv.
4. Leading by the hand.

hopes are to be crush'd at once, by my Aunt's consent and approbation! – and *I* am myself, the only dupe at last! [*Walking about in heat.*] – But here, Sir, here is the picture – *Beverley's* picture! [*taking a miniature from her bosom*] which I have worn, night and day, in spite of threats and entreaties! – There, Sir, [*flings it to him*] and be assured I throw the original from my heart as easily!

ABSOLUTE: Nay, nay, Ma'am, we will not differ as to that. – Here, [*taking out a picture*] here is Miss Lydia Languish. – What a difference! – aye, *there* is the heav'nly assenting smile, that first gave soul and spirit to my hopes! – those are the lips which seal'd a vow, as yet scarce dry in Cupid's calendar! – and *there* the *half* resentful blush, that *would* have check'd the ardour of my thanks – Well, all that's past! – all over indeed! – There, Madam – in *beauty*, that copy is not equal to you, but in my mind its merit over the original, in being still the same, is such – that – I cannot find in my heart to *part with* it. [*Puts it up again.*]

LYDIA: [*Softening*] 'Tis *your own* doing, Sir – I, I, I suppose you are perfectly satisfied.

ABSOLUTE: O, most certainly – sure now this is much better than being in love! – ha! ha! ha! – there's some spirit in *this*! – What signifies breaking some scores of solemn promises: – all that's of no consequence you know. – To be sure people will say, that Miss didn't know her own mind – but never mind that: – or perhaps they may be ill-natured enough to hint, that the gentleman grew tired of the lady and forsook her – but don't let that fret you.

LYDIA: There's no bearing his insolence. [*Bursts into tears.*]

[*Enter* MRS. MALAPROP *and* SIR ANTHONY.]

MRS. MALAPROP: [*Entering*] Come, we must interrupt your billing and cooing a while.

LYDIA: This is worse than your treachery and deceit, you base ingrate! [*Sobbing.*]

SIR ANTHONY: What the devil's the matter now! – Z—ds! Mrs. Malaprop, this is the *oddest billing* and *cooing* I ever heard! – but what the deuce is the meaning of it? – I'm quite astonished

ABSOLUTE: Ask the lady, Sir.

MRS. MALAPROP: O mercy! – I'm quite analys'd[1] for my part! – why, Lydia, what is the reason of this?

LYDIA: Ask the gentleman, Ma'am.

SIR ANTHONY: Z—ds! I shall be in a phrenzy! – why Jack, you are not come out to be any one else, are you?

MRS. MALAPROP: Aye, Sir, there's no more *trick*, is there? – you are not like Cerberus,[2] *three* Gentlemen, at once, are you?

1. Paralysed.
2. Cerberus was the three-headed dog, guarding the entrance to Hades.

ABSOLUTE: You'll not let me speak – I say the lady can account for this much better than I can.

LYDIA: Ma'am, you once commanded me never to think of Beverley again – there is the man – I now obey you: – for, from this moment, I renounce him for ever. [*Exit* LYDIA.]

MRS. MALAPROP: O mercy! and miracles! what a turn here is – why sure, Captain, you haven't behaved disrespectfully to my Niece.

SIR ANTHONY: Ha! ha! ha! – ha! ha! ha! – now I see it – Ha! ha! ha! – now I see it – you have been too lively, Jack.

ABSOLUTE: Nay, Sir, upon my word –

SIR ANTHONY: Come, no lying, Jack – I'm sure *'twas* so.

MRS. MALAPROP: O Lud! Sir Anthony! – O fie, Captain!

ABSOLUTE: Upon my soul, Ma'am –

SIR ANTHONY: Come, no excuses, Jack: – why, your father, you rogue, was so before you: – the blood of the Absolutes was always impatient. – Ha! ha! ha! poor little Lydia! – why, you've frightened her, you Dog, you have.

ABSOLUTE: By all that's good, Sir –

SIR ANTHONY: Z—ds! say no more, I tell you. – Mrs. Malaprop shall make your peace. – You must make his peace, Mrs. Malaprop; – you must tell her 'tis Jack's way – tell her 'tis all our ways – it runs in the blood of our family! – Come, get on, Jack – ha! ha! ha! Mrs. Malaprop – a young villain! [*Pushes him out.*]

MRS. MALAPROP: O! Sir Anthony! – O fie, Captain! [*Exeunt severally.*]

Act IV, Scene III

[*The* North-Parade.
Enter SIR LUCIUS O'TRIGGER.]

SIR LUCIUS: I wonder where this Capt. Absolute hides himself. – Upon my conscience! – these officers are always in one's way in love affairs: I remember I might have married Lady Dorothy Carmine, if it had not been for a little rogue of a Major, who ran away with her before she could get a sight of me! – And I wonder too what it is the ladies can see in them to be so fond of them – unless it be a touch of the old serpent in 'em, that makes the little creatures be caught, like vipers with a bit of red cloth. – Hah! – isn't this the Captain coming? – faith it is! – There is a probability of succeeding about that fellow, that is mighty provoking! – Who the devil is he talking to? [*Steps aside.*]

[*Enter* CAPT. ABSOLUTE.]

ABSOLUTE: To what fine purpose I have been plotting! a noble reward for all my schemes, upon my soul! – a little gypsey! – I did not think her romance could have made her so d—nd absurd either – S'death, I never was in a worse humour in my life – I could cut my own throat, or any other person's, with the greatest pleasure in the world!

SIR LUCIUS: O, faith! I'm in the luck of it – I never could have found him in a sweeter temper for my purpose – to be sure I'm just come in the nick! now to enter into conversation with him, and so quarrel genteelly. [SIR LUCIUS *goes up to* ABSOLUTE.] – With regard to that matter, Captain, I must beg leave to differ in opinion with you.

ABSOLUTE: Upon my word then, you must be a very subtle disputant: – because, Sir, I happen'd just then to be giving no opinion at all.

SIR LUCIUS: That's no reason. – For give me leave to tell you, a man may *think* an untruth as well as *speak* one.

ABSOLUTE: Very true, Sir, but if the man never utters his thoughts, I should think they might stand a chance of escaping controversy.

SIR LUCIUS: Then, Sir, you differ in opinion with me, which amounts to the same thing.

ABSOLUTE: Hark'ee, Sir Lucius, – if I had not before known you to be a gentleman, upon my soul, I should not have discovered it at this interview: for what you can drive at, unless you mean to quarrel with me, I cannot conceive!

SIR LUCIUS: I humbly thank you, Sir, for the quickness of your apprehension, [*Bowing.*] – you have nam'd the very thing I would be at.

ABSOLUTE: Very well, Sir – I shall certainly not baulk your inclinations: but I should be glad you would please to explain your motives.

SIR LUCIUS: Pray, Sir, be easy – the quarrel is a very pretty quarrel as it stands – we should only spoil it, by trying to explain it. – However, your memory is very short – or you could not have forgot an affront you pass'd on me within this week. – So no more, but name your time and place.

ABSOLUTE: Well, Sir, since you are so bent on it, the sooner the better; – let it be this evening – here, by the Spring-Gardens.[1] – We shall scarcely be interrupted.

SIR LUCIUS: Faith! that same interruption in affairs of this nature, shews very great ill-breeding. – I don't know what's the reason, but in England, if a thing of this kind gets wind, people make such a pother, that a gentleman can never fight in peace and quietness. – However, if it's the same to you, Captain, I should take it as a particular kindness, if you'd let us meet in King's-Mead Fields, as a little business will call me there about six o'clock, and I may dispatch both matters at once.

ABSOLUTE: 'Tis the same to me exactly. – A little after six, then we will discuss this matter more seriously.

SIR LUCIUS: If you please, Sir, there will be very pretty small-sword light, tho'

1. A summer meeting place across Pulteney Bridge.

it won't do for a long shot. – So that matter's settled! and my mind's at ease. [*Exit* SIR LUCIUS.]

[*Enter* FAULKLAND, *meeting* ABSOLUTE.]

ABSOLUTE: Well met. – I was going to look for you. – O, Faulkland! all the Dæmons of spite and disappointment have conspired against me! I'm so vex'd, that if I had not the prospect of a resource in being knock'd o'the head by and bye, I should scarce have spirits to tell you the cause.

FAULKLAND: What can you mean? – Has Lydia chang'd her mind? – I should have thought her duty and inclination would now have pointed to the same object.

ABSOLUTE: Aye, just as the eyes do of a person who squints: – when her love eye was fix'd on me – t'other – her eye of duty, was finely obliqued: – but when duty bid her point that the same way – off t'other turn'd on a swivel, and secured its retreat with a frown!

FAULKLAND: But what's the resource you –

ABSOLUTE: O, to wind up the whole, a good natured Irishman here has [*mimicking* SIR LUCIUS] beg'd leave to have the pleasure of cutting my throat – and I mean to indulge him – that's all.

FAULKLAND: Prithee, be serious.

ABSOLUTE: 'Tis fact, upon my soul. – Sir Lucius O'Trigger – you know him by sight – for some affront, which I am sure I never intended, has obliged me to meet him this evening at six o'clock: – 'tis on that account I wish'd to see you – you must go with me.

FAULKLAND: Nay, there must be some mistake, sure. – Sir Lucius shall explain himself – and I dare say matters may be accommodated: – but this evening, did you say? – I wish it had been any other time.

ABSOLUTE: Why? – there will be light enough: – there will (as Sir Lucius says) 'be very pretty small-sword light, tho' it won't do for a long shot.' – Confound his long shots!

FAULKLAND: But I am myself a good deal ruffled, by a difference I have had with Julia – my vile tormenting temper has made me treat her so cruelly, that I shall not be myself till we are reconciled.

ABSOLUTE: By Heav'ns, Faulkland, you don't deserve her.

[*Enter* SERVANT, *gives* FAULKLAND *a letter*.]

FAULKLAND: O Jack! this is from Julia – I dread to open it – I fear it may be to take a last leave – perhaps to bid me return her letters – and restore – O! how I suffer for my folly!

ABSOLUTE: Here – let me see. [*Takes the letter and opens it.*]
Aye, a final sentence indeed! – 'tis all over with you, faith!

FAULKLAND: Nay, Jack – don't keep me in suspence.

ABSOLUTE: Hear then. – '*As I am convinced that my dear* Faulkland's *own reflections have already upbraided him for his last unkindness to me, I will not add a word on the subject. – I wish to speak with you as soon as possible. – Yours ever and truly,* Julia.' – There's stubborness and resentment for you!

[*Gives him the letter.*]

Why, man, you don't seem one whit the happier at this.

FAULKLAND: O, yes, I am – but – but –

ABSOLUTE: Confound your *buts.* – You never hear any thing that would make another man bless himself, but you immediately d—n it with a *but.*

FAULKLAND: Now, Jack, as you are my friend, own honestly – don't you think there is something forward – something indelicate in this haste to forgive? – Women should never sue for reconciliation: – that should always come from us. – They should retain their coldness till *woo'd* to kindness – and their *pardon,* like their *love,* should 'not unsought be won.'[1]

ABSOLUTE: I have not patience to listen to you: – thou'rt incorrigible! – so say no more on the subject. – I must go to settle a few matters – let me see you before six – remember – at my lodgings. – A poor industrious devil like me, who have toil'd, and drudg'd, and plotted to gain my ends, and am at last disappointed by other people's folly – may in pity be allowed to swear and grumble a little – but a captious sceptic in love, – a slave to fretfulness and whim – who has no difficulties but of his own creating – is a subject more fit for ridicule than compassion! [*Exit* ABSOLUTE.]

FAULKLAND: I feel his reproaches! – yet I would not change this too exquisite nicety, for the gross content with which *he* tramples on the thorns of love. – His engaging me in this duel, has started an idea in my head, which I will instantly pursue. – I'll use it as the touch-stone of Julia's sincerity and disinterestedness – if her love prove pure and sterling ore – my name will rest on it with honour! – and once I've stamp'd it there, I lay aside my doubts for ever: – but if the dross of selfishness, the allay of pride predominate – 'twill be best to leave her as a toy for some less cautious Fool to sigh for. [*Exit* FAULKLAND.]

Act V, Scene I

[JULIA's *Dressing-room.*
JULIA, *sola.*]

JULIA:How this message has alarmed me! what dreadful accident can he mean! why such charge to be alone? – O Faulkland! – how many unhappy moments! – how many tears have you cost me!

[*Enter* FAULKLAND, *muffled up in a Riding-coat.*]

1. A quotation from *Paradise Lost*, viii, 503.

JULIA: What means this? – why this caution, Faulkland?

FAULKLAND: Alas! Julia, I am come to take a long farewell.

JULIA: Heav'ns! what do you mean?

FAULKLAND: You see before you a wretch, whose life is forfeited. – Nay, start not! – the infirmity of my temper has drawn all this misery on me. – I left you fretful and passionate – an untoward accident drew me into a quarrel – the event is, that I must fly this kingdom instantly. – O Julia, had I been so fortunate as to have call'd you mine entirely, before this mischance had fallen on me, I should not so deeply dread my banishment! –

JULIA: My soul is oppress'd with sorrow at the nature of your misfortune: had these adverse circumstances arisen from a less fatal cause, I should have felt strong comfort in the thought that I could now chase from your bosom every doubt of the warm sincerity of my love. – My heart has long known no other guardian – I now entrust my person to your honour – we will fly together. – When safe from pursuit, my Father's will may be fulfilled – and I receive a legal claim to be the partner of your sorrows, and tenderest comforter. Then on the bosom of your wedded Julia, you may lull your keen regret to slumbering; while virtuous love, with a Cherub's hand, shall smooth the brow of upbraiding thought, and pluck the thorn from compunction.

FAULKLAND: O Julia! I am bankrupt in gratitude! but the time is so pressing, it calls on you for so hasty a resolution. – Would you not wish some hours to weigh the advantages you forego, and what little compensation poor Faulkland can make you beside his solitary love?

JULIA: I ask not a moment. – No, Faulkland, I have lov'd you for yourself: and if I now, more than ever, prize the solemn engagement which so long has pledged us to each other, it is because it leaves no room for hard aspersions on my fame, and puts the seal of duty to an act of love. – But let us not linger. – Perhaps this delay –

FAULKLAND: 'Twill be better I should not venture out again till dark. – Yet am I griev'd to think what numberless distresses will press heavy on your gentle disposition!

JULIA: Perhaps your fortune may be forfeited by this unhappy act. – I know not whether 'tis so – but sure that alone can never make us unhappy. The little I have will be sufficient to support us; and exile never should be splendid.

FAULKLAND: Aye, but in such an abject state of life, my wounded pride perhaps may increase the natural fretfulness of my temper, till I become a rude, morose companion, beyond your patience to endure. Perhaps the recollection of a deed, my conscience cannot justify, may haunt me in such gloomy and unsocial fits, that I shall hate the tenderness that would relieve me, break from your arms, and quarrel with your fondness!

JULIA: If your thoughts should assume so unhappy a bent, you will the more want some mild and affectionate spirit to watch over and console you: –

One who, by bearing *your* infirmities with gentleness and resignation, may teach you *so* to bear the evils of your fortune.

FAULKLAND: Julia, I have proved you to the quick! and with this useless device I throw away all my doubts. How shall I plead to be forgiven this last unworthy effect of my restless, unsatisfied disposition ?

JULIA: Has no such disaster happened as you related?

FAULKLAND: I am ashamed to own that it was all pretended; yet in pity, Julia, do not kill me with resenting a fault which never can be repeated: But sealing, this once, my pardon, let me to-morrow, in the face of Heaven, receive my future guide and monitress, and expiate my past folly, by years of tender adoration.

JULIA: Hold, Faulkland! – that you are free from a crime, which I before fear'd to name, Heaven knows how sincerely I rejoice! – These are tears of thankfulness for that! But that your cruel doubts should have urged you to an imposition that has wrung my heart, gives me now a pang, more keen than I can express!

FAULKLAND: By Heav'ns! Julia –

JULIA: Yet hear me. – My Father lov'd you, Falkland and you preserv'd the life that tender parent gave me; in his presence I pledged my hand – joyfully pledged it – where before I had given my heart. When, soon after, I lost that parent, it seem'd to me that Providence had, in Faulkland, shewn me whither to transfer, without a pause, my grateful duty, as well as my affection: Hence I have been content to bear from you what pride and delicacy would have forbid me from another. – I will not upbraid you, by repeating how you have trifled with my sincerity. –

FAULKLAND: I confess it all! yet hear –

JULIA: After such a year of trial – I might have flattered myself that I should not have been insulted with a new probation of my sincerity, as cruel as unnecessary! I now see it is not in your nature to be content, or confident in love. With this conviction – I never will be yours. While I had hopes that my persevering attention, and unreproaching kindness might in time reform your temper, I should have been happy to have gain'd a dearer influence over you; but I will not furnish you with a licensed power to keep alive an incorrigible fault, at the expence of one who never would contend with you.

FAULKLAND: Nay, but Julia, by my soul and honour, if after this –

JULIA: But one word more. – As my faith has once been given to you, I never will barter it with another. – I shall pray for your happiness with the truest sincerity; and the dearest blessing I can ask of Heaven to send you, will be to charm you from that unhappy temper, which alone has prevented the performance of our solemn engagement. – All I request of *you* is, that you will yourself reflect upon this infirmity, and when you number up the many true delights it has deprived you of – let it not be your *least* regret, that it lost you the love of one – who would have follow'd you in beggary through the world! [*Exit.*]

FAULKLAND: She's gone! – for ever! – There was an awful resolution in her manner, that rivetted me to my place. – O Fool! – Dolt! – Barbarian! – Curst as I am, with more imperfections than my fellow-wretches, kind Fortune sent a heaven-gifted cherub to my aid, and, like a ruffian, I have driven her from my side! – I must now haste to my appointment. – Well my mind is tuned for such a scene. – I shall wish only to become a principal in it, and reverse the tale my cursed folly put me upon forging here. – O Love! – Tormentor! – Fiend! – whose influence, like the Moon's, acting on men of dull souls, makes idiots of them, but meeting subtler spirits, betrays their course, and urges sensibility to madness! [*Exit.*]

[*Enter* MAID *and* LYDIA.]

MAID: My Mistress, Ma'am, I know, was here just now – perhaps she is only in the next room. [*Exit* MAID.]

LYDIA: Heigh ho! – Though he has used me so, this fellow runs strangely in my head. I believe one lecture from my grave Cousin will make me recall him.

[*Enter* JULIA.]

LYDIA: O Julia, I am come to you with such an appetite for consolation. – Lud! Child, what's the matter with you? – You have been crying! – I'll be hanged, if that Faulkland has not been tormenting you!

JULIA: You mistake the cause of my uneasiness. – Something *has* flurried me a little. – Nothing that you can guess at. – I would not accuse Faulkland to a Sister! [*Aside.*]

LYDIA: Ah! whatever vexations you may have, I can assure you mine surpass them. – You know who Beverley proves to be?

JULIA: I will now own to you, Lydia, that Mr. Faulkland had before inform'd me of the whole affair. Had young Absolute been the person you took him for, I should not have accepted your confidence on the subject, without a serious endeavour to counteract your caprice.

LYDIA: So, then, I see I have been deceived by every one! – but I don't care – I'll never have him.

JULIA: Nay, Lydia –

LYDIA: Why, is it not provoking; when I thought we were coming to the prettiest distress imaginable, to find myself made a mere Smithfield bargain[1] of at last – There had I projected one of the most sentimental elopements! – so becoming a disguise! – so amiable a ladder of Ropes! – Conscious Moon – four horses – Scotch parson[2] – with such surprise to Mrs. Malaprop – and such paragraphs in the News-papers! – O, I shall die with disappointment.

1. A deal, as in the Smithfield meat market, in which money is the main consideration.
2. Scottish marriage laws permitted the marriage of young people under twenty-one without parental consent.

JULIA: I don't wonder at it!

LYDIA: Now – sad reverse! – what have I to expect, but, after a deal of flimsy preparation with a bishop's licence, and my Aunt's blessing, to go simpering up to the Altar; or perhaps be cried three times in a country-church,[1] and have an unmannerly fat clerk ask the consent of every butcher in the parish to join John Absolute and Lydia Languish, Spinster! O, that I should live to hear myself called Spinster!

JULIA: Melancholy, indeed!

LYDIA: How mortifying, to remember the dear delicious shifts I used to be put to, to gain half a minute's conversation with this fellow! – How often have I stole forth, in the coldest night in January, and found him in the garden, stuck like a dripping statue! – There would he kneel to me in the snow, and sneeze and cough so pathetically! he shivering with cold, and I with apprehension! and while the freezing blast numb'd our joints, how warmly would he press me to pity his flame, and glow with mutual ardour! – Ah, Julia! that was something like being in love.

JULIA: If I were in spirits, Lydia, I should chide you only by laughing heartily at you: but it suits more the situation of my mind, at present, earnestly to entreat you, not to let a man, who loves you with sincerity, suffer that unhappiness from your caprice, which I know too well caprice can inflict.

LYDIA: O Lud! what has brought my Aunt here!

[*Enter* MRS. MALAPROP, FAG, *and* DAVID.]

MRS. MALAPROP: So! so! here's fine work! – here's fine suicide, paracide,[2] and simulation[3] going on in the fields! and Sir Anthony not to be found to prevent the antistrophe![4]

JULIA: For Heaven's sake, Madam, what's the meaning of this?

MRS. MALAPROP: That gentleman can tell you – 'twas he enveloped[5] the affair to me.

LYDIA: Do, Sir, will you inform us. [*To* FAG.]

FAG: Ma'am, I should hold myself very deficient in every requisite that forms the man of breeding, if I delay'd a moment to give all the information in my power to a lady so deeply interested in the affair as you are.

LYDIA: But quick! quick, Sir!

FAG: True, Ma'am, as you say, one should be quick in divulging matters of this nature; for should we be tedious, perhaps while we are flourishing[6] on the subject, two or three lives may be lost!

1. A reference to the reading of the banns.
2. Parricide.
3. Agitation.
4. Catastrophe.
5. Developed or unfolded.
6. Waxing lyrical.

LYDIA: O patience! – Do, Ma'am, for Heaven's sake! tell us what is the matter?

MRS. MALAPROP: Why, murder's the matter! slaughter's the matter! killing's the matter! – but he can tell you the perpendiculars.[1]

LYDIA: Then, prythee, Sir, be brief.

FAG: Why then, Ma'am – as to murder – I cannot take upon me to say – and as to slaughter, or man-slaughter, that will be as the jury finds it.

LYDIA: But who, Sir – who are engaged in this?

FAG: Faith, Ma'am, one is a young gentleman whom I should be very sorry any thing was to happen to – a very pretty behaved gentleman! We have lived much together, and always on terms.

LYDIA: But who is this? who! who! who!

FAG: My Master, Ma'am – my Master – I speak of my Master.

LYDIA: Heavens! What, Captain Absolute!

MRS. MALAPROP: O, to be sure, you are frightened now!

JULIA: But who are with him, Sir?

FAG: As to the rest, Ma'am, this gentleman can inform you better than I.

JULIA: Do speak, friend. [*To* DAVID.]

DAVID: Look'ee, my Lady – by the Mass! there's mischief going on. – Folks don't use to meet for amusement with fire-arms, firelocks,[2] fire-engines, fire-screens, fire-office, and the devil knows what other crackers besides! – This, my Lady, I say, has an angry favour.

JULIA: But who is there beside Captain Absolute, friend?

DAVID: My poor Master – under favour, for mentioning him first. – You know me, my Lady – I am David – and my Master of course is, or *was,* Squire Acres. – Then comes Squire Faulkland.

JULIA: Do, Ma'am, let us instantly endeavour to prevent mischief

MRS. MALAPROP: O fie – it would be very inelegant in us: – we should only participate[3] things.

DAVID: Ah! do, Mrs. Aunt, save a few lives – they are desperately given, believe me. – Above all, there is that blood-thirsty Philistine, Sir Lucius O'Trigger.

MRS. MALAPROP: Sir Lucius O'Trigger! – O mercy! have they drawn poor little dear Sir Lucius into the scrape? – why, how, how you stand, girl! you have no more feeling than one of the Derbyshire Putrefactions![4]

LYDIA: What are we to do, Madam?

MRS. MALAPROP: Why, fly with the utmost felicity[5] to be sure, to prevent mischief: – here, friend – you can shew us the place?

FAG: If you please, Ma'am, I will conduct you. – David, do you look for Sir Anthony. [*Exit* DAVID.]

1. Particulars.
2. Muskets.
3. Precipitate.
4. Petrifactions, i.e. fossils.
5. Alacrity

MRS. MALAPROP: Come, girls!—this gentleman will exhort[1] us.—Come, Sir, you're our envoy—lead the way, and we'll precede.[2]

FAG: Not a step before the ladies for the world!

MRS. MALAPROP: You're sure you know the spot.

FAG: I think I can find it, Ma'am; and one good thing is, we shall hear the report of the pistols as we draw near, so we can't well miss them; never fear, Ma'am, never fear. [*Exeunt, he talking.*]

Act V, Scene II

[South-Parade.
Enter ABSOLUTE, *putting his sword under his greatcoat.*]

ABSOLUTE: A sword seen in the streets of Bath would raise as great an alarm as a mad-dog.[3] – How provoking this is in Faulkland! – never punctual! I shall be obliged to go without him at last. – O, the devil! here's Sir Anthony! – how shall I escape him?
[*Muffles up his, face, and takes a circle to go off.*]

[*Enter* SIR ANTHONY.]

SIR ANTHONY: How one may be deceived at a little distance! only that I see he don't know me, I could have sworn that was Jack! – Hey! – 'Gad's life; it is. – Why, Jack – what are you afraid of ? – hey! sure I'm right. – why, Jack – Jack Absolute! – Jack Absolute! [*Goes up to him.*]

ABSOLUTE: Really, Sir, you have the advantage of me: – I don't remember ever to have had the honour – my name is Saunderson, at your service.

SIR ANTHONY: Sir, I beg your pardon – I took you – hey! – why, z—ds! it is – Stay – [*Looks up to his face.*]
So, so – your humble servant, Mr. Saunderson! – Why, you scoundrel, what tricks are you after now?

ABSOLUTE: O! a joke, Sir, a joke! – I came here on purpose to look for you, Sir.

SIR ANTHONY: You did! well, I am glad you were so lucky: – but what are you muffled up so for? – what's this for? – hey?

ABSOLUTE: 'Tis cool, Sir; isn't it? – rather chilly somehow: – but I shall be late – I have a particular engagement.

SIR ANTHONY: Stay. – why, I thought you were looking for me? – Pray, Jack, where is't you are going?

ABSOLUTE: Going, Sir!

SIR ANTHONY: Aye – where are you going?

ABSOLUTE: Where am I going?

1. Escort.
2. Proceed.
3. Because of Beau Nash's prohibition.

SIR ANTHONY: You unmannerly puppy!

ABSOLUTE: I was going, Sir, to – to – to – to Lydia – Sir to Lydia – to make matters up if I could; – and I was looking for you, Sir, to – to

SIR ANTHONY: To go with you, I suppose – Well, come along.

ABSOLUTE: O! z—ds! no, Sir, not for the world! – I wish'd to meet with you, Sir, to – to – to – You find it cool, I'm sure, Sir – you'd better not stay out.

SIR ANTHONY: Cool! – not at all – Well, Jack – and what will you say to Lydia?

ABSOLUTE: O, Sir, beg her pardon, humour her – promise and vow: – but I detain you, Sir – consider the cold air on your gout.

SIR ANTHONY: O, not at all! – not at all! – I'm in no hurry. – Ah! Jack, you youngsters when once you are wounded here.

[*Putting his hand to Absolute's breast.*]

Hey! what the deuce have you got here?

ABSOLUTE: Nothing, Sir – nothing.

SIR ANTHONY: What's this? – here's something d—d hard!

ABSOLUTE: O, trinkets, Sir! trinkets – a bauble for Lydia!

SIR ANTHONY: Nay, let me see your taste. [*Pulls his coat open, the sword falls.*] Trinkets! – a bauble for Lydia! – z—ds! sirrah, you are not going to cut her throat, are you?

ABSOLUTE: Ha! ha! ha! – I thought it would divert you, Sir, tho' I didn't mean to tell you till afterwards.

SIR ANTHONY: You didn't? – Yes, this is a very diverting trinket, truly.

ABSOLUTE: Sir, I'll explain to you. – You know, Sir, Lydia is romantic – dev'lish romantic, and very absurd of course: – now, Sir, I intend, if she refuses to forgive me – to unsheath this sword – and swear – I'll fall upon its point, and expire at her feet!

SIR ANTHONY: Fall upon a fiddle-stick's end! – why, I suppose it is the very thing that would please her – Get along, you Fool. –

ABSOLUTE: Well, Sir, you shall hear of my success – you shall hear. – 'O, Lydia! – forgive me, or this pointed steel' – says I.

SIR ANTHONY: 'O, Booby! stab away, and welcome' – says she – Get along! – and d—n your trinkets! [*Exit* ABSOLUTE.]

[*Enter* DAVID, *running.*]

DAVID: Stop him! stop him! Murder! Thief! Fire! – Stop fire! Stop fire! – O! Sir Anthony – call! call! bid 'em stop! Murder! Fire!

SIR ANTHONY: Fire! Murder! where ?

DAVID: Oons! he's out of sight! and I'm out of breath, for my part! O, Sir Anthony, why didn't you stop him? why didn't you stop him?

SIR ANTHONY: Z—ds! the fellow's mad! – Stop whom? stop Jack?

DAVID: Aye, the Captain, Sir! – there's murder and slaughter –

SIR ANTHONY: Murder!

DAVID: Aye, please you, Sir Anthony, there's all kinds of murder, all sorts of slaughter to be seen in the fields: there's fighting going on, Sir – bloody sword-and-gun fighting!

SIR ANTHONY: Who are going to fight, Dunce?
DAVID: Every body that I know of, Sir Anthony: – every body is going to fight, my poor Master, Sir Lucius O'Trigger, your son, the Captain –
SIR ANTHONY: O, the Dog! – I see his tricks: – do you know the place?
DAVID: King's-Mead-Fields.
SIR ANTHONY: You know the way?
DAVID: Not an inch; – but I'll call the Mayor – Aldermen – Constables – Church-wardens – and Beadles – we can't be too many to part them.
SIR ANTHONY: Come along – give me your shoulder![1] we'll get assistance as we go – the lying villain! – Well, I shall be in such a phrenzy – So this was the history of his d—d trinkets! I'll bauble him! [*Exeunt.*]

Act V, Scene III

[King's-Mead-Fields.
SIR LUCIUS *and* ACRES, *with pistols.*]

ACRES: By my valour! then, Sir Lucius, forty yards is a good distance – Odds levels and aims! – I say it is a good distance.
SIR LUCIUS: Is it for muskets or small field-pieces?[2] upon my conscience, Mr. Acres, you must leave those things to me. – Stay now – I'll shew you [*Measures paces along the stage.*] there now, that is a very pretty distance – a pretty gentleman's distance.
ACRES: Z—ds! we might as well fight in a sentry-box! – I tell you, Sir Lucius, the farther he is off, the cooler I shall take my aim.
SIR LUCIUS: Faith! then I suppose you would aim at him best of all if he was out of sight!
ACRES: No, Sir Lucius – but I should think forty or eight and thirty yards –
SIR LUCIUS: Pho! pho! nonsense! three or four feet between the mouths of your pistols is as good as a mile.
ACRES: Odds bullets, no! – by my valour! there is no merit in killing him so near: – no, my dear Sir Lucius, let me bring him down at a long shot: – a long shot, Sir Lucius, if you love me!
SIR LUCIUS: Well – the gentleman's friend and I must settle that. – But tell me now, Mr. Acres, in case of an accident, is there any little will or commission I could execute for you?
ACRES: I am much obliged to you, Sir Lucius – but I don't understand –
SIR LUCIUS: Why, you may think there's no being shot at without a little risk – and if an unlucky bullet should carry a *Quietus*[3] with it – I say it will be no time then to be bothering you about family matters.

1. Sir Anthony needs support because of his gout.
2. Cannons.
3. Death.

ACRES: A *Quietus*!

SIR LUCIUS: For instance, now – if that should be the case – would you chuse to be pickled and sent home? – or would it be the same to you to lie here in the Abbey? – I'm told there is very snug lying in the Abbey.

ACRES: Pickled! – Snug lying in the Abbey! – Odds tremors! Sir Lucius, don't talk so!

SIR LUCIUS: I suppose, Mr. Acres, you never were engaged in an affair of this kind before?

ACRES: No, Sir Lucius, never before.

SIR LUCIUS: Ah! that's a pity! – there's nothing, like being used to a thing. – Pray now, how would you receive the gentleman's shot?

ACRES: Odds files![1] – I've practised that – there, Sir Lucius – there [*Puts himself in an attitude.*] – a side-front, hey? – Odd! I'll make myself small enough: – I'll stand edge-ways.

SIR LUCIUS: Now – you're quite out – for if you stand so when I take my aim – [*Levelling at him.*]

ACRES: Z—ds! Sir Lucius – are you sure it is not cock'd?

SIR LUCIUS: Never fear.

ACRES: But – but – you don't know – it may go off of its own head![2]

SIR LUCIUS: Pho! be easy – Well, now if I hit you in the body, my bullet has a double chance – for if it misses a vital part on your right side 'twill be very hard if it don't succeed on the left!

ACRES: A vital part!

SIR LUCIUS: But, there – fix yourself so – [*Placing him.*] let him see the broad side of your full front – there – now a ball or two may pass clean thro' your body, and never do any harm at all.

ACRES: Clean thro' me! – a ball or two clean thro' me!

SIR LUCIUS: Aye – may they – and it is much the genteelest attitude into the bargain.

ACRES: Look'ee! Sir Lucius – I'd just as leive be shot in an aukward posture as a genteel one – so, by my valour! I will stand edge-ways.

SIR LUCIUS: [*Looking at his watch.*] Sure they don't mean to disappoint us. – Hah? – no faith – I think I see them coming.

ACRES: Hey! – what! – coming!

SIR LUCIUS: Aye – Who are those yonder getting over the stile?

ACRES: There are two of them, indeed! – well – let them come – hey, Sir Lucius! – we – we – we – we – won't run

SIR LUCIUS: Run!

ACRES: No – I say – we *won't* run, by my valour!

SIR LUCIUS: What the devil's the matter with you ?

1. Foils, or fencing swords.
2. On its own.

ACRES: Nothing – nothing – my dear friend – my dear Sir Lucius but – I – I – I don't feel quite so bold, somehow – as I did.

SIR LUCIUS: O fie! – consider your honour.

ACRES: Aye – true – my honour – Do, Sir Lucius, edge in a word or two every now and then about my honour.

SIR LUCIUS: Well, here they're coming. [*Looking.*]

ACRES: Sir Lucius – if I wa'n't with you, I should almost think I was afraid – if my valour should leave me! – Valour will come and go.

SIR LUCIUS: Then, pray keep it fast, while you have it.

ACRES: Sir Lucius – I doubt it is going – yes – my valour is certainly going! – it is sneaking off! – I feel it oozing out as it were at the palms of my hands!

SIR LUCIUS: Your honour – your honour – Here they are.

ACRES: O mercy! – now – that I were safe at *Clod-hall!* or could be shot before I was aware!

[*Enter* FAULKLAND *and* ABSOLUTE.]

SIR LUCIUS: Gentlemen, your most obedient – hah! – what Captain Absolute! – So, I suppose, Sir, you are come here, just like myself – to do a kind office, first for your friend—then to proceed to business on your own account.

ACRES: What, Jack! – my dear Jack! – my dear friend!

ABSOLUTE: Heark'ee, Bob, *Beverley's* at hand.

SIR LUCIUS: Well, Mr. Acres – I don't blame your saluting the gentleman civilly. – So, Mr. Beverley, [*to* FAULKLAND] if you'll chuse your weapons, the Captain and I will measure the ground.

FAULKLAND: *My* weapons, Sir.

ACRES: Odds life! Sir Lucius, I'm not going to fight Mr. Faulkland; these are my particular friends.

SIR LUCIUS: What, Sir, did not you come here to fight Mr. Acres ?

FAULKLAND: Not I, upon my word, Sir.

SIR LUCIUS: Well, now, that's mighty provoking! But I hope, Mr. Faulkland, as there are three of us come on purpose for the game – you won't be so cantanckerous as to spoil the party by sitting out.

ABSOLUTE: O pray, Faulkland, fight to oblige Sir Lucius.

FAULKLAND: Nay, if Mr. Acres is so bent on the matter.

ACRES: No, no, Mr. Faulkland – I'll bear my disappointment like a Christian – Look'ee, Sir Lucius, there's no occasion at all for me to fight; and if it is the same to you, I'd as lieve let it alone.

SIR LUCIUS: Observe me, Mr. Acres – I must not be trifled with. You have certainly challenged somebody – and you came here to fight him – Now, if that gentleman is willing to represent him – I can't see, for my soul, why it isn't just the same thing.

ACRES: Why no – Sir Lucius – I tell you, 'tis one Beverley I've challenged – a fellow, you see, that dare not shew his face! If *he* were here, I'd make him give up his pretensions directly! –

ABSOLUTE: Hold, Bob – let me set you right – there is no such man as *Beverley* in the case. – The person who assumed that name is before you; and as his pretensions are the same in both characters, he is ready to support them in whatever way you please.

SIR LUCIUS: Well, this is lucky – Now you have an opportunity –

ACRES: What, quarrel with my dear friend Jack Absolute – not if he were fifty Beverleys! Z—ds! Sir Lucius, you would not have me be so unnatural.

SIR LUCIUS: Upon my conscience, Mr. Acres, your valour has *oozed* away with a vengeance!

ACRES: Not in the least! Odds Backs,[1] and Abettors! I'll be your second with all my heart – and if you should get a *Quietus,* you may command me entirely. I'll get you a *snug lying* in the *Abbey here;* or *pickle* you, and send you over to Blunderbuss-hall, or any thing of the kind with the greatest pleasure.

SIR LUCIUS: Pho! pho! you are little better than a coward.

ACRES: Mind, gentlemen, he calls me a *Coward;* Coward was the word, by my valour!

SIR LUCIUS: Well, Sir?

ACRES: Look'ee, Sir Lucius, 'tisn't that I mind the word Coward – *Coward* may be said in joke. – But if you had call'd me a *Poltroon,* Odds Daggers and Balls!

SIR LUCIUS: Well, Sir?

ACRES: – I should have thought you a very ill-bred man.

SIR LUCIUS: Pho! you are beneath my notice.

ABSOLUTE: Nay, Sir Lucius, you can't have a better second than my friend, Acres – He is a most *determined dog* – call'd in the country, *Fighting Bob.* – He generally *kills a man a week;* don't you, Bob?

ACRES: Aye – at home!

SIR LUCIUS: Well then, Captain, 'tis we must begin – so come out, my little counsellor, [*Draws his sword.*] and ask the gentleman, whether he will resign the lady, without forcing you to proceed against him?

ABSOLUTE: Come on then, Sir; [*draws*] since you won't let it be an amicable suit, here's my reply.

[*Enter* SIR ANTHONY, DAVID, *and the* WOMEN.]

DAVID: Knock 'em all down, sweet Sir Anthony, knock down my Master in particular – and bind his hands over to their good behaviour!

SIR ANTHONY: Put up, Jack, put up, or I shall be in a frenzy – how came you in a duel, Sir?

ABSOLUTE: Faith, Sir, that gentleman can tell you better than I; 'twas he call'd on me, and you know, Sir, I serve his Majesty.

1. Seconds in a duel.

SIR ANTHONY: Here's a pretty fellow; I catch him going to cut a man's throat, and he tells me, he serves his Majesty! – Zounds! sirrah, then how durst you draw the King's sword against one of his subjects?

ABSOLUTE: Sir, I tell you! That gentleman call'd me out, without explaining his reasons.

SIR ANTHONY: Gad! Sir, how came you to call my son out, without explaining your reasons?

SIR LUCIUS: Your son, Sir, insulted me in a manner which my honour could not brook.

SIR ANTHONY: Zounds! Jack, how durst you insult the gentleman in a manner which his honour could not brook?

MRS. MALAPROP: Come, come, let's have no Honour before ladies – Captain Absolute, come here – How could you intimidate us so? – Here's Lydia has been terrified to death for you.

ABSOLUTE: For fear I should be kill'd, or escape, Ma'am?

MRS. MALAPROP: Nay, no delusions[1] to the past – Lydia is convinc'd; speak child.

SIR LUCIUS: With your leave, Ma'am, I must put in a word here – I believe I could interpret the young lady's silence – Now mark –

LYDIA: What is it you mean, Sir?

SIR LUCIUS: Come, come, Delia, we must be serious now – this is no time for trifling.

LYDIA: 'Tis true, Sir; and your reproof bids me offer this gentleman my hand, and solicit the return of his affections.

ABSOLUTE: O! my little angel, say you so? – Sir Lucius – I perceive there must be some mistake here – with regard to the affront, which you affirm I have given you – I can only say, that it could not have been intentional. – And as you must be convinced, that I should not fear to support a real injury – you shall now see that I am not ashamed to atone for an inadvertency – I ask your pardon. – But for this lady, while honour'd with her approbation, I will support my claim against any man whatever.

SIR ANTHONY: Well said, Jack, and I'll stand by you, my Boy.

ACRES: Mind, I give up all my claim – I make no pretensions to any thing in the world – and if I can't get a wife, without fighting for her, by my Valour! I'll live a bachelor.

SIR LUCIUS: Captain, give me your hand – an affront handsomely acknowledged becomes an obligation – and as for the Lady if she chuses to deny her own hand writing here – [*Takes out letters.*]

MRS. MALAPROP: O, he will dissolve[2] my mystery! – Sir Lucius, perhaps there's some mistake – perhaps, I can illuminate –

SIR LUCIUS: Pray, old gentlewoman, don't interfere, where you have no business. – Miss Languish, are you my Delia, or not?

1. Allusions.
2. Discover or reveal.

LYDIA: Indeed, Sir Lucius, I am not. [LYDIA *and* ABSOLUTE *walk aside.*]

MRS. MALAPROP: Sir Lucius O'Trigger – ungrateful as you are – I own the soft impeachment[1] – pardon my blushes, I am Delia.

SIR LUCIUS: You Delia – pho! pho! be easy.[2]

MRS. MALAPROP: Why, thou barbarous Vandyke – those letters are mine – When you are more sensible of my benignity – perhaps I may be brought to encourage your addresses.

SIR LUCIUS: Mrs. Malaprop I am extremely sensible of your condescension; and whether you or Lucy have put this trick upon me, I am equally beholden to you. – And to shew you I'm not ungrateful, Captain Absolute! since you have taken that lady from me, I'll give you my Delia into the bargain.

ABSOLUTE: I am much obliged to you, Sir Lucius; but here's our friend, fighting Bob, unprovided for.

SIR LUCIUS: Hah! little Valour – here, will you make your fortune?

ACRES: Odds Wrinkles! No. – But give me your hand, Sir Lucius, forget and forgive; but if ever I give you a chance of *pickling* me again, say Bob Acres is a Dunce, that's all.

SIR ANTHONY: Come, Mrs. Malaprop, don't be cast down – you are in your bloom yet.

MRS. MALAPROP: O Sir Anthony! – men are all barbarians –

[*All retire but* JULIA *and* FAULKLAND.]

JULIA: He seems dejected and unhappy – not sullen – there was some foundation, however, for the tale he told me – O woman! how true should be your judgment, when your resolution is so weak!

FAULKLAND: Julia! – how can I sue for what I so little deserve? I dare not presume – yet Hope is the child of Penitence.

JULIA: Oh! Faulkland, you have not been more faulty in your unkind treatment of me, than I am now in wanting inclination to resent it. As my heart honestly bids me place my weakness to the account of love, I should be ungenerous not to admit the same plea for yours.

FAULKLAND: Now I shall be blest indeed! [SIR ANTHONY *comes forward.*]

SIR ANTHONY: What's going on here? – So you have been quarrelling too, I warrant. – Come, Julia, I never interfered before; but let me have a hand in the matter at last. – All the faults I have ever seen in my friend Faulkland, seemed to proceed from what he calls the *delicacy* and *warmth* of his affection for you – There, marry him directly, Julia, you'll find he'll mend surprisingly! [*The rest come forward.*]

SIR LUCIUS: Come now, I hope there is no dissatisfied person, but what is content; for as I have been disappointed myself, it will be very hard if I have not the satisfaction of seeing other people succeed better –

ACRES: You are right, Sir Lucius. – So, Jack, I wish you joy – Mr. Faulkland

1. Accusation.
2. Take it easy.

the same. – Ladies, – come now, to shew you I'm neither vex'd nor angry, Odds Tabors and Pipes! I'll order the fiddles in half an hour, to the New Rooms[1] – and I insist on your all meeting me there.

SIR ANTHONY: Gad! Sir, I like your spirit; and at night we single lads will drink a health to the young couples, and a husband to Mrs. Malaprop.

FAULKLAND: Our partners are stolen from us, Jack – I hope to be congratulated by each other – *yours* for having checked in time, the errors of an ill-directed Imagination, which might have betray'd an innocent heart; and *mine*, for having, by her gentleness and candour, reformed the unhappy temper of one, who by it made wretched whom he loved most, and tortured the heart he ought to have ador'd.

ABSOLUTE: Well, Faulkland, we have both tasted the Bitters, as well as the Sweets of Love – with this difference only, that *you* always prepared the bitter cup for yourself, while *I* –

LYDIA: Was always obliged to *me* for it, hey! Mr. Modesty? – But come, no more of that – our happiness is now as unallay'd as general.

JULIA: Then let us study to preserve it so: and while Hope pictures to us a flattering scene of future Bliss, let us deny its pencil those colours which are too bright to be lasting. – When Hearts deserving Happiness would unite their fortunes, Virtue would crown them with an unfading garland of modest, hurtless flowers; but ill-judging Passion will force the gaudier Rose into the wreath, whose thorn offends them, when its Leaves are dropt!

Epilogue[2]

BY THE AUTHOR
Spoken by MRS. BULKLEY

Ladies for *You* – I heard our Poet say –
He'd try to coax some *Moral* from his Play:
'One moral's plain' – cried I – 'without more fuss;
Man's social happiness all rests on Us –
Thro' all the Drama – whether damn'd or not –
Love gilds the *Scene*, and *Women* guide the *plot*.
From ev'ry rank – obedience is our due –
D'ye doubt? – The world's great stage shall prove it true.'

The Cit – well skill'd to shun domestic strife –

1. The New Assembly Rooms, opened in 1771.
2. In both the first and third editions of the play, the Epilogue was printed immediately after the Prologue. The version printed here is the corrected one from the third edition.

Will sup abroad; – but first – he'll ask his *wife:*
John Trot, his friend for once, will do the same,
But then – he'll just *step home to tell his dame.* –

The *surly 'Squire* – at noon resolves to rule,
And half the day – Zounds! Madam is a fool!
Convinc'd at night – the vanquish'd Victor says,
Ah! Kate! *you women have such coaxing ways!* –

The jolly Toper[1] chides each tardy blade,[2] –
Till reeling Bacchus calls on Love for aid.
Then with each Toast, he sees fair bumpers swim,
And kisses Chloe on the sparkling Brim!

Nay, I have heard that Statesmen – great and wise –
Will *sometimes* counsel with a Lady's eyes;
The servile suitors – watch her various face,
She smiles preferment – or she frowns disgrace,
Curtsies a pension here – there nods a place.

Nor with less awe, in scenes of humbler life,
Is *view'd the mistress,* or is *heard the wife.*
The poorest Peasant of the poorest soil,
The child of Poverty, and heir to Toil –
Early from radiant Love's impartial light,
Steals one small spark, to cheer his world of night:
Dear spark! – that oft thro' winter's chilling woes,
Is all the warmth his little cottage knows!

The wand'ring *Tar* – who, not for *years,* has press'd
The widow'd partner of his *day* of rest –
On the cold deck – far from her arms remov'd –
Still hums the ditty, which his Susan lov'd:
And while around the cadence rude is blown,
The Boatswain whistles in a softer tone.
The Soldier, fairly proud of wounds and toil,
Pants for the *triumph* of his Nancy's smile;
But ere the battle, should he list' her cries,
The Lover trembles – and the Hero dies!
That heart, by war and honour steel'd to fear,
Droops on a sigh, and sickens at a tear!

1. Hard drinker.
2. Young spark.

But Ye more cautious – ye nice judging few,
Who give to Beauty only Beauty's due,
Tho' friends to Love – *Ye* view with deep regret
Our conquests marr'd – and triumphs incomplete,
'Till polish'd Wit more lasting charms disclose,
And judgment fix the darts which Beauty throws!
– In female breasts did Sense and Merit rule,
The Lover's mind would ask no other school;
Sham'd into sense – the Scholars of our eyes,
Our Beaux from *Gallantry* would soon be wise;
Would gladly light, their homage to improve,
The Lamp of Knowledge at the Torch of Love.

She Stoops to Conquer

OLIVER GOLDSMITH

INTRODUCTION

Little is known of Goldsmith's early life in Ireland. Even his date of birth is uncertain; some biographers claim it was 1728, most settle for 1730. He was born the son of a poor clergyman (later idealised in the figure of Dr Primrose in his novel *The Vicar of Wakefield*), and spent most of his youth in the village of Lissoy. Given the genteel poverty of his upbringing, Goldsmith had to struggle first for his education and then for his livelihood. He entered Trinity College, Dublin in 1745 as a sizar, which meant he was granted free tuition in return for working as a servant for his tutors. In 1752 he moved to Edinburgh to study medicine, but left without a degree. He spent several years working his way through Europe, combining study with busking and also trying his hand at university disputations for a fee. In 1756 he returned to London. Having dabbled with a variety of ill-suited careers (these included work as an apothecary's assistant, a proof-reader and usher in a boys' school), he eventually began to earn a living of sorts as a Grub Street journalist and hack writer. He was soon writing regular features for the *Monthly Review*, as well as entertaining letters from an imaginary Chinese visitor to England.

Goldsmith's first substantive piece of work, which attracted serious attention, was his essay entitled *An Enquiry into the Present State of Polite Learning in Europe* (1759). This was followed in 1764 by a lengthy poem, *The Traveller or a Prospect of Society*, which gained him admittance to the circle of writers and artists gathered around Dr Johnson. Two years later, in 1766, he went on to write his first, much acclaimed novel, *The Vicar of Wakefield*. At this point, he began work on his first play, *The Good Natur'd Man*. However, in his essay on the *Present State of Polite Learning in Europe,* he had already sketched out the distinctive and myriad difficulties confronting the would-be dramatist in Georgian England. These included the Licenser, who had power to exercise draconian censorship on behalf of the Lord Chamberlain; the Managers of the two patent houses at Drury Lane and Covent Garden who were disinclined to risk offending the taste of the town with new plays when there was a large stock of older plays, suitably bowdlerised, on which they could rely; and the Reviews, written in an often vituperative style by Grub Street hacks. Goldsmith now experienced some of these difficulties at first hand. He managed to avoid any problems with the Licenser by ensuring that his play (in marked contrast to his poetry and essays) omitted any reference to contemporary political or social issues. The managers proved more difficult to please. Garrick at Drury Lane prevaricated for many months, even though Goldsmith's literary friends and allies spoke on his behalf. In sheer exasperation, Goldsmith offered his play to Garrick's rival, George Colman at Covent Garden. Perhaps because he was a relatively new and inexperienced manager, Colman felt less able to withstand the pressure of Goldsmith's powerful friends. He accepted the play, which was given its first performance on 29 January 1768: it ran for ten performances. Although this was a respectable total, it was not the unqualified success for which Goldsmith had hoped. Audiences and reviewers found some of the scenes too 'low'; in particular Goldsmith was advised in no uncertain terms by the reviewers to omit the farcical bailiff scene. After the first night, Goldsmith followed their advice, but the whole experience must have been distinctly dispiriting.

In 1770 Goldsmith enjoyed a much needed critical success with his poem *The Deserted Village*. Set in Ireland, the poem expresses a cogent critique of contemporary social values. A country squire has uprooted a whole village in order to satisfy his wish for a landscaped garden. The delicate balance of country life that Goldsmith imagines in some distant feudal past is shattered by modern avarice and selfishness. Almost foreshadowing the insights of today's ecologists, Goldsmith warns of the dangers inherent in allowing human greed to interfere with nature. His poem was a powerfully written piece, full of romantic nostalgia for a long-lost golden age; its success undoubtedly helped to restore Goldsmith's confidence.

By 1771, Goldsmith was at work on his second play, *The Mistakes of a Night*. It was not to be given its final title, *She Stoops to Conquer*, until the day before its opening night at Covent Garden on 15 March 1773. Once again, Goldsmith had grave difficulties in having his play accepted. As before, Garrick was evasive, although he eventually contributed a Prologue to the play. Eventually it was only bullying from Dr Johnson himself that persuaded Colman, much against his will, to put on a play he was convinced would not succeed. What made Colman hesitate was Goldsmith's inclination to write 'low' rather than genteel comedy, and also his outspoken attack on the popular sentimental form of comic writing. Such was Goldsmith's dislike of sentimental drama that he went to the trouble of publishing an *Essay on the Theatre*, which attacked the genre, only a matter of months before the opening night of his own play. No wonder Colman was apprehensive about the way an audience would respond to Goldsmith's latest work.

In the event, Colman's fears were unfounded. *She Stoops to Conquer* proved to be an outstanding popular success. Although Goldsmith claimed to have written a satiric comedy that was firmly opposed to a sentimental approach, there was more than enough warm-hearted benevolence in the play to make it acceptable to contemporary audiences. Provoking laughter that was good-natured rather than malicious, Goldsmith's new play was written to delight rather than to disturb.

She Stoops to Conquer

The basic idea for the play was borrowed from one of the most successful comedies of the period, Isaac Bickerstaffe's *Love in a Village* (1762). Goldsmith makes use of Bickerstaffe's plot involving two pairs of young lovers; he also takes over the figure of Hodge, a comic outspoken serving-man, as the basis for his figure Tony Lumpkin. However, Goldsmith brilliantly embellishes his literary thefts in such a way that they are hardly recognisable.

The plot of *She Stoops to Conquer* is simple enough. Two young men, Marlow and Hastings, come to the countryside to court two young ladies. Marlow is to visit a young lady called Kate Hardcastle, chosen for him by his father as a suitable bride. Mr Hardcastle is an old friend of Sir Charles Marlow and this marriage will bring their two families even closer together. Hastings wishes to visit Constance Neville who is related to Mrs Hardcastle, the stepmother of Kate Hardcastle.

Mr and Mrs Hardcastle are a delightfully eccentric couple, coping with the strains of a second marriage. Both have children from their first marriages. Mr Hardcastle enjoys a particularly close relationship with his daughter Kate. His wife has one son from her previous marriage, a boy called Tony Lumpkin. She has so spoilt and pampered him that he has now become quite unmanageable. Full of tricks and pranks, he far prefers the atmosphere of the local alehouse to the boredom of life at home. His mother wishes him to marry Miss Neville, but Tony far prefers a buxom country girl called Bett Bouncer.

Tony mischievously starts the action in motion when Marlow and Hastings arrive at his alehouse, asking directions to Mr Hardcastle's house. Launching with gusto into his latest prank, he claims that they are miles away from the house and pretends that the house is in fact an inn where they can stay in some comfort overnight. That is where the mistakes of a night begin. Marlow, who has a reputation for shyness, naturally assumes that Hardcastle is an innkeeper and orders him around with some arrogance. Hastings quickly discovers the true situation but decides not to tell Marlow. When Marlow is introduced to Miss Hardcastle (who 'happens' to have alighted at the inn), he is too shy to even look at her, let alone speak to her. This gives her the opportunity in a later scene to pretend to be a barmaid. The effect on Marlow is miraculous. He immediately talks to her with considerable verve and animation and does his best to extract a kiss from her. Meanwhile, Hastings's intention of eloping with Miss Neville is thwarted by Mrs Hardcastle, who not only refuses to hand over the younger woman's jewels but insists that she be driven to her aunt's who will act as a severe guardian for the next few years. This time Tony Lumpkin comes to the rescue by driving his mother and Miss Neville in circles around the house, only to end up in the horse pond.

Eventually, all the mistakes of the night are resolved. Marlow is told the real identity of his host and daughter and learns to face them both without succumbing to tongue-tied silence. Tony renounces any claim on Miss Neville, which leaves her free to marry Hastings. Sir Charles Marlow and Mr Hardcastle are delighted at both matches. The only real loser in the play is Mrs Hardcastle who discovers to her cost the consequences of spoiling her son.

The various characters are drawn in such a way as to permit good comic actors to fill out the parts with something of their own personalities. Despite his relative lack of experience in playwriting,

Goldsmith seems to have a remarkably sure touch here. He seems to know intuitively what will work on stage and what will not. There is also enough real human experience behind his character drawing to make his figures more substantial than one might otherwise expect from such a light comedy.

Goldsmith himself was just like young Marlow. Brash and outspoken in the company of barmaids and other working-class women, but shy and tongue-tied when in the company of women of his own class and standing. In the figure of Marlow Goldsmith raises the whole issue of personality. Is there such a thing as personality, or are we just a set of contrasting responses, depending on the 'other' with whom we are interacting for the way we respond? In Marlow's case, the issue is brought to a head because of his excessive shyness with women of his own class. But even in his dealings with Mr Hardcastle, Marlow is a completely different person when he thinks Hardcastle is a mere innkeeper. Is personality therefore, in the way we normally understand it, merely a question of social conditioning, a set of socially drilled responses with which we confront different and contrasting individuals?

There was another aspect of Goldsmith's personality reflected in the play. This was his relationship with his mother. In the figure of the oafish, ill-mannered and impossibly spoilt Tony Lumpkin, Goldsmith showed an image of himself in his youth, rewarding his own mother for the care she had shown him with thoughtless ingratitude. In the same way that much of the emotional energy in Ibsen's play *Peer Gynt* is based on the author's intense and emotionally unresolved relationship with his mother, Goldsmith's play derives much of its strength from the playwright's painful memories of the way he had treated his doting mother so selfishly and ungratefully.

Another issue explored with gentle tact and good humour in the play is the question of second marriages, where there are children from the first marriages. The tensions created are shown with deft precision in the very first scene of the play involving Tony Lumpkin and Mr and Mrs Hardcastle. Mr Hardcastle despairs of Tony ever turning into something approximating to a responsible human being. His wife will hear nothing of the matter: Tony is the apple of her eye. Whatever he does, she defends and excuses him. Her love for Tony is quite blind. She is too indulgent and self-indulgent to permit any critique of her beloved son, who reminds her so vividly of her wayward first husband. The relationship is only held together because Mr Hardcastle accepts his wife, with all her faults, and expresses his critique of Tony with no more than gentle exasperation. His is a voice of sweet reason, an old-fashioned, romantic Tory voice of the kind Goldsmith prized so highly. The scene where he discovers his wife newly emerged from the horse pond, while she imagines that he is a highwayman on Crack-Skull Common is a masterly demonstration of their contrasting responses. Even here, when she thinks her own life is in danger, she pleads for the life of her son. Tony *is* her life, she is completely besotted with him and will defend him against all odds. Confronted by this world of hysterical unreason, Hardcastle is merely bemused and treats his wife with his usual gentle good humour:

> Sure, Dorothy, you have not lost your wits? So far from home, when you are within forty yards of your own door. [*To him.*] This is one of your old tricks, you graceless rogue you. [*To her.*] Don't you know the gate, and the mulberry-tree; and don't you remember the horsepond, my dear?

Goldsmith seems to suggest that for relationships to work there has to be one party at least with a still emotional centre who has sound common sense. In his own life, these were qualities he noticeably lacked but he clearly admired them as a romantic ideal. In *She Stoops to Conquer*, not only Mr Hardcastle but his daughter Kate and also Miss Neville are blessed with just such common sense. It is this that guarantees the success of the relationships they are involved in as well as the success of Goldsmith's play. The underlying message is a warm and comforting one. Personality may be a fiction, love can lead to folly, even motherly devotion to self-indulgence, but sound common sense brings stability and happiness to those who cultivate it.

The message was one to which Goldsmith's contemporaries responded with great warmth. It was also a message of deep personal significance. The one quality that Goldsmith lacked was common sense. Even his closest friends regarded him as a walking contradiction: a man envied and yet mocked; a man of fine feelings and yet a solitary and lonely figure who was afraid of his own feelings. He was a friend of the great and the good; men such as Dr Johnson, Sir Joshua Reynolds, Garrick and Thomas Percy knew him intimately. And yet he often seemed ridiculous in company, speaking non-stop as if he were terrified of any moment of silence.

He castigated greed and corruption in his essays and poems, and yet he himself dressed in ridiculously expensive clothes and was for ever in debt. He wrote as an idealist, but gambled away his earnings at a game of cards. He would prefer to spend his last penny on a bottle of claret rather than pay off a single creditor. No wonder he wrote so warmly of characters whose life was shaped by the voice of sweet reason.

Goldsmith was a Jack the Lad who lived on his wits and finally died when his wits could no longer cope. Even as his audiences laughed at the festive comedy he had written in *She Stoops to Conquer*, Goldsmith sank into yet another pit of financial despair. He became desperately ill but still insisted on playing the fool. Although he had never qualified as a doctor, he prescribed himself powders that in fact helped to kill him. He died in April 1774. His friends were shocked at the suddenness of his death and equally shocked to discover the extent of his debts. Goldsmith had spent much of his life running away from real experience. He preferred to gamble rather than face reality. His last gamble with Dr James's fever powders did not pay off. His friends, however, remembered him with great warmth. Dr Johnson's epitaph sums up what he had achieved in their eyes: 'There was hardly any kind of writing that he did not touch upon, and he touched none that he did not adorn.' Goldsmith may have been a clown, but he was also a very great man.

The original cast members of *She Stoops to Conquer* in a scene from Act V: Mr Shuter as Mr Hardcastle, Mrs Green as Mrs Hardcastle and Mr Quick as Tony Lumkin. Mezzotint by W. Humphrey after a painting by T. Parkinson, 1775.

She Stoops to Conquer

OR,

The Mistakes of a Night.

A
COMEDY.

AS IT IS ACTED AT THE
THEATRE-ROYAL
IN
COVENT-GARDEN.

WRITTEN BY
Doctor GOLDSMITH

LONDON:
Printed for F. Newberry, in St. Paul's Church-Yard
M DCC LXXIII

TO SAMUEL JOHNSON, L.L.D.

Dear Sir,
By inscribing this slight performance to you, I do not mean so much to compliment you as myself. It may do me some honour to inform the public, that I have lived many years in intimacy with you. It may serve the interests of mankind also to inform them, that the greatest wit may be found in a character, without impairing the most unaffected piety.

I have, particularly, reason to thank you for your partiality to this performance. The undertaking a comedy, not merely sentimental, was very dangerous; and Mr. Colman, who saw this piece in its various stages, always thought it so.[1] However I ventured to trust it to the public; and though it was necessarily delayed till late in the season, I have every reason to be grateful.

I am, Dear Sir,
Your most sincere friend,
And admirer,
OLIVER GOLDSMITH.

Prologue

BY DAVID GARRICK, Esq.

[*Enter Mr.* WOODWARD,
Dressed in Black, and holding a Handkerchief to his Eyes.]

Excuse me, Sirs, I pray – I can't yet speak –
I'm crying now – and have been all the week!
'Tis not alone this mourning suit, *good masters;*
I've that within – *for which there are no plaisters!*
Pray wou'd you know the reason why I'm crying?
The Comic muse, long sick, is now a dying!
And if she goes, my tears will never stop;
For as a play'r, I can't squeeze out one drop:
I am undone, that's all – shall lose my bread –
I'd rather, but that's nothing – lose my head.
When the sweet maid is laid upon the bier,
Shuter[2] *and I shall be chief mourners here.*
To her *a mawkish drab of spurious breed,*

1. Colman, the patent holder and manager of Covent Garden, was concerned at Goldsmith's attack on sentimental comedy.
2. Ned Shuter, a well-known comic actor playing the role of Hardcastle.

Who deals in sentimentals *will succeed!*
Poor Ned *and I are dead to all intents,*
We can as soon speak Greek as sentiments!
Both nervous grown, to keep our spirits up,
We now and then take down a hearty cup.
What shall we do? – If Comedy forsake us!
They'll turn us out, and no one else will take us,
But why can't I be moral? – Let me try –
My heart thus pressing – fix'd my face and eye –
With a sententious look, that nothing means,
(Faces are blocks, in sentimental scenes)
Thus I begin – All is not gold that glitters,
Pleasure seems sweet, but proves a glass of bitters.
When ign'rance enters, folly is at hand;
Learning is better far than house and land:
Let not your virtue trip, who trips may stumble,
And virtue is not virtuc, if she tumble.
I give it up – morals won't do for me;
To make you laugh I must play tragedy.
One hope remains – hearing the maid was ill,
A doctor[1] *comes this night to shew his skill.*
To cheer her heart, and give your muscles motion,
He in five draughts prepar'd, presents a potion:
A kind of magic charm – for be assur'd,
If you will swallow it, the maid is cur'd:
But desp'rate the Doctor, and her case is,
If you reject the dose, and make wry faces!
This truth he boasts, will boast it while he lives,
No pois'nous drugs *are mix'd in what he gives;*
Should he succeed, you'll give him his degree;
If not, within he will receive no fee!
The college you, *must his pretensions back,*
Pronounce him regular, *or dub him* quack.

1. Dr Goldsmith. But Garrick goes on to comment ironically on Goldsmith's self-awarded qualifications.

Dramatis Personae

SIR CHARLES MARLOW,	*Mr. Gardner.*
Young MARLOW (his Son),	*Mr. Lewes.*
HARDCASTLE,	*Mr. Shuter.*
HASTINGS,	*Mr. Dubellamy.*
TONY LUMPKIN,	*Mr. Quick.*
DIGGORY,	*Mr. Saunders.*
MRS. HARDCASTLE,	*Mrs. Green.*
MISS HARDCASTLE,	*Mrs. Bulkely.*
MISS NEVILLE,	*Mrs. Kniveton.*
MAID,	*Miss Willems.*

Landlord, Servants, &c. &c.

Act I, [Scene I]

[SCENE, *A Chamber in an old fashioned House.*
Enter MRS. HARDCASTLE *and* MR. HARDCASTLE.]

MRS. HARDCASTLE: I vow, Mr. Hardcastle, you're very particular. Is there a creature in the whole country, but ourselves, that does not take a trip to town now and then, to rub off the rust a little? There's the two Miss Hoggs, and our neighbour, Mrs. Grigsby, go to take a month's polishing every winter.

HARDCASTLE: Ay, and bring back vanity and affectation to last them the whole year. I wonder why London cannot keep its own fools at home. In my time, the follies of the town crept slowly among us, but now they travel faster than a stage-coach. Its fopperies come down, not only as inside passengers, but in the very basket.[1]

MRS. HARDCASTLE: Ay, *your* times were fine times, indeed; you have been telling us of *them* for many a long year. Here we live in an old rumbling mansion, that looks for all the world like an inn, but that we never see company. Our best visitors are old Mrs. Oddfish, the curate's wife, and little Cripplegate, the lame dancing-master: And all our entertainment your old stories of Prince Eugene and the Duke of Marlborough.[2] I hate such old-fashioned trumpery.

HARDCASTLE: And I love it. I love every thing that's old: old friends, old times, old manners, old books, old wine; and, I believe, Dorothy, [*Taking her hand.*] you'll own I have been pretty fond of an old wife.

1. The exterior back seat or baggage container.
2. Respectively, leaders of the Austrian and English armies in the War of the Spanish Succession, which took place in the first decade of the eighteenth century.

MRS. HARDCASTLE: Lord, Mr. Hardcastle, you're for ever at your Dorothy's and your old wife's. You may be a Darby, but I'll be no Joan, I promise you. I'm not so old as you'd make me, by more than one good year. Add twenty to twenty, and make money of that.

HARDCASTLE: Let me see; twenty added to twenty, makes just fifty and seven.

MRS. HARDCASTLE: It's false, Mr. Hardcastle: I was but twenty when I was brought to bed of Tony, that I had by Mr. Lumpkin, my first husband; and he's not come to years of discretion yet.

HARDCASTLE: Nor ever will, I dare answer for him. Ay, you have taught *him* finely.

MRS. HARDCASTLE: No matter, Tony Lumpkin has a good fortune. My son is not to live by his learning. I don't think a boy wants much learning to spend fifteen hundred a year.

HARDCASTLE: Learning, quotha! A mere composition of tricks and mischief.

MRS. HARDCASTLE: Humour, my dear: nothing but humour. Come, Mr. Hardcastle, you must allow the boy a little humour.

HARDCASTLE: I'd sooner allow him an horse-pond. If burning the footmen's shoes, frighting the maids, and worrying the kittens, be humour, he has it. It was but yesterday he fastened my wig to the back of my chair, and when I went to make a bow, I popt my bald head in Mrs. Frizzle's face.

MRS. HARDCASTLE: And am I to blame? The poor boy was always too sickly to do any good. A school would be his death. When he comes to be a little stronger, who knows what a year or two's Latin may do for him?

HARDCASTLE: Latin for him! A cat and fiddle. No, no, the ale-house and the stable are the only schools he'll ever go to.

MRS. HARDCASTLE: Well, we must not snub the poor boy now, for I believe we shan't have him long among us. Any body that looks in his face may see he's consumptive.

HARDCASTLE: Ay, if growing too fat be one of the symptoms.

MRS. HARDCASTLE: He coughs sometimes.

HARDCASTLE: Yes, when his liquor goes the wrong way.

MRS. HARDCASTLE: I'm actually afraid of his lungs.

HARDCASTLE: And truly so am I; for he sometimes whoops like a speaking trumpet – [TONY *hallooing behind the Scenes.*] – O there he goes – A very consumptive figure, truly.

[*Enter* TONY, *crossing the Stage.*]

MRS. HARDCASTLE: Tony, where are you going, my charmer? Won't you give papa and I a little of your company, lovee?

TONY: I'm in haste, mother, I cannot stay.

MRS. HARDCASTLE: You shan't venture out this raw evening, my dear: You look most shockingly.

TONY: I can't stay, I tell you. The Three Pigeons expects me down every moment. There's some fun going forward.

HARDCASTLE: Ay; the ale-house, the old place: I thought so.

MRS. HARDCASTLE: A low, paltry set of fellows.

TONY: Not so low neither. There's Dick Muggins the exciseman, Jack Slang the horse doctor, Little Aminadab that grinds the music box, and Tom Twist that spins the pewter platter.

MRS. HARDCASTLE: Pray, my dear, disappoint them for one night at least.

TONY: As for disappointing *them,* I should not so much mind; but I can't abide to disappoint *myself.*

MRS. HARDCASTLE: [*Detaining him.*] You shan't go.

TONY: I will, I tell you.

MRS. HARDCASTLE: I say you shan't.

TONY: We'll see which is strongest, you or I. [*Exit, hawling her out.*]

[HARDCASTLE, *solus.*]

HARDCASTLE: Ay, there goes a pair that only spoil each other. But is not the whole age in a combination to drive sense and discretion out of doors? There's my pretty darling Kate; the fashions of the times have almost infected her too. By living a year or two in town, she is as fond of gauze, and French frippery, as the best of them.

[*Enter* MISS HARDCASTLE]

HARDCASTLE: Blessings on my pretty innocence! Drest out as usual my Kate. Goodness! What a quantity of superfluous silk hast thou got about thee, girl! I could never teach the fools of this age, that the indigent world could be cloathed out of the trimmings of the vain.

MISS HARDCASTLE: You know our agreement, Sir. You allow me the morning to receive and pay visits, and to dress in my own manner; and in the evening, I put on my housewife's dress to please you.

HARDCASTLE: Well, remember I insist on the terms of our agreement; and, by the bye, I believe I shall have occasion to try your obedience this very evening.

MISS HARDCASTLE: I protest, Sir, I don't comprehend your meaning.

HARDCASTLE: Then, to be plain with you, Kate, I expect the young gentleman I have chosen to be your husband from town this very day. I have his father's letter, in which he informs me his son is set out, and that he intends to follow himself shortly after.

MISS HARDCASTLE: Indeed! I wish I had known something of this before. Bless me, how shall I behave? It's a thousand to one I shan't like him; our meeting will be so formal, and so like a thing of business, that I shall find no room for friendship or esteem.

HARDCASTLE: Depend upon it, child, I'll never controul your choice; but Mr. Marlow, whom I have pitched upon, is the son of my old friend, Sir Charles Marlow, of whom you have heard me talk so often. The young gentleman has been bred a scholar, and is designed for an employment in the service of his country. I am told he's a man of an excellent understanding.

MISS HARDCASTLE: Is he?

HARDCASTLE: Very generous.

MISS HARDCASTLE: I believe I shall like him.

HARDCASTLE: Young and brave.

MISS HARDCASTLE: I'm sure I shall like him.

HARDCASTLE: And very handsome.

MISS HARDCASTLE: My dear Papa, say no more [*Kissing his hand.*] he's mine, I'll have him.

HARDCASTLE: And to crown all, Kate, he's one of the most bashful and reserved young fellows in all the world.

MISS HARDCASTLE: Eh! you have frozen me to death again. That word reserved, has undone all the rest of his accomplishments. A reserved lover, it is said, always makes a suspicious husband.

HARDCASTLE: On the contrary, modesty seldom resides in a breast that is not enriched with nobler virtues. It was the very feature in his character that first struck me.

MISS HARDCASTLE: He must have more striking features to catch me, I promise you. However, if he be so young, so handsome, and so every thing, as you mention, I believe he'll do still. I think I'll have him.

HARDCASTLE: Ay, Kate, but there is still an obstacle. Its more than an even wager, he may not have *you*.

MISS HARDCASTLE: My dear Papa, why will you mortify one so? – Well, if he refuses, instead of breaking my heart at his indifference, I'll only break my glass for its flattery. Set my cap to some newer fashion, and look out for some less difficult admirer.

HARDCASTLE: Bravely resolved! In the mean time I'll go prepare the servants for his reception; as we seldom see company they want as much training as a company of recruits, the first day's muster. [*Exit.*]

[MISS HARDCASTLE, *sola.*]

MISS HARDCASTLE: Lud, this news of Papa's, puts me all in a flutter. Young, handsome; these he put last; but I put them foremost. Sensible, good-natured; I like all that. But then reserved, and sheepish, that's much against him. Yet can't he be cured of his timidity, by being taught to be proud of his wife? Yes, and can't I – But I vow I'm disposing of the husband, before I have secured the lover.

[*Enter* MISS NEVILLE.]

MISS HARDCASTLE: I'm glad you're come, Neville, my dear. Tell me, Constance, how do I look this evening? Is there any thing whimsical about me? Is it one of my well looking days, child? Am I in face to day?

MISS NEVILLE: Perfectly, my dear. Yet now I look again – bless me ! – sure no accident has happened among the canary birds or the gold fishes. Has your brother or the cat been meddling? Or has the last novel been too moving?

MISS HARDCASTLE: No; nothing of all this. I have been threatened – I can scarce get it out – I have been threatened with a lover.

MISS NEVILLE: And his name –

MISS HARDCASTLE: Is Marlow.

MISS NEVILLE: Indeed!

MISS HARDCASTLE: The son of Sir Charles Marlow.

MISS NEVILLE: As I live, the most intimate friend of Mr. Hastings, *my* admirer. They are never asunder. I believe you must have seen him when we lived in town.

MISS HARDCASTLE: Never.

MISS NEVILLE: He's a very singular character, I assure you. Among women of reputation and virtue, he is the modestest man alive; but his acquaintance give him a very different character among creatures of another stamp: you understand me.

MISS HARDCASTLE: An odd character, indeed. I shall never be able to manage him. What shall I do? Pshaw, think no more of him, but trust to occurrences for success. But how goes on your own affair my dear, has my mother been courting you for my brother Tony, as usual?

MISS NEVILLE: I have just come from one of our agreeable tête-à-têtes. She has been saying a hundred tender things, and setting off her pretty monster as the very pink of perfection.

MISS HARDCASTLE: And her partiality is such, that she actually thinks him so. A fortune like yours is no small temptation. Besides, as she has the sole management of it, I'm not surprized to see her unwilling to let it go out of the family.

MISS NEVILLE: A fortune like mine, which chiefly consists in jewels, is no such mighty temptation. But at any rate if my dear Hastings be but constant, I make no doubt to be too hard for her at last. However, I let her suppose that I am in love with her son, and she never once dreams that my affections are fixed upon another.

MISS HARDCASTLE: My good brother holds out stoutly. I could almost love him for hating you so.

MISS NEVILLE: It is a good natured creature at bottom, and I'm sure would wish to see me married to any body but himself. But my aunt's bell rings for our afternoon's walk round the improvements. Allons. Courage is necessary as our affairs are critical.

MISS HARDCASTLE: Would it were bed time and all were well. [*Exeunt.*]

[Act I, Scene II]

[SCENE, *An Alehouse Room. Several shabby fellows, with Punch and Tobacco.* TONY *at the head of the Table, a little higher than the rest: A mallet in his hand.*]

OMNES: Hurrea, hurrea, hurrea, bravo.
FIRST FELLOW: Now, gentlemen, silence for a song. The 'Squire is going to knock himself down for a song.
OMNES: Ay, a song, a song.
TONY: Then I'll sing you, gentlemen, a song I made upon this ale-house, the Three Pigeons.

SONG.

Let school-masters puzzle their brain,
With grammar, and nonsense, and learning;
Good liquor, I stoutly maintain,
Gives genus *a better discerning.*
Let them brag of their Heathenish Gods,
Their Lethes, their Styxes, and Stygians;[1]
Their Quis, and their Quæs, and their Quods,[2]
They're all but a parcel of Pigeons.[3]
Toroddle, toroddle, toroll.

When Methodist preachers come down,
A preaching that drinking is sinful,
I'll wager the rascals a crown,
They always preach best with a skinful.
But when you come down with your pence,
For a slice of their scurvy religion,
I'll leave it to all men of sense,
But you my good friend are the pigeon.
Toroddle, toroddle, toroll.

Then come, put the jorum[4] *about,*
And let us be merry and clever,
Our hearts and our liquors are stout,
Here's the Three Jolly Pigeons for ever.
Let some cry up woodcock or hare,
Your bustards, your ducks, and your widgeons;
But of all the birds in the air,

1. Rivers of the classical underworld.
2. Latin relative pronouns, learnt by heart by all schoolboys.
3. Fools.
4. Bowl of punch.

Here's a health to the Three Jolly Pigeons.
Toroddle, toroddle, toroll.

OMNES: Bravo, bravo.

FIRST FELLOW: The 'Squire has got spunk in him.

SECOND FELLOW: I love to hear him sing, bekeays he never gives us nothing that's *low*.

THIRD FELLOW: O damn any thing that's *low*, I cannot bear it.

FOURTH FELLOW: The genteel thing is the genteel thing at any time. If so be that a gentleman bees in a concatenation accordingly.

THIRD FELLOW: I like the maxum of it, Master Muggins. What, tho' I am obligated to dance a bear, a man may be a gentleman for all that. May this be my poison if my bear ever dances but to the very genteelest of tunes. Water Parted,[1] or the minuet in Ariadne.[2]

SECOND FELLOW: What a pity it is the 'Squire is not come to his own. It would be well for all the publicans within ten miles round of him.

TONY: Ecod and so it would Master Slang. I'd then shew what it was to keep choice of company.

SECOND FELLOW: O he takes after his own father for that. To be sure old 'Squire Lumpkin was the finest gentleman I ever set my eyes on. For winding the streight horn, or beating a thicket for a hare, or a wench, he never had his fellow. It was a saying in the place, that he kept the best horses, dogs and girls in the whole county.

TONY: Ecod, and when I'm of age I'll be no bastard[3] I promise you. I have been thinking of Bett Bouncer and the miller's grey mare to begin with. But come, my boys, drink about and be merry, for you pay no reckoning. Well Stingo,[4] what's the matter?

[*Enter* LANDLORD.]

LANDLORD: There be two gentlemen in a post-chaise at the door. They have lost their way upo' the forest; and they are talking something about Mr. Hardcastle.

TONY: As sure as can be one of them must be the gentleman that's coming down to court my sister. Do they seem to be Londoners?

LANDLORD: I believe they may. They look woundily like Frenchmen.

TONY: Then desire them to step this way, and I'll set them right in a twinkling. [*Exit* LANDLORD.] Gentlemen, as they mayn't be good enough company for you, step down for a moment, and I'll be with you in the squeezing of a lemon. [*Exeunt Mob.*]

1. An aria from Thomas Arne's opera *Artaxerxes.*
2. Handel's opera *Arianna in Creta.*
3. Changeling.
4. Strong ale, a nickname for the Landlord.

[TONY, *solus*.]

TONY: Father-in-law[1] has been calling me whelp, and hound, this half year. Now if I pleased, I could be so revenged upon the old grumbletonian. But then I'm afraid – afraid of what! I shall soon be worth fifteen hundred a year, and let him frighten me out of *that* if he can.

[*Enter* LANDLORD, *conducting* MARLOW *and* HASTINGS.]

MARLOW: What a tedious uncomfortable day have we had of it! We were told it was but forty miles across the country, and we have come above threescore.

HASTINGS: And all Marlow, from that unaccountable reserve of yours, that would not let us enquire more frequently on the way.

MARLOW: I own, Hastings, I am unwilling to lay myself under an obligation to every one I meet; and often, stand the chance of an unmannerly answer.

HASTINGS: At present, however, we are not likely to receive any answer.

TONY: No offence, gentlemen. But I'm told you have been enquiring for one Mr. Hardcastle, in these parts. Do you know what part of the country you are in?

HASTINGS: Not in the least Sir, but should thank you for information.

TONY: Nor the way you came?

HASTINGS: No, Sir; but if you can inform us –

TONY: Why, gentlemen, if you know neither the road you are going, nor where you are, nor the road you came, the first thing I have to inform you is, that – You have lost your way.

MARLOW: We wanted no ghost to tell us that.

TONY: Pray, gentlemen, may I be so bold as to ask the place from whence you came?

MARLOW: That's not necessary towards directing us where we are to go.

TONY: No offence; but question for question is all fair, you know. Pray, gentlemen, is not this same Hardcastle a cross-grain'd, oldfashion'd, whimsical fellow, with an ugly face; a daughter, and a pretty son?

HASTINGS: We have not seen the gentleman, but he has the family you mention.

TONY: The daughter, a tall trapesing, trolloping, talkative maypole – The son, a pretty, well-bred, agreeable youth, that every body is fond of.

MARLOW: Our information differs in this. The daughter is said to be well-bred and beautiful; the son, an aukward booby, reared up, and spoiled at his mother's apron-string.

TONY: He-he-hem – Then, gentlemen, all I have to tell you is, that you won't reach Mr. Hardcastle's house this night, I believe.

1. Step-father.

HASTINGS: Unfortunate!

TONY: It's a damn'd long, dark, boggy, dirty, dangerous way. Stingo, tell the gentlemen the way to Mr. Hardcastle's; [*Winking upon the* LANDLORD.] Mr. Hardcastle's, of Quagmire Marsh, you understand me.

LANDLORD: Master Hardcastle's! Lock-a-daisy, my masters, you're come a deadly deal wrong! When you came to the bottom of the hill, you should have cross'd down Squash-lane.

MARLOW: Cross down Squash-lane!

LANDLORD: Then you were to keep streight forward, 'till you came to four roads.

MARLOW: Come to where four roads meet!

TONY: Ay; but you must be sure to take only one of them.

MARLOW: O Sir, you're facetious.

TONY: Then keeping to the right, you are to go side-ways till you come upon Crack-skull common: there you must look sharp for the track of the wheel, and go forward, 'till you come to farmer Murrain's barn. Coming to the farmer's barn, you are to turn to the right, and then to the left, and then to the right about again, till you find out the old mill –

MARLOW: Zounds, man! we could as soon find out the longitude![1]

HASTINGS: What's to be done, Marlow?

MARLOW: This house promises but a poor reception; though perhaps the Landlord can accommodate us.

LANDLORD: Alack, master, we have but one spare bed in the whole house.

TONY: And to my knowledge, that's taken up by three lodgers already. [*After a pause, in which the rest seem disconcerted.*] I have hit it. Don't you think, Stingo, our landlady could accommodate the gentlemen by the fire-side, with – three chairs and a bolster?

HASTINGS: I hate sleeping by the fire-side.

MARLOW: And I detest your three chairs and a bolster.

TONY: You do, do you? – then let me see – what if you go on a mile further, to the Buck's Head; the old Buck's Head on the hill, one of the best inns in the whole county?

HASTINGS: O ho! so we have escaped an adventure for this night, however.

LANDLORD: [*Apart to* TONY.] Sure, you ben't sending them to your father's as an inn, be you?

TONY: Mum, you fool you. Let *them* find that out. [*To them.*] You have only to keep on streight forward, till you come to a large old house by the road side. You'll see a pair of large horns over the door. That's the sign. Drive up the yard, and call stoutly about you.

HASTINGS: Sir, we are obliged to you. The servants can't miss the way?

TONY: No, no: But I tell you though, the landlord is rich, and going to leave off business; so he wants to be thought a Gentleman, saving your

1. A reliable method of determining longitude had eluded scientists for centuries. A solution was found by June 1773. See Dava Sobel, *Longitude* (London, 1996).

presence, he! he! he! He'll be for giving you his company, and ecod if you mind him, he'll persuade you that his mother was an alderman, and his aunt a justice of peace.

LANDLORD: A troublesome old blade to be sure; but a keeps as good wines and beds as any in the whole country.

MARLOW: Well, if he supplies us with these, we shall want no further connexion.[1] We are to turn to the right, did you say?

TONY: No, no; streight forward. I'll just step myself, and shew you a piece of the way. [*To the* LANDLORD.] Mum.

LANDLORD: Ah, bless your heart, for a sweet, pleasant – damn'd mischievous son of a whore. [*Exeunt.*]

Act II

[SCENE, *An old-fashioned House.*
Enter HARDCASTLE, *followed by three or four aukward* SERVANTS.]

HARDCASTLE: Well, I hope you're perfect in the table exercise I have been teaching you these three days. You all know your posts and your places, and can shew that you have been used to good company, without ever stirring from home.

OMNES: Ay, ay.

HARDCASTLE: When company comes, you are not to pop out and stare, and then run in again, like frighted rabbits in a warren.

OMNES: No, no.

HARDCASTLE: You, Diggory, whom I have taken from the barn, are to make a shew at the side-table; and you, Roger, whom I have advanced from the plough, are to place yourself behind *my* chair. But you're not to stand so, with your hands in your pockets. Take your hands from your pockets, Roger; and from your head, you blockhead you. See how Diggory carries his hands. They're a little too stiff, indeed, but that's no great matter.

DIGGORY: Ay, mind how I hold them. I learned to hold my hands this way, when I was upon drill for the militia. And so being upon drill –

HARDCASTLE: You must not be so talkative, Diggory. You must be all attention to the guests. You must hear us talk, and not think of talking; you must see us drink, and not think of drinking; you must see us eat, and not think of eating.

DIGGORY: By the laws, your worship, that's parfectly unpossible. Whenever Diggory sees yeating going forward, ecod he's always wishing for a mouthful himself.

HARDCASTLE: Blockhead! Is not a belly-full in the kitchen as good as a belly-full in the parlour? Stay your stomach with that reflection.

1. Relationship.

DIGGORY: Ecod I thank your worship, I'll make a shift to stay my stomach with a slice of cold beef in the pantry.

HARDCASTLE: Diggory, you are too talkative. Then if I happen to say a good thing, or tell a good story at table, you must not all burst out a-laughing, as if you made part of the company.

DIGGORY: Then ecod your worship must not tell the Story of Ould Grouse in the gun-room: I can't help laughing at that – he! he! he! – for the soul of me. We have laughed at that these twenty years – ha! ha! ha!

HARDCASTLE: Ha! ha! ha! The story is a good one. Well, honest Diggory, you may laugh at that – but still remember to be attentive. Suppose one of the company should call for a glass of wine, how will you behave? A glass of wine, Sir, if you please [*To* DIGGORY.] – Eh, why don't you move?

DIGGORY: Ecod, your worship, I never have courage till I see the eatables and drinkables brought upo' the table, and then I'm as bauld as a lion.

HARDCASTLE: What, will no body move?

FIRST SERVANT: I'm not to leave this pleace.

SECOND SERVANT: I'm sure it's no pleace of mine.

THIRD SERVANT: Nor mine, for sartain.

DIGGORY: Wauns, and I'm sure it canna be mine.

HARDCASTLE: You numbskulls! and so while, like your betters, you are quarrelling for places, the guests must be starved. O you dunces! I find I must begin all over again. – But don't I hear a coach drive into the yard? To your posts, you blockheads. I'll go in the mean time and give my old friend's son a hearty reception at the gate. [*Exit* HARDCASTLE.]

DIGGORY: By the elevens, my pleace is gone quite out of my head.

ROGER: I know that my pleace is to be every where.

FIRST SERVANT: Where the devil is mine?

SECOND SERVANT: My pleace is to be no where at all; and so Ize go about my business. [*Exeunt* SERVANTS, *running about as if frighted, different ways.*]

[*Enter* SERVANT *with Candles, shewing in* MARLOW *and* HASTINGS.]

SERVANT: Welcome, gentlemen, very welcome. This way.

HASTINGS: After the disappointments of the day, welcome once more, Charles, to the comforts of a clean room and a good fire. Upon my word, a very well-looking house; antique, but creditable.

MARLOW: The usual fate of a large mansion. Having first ruined the master by good housekeeping, it at last comes to levy contributions as an inn.

HASTINGS: As you say, we passengers are to be taxed to pay all these fineries. I have often seen a good sideboard, or a marble chimney-piece, tho' not actually put in the bill, enflame a reckoning confoundedly.

MARLOW: Travellers, George, must pay in all places. The only difference is, that in good inns, you pay dearly for luxuries; in bad ones, you are fleeced and starved.

HASTINGS: You have lived pretty much among them. In truth, I have been often surprized, that you who have seen so much of the world, with your natural good sense, and your many opportunities, could never yet acquire a requisite share of assurance.

MARLOW: The Englishman's malady. But tell me, George, where could I have learned that assurance you talk of? My life has been chiefly spent in a college, or an inn, in seclusion from that lovely part of the creation that chiefly teach men confidence. I don't know that I was ever familiarly acquainted with a single modest woman – except my mother – But among females of another class you know –

HASTINGS: Ay, among them you are impudent enough of all conscience.

MARLOW: They are of *us* you know.

HASTINGS: But in the company of women of reputation I never saw such an ideot, such a trembler; you look for all the world as if you wanted an opportunity of stealing out of the room.

MARLOW: Why man that's because I *do* want to steal out of the room. Faith, I have often formed a resolution to break the ice, and rattle away at any rate. But I don't know how, a single glance from a pair of fine eyes has totally overset my resolution. An impudent fellow may counterfeit modesty, but I'll be hanged if a modest man can ever counterfeit impudence.

HASTINGS: If you could but say half the fine things to them that I have heard you lavish upon the bar-maid of an inn, or even a college bed maker –

MARLOW: Why, George, I can't say fine things to them. They freeze, they petrify me. They may talk of a comet, or a burning mountain, or some such bagatelle. But to me, a modest woman, drest out in all her finery, is the most tremendous object of the whole creation.

HASTINGS: Ha! ha! ha! At this rate, man, how can you ever expect to marry!

MARLOW: Never, unless as among kings and princes, my bride were to be courted by proxy. If, indeed, like an Eastern bridegroom, one were to be introduced to a wife he never saw before, it might be endured. But to go through all the terrors of a formal courtship, together with the episode of aunts, grandmothers and cousins, and at last to blurt out the broad staring question, of, *madam will you marry me*? No, no, that's a strain much above me I assure you.

HASTINGS: I pity you. But how do you intend behaving to the lady you are come down to visit at the request of your father?

MARLOW: As I behave to all other ladies. Bow very low. Answer yes, or no, to all her demands – But for the rest, I don't think I shall venture to look in her face, till I see my father's again.

HASTINGS: I'm surprized that one who is so warm a friend can be so cool a lover.

MARLOW: To be explicit, my dear Hastings, my chief inducement down was to be instrumental in forwarding your happiness, not my own. Miss Neville loves you, the family don't know you, as my friend you are sure of a reception, and let honour do the rest.

HASTINGS: My dear Marlow! But I'll suppress the emotion. Were I a wretch, meanly seeking to carry off a fortune, you should be the last man in the world I would apply to for assistance. But Miss Neville's person is all I ask, and that is mine, both from her deceased father's consent, and her own inclination.

MARLOW: Happy man! You have talents and art to captivate any woman. I'm doom'd to adore the sex, and yet to converse with the only part of it I despise. This stammer in my address, and this aukward prepossessing visage of mine, can never permit me to soar above the reach of a milliner's 'prentice, or one of the dutchesses of Drury-lane.[1] Pshaw! this fellow here to interrupt us.

[*Enter* HARDCASTLE.]

HARDCASTLE: Gentlemen, once more you are heartily welcome. Which is Mr. Marlow? Sir, you're heartily welcome. It's not my way, you see, to receive my friends with my back to the fire. I like to give them a hearty reception in the old stile at my gate. I like to see their horses and trunks taken care of.

MARLOW: [*Aside.*] He has got our names from the servants already. [*To Him.*] We approve your caution and hospitality, Sir. [*To* HASTINGS.] I have been thinking, George, of changing our travelling dresses in the morning. I am grown confoundedly ashamed of mine.

HARDCASTLE: I beg, Mr. Marlow, you'll use no ceremony in this house.

HASTINGS: I fancy, Charles, you're right: the first blow is half the battle. I intend opening the campaign with the white and gold.

HARDCASTLE: Mr. Marlow – Mr. Hastings – gentlemen – pray be under no constraint in this house. This is Liberty-hall, gentlemen. You may do just as you please here.

MARLOW: Yet, George, if we open the campaign too fiercely at first, we may want ammunition before it is over. I think to reserve the embroidery to secure a retreat.

HARDCASTLE: Your talking of a retreat, Mr. Marlow, puts me in mind of the Duke of Marlborough, when we went to besiege Denain. He first summoned the garrison.

MARLOW: Don't you think the *ventre dor* waistcoat will do with the plain brown?

HARDCASTLE: He first summoned the garrison, which might consist of about five thousand men –

HASTINGS: I think not: Brown and yellow mix but very poorly.

HARDCASTLE: I say, gentlemen, as I was telling you, he summoned the garrison, which might consist of about five thousand men –

MARLOW: The girls like finery.

1. One of the prostitutes who worked outside the theatre.

HARDCASTLE: Which might consist of about five thousand men, well appointed with stores, ammunition, and other implements of war. Now, says the Duke of Marlborough, to George Brooks, that stood next to him – You must have heard of George Brooks; I'll pawn my Dukedom, says he, but I take that garrison without spilling a drop of blood. So –

MARLOW: What, my good friend, if you gave us a glass of punch in the mean time, it would help us to carry on the siege with vigour.

HARDCASTLE: Punch, Sir! [*Aside.*] This is the most unaccountable kind of modesty I ever met with.

MARLOW: Yes, Sir, Punch. A glass of warm punch, after our journey, will be comfortable. This is Liberty-Hall, you know.

HARDCASTLE: Here's Cup, Sir.

MARLOW: [*Aside.*] So this fellow, in his Liberty-hall, will only let us have just what he pleases.

HARDCASTLE: [*Taking the Cup.*] I hope you'll find it to your mind. I have prepared it with my own hands, and I believe you'll own the ingredients are tolerable. Will you, be so good as to pledge me, Sir? Here, Mr. Marlow, here is to our better acquaintance. [*Drinks.*]

MARLOW: [*Aside.*] A very impudent fellow this! but he's a character, and I'll humour him a little. Sir, my service to you. [*Drinks.*]

HASTINGS: [*Aside.*] I see this fellow wants to give us his company, and forgets that he's an innkeeper, before he has learned to be a gentleman.

MARLOW: From the excellence of your cup, my old friend, I suppose you have a good deal of business in this part of the country. Warm work, now and then, at elections, I suppose.

HARDCASTLE: No, Sir, I have long given that work over. Since our betters have hit upon the expedient of electing each other, there's no business *for us that sell ale.*[1]

HASTINGS: So, then you have no turn for politics I find.

HARDCASTLE: Not in the least. There was a time, indeed, I fretted myself about the mistakes of government, like other people; but finding myself every day grow more angry, and the government growing no better, I left it to mend itself. Since that, I no more trouble my head about *Heyder Ally*, or *Ally Cawn*, than about *Ally Croaker*.[2] Sir, my service to you.

HASTINGS: So that with eating above stairs, and drinking below, with receiving your friends within, and amusing them without, you lead a good pleasant bustling life of it.

HARDCASTLE: I do stir about a great deal, that's certain. Half the differences of the parish are adjusted in this very parlour.

MARLOW: [*After drinking.*] And you have an argument in your cup, old gentleman, better than any in Westminster-hall.

1. Presumably a reference to the proverbial expression, 'thus it must be, if we sell ale', i.e. if we are engaged in commerce. But it is taken literally by Marlow and Hastings
2. The first two were foreign potentates and the latter a character in an Irish song .

HARDCASTLE: Ay, young gentleman, that, and a little philosophy.

MARLOW: [*Aside.*] Well, this is the first time I ever heard of an inn-keeper's philosophy.

HASTINGS: So then, like an experienced general, you attack them on every quarter. If you find their reason manageable, you attack it with your philosophy; if you find they have no reason, you attack them with this. Here's your health, my philosopher. [*Drinks.*]

HARDCASTLE: Good, very good, thank you; ha, ha. Your Generalship puts me in mind of Prince Eugene, when he fought the Turks at the battle of Belgrade. You shall hear.

MARLOW: Instead of the battle of Belgrade, I believe it's almost time to talk about supper. What has your philosophy got in the house for supper?

HARDCASTLE: For Supper, Sir! [*Aside.*] Was ever such a request to a man in his own house!

MARLOW: Yes, Sir, supper Sir; I begin to feel an appetite. I shall make devilish work to-night in the larder, I promise you.

HARDCASTLE: [*Aside.*] Such a brazen dog sure never my eyes beheld. [*to him*] Why really, Sir, as for supper I can't well tell. My Dorothy, and the cook maid, settle these things between them. I leave these kind of things entirely to them.

MARLOW: You do, do you?

HARDCASTLE: Entirely. By-the-bye, I believe they are in actual consultation upon what's for supper this moment in the kitchen.

MARLOW: Then I beg they'll admit *me* as one of their privy council. It's a way I have got. When I travel, I always chuse to regulate my own supper. Let the cook be called. No offence I hope, Sir.

HARDCASTLE: O no, Sir, none in the least; yet I don't know how: our Bridget, the cook maid, is not very communicative upon these occasions. Should we send for her, she might scold us all out of the house.

HASTINGS: Let's see your list of the larder then. I ask it as a favour. I always match my appetite to my bill of fare.

MARLOW: [*To* HARDCASTLE, *who looks at them with surprize.*] Sir, he's very right, and it's my way too.

HARDCASTLE: Sir, you have a right to command here. Here, Roger, bring us the bill of fare for to night's supper. I believe it's drawn out. Your manner, Mr. Hastings, puts me in mind of my uncle, Colonel Wallop. It was a saying of his, that no man was sure of his supper till he had eaten it.

[*Enter* ROGER, *who gives a Bill of Fare.*][1]

HASTINGS: [*Aside.*] All upon the high ropes! His uncle a Colonel! We shall soon hear of his mother being a justice of peace. But let's hear the bill of fare.

1. This stage direction was omitted from the first editions of the play.

MARLOW: [*Perusing.*] What's here? For the first course; for the second course; for the desert. The devil, Sir, do you think we have brought down the whole Joiners Company, or the Corporation of Bedford, to eat up such a supper? Two or three little things, clean and comfortable, will do.

HASTINGS: But, let's hear it.

MARLOW: [*Reading.*] For the first course at the top, a pig, and pruin sauce.

HASTINGS: Damn your pig, I say.

MARLOW: And damn your pruin sauce, say I.

HARDCASTLE: And yet, gentlemen, to men that are hungry, pig, with pruin sauce, is very good eating.

MARLOW: At the bottom, a calve's tongue and brains.

HASTINGS: Let your brains be knock'd out, my good Sir; I don't like them.

MARLOW: Or you may clap them on a plate by themselves. I do.

HARDCASTLE: [*Aside.*] Their impudence confounds me. [*To them.*] Gentlemen, you are my guests, make what alterations you please. Is there any thing else you wish to retrench or alter, gentlemen?

MARLOW: Item. A pork pie, a boiled rabbet and sausages, a florentine, a shaking pudding, and a dish of tiff-taff-taffety cream![1]

HASTINGS: Confound your made dishes, I shall be as much at a loss in this house as at a green and yellow dinner at the French ambassador's table. I'm for plain eating.

HARDCASTLE: I'm sorry, gentlemen, that I have nothing you like, but if there be any thing you have a particular fancy to –

MARLOW: Why, really, Sir, your bill of fare is so exquisite, that any one part of it is full as good as another. Send us what you please. So much for supper. And now to see that our beds are air'd, and properly taken care of.

HARDCASTLE: I entreat you'll leave all that to me. You shall not stir a step.

MARLOW: Leave that to you! I protest, Sir, you must excuse me, I always look to these things myself.

HARDCASTLE: I must insist, Sir, you'll make yourself easy on that head.

MARLOW: You see I'm resolved on it. [*Aside.*] A very troublesome fellow this, as ever I met with.

HARDCASTLE: Well, Sir, I'm resolved at least to attend you. [*Aside.*] This may be modern modesty, but I never saw any thing look so like old-fashioned impudence. [*Exeunt* MARLOW *and* HARDCASTLE.]

[HASTINGS, *solus.*]

HASTINGS: So I find this fellow's civilities begin to grow troublesome. But who can be angry at those assiduities which are meant to please him? Ha! what do I see? Miss Neville, by all that's happy!

[*Enter* MISS NEVILLE.]

1. A dish of fine cream, as smooth as taffeta.

MISS NEVILLE: My dear Hastings! To what unexpected good fortune? to what accident am I to ascribe this happy meeting?

HASTINGS: Rather let me ask the same question, as I could never have hoped to meet my dearest Constance at an inn.

MISS NEVILLE: An inn! sure you mistake! my aunt, my guardian, lives here. What could induce you to think this house an inn?

HASTINGS: My friend Mr. Marlow, with whom I came down, and I, have been sent here as to an inn, I assure you. A young fellow whom we accidentally met at a house hard by directed us hither.

MISS NEVILLE: Certainly it must be one of my hopeful cousin's tricks, of whom you have heard me talk so often, ha! ha! ha! ha

HASTINGS: He whom your aunt intends for you? He of whom I have such just apprehensions?

MISS NEVILLE: You have nothing to fear from him, I assure you. You'd adore him if you knew how heartily he despises me. My aunt knows it too, and has undertaken to court me for him, and actually begins to think she has made a conquest.

HASTINGS: Thou dear dissembler! You must know, my Constance, I have just seized this happy opportunity of my friend's visit here to get admittance into the family. The horses that carried us down are now fatigued with their journey, but they'll soon be refreshed; and then if my dearest girl will trust in her faithful Hastings, we shall soon be landed in France, where even among slaves the laws of marriage are respected.

MISS NEVILLE: I have often told you, that though ready to obey you, I yet should leave my little fortune behind with reluctance. The greatest part of it was left me by my uncle, the India Director, and chiefly consists in jewels. I have been for some time persuading my aunt to let me wear them. I fancy I'm very near succeeding. The instant they are put into my possession you shall find me ready to make them and myself yours.

HASTINGS: Perish the baubles! Your person is all I desire. In the meantime, my friend Marlow must not be let into his mistake. I know the strange reserve of his temper is such, that if abruptly informed of it, he would instantly quit the house before our plan was ripe for execution.

MISS NEVILLE: But how shall we keep him in the deception? Miss Hardcastle is just returned from walking; what if we still continue to deceive him? – This, this way – [*They confer.*]

[*Enter* MARLOW.]

MARLOW: The assiduities of these good people teize me beyond bearing. My host seems to think it ill manners to leave me alone, and so he claps not only himself but his old-fashioned wife on my back. They talk of coming to sup with us too; and then, I suppose, we are to run the gauntlet thro' all the rest of the family. – What have we got here! –

HASTINGS: My dear Charles! Let me congratulate you! – The most fortunate accident! – Who do you think is just alighted?

MARLOW: Cannot guess.

HASTINGS: Our mistresses my boy, Miss Hardcastle and Miss Neville. Give me leave to introduce Miss Constance Neville to your acquaintance. Happening to dine in the neighbourhood, they called on their return to take fresh horses here. Miss Hardcastle has just stept into the next room, and will be back in an instant. Wasn't it lucky? eh!

MARLOW: [*Aside.*] I have just been mortified enough of all conscience, and here comes something to complete my embarrassment.

HASTINGS: Well! but wasn't it the most fortunate thing in the world?

MARLOW: Oh! yes. Very fortunate – most joyful encounter – But our dresses, George, you know, are in disorder – What if we should postpone the happiness 'till to-morrow? – To-morrow at her own house – It will be every bit as convenient – And rather more respectful – To-morrow let it be. [*Offering to go.*]

MISS NEVILLE: By no means, Sir. Your ceremony will displease her. The disorder of your dress will shew the ardour of your impatience. Besides, she knows you are in the house, and will permit you to see her.

MARLOW: O! the devil! how shall I support it? Hem! hem! Hastings, you must not go. You are to assist me, you know. I shall be confoundedly ridiculous. Yet, hang it! I'll take courage. Hem!

HASTINGS: Pshaw man! it's but the first plunge, and all's over. She's but a woman, you know.

MARLOW: And of all women, she that I dread most to encounter!

[*Enter* MISS HARDCASTLE *as returned from walking, a Bonnet, &c.*]

HASTINGS: [*Introducing them.*] Miss Hardcastle, Mr. Marlow, I'm proud of bringing two persons of such merit together, that only want to know, to esteem each other.

MISS HARDCASTLE: [*Aside.*] Now, for meeting my modest gentleman with a demure face, and quite in his own manner. [*After a pause, in which he appears very uneasy and disconcerted.*] I'm glad of your safe arrival, Sir – I'm told you had some accidents by the way.

MARLOW: Only a few madam. Yes, we had some. Yes, Madam, a good many accidents, but should be sorry – Madam – or rather glad of any accidents – that are so agreeably concluded. Hem!

HASTINGS: [*To him.*] You never spoke better in your whole life. Keep it up, and I'll insure you the victory.

MISS HARDCASTLE: I'm afraid you flatter, Sir. You that have seen so much of the finest company can find little entertainment in an obscure corner of the country.

MARLOW: [*Gathering courage.*] I have lived, indeed, in the world, Madam; but I have kept very little company. I have been but an observer upon life, Madam, while others were enjoying it.

MISS NEVILLE: But that, I am told, is the way to enjoy it at last.

HASTINGS: [*To him.*] Cicero never spoke better. Once more, and you are confirm'd in assurance for ever.

MARLOW: [*To him.*] Hem! Stand by me then, and when I'm down, throw in a word or two to set me up again.

MISS HARDCASTLE: An observer, like you, upon life, were, I fear, disagreeably employed, since you must have had much more to censure than to approve.

MARLOW: Pardon me, Madam. I was always willing to be amused. The folly of most people is rather an object of mirth than uneasiness.

HASTINGS: [*To him.*] Bravo, Bravo. Never spoke so well in your whole life. Well! Miss Hardcastle, I see that you and Mr. Marlow are going to be very good company. I believe our being here will but embarrass the interview.

MARLOW: Not in the least, Mr. Hastings. We like your company of all things. [*To him.*] Zounds! George, sure you won't go? How can you leave us?

HASTINGS: Our presence will but spoil conversation, so we'll retire to the next room. [*To him.*] You don't consider, man, that we are to manage a little tête-à-tête of our own. [*Exeunt.*]

MISS HARDCASTLE: [*After a pause.*] But you have not been wholly an observer, I presume, Sir: The ladies I should hope have employed some part of your addresses.

MARLOW: [*Relapsing into timidity.*] Pardon me, Madam, I – I – I – as yet have studied – only – to – deserve them.

MISS HARDCASTLE: And that some say is the very worst way to obtain them.

MARLOW: Perhaps so, madam. But I love to converse only with the more grave and sensible part of the sex. – But I'm afraid I grow tiresome.

MISS HARDCASTLE: Not at all, Sir; there is nothing I like so much as grave conversation myself; I could hear it for ever. Indeed I have often been surprized how a man of *sentiment* could ever admire those light airy pleasures, where nothing reaches the heart.

MARLOW: It's – a disease – of the mind, madam. In the variety of tastes there must be some who wanting a relish – for – um-a-um.

MISS HARDCASTLE: I understand you, Sir. There must be some, who wanting a relish for refined pleasures, pretend to despise what they are incapable of tasting.

MARLOW: My meaning, madam, but infinitely better expressed. And I can't help observing – a –

MISS HARDCASTLE: [*Aside.*] Who could ever suppose this fellow impudent upon some occasions. [*To him.*] You were going to observe, Sir –

MARLOW: I was observing, madam – I protest, madam, I forget what I was going to observe.

MISS HARDCASTLE: [*Aside.*] I vow and so do I. [*To him.*] You were observing, Sir, that in this age of hypocrisy – something about hypocrisy, Sir.

MARLOW: Yes, madam. In this age of hypocrisy there are few who upon strict enquiry do not – a – a – a –

MISS HARDCASTLE: I understand you perfectly, Sir.

MARLOW: [*Aside.*] Egad! and that's more than I do myself.

MISS HARDCASTLE: You mean that in this hypocritical age there are few that do not condemn in public what they practise in private, and think they pay every debt to virtue when they praise it.

MARLOW: True, madam; those who have most virtue in their mouths, have least of it in their bosoms. But I'm sure I tire you, madam.

MISS HARDCASTLE: Not in the least, Sir; there's something so agreeable and spirited in your manner, such life and force – pray, Sir, go on.

MARLOW: Yes, madam. I was saying – that there are some occasions – when a total want of courage, madam, destroys all the – and puts us – upon a – a – a –

MISS HARDCASTLE: I agree with you entirely, a want of courage upon some occasions assumes the appearance of ignorance, and betrays us when we most want to excel. I beg you'll proceed.

MARLOW: Yes, Madam. Morally speaking, madam – But I see Miss Neville expecting us in the next room. I would not intrude for the world.

MISS HARDCASTLE: I protest, Sir, I never was more agreeably entertained in all my life. Pray go on.

MARLOW: Yes, madam. I was – But she beckons us to join her. Madam, shall I do myself the honour to attend you?

MISS HARDCASTLE: Well then, I'll follow.

MARLOW: [*Aside.*] This pretty smooth dialogue has done for me. [*Exit.*]

[MISS HARDCASTLE, *sola.*]

MISS HARDCASTLE: Ha! ha! ha! Was there ever such a sober sentimental interview? I'm certain he scarce look'd in my face the whole time. Yet the fellow, but for his unaccountable bashfulness, is pretty well too. He has good sense, but then so buried in his fears, that it fatigues one more than ignorance. If I could teach him a little confidence, it would be doing somebody that I know of a piece of service. But who is that somebody? – that, faith, is a question I can scarce answer. [*Exit.*]

[*Enter* TONY *and* MISS NEVILLE, *followed by* MRS. HARDCASTLE *and* HASTINGS.]

TONY: What do you follow me for, cousin Con? I wonder you're not ashamed to be so very engaging.

MISS NEVILLE: I hope, cousin, one may speak to one's own relations, and not be to blame.

TONY: Ay, but I know what sort of a relation you want to make me though; but it won't do. I tell you, cousin Con, it won't do, so I beg you'll keep your distance, I want no nearer relationship.

[*She follows coqueting him to the back scene.*]

MRS. HARDCASTLE: Well! I vow, Mr. Hastings, you are very entertaining. There's nothing in the world I love to talk of so much as London, and the fashions, though I was never there myself.

HASTINGS: Never there! You amaze me! From your air and manner, I concluded you had been bred all your life either at Ranelagh, St. James's, or Tower Wharf.[1]

MRS. HARDCASTLE: O! Sir, you're only pleased to say so. We Country persons can have no manner at all. I'm in love with the town, and that serves to raise me above some of our neighbouring rustics; but who can have a manner, that has never seen the Pantheon, the Grotto Gardens, the Borough,[2] and such places where the Nobility chiefly resort? All I can do, is to enjoy London at second-hand. I take care to know every tête-à-tête from the Scandalous Magazine,[3] and have all the fashions, as they come out, in a letter from the two Miss Rickets of Crooked-lane. Pray how do you like this head, Mr. Hastings?

HASTINGS: Extremely elegant and degagée, upon my word, Madam. Your Friseur is a Frenchman, I suppose?

MRS. HARDCASTLE: I protest I dressed it myself from a print in the Ladies Memorandum-book for the last year.

HASTINGS: Indeed. Such a head in a side-box, at the Playhouse, would draw as many gazers as my Lady May'ress at a City Ball.

MRS. HARDCASTLE: I vow, since inoculation began,[4] there is no such thing to be seen as a plain woman; so one must dress a little particular or one may escape in the crowd.

HASTINGS: But that can never be your case, Madam, in any dress. [*Bowing*.]

MRS. HARDCASTLE: Yet, what signifies *my* dressing when I have such a piece of antiquity by my side as Mr. Hardcastle: all I can say will never argue down a single button from his cloaths. I have often wanted him to throw off his great flaxen wig, and where he was bald, to plaister it over like my Lord Pately, with powder.

HASTINGS: You are right, Madam; for, as among the ladies, there are none ugly, so among the men there are none old.

MRS. HARDCASTLE: But what do you think his answer was? Why, with his usual Gothic vivacity, he said I only wanted him to throw off his wig to convert it into a tête for my own wearing.

HASTINGS: Intolerable! At your age you may wear what you please, and it must become you.

1. Tower Wharf was certainly not a fashionable place. Hastings is having fun at her expense.
2. The Pantheon was in Oxford Street, the Grotto Gardens were less fashionable than Ranelagh and the Borough of Southwark was by this date not a place where the nobility resorted.
3. *The Town and Country Magazine*.
4. Inoculation against smallpox.

MRS. HARDCASTLE: Pray, Mr. Hastings, what do you take to be the most fashionable age about town?

HASTINGS: Some time ago, forty was all the mode; but I'm told the ladies intend to bring up fifty for the ensuing winter.

MRS. HARDCASTLE: Seriously. Then I shall be too young for the fashion.

HASTINGS: No lady begins now to put on jewels 'till she's past forty. For instance, Miss there, in a polite circle, would be considered as a child, as a mere maker of samplers.

MRS. HARDCASTLE: And yet Mrs. Niece thinks herself as much a woman, and is as fond of jewels as the oldest of us all.

HASTINGS: Your niece, is she? And that young gentleman, a brother of yours, I should presume?

MRS. HARDCASTLE: My son, Sir. They are contracted to each other. Observe their little sports. They fall in and out ten times a day, as if they were man and wife already. [*To them*] Well Tony, child, what soft things are you saying to your cousin Constance this evening?

TONY: I have been saying no soft things; but that it's very hard to be followed about so. Ecod! I've not a place in the house now that's left to myself but the stable.

MRS. HARDCASTLE: Never mind him, Con. my dear. He's in another story behind your back.

MISS NEVILLE: There's something generous in my cousin's manner. He falls out before faces to be forgiven in private.

TONY: That's a damned confounded – crack.

MRS. HARDCASTLE: Ah! he's a sly one. Don't you think they're like each other about the mouth, Mr. Hastings? The Blenkinsop mouth to a T. They're of a size too. Back to back, my pretties, that Mr. Hastings may see you. Come Tony.

TONY: You had as good not make me, I tell you. [*Measuring.*]

MISS NEVILLE: O lud! he has almost cracked my head.

MRS. HARDCASTLE: O the monster! For shame, Tony. You a man, and behave so!

TONY: If I'm a man, let me have my fortin. Ecod! I'll not be made a fool of no longer.

MRS. HARDCASTLE: Is this, ungrateful boy, all that I'm to get for the pains I have taken in your education? I that have rock'd you in your cradle, and fed that pretty mouth with a spoon! Did not I work that waistcoat to make you genteel? Did not I prescribe for you every day, and weep while the receipt was operating?

TONY: Ecod! you had reason to weep, for you have been dosing me ever since I was born. I have gone through every receipt in the complete huswife ten times over; and you have thoughts of coursing me through *Quincy*[1] next spring. But, Ecod! I tell you, I'll not be made a fool of no longer.

1. John Quincy's *Compleat English Dispensatory*.

MRS. HARDCASTLE: Wasn't it all for your good, viper? Wasn't it all for your good?

TONY: I wish you'd let me and my good alone then. Snubbing this way when I'm in spirits. If I'm to have any good, let it come of itself; not to keep dinging it, dinging it into one so.

MRS. HARDCASTLE: That's false; I never see you when you're in spirits. No, Tony, you then go to the alehouse or kennel. I'm never to be delighted with your agreeable, wild notes, unfeeling monster!

TONY: Ecod! Mamma, your own notes are the wildest of the two.

MRS. HARDCASTLE: Was ever the like? But I see he wants to break my heart, I see he does.

HASTINGS: Dear Madam, permit me to lecture the young gentleman a little. I'm certain I can persuade him to his duty.

MRS. HARDCASTLE: Well! I must retire. Come, Constance, my love. You see Mr. Hastings, the wretchedness of my situation: Was ever poor woman so plagued with a dear, sweet, pretty, provoking, undutiful boy.

[*Exeunt* MRS. HARDCASTLE *and* MISS NEVILLE.]

[HASTINGS, TONY.]

TONY: [*Singing.*] *There was a young man riding by, and fain would have his will. Rang do didlo dee.* Don't mind her. Let her cry. It's the comfort of her heart. I have seen her and sister cry over a book for an hour together, and they said, they liked the book the better the more it made them cry.

HASTINGS: Then you're no friend to the ladies, I find, my pretty young gentleman?

TONY: That's as I find 'um.

HASTINGS: Not to her of your mother's chusing, I dare answer? And yet she appears to me a pretty well-tempered girl.

TONY: That's because you don't know her as well as I. Ecod! I know every inch about her; and there's not a more bitter cantanckerous toad in all Christendom.

HASTINGS: [*Aside.*] Pretty encouragement this for a lover!

TONY: I have seen her since the height of that. She has as many tricks as a hare in a thicket, or a colt the first day's breaking.

HASTINGS: To me she appears sensible and silent!

TONY: Ay, before company. But when she's with her play-mates she's as loud as a hog in a gate.

HASTINGS: But there is a meek modesty about her that charms me.

TONY: Yes, but curb her never so little, she kicks up, and you're flung in a ditch.

HASTINGS: Well, but you must allow her a little beauty. – Yes, you must allow her some beauty.

TONY: Bandbox! She's all a made up thing, mun. Ah! could you but see Bet Bouncer of these parts, you might then talk of beauty. Ecod, she has two eyes as black as sloes, and cheeks as broad and red as a pulpit cushion. She'd make two of she.

HASTINGS: Well, what say you to a friend that would take this bitter bargain off your hands?

TONY: Anon.

HASTINGS: Would you thank him that would take Miss Neville and leave you to happiness and your dear Betsy?

TONY: Ay; but where is there such a friend, for who would take *her*?

HASTINGS: I am he. If you but assist me, I'll engage to whip her off to France, and you shall never hear more of her.

TONY: Assist you! Ecod I will, to the last drop of my blood. I'll clap a pair of horses to your chaise that shall trundle you off in a twinkling, and may be get you a part of her fortin beside, in jewels, that you little dream of.

HASTINGS: My dear squire, this looks like a lad of spirit.

TONY: Come along then, and you shall see more of my spirit before you have done with me [*singing*].

We are the boys
That fears no noise
Where the thundering cannons roar. [*Exeunt.*]

Act III

[*Enter* HARDCASTLE, *solus.*]

HARDCASTLE: What could my old friend Sir Charles mean by recommending his son as the modestest young man in town? To me he appears the most impudent piece of brass that ever spoke with a tongue. He has taken possession of the easy chair by the fire-side already. He took off his boots in the parlour, and desired me to see them taken care of. I'm desirous to know how his impudence affects my daughter. – She will certainly be shocked at it.

[*Enter* MISS HARDCASTLE, *plainly dress'd.*]

HARDCASTLE: Well, my Kate, I see you have changed your dress as I bid you; and yet, I believe, there was no great occasion.

MISS HARDCASTLE: I find such a pleasure, Sir, in obeying your commands, that I take care to observe them without ever debating their propriety.

HARDCASTLE: And yet, Kate, I sometimes give you some cause, particularly when I recommended my *modest* gentleman to you as a lover to-day.

MISS HARDCASTLE: You taught me to expect something extraordinary, and I find the original exceeds the description.

HARDCASTLE: I was never so surprized in my life! He has quite confounded all my faculties!

MISS HARDCASTLE: I never saw any thing like it: And a man of the world too!

HARDCASTLE: Ay, he learned it all abroad, – what a fool was I, to think a young man could learn modesty by travelling. He might as soon learn wit at a masquerade.

MISS HARDCASTLE: It seems all natural to him.

HARDCASTLE: A good deal assisted by bad company and a French dancing-master.

MISS HARDCASTLE: Sure you mistake, papa! a French dancing-master could never have taught him that timid look, – that aukward address, – that bashful manner –

HARDCASTLE: Whose look? whose manner? child!

MISS HARDCASTLE: Mr. Marlow's: his mauvaise honte,[1] his timidity struck me at the first sight.

HARDCASTLE: Then your first sight deceived you; for I think him one of the most brazen first sights that ever astonished my senses.

MISS HARDCASTLE: Sure, Sir, you rally! I never saw any one so modest.

HARDCASTLE: And can you be serious! I never saw such a bouncing swaggering puppy since I was born. Bully Dawson[2] was but a fool to him.

MISS HARDCASTLE: Surprizing! He met me with a respectful bow, a stammering voice, and a look fixed on the ground.

HARDCASTLE: He met me with loud voice, a lordly air, and a familiarity that made my blood freeze again.

MISS HARDCASTLE: He treated me with diffidence and respect; censured the manners of the age; admired the prudence of girls that never laughed; tired me with apologies for being tiresome; then left the room with a bow, and, madam, I would not for the world detain you.

HARDCASTLE: He spoke to me as if he knew me all his life before. Asked twenty questions, and never waited for an answer. Interrupted my best remarks with some silly pun, and when I was in my best story of the Duke of Marlborough and Prince Eugene, he asked if I had not a good hand at making punch. Yes, Kate, he ask'd your father if he was a maker of punch!

MISS HARDCASTLE: One of us must certainly be mistaken.

HARDCASTLE: If he be what he has shewn himself, I'm determined he shall never have my consent.

MISS HARDCASTLE: And if he be the sullen thing I take him, he shall never have mine.

HARDCASTLE: In one thing then we are agreed – to reject him.

MISS HARDCASTLE: Yes. But upon conditions. For if you should find him less impudent, and I more presuming; if you find him more respectful, and I more importunate – I don't know – the fellow is well enough for a man – Certainly we don't meet many such at a horse race in the country.

1. Self-consciousness.
2. A famous bully from earlier in the century.

HARDCASTLE: If we should find him so – But that's impossible. The first appearance has done my business. I'm seldom deceived in that.

MISS HARDCASTLE: And yet there may be many good qualities under that first appearance.

HARDCASTLE: Ay, when a girl finds a fellow's outside to her taste, she then sets about guessing the rest of his furniture.[1] With her, a smooth face stands for good sense, and a genteel figure for every virtue.

MISS HARDCASTLE: I hope, Sir, a conversation begun with a compliment to my good sense won't end with a sneer at my understanding?

HARDCASTLE: Pardon me, Kate. But if young Mr. Brazen can find the art of reconciling contradictions, he may please us both, perhaps.

MISS HARDCASTLE: And as one of us must be mistaken, what if we go to make further discoveries?

HARDCASTLE: Agreed. But depend on't I'm in the right.

MISS HARDCASTLE: And depend on't I'm not much in the wrong. [*Exeunt*.]

[*Enter* TONY *running in with a Casket*.]

TONY: Ecod! I have got them. Here they are. My Cousin Con's necklaces, bobs[2] and all. My mother shan't cheat the poor souls out of their fortune neither. O! my genus, is that you?

[*Enter* HASTINGS.]

HASTINGS: My dear friend, how have you managed with your mother? I hope you have amused her with pretending love for your cousin, and that you are willing to be reconciled at last? Our horses will be refreshed in a short time, and we shall soon be ready to set off.

TONY: And here's something to bear your charges by the way. [*Giving the casket*.] Your sweetheart's jewels. Keep them, and hang those, I say, that would rob you of one of them.

HASTINGS: But how have you procured them from your mother?

TONY: Ask me no questions, and I'll tell you no fibs. I procured them by the rule of thumb. If I had not a key to every drawer in mother's bureau, how could I go to the alehouse so often as I do? An honest man may rob himself of his own at any time.

HASTINGS: Thousands do it every day. But to be plain with you; Miss Neville is endeavouring to procure them from her aunt this very instant. If she succeeds, it will be the most delicate way at least of obtaining them.

TONY: Well, keep them, till you know how it will be. But I know how it will be well enough, she'd as soon part with the only sound tooth in her head.

1. The normal meaning of 'equipment' would have too obvious sexual connotations. Presumably, Hardcastle means 'qualities'.
2. Pendant ear-rings.

HASTINGS: But I dread the effects of her resentment, when she finds she has lost them.

TONY: Never you mind her resentment, leave *me* to manage that. I don't value her resentment the bounce of a cracker.[1] Zounds! here they are. Morrice. Prance.[2] [*Exit* HASTINGS.]

[TONY, MRS. HARDCASTLE, MISS NEVILLE.]

MRS. HARDCASTLE: Indeed, Constance, you amaze me. Such a girl as you want jewels? It will be time enough for jewels, my dear, twenty years hence, when your beauty begins to want repairs.

MISS NEVILLE: But what will repair beauty at forty, will certainly improve it at twenty, Madam.

MRS. HARDCASTLE: Yours, my dear, can admit of none. That natural blush is beyond a thousand ornaments. Besides, child, jewels are quite out at present. Don't you see half the ladies of our acquaintance, my Lady Kill day light, and Mrs. Crump, and the rest of them, carry their jewels to town, and bring nothing but Paste and Marcasites[3] back.

MISS NEVILLE: But who knows, Madam, but somebody that shall be nameless would like me best with all my little finery about me?

MRS. HARDCASTLE: Consult your glass, my dear, and then see, if with such a pair of eyes, you want any better sparklers. What do you think, Tony, my dear, does your cousin Con. want any jewels, in your eyes, to set off her beauty.

TONY: That's as thereafter may be.

MISS NEVILLE: My dear aunt, if you knew how it would oblige me.

MRS. HARDCASTLE: A parcel of old-fashioned rose and table-cut things.[4] They would make you look like the court of king Solomon at a puppet-shew. Besides, I believe I can't readily come at them. They may be missing for aught I know to the contrary.

TONY: [*Apart to* MRS. HARDCASTLE.] Then why don't you tell her so at once, as she's so longing for them. Tell her they're lost. It's the only way to quiet her. Say they're lost, and call me to bear witness.

MRS. HARDCASTLE: [*Apart to* TONY.] You know, my dear, I'm only keeping them for you. So if I say they're gone, you'll bear me witness, will you? He! he! he!

TONY: Never fear me. Ecod! I'll say I saw them taken out with my own eyes.

MISS NEVILLE: I desire them but for a day, Madam. Just to be permitted to shew them as relicks, and then they may be lock'd up again.

MRS. HARDCASTLE: To be plain with you, my dear Constance; if I could find

1. The bang of a fire-cracker.
2. Tony's highly individual slang suggesting that Hastings should leave and leave quickly.
3. Imitation jewellery made of crystallized iron pyrites.
4. The reference is to an old-fashioned way of cutting diamonds.

them, you should have them. They're missing, I assure you. Lost, for aught I know; but we must have patience wherever they are.

MISS NEVILLE: I'll not believe it; this is but a shallow pretence to deny me. I know they're too valuable to be so slightly kept, and as you are to answer for the loss.

MRS. HARDCASTLE: Don't be alarm'd, Constance. If they be lost, I must restore an equivalent. But my son knows they are missing, and not to be found.

TONY: That I can bear witness to. They are missing, and not to be found, I'll take my oath on't.

MRS. HARDCASTLE: You must learn resignation, my dear; for tho' we lose our fortune, yet we should not lose our patience. See me, how calm I am.

MISS NEVILLE: Ay, people are generally calm at the misfortunes of others.

MRS. HARDCASTLE: Now, I wonder a girl of your good sense should waste a thought upon such trumpery. We shall soon find them; and, in the mean time, you shall make use of my garnets[1] till your jewels be found.

MISS NEVILLE: I detest garnets.

MRS. HARDCASTLE: The most becoming things in the world to set off a clear complexion. You have often seen how well they look upon me. You *shall* have them. [*Exit*.]

MISS NEVILLE: I dislike them of all things. You shan't stir. – Was ever any thing so provoking to mislay my own jewels, and force me to wear her trumpery.

TONY: Don't be a fool. If she gives you the garnets, take what you can get. The jewels are your own already. I have stolen them out of her bureau, and she does not know it. Fly to your spark, he'll tell you more of the matter. Leave me to manage *her*.

MISS NEVILLE: My dear cousin.

TONY: Vanish. She's here, and has missed them already. Zounds! how she fidgets and spits about like a Catharine wheel.

[*Enter* MRS. HARDCASTLE.]

MRS. HARDCASTLE: Confusion! thieves! robbers! We are cheated, plundered, broke open, undone.

TONY: What's the matter, what's the matter, mamma? I hope nothing has happened to any of the good family

MRS. HARDCASTLE: We are robbed. My bureau has been broke open, the jewels taken out, and I'm undone.

TONY: Oh! is that all? Ha, ha, ha. By the laws, I never saw it better acted in my life. Ecod, I thought you was ruin'd in earnest, ha, ha, ha.

MRS. HARDCASTLE: Why boy, I *am* ruin'd in earnest. My bureau has been broke open, and all taken away.

TONY: Stick to that; ha, ha, ha; stick to that I'll bear witness, you know, call me to bear witness.

1. Ruby-coloured, silicate-based stones used in imitation jewellery.

MRS. HARDCASTLE: I tell you, Tony, by all that's precious, the jewels are gone, and I shall be ruin'd for ever.

TONY: Sure I know they're gone, and I am to say so.

MRS. HARDCASTLE: My dearest Tony, but hear me. They're gone, I say.

TONY: By the laws, mamma, you make me for to laugh, ha, ha. I know who took them well enough, ha, ha, ha.

MRS. HARDCASTLE: Was there ever such a blockhead, that can't tell the difference between jest and earnest. I tell you I'm not in jest, booby.

TONY: That's right, that's right: You must be in a bitter passion, and then nobody will suspect either of us. I'll bear witness that they are gone.

MRS. HARDCASTLE: Was there ever such a cross-grain'd brute, that won't hear me! Can you bear witness that you're no better than a fool? Was ever poor woman so beset with fools on one hand, and thieves on the other.

TONY: I can bear witness to that.

MRS. HARDCASTLE: Bear witness again, you blockhead you, and I'll turn you out of the room directly. My poor niece, what will become of *her*! Do you laugh, you unfeeling brute, as if you enjoy'd my distress?

TONY: I can bear witness to that.

MRS. HARDCASTLE: Do you insult me, monster? I'll teach you to vex your mother, I will.

TONY: I can bear witness to that. [*He runs off, she follows him.*]

[*Enter* MISS HARDCASTLE *and* MAID.]

MISS HARDCASTLE: What an unaccountable creature is that brother of mine, to send them to the house as an inn, ha, ha. I don't wonder at his impudence.

MAID: But what is more, madam, the young gentleman as you passed by in your present dress, ask'd me if you were the bar maid? He mistook you for the bar maid, madam.

MISS HARDCASTLE: Did he? Then as I live I'm resolved to keep up the delusion. Tell me, Pimple, how do you like my present dress. Don't you think I look something like Cherry in the Beaux Stratagem?[1]

MAID: It's the dress, madam, that every lady wears in the country, but when she visits or receives company.

MISS HARDCASTLE: And are you sure he does not remember my face or person?

MAID: Certain of it.

MISS HARDCASTLE: I vow I thought so; for though we spoke for some time together, yet his fears were such, that he never once looked up during the interview. Indeed, if he had, my bonnet would have kept him from seeing me.

1. Cherry is the inn-keeper's daughter in Farquhar's play who attempts to marry Archer, a gentleman disguised as a valet.

MAID: But what do you hope from keeping him in his mistake?

MISS HARDCASTLE: In the first place, I shall be *seen*, and that is no small advantage to a girl who brings her face to market. Then I shall perhaps make an acquaintance and that's no small victory gained over one who never addresses any but the wildest of her sex. But my chief aim is to take my gentleman off his guard, and like an invisible champion of romance examine the giant's force before I offer to combat.

MAID: But are you sure you can act your part, and disguise your voice, so that he may mistake that, as he has already mistaken your person?

MISS HARDCASTLE: Never fear me. I think I have got the true bar cant. – Did your honour call? – Attend the Lion there. – Pipes and tobacco for the Angel. – The Lamb has been outrageous this half hour.[1]

MAID: It will do, madam. But he's here. [*Exit* MAID.]

[*Enter* MARLOW.]

MARLOW: What a bawling in every part of the house; I have scarce a moment's repose. If I go to the best room, there I find my host and his story. If I fly to the gallery, there we have my hostess with her curtesy down to the ground. I have at last got a moment to myself, and now for recollection. [*Walks and muses.*]

MISS HARDCASTLE: Did you call, Sir? did your honour call?

MARLOW: [*Musing.*] As for Miss Hardcastle, she's too grave and sentimental for me.

MISS HARDCASTLE: Did your honour call?

[*She still places herself before him, he turning away.*]

MARLOW: No, child [*Musing.*] Besides from the glimpse I had of her, I think she squints.

MISS HARDCASTLE: I'm sure, Sir, I heard the bell ring.

MARLOW: No, No. [*Musing.*] I have pleased my father, however, by coming down, and I'll to-morrow please myself by returning.

[*Taking out his tablets,[2] and perusing.*]

MISS HARDCASTLE: Perhaps the other gentleman called, Sir.

MARLOW: I tell you, no.

MISS HARDCASTLE: I should be glad to know, Sir. We have such a parcel of servants.

MARLOW: No, no, I tell you. [*Looks full in her face.*] Yes, child, I think I did call. I wanted – I wanted – I vow, child, you are vastly handsome.

1. The names of different rooms.
2. Notebook.

MISS HARDCASTLE: O la, Sir, you'll make one asham'd.

MARLOW: Never saw a more sprightly malicious eye. Yes, yes, my dear, I did call. Have you got any of your – a – what d'ye call it in the house?

MISS HARDCASTLE: No, Sir, we have been out of that these ten days.

MARLOW: One may call in this house, I find, to very little purpose. Suppose I should call for a taste, just by way of trial, of the nectar of your lips; perhaps I might be disappointed in that too.

MISS HARDCASTLE: Nectar! nectar! that's a liquor there's no call for in these parts. French, I suppose. We keep no French wines here, Sir.

MARLOW: Of true English growth, I assure you.

MISS HARDCASTLE: Then it's odd I should not know it. We brew all sorts of wines in this house, and I have lived here these eighteen years.

MARLOW: Eighteen years! Why one would think, child, you kept the bar before you were born. How old are you?

MISS HARDCASTLE: O! Sir, I must not tell my age. They say women and music should never be dated.

MARLOW: To guess at this distance, you can't be much above forty. [*Approaching.*] Yet nearer I don't think so much. [*Approaching.*] By coming close to some women they look younger still; but when we come very close indeed. [*Attempting to kiss her.*]

MISS HARDCASTLE: Pray, Sir, keep your distance. One would think you wanted to know one's age as they do horses, by mark of mouth.

MARLOW: I protest, child, you use me extremely ill. If you keep me at this distance, how is it possible you and I can be ever acquainted?

MISS HARDCASTLE: And who wants to be acquainted with you? I want no such acquaintance, not I. I'm sure you did not treat Miss Hardcastle that was here awhile ago in this obstropalous[1] manner. I'll warrant me, before her you look'd dash'd, and kept bowing to the ground, and talk'd, for all the world, as if you was before a justice of peace.

MARLOW: [*Aside.*] Egad! she has hit it, sure enough. [*To her.*] In awe of her, child? Ha! ha! ha! A mere, aukward, squinting thing, no, no. I find you don't know me. I laugh'd, and rallied her a little; but I was unwilling to be too severe. No, I could not be too severe, *curse me*!

MISS HARDCASTLE: O! then, Sir, you are a favourite, I find, among the ladies?

MARLOW: Yes, my dear, a great favourite. And yet, hang me, I don't see what they find in me to follow. At the Ladies Club in town,[2] I'm called their agreeable Rattle. Rattle, child, is not my real name, but one I'm known by. My name is Solomons. Mr. Solomons, my dear, at your service. [*Offering to salute her.*][3]

MISS HARDCASTLE: Hold, Sir; you were introducing me to your club, not to yourself. And you're so great a favourite there you say?

1. Obstreperous.
2. The reference is to a famous female coterie.
3. Kiss.

MARLOW: Yes, my dear. There's Mrs. Mantrap, Lady Betty Blackleg, the Countess of Sligo, Mrs. Langhorns, old Miss Biddy Buckskin, and your humble servant, keep up the spirit of the place.[1]

MISS HARDCASTLE: Then it's a very merry place, I suppose.

MARLOW: Yes, as merry as cards, suppers, wine, and old women can make us.

MISS HARDCASTLE: And their agreeable Rattle, ha! ha! ha!

MARLOW: [*Aside.*] Egad! I don't quite like this chit. She looks knowing, methinks. You laugh, child!

MISS HARDCASTLE: I can't but laugh to think what time they all have for minding their work or their family.

MARLOW: [*Aside.*] All's well, she don't laugh at me. [*To her.*] Do you ever work, child?

MISS HARDCASTLE: Ay, sure. There's not a screen or a quilt in the whole house but what can bear witness to that.

MARLOW: Odso! Then you must shew me your embroidery. I embroider and draw patterns myself a little. If you want a judge of your work you must apply to me. [*Seizing her hand.*]

MISS HARDCASTLE: Ay, but the colours don't look well by candle light. You shall see all in the morning. [*Struggling.*]

MARLOW: And why not now, my angel? Such beauty fires beyond the power of resistance. – Pshaw! the father here! My old luck: I never nick'd seven that I did not throw ames ace three times following.[2] [*Exit* MARLOW.]

[*Enter* HARDCASTLE, *who stands in surprize.*]

HARDCASTLE: So, madam! So I find *this* is your *modest* lover. This is your humble admirer that kept his eyes fixed on the ground, and only ador'd at humble distance. Kate, Kate, art thou not asham'd to deceive your father so?

MISS HARDCASTLE: Never trust me, dear papa, but he's still the modest man I first took him for, you'll be convinced of it as well as I.

HARDCASTLE: By the hand of my body I believe his impudence is infectious! Didn't I see him seize your hand? Didn't I see him hawl you about like a milk maid? and now you talk of his respect and his modesty, forsooth!

MISS HARDCASTLE: But if I shortly convince you of his modesty, that he has only the faults that will pass off with time, and the virtues that will improve with age, I hope you'll forgive him.

HARDCASTLE: The girl would actually make one run mad! I tell you I'll not be convinced. I am convinced. He has scarcely been three hours in the house, and he has already encroached on all my prerogatives. You may

1. The names are pure invention, apart from the last, who was an actual member of the coterie.
2. The reference is to a game of dice where a high throw is followed by three low throws.

like his impudence, and call it modesty. But my son-in-law, madam, must have very different qualifications.

MISS HARDCASTLE: Sir, I ask but this night to convince you.

HARDCASTLE: You shall not have half the time, for I have thoughts of turning him out this very hour.

MISS HARDCASTLE: Give me that hour then, and I hope to satisfy you.

HARDCASTLE: Well, an hour let it be then. But I'll have no trifling with your father. All fair and open, do you mind me?

MISS HARDCASTLE: I hope, Sir, you have ever found that I considered your commands as my pride; for your kindness is such, that my duty as yet has been inclination. [*Exeunt.*]

Act IV

[*Enter* HASTINGS *and* MISS NEVILLE.]

HASTINGS: You surprise me! Sir Charles Marlow expected here this night? Where have you had your information?

MISS NEVILLE: You may depend upon it. I just saw his letter to Mr. Hardcastle, in which he tells him he intends setting out a few hours after his son.

HASTINGS: Then, my Constance, all must be completed before he arrives. He knows me; and should he find me here, would discover my name, and perhaps my designs, to the rest of the family.

MISS NEVILLE: The jewels, I hope, are safe.

HASTINGS: Yes, yes. I have sent them to Marlow, who keeps the keys of our baggage. In the meantime, I'll go to prepare matters for our elopement. I have had the Squire's promise of a fresh pair of horses; and, if I should not see him again, will write him further directions. [*Exit.*]

MISS NEVILLE: Well! success attend you. In the meantime, I'll go amuse my aunt with the old pretence of a violent passion for my cousin. [*Exit.*]

[*Enter* MARLOW, *followed by a* SERVANT.]

MARLOW: I wonder what Hastings could mean by sending me so valuable a thing as a casket to keep for him, when he knows the only place I have is the seat of a post-coach at an Inn-door. Have you deposited the casket with the landlady, as I ordered you? Have you put it into her own hands?

SERVANT: Yes, your honour.

MARLOW: She said she'd keep it safe, did she?

SERVANT: Yes, she said she'd keep it safe enough; she ask'd me how I came by it? and she said she had a great mind to make me give an account of myself. [*Exit* SERVANT.]

MARLOW: Ha! ha! ha! They're safe however. What an unaccountable set of beings have we got amongst! This little bar-maid though runs in my head most strangely, and drives out the absurdities of all the rest of the family. She's mine, she must be mine, or I'm greatly mistaken.

[*Enter* HASTINGS.]

HASTINGS: Bless me! I quite forgot to tell her that I intended to prepare at the bottom of the garden. Marlow here, and in spirits too!

MARLOW: Give me joy, George! Crown me, shadow me with laurels! Well, George, after all, we modest fellows don't want for success among the women.

HASTINGS: Some women you mean. But what success has your honour's modesty been crowned with now, that it grows so insolent upon us?

MARLOW: Didn't you see the tempting, brisk, lovely, little thing that runs about the house with a bunch of keys to its girdle?

HASTINGS: Well! and what then?

MARLOW: She's mine, you rogue you. Such fire, such motion, such eyes, such lips – but, egad! she would not let me kiss them though.

HASTINGS: But are you so sure, so very sure of her?

MARLOW: Why man, she talk'd of shewing me her work above-stairs,[1] and I am to improve the pattern.

HASTINGS: But how can *you*, Charles, go about to rob a woman of her honour?

MARLOW: Pshaw! pshaw! we all know the honour of the bar-maid of an inn. I don't intend to *rob* her, take my word for it, there's nothing in this house, I shan't honestly *pay* for.

HASTINGS: I believe the girl has virtue.

MARLOW: And if she has, I should be the last man in the world that would attempt to corrupt it.

HASTINGS: You have taken care, I hope, of the casket I sent you to lock up? It's in safety?

MARLOW: Yes, yes. It's safe enough. I have taken care of it. But how could you think the seat of a post-coach at an Inn-door a place of safety? Ah! numbskull! I have taken better precautions for you than you did for yourself. – I have –

HASTINGS: What!

MARLOW: I have sent it to the landlady to keep for you.

HASTINGS: To the landlady!

MARLOW: The landlady.

HASTINGS: You did.

MARLOW: I did. She's to be answerable for its forth-coming, you know.

HASTINGS: Yes, she'll bring it forth, with a witness.[2]

MARLOW: Wasn't I right? I believe you'll allow that I acted prudently upon this occasion?

1. Upstairs, presumably in her bedroom.
2. With a vengeance.

HASTINGS: [*Aside.*] He must not see my uneasiness.

MARLOW: You seem a little disconcerted though, methinks. Sure nothing has happened?

HASTINGS: No, nothing. Never was in better spirits in all my life. And so you left it with the landlady, who, no doubt, very readily undertook the charge?

MARLOW: Rather too readily. For she not only kept the casket; but, thro' her great precaution, was going to keep the messenger too. Ha! ha! ha!

HASTINGS: He! he! he! They're safe however.

MARLOW: As a guinea in a miser's purse.

HASTINGS: [*Aside.*] So now all hopes of fortune are at an end, and we must set off without it. [*To him.*] Well, Charles, I'll leave you to your meditations on the pretty bar-maid, and, he! he! he! may you be as successful for yourself as you have been for me. [*Exit.*]

MARLOW: Thank ye, George! I ask no more. Ha! ha! ha!

[*Enter* HARDCASTLE.]

HARDCASTLE: I no longer know my own house. It's turned all topsey-turvey. His servants have got drunk already. I'll bear it no longer, and yet, from my respect for his father, I'll be calm. [*To him.*] Mr. Marlow, your servant. I'm your very humble servant. [*Bowing low.*]

MARLOW: Sir, your humble servant. [*Aside.*] What's to be the wonder now?

HARDCASTLE: I believe, Sir, you must be sensible, Sir, that no man alive ought to be more welcome than your father's son, Sir. I hope you think so?

MARLOW: I do from my soul, Sir. I don't want much intreaty. I generally make my father's son welcome wherever he goes.

HARDCASTLE: I believe you do, from my soul, Sir. But tho' I say nothing to your own conduct, that of your Servants is insufferable. Their manner of drinking is setting a very bad example in this house, I assure you.

MARLOW: I protest, my very good Sir, that's no fault of mine. If they don't drink as they ought *they* are to blame. I ordered them not to spare the cellar. I did, I assure you. [*To the side scene.*] Here, let one of my servants come up. [*To him.*] My positive directions were, that as I did not drink myself, they should make up for my deficiencies below.

HARDCASTLE: Then they had your orders for what they do! I'm satisfied!

MARLOW: They had, I assure you. You shall hear from one of themselves.

[*Enter* SERVANT *drunk.*]

MARLOW: You, Jeremy! Come forward, sirrah! What were my orders? Were you not told to drink freely, and call for what you thought fit, for the good of the house?

HARDCASTLE: [*Aside.*] I begin to lose my patience.

JEREMY: Please your honour, liberty and Fleet-street for ever! Tho' I'm but a servant, I'm as good as another man. I'll drink for no man before supper,

Sir, dammy! Good liquor will sit upon a good supper, but a good supper will not sit upon – hiccup – upon my conscience, Sir.

MARLOW: You see, my old friend, the fellow is as drunk as he can possibly be. I don't know what you'd have more, unless you'd have the poor devil soused in a beer-barrel.

HARDCASTLE: Zounds! He'll drive me distracted if I contain myself any longer. Mr. Marlow. Sir; I have submitted to your insolence for more than four hours, and I see no likelihood of its coming to an end. I'm now resolved to be master here, Sir, and I desire that you and your drunken pack may leave my house directly.

MARLOW: Leave your house! – Sure you jest, my good friend? What, when I'm doing what I can to please you.

HARDCASTLE: I tell you, Sir, you don't please me; so I desire you'll leave my house.

MARLOW: Sure you cannot be serious? At this time o'night, and such a night. You only mean to banter me?

HARDCASTLE: I tell you, Sir, I'm serious; and, now that my passions are rouzed, I say this house is mine, Sir; this house is mine, and I command you to leave it directly.

MARLOW: Ha! ha! ha! A puddle in a storm. I shan't stir a step, I assure you. [*In a serious tone.*] This, your house, fellow! It's my house. This is my house. Mine, while I chuse to stay. What right have you to bid me leave this house, Sir? I never met with such impudence, curse me, never in my whole life before.

HARDCASTLE: Nor I, confound me if ever I did. To come to my house, to call for what he likes, to turn me out of my own chair, to insult the family, to order his servants to get drunk, and then to tell me *This house is mine, Sir*. By all that's impudent it makes me laugh. Ha! ha! ha! Pray, Sir, [*Bantering.*] as you take the house, what think you of taking the rest of the furniture? There's a pair of silver candlesticks, and there's a fire-screen, and here's a pair of brazen nosed bellows, perhaps you may take a fancy to them?

MARLOW: Bring me your bill, Sir, bring me your bill, and let's make no more words about it.

HARDCASTLE: There are a set of prints too. What think you of the rake's progress for your own apartment?

MARLOW: Bring me your bill, I say; and I'll leave you and your infernal house directly.

HARDCASTLE: Then there's a mahogony table, that you may see your own face in.

MARLOW: My bill, I say.

HARDCASTLE: I had forgot the great chair, for your own particular slumbers, after a hearty meal.

MARLOW: Zounds! bring me my bill, I say, and let's hear no more on't.

HARDCASTLE: Young man, young man, from your father's letter to me, I was taught to expect a well-bred modest man, as a visitor here, but now I find him no better than a coxcomb and a bully; but he will be down here presently, and shall hear more of it. [*Exit.*]

MARLOW: How's this! Sure I have not mistaken the house! Every thing looks like an inn. The servants cry, coming. The attendance is aukward; the bar-maid too to attend us. But she's here, and will further inform me. Whither so fast, child. A word with you.

[*Enter* MISS HARDCASTLE.]

MISS HARDCASTLE: Let it be short then. I'm in a hurry. [*Aside.*] (I believe he begins to find out his mistake, but its too soon quite to undeceive him.)

MARLOW: Pray, child, answer me one question. What are you, and what may your business in this house be?

MISS HARDCASTLE: A relation of the family, Sir.

MARLOW: What. A poor relation?

MISS HARDCASTLE: Yes, Sir. A poor relation appointed to keep the keys, and to see that the guests want nothing in my power to give them.

MARLOW: That is, you act as the bar-maid of this inn.

MISS HARDCASTLE: Inn. O law – What brought that in your head. One of the best families in the county keep an inn. Ha, ha, ha, old Mr. Hardcastle's house an inn.

MARLOW: Mr. Hardcastle's house! Is this house Mr. Hardcastle's house, child!

MISS HARDCASTLE: Ay, sure. Whose else should it be.

MARLOW: So then all's out, and I have been damnably imposed on. O, confound my stupid head, I shall be laugh'd at over the whole town. I shall be stuck up in caricatura in all the print-shops. The Dullissimo Maccaroni.[1] To mistake this house of all others for an inn, and my father's old friend for an inn-keeper. What a swaggering puppy must he take me for. What a silly puppy do I find myself. There again, may I be hang'd, my dear, but I mistook you for the bar-maid.

MISS HARDCASTLE: Dear me! dear me! I'm sure there's nothing in my *behavour* to put me upon a level with one of that stamp.

MARLOW: Nothing, my dear, nothing. But I was in for a list of blunders, and could not help making you a subscriber. My stupidity saw every thing the wrong way. I mistook your assiduity for assurance, and your simplicity for allurement. But it's over – This house I no more shew *my* face in.

MISS HARDCASTLE: I hope, Sir, I have done nothing to disoblige you. I'm sure I should be sorry to affront any gentleman who has been so polite, and said so many civil things to me. I'm sure I should be sorry [*Pretending to cry.*] if he left the family upon my account. I'm sure I should be sorry, people said any thing amiss, since I have no fortune but my character.

1. Macaronis were fops. The reference is to a set of illustrations of fops of all kinds in Darly's Comic Prints.

MARLOW: [*Aside.*] By heaven, she weeps. This is the first mark of tenderness I ever had from a modest woman, and it touches me; [*To her.*] Excuse me, my lovely girl, you are the only part of the family I leave with reluctance. But to be plain with you, the difference of our birth, fortune and education, make an honourable connexion impossible; and I can never harbour a thought of seducing simplicity that trusted in my honour, or bringing ruin upon one, whose only fault was being too lovely.

MISS HARDCASTLE: [*Aside.*] Generous man! I now begin to admire him. [*To him.*] But I'm sure my family is as good as miss Hardcastle's, and though I'm poor, that's no great misfortune to a contented mind, and, until this moment, I never thought that it was bad to want fortune.

MARLOW: And why now, my pretty simplicity?

MISS HARDCASTLE: Because it puts me at a distance from one, that if I had a thousand pound I would give it all to.

MARLOW: [*Aside.*] This simplicity bewitches me, so that if I stay I'm undone. I must make one bold effort, and leave her. [*To her.*] Your partiality in my favour, my dear, touches me most sensibly, and were I to live for myself alone, I could easily fix my choice. But I owe too much to the opinion of the world, too much to the authority of a father, so that – I can scarcely speak it – it affects me. Farewell. [*Exit.*]

MISS HARDCASTLE: I never knew half his merit till now. He shall not go, if I have power or art to detain him. I'll still preserve the character in which I stoop'd to conquer, but will undeceive my papa, who, perhaps, may laugh him out of his resolution. [*Exit.*]

[*Enter* TONY, MISS NEVILLE.]

TONY: Ay, you may steal for yourselves the next time. I have done my duty. She has got the jewels again, that's a sure thing; but she believes it was all a mistake of the servants.

MISS NEVILLE: But, my dear cousin, sure you won't forsake us in this distress. If she in the least suspects that I am going off, I shall certainly be locked up, or sent to my aunt Pedigree's, which is ten times worse.

TONY: To be sure, aunts of all kinds are damn'd bad things. But what can I do? I have got you a pair of horses that will fly like Whistlejacket,[1] and I'm sure you can't say but I have courted you nicely before her face. Here she comes, we must court a bit or two more, for fear she should suspect us. [*They retire, and seem to fondle.*]

[*Enter* MRS. HARDCASTLE.]

MRS. HARDCASTLE: Well, I was greatly fluttered, to be sure. But my son tells me it was all a mistake of the servants. I shan't be easy, however, till they

1. Whistlejacket was a famous racehorse in the 1750s.

are fairly married, and then let her keep her own fortune. But what do I see! Fondling together, as I'm alive. I never saw Tony so sprightly before. Ah! have I caught you, my pretty doves! What, billing, exchanging stolen glances, and broken murmurs. Ah!

TONY: As for murmurs, mother, we grumble a little now and then, to be sure. But there's no love lost between us.

MRS. HARDCASTLE: A mere sprinkling, Tony, upon the flame, only to make it burn brighter.

MISS NEVILLE: Cousin Tony promises to give us more of his company at home. Indeed, he shan't leave us any more. It won't leave us cousin Tony, will it?

TONY: O! it's a pretty creature. No, I'd sooner leave my horse in a pound, than leave you when you smile upon one so. Your laugh makes you so becoming.

MISS NEVILLE: Agreeable cousin! Who can help admiring that natural humour, that pleasant, broad, red, thoughtless, [*Patting his cheek.*] ah! it's a bold face.

MRS. HARDCASTLE: Pretty innocence.

TONY: I'm sure I always lov'd cousin Con's hazle eyes, and her pretty long fingers, that she twists this way and that, over the haspicholls,[1] like a parcel of bobbins.[2]

MRS. HARDCASTLE: Ah, he would charm the bird from the tree. I was never so happy before. My boy takes after his father, poor Mr. Lumpkin, exactly. The jewels, my dear Con, shall be yours incontinently. You shall have them. Isn't he a sweet boy, my dear? You shall be married to-morrow, and we'll put off the rest of his education, like Dr. Drowsy's sermons, to a fitter opportunity.

[*Enter* DIGGORY.]

DIGGORY: Where's the 'Squire? I have got a letter for your worship.

TONY: Give it to my mamma. She reads all my letters first.

DIGGORY: I had orders to deliver it into your own hands.

TONY: Who does it come from?

DIGGORY: Your worship mun ask that o' the letter itself.

TONY: I could wish to know, tho'. [*Turning the letter, and gazing on it.*]

MISS NEVILLE: [*Aside.*] Undone, undone. A letter to him from Hastings. I know the hand. If my aunt sees it, we are ruined for ever. I'll keep her employ'd a little if I can. [*To Mrs. Hardcastle.*] But I have not told you, Madam, of my cousin's smart answer just now to Mr. Marlow. We so laugh'd – You must know, Madam – this way a little, for he must not hear us. [*They confer.*]

TONY: [*Still gazing.*] A damn'd cramp piece of penmanship, as ever I saw in

1. The harpsichord.
2. Used in lace-making.

my life. I can read your print-hand very well. But here there are such handles, and shanks, and dashes, that one can scarce tell the head from the tail. *To Anthony Lumpkin, Esquire*. It's very odd, I can read the outside of my letters, where my own name is, well enough. But when I come to open it, it's all – buzz. That's hard, very hard; for the inside of the letter is always the cream of the correspondence.

MRS. HARDCASTLE: Ha, ha, ha. Very well, very well. And so my son was too hard for the philosopher.

MISS NEVILLE: Yes, Madam; but you must hear the rest, Madam. A little more this way, or he may hear us. You'll hear how he puzzled him again.

MRS. HARDCASTLE: He seems strangely puzzled now himself, methinks.

TONY: [*Still gazing.*] A damn'd up and down hand, as if it was disguised in liquor. [*Reading.*] *Dear Sir*. Ay, that's that. Then there's an *M*, and a *T*, and an *S*, but whether the next be an *izzard* or an *R*, confound me, I cannot tell.

MRS. HARDCASTLE: What's that, my dear. Can I give you any assistance?

MISS NEVILLE: Pray, aunt, let me read it. No body reads a cramp hand better than I. [*Twitching the letter from her.*] Do you know who it is from?

TONY: Can't tell, except from Dick Ginger the feeder.[1]

MISS NEVILLE: Ay, so it is, [*Pretending to read.*] Dear Squire, Hoping that you're in health, as I am at this present. The gentlemen of the Shake bag club has cut the gentlemen of goose-green quite out of feather.[2] The odds – um – odd battle – um – long fighting – um here, here, it's all about cocks, and fighting; it's of no consequence, here, put it up, put it up. [*Thrusting the crumpled letter upon him.*]

TONY: But I tell you, Miss, it's of all the consequence in the world. I would not lose the rest of it for a guinea. Here, mother, do you make it out. Of no consequence! [*Giving Mrs. Hardcastle the letter.*]

MRS. HARDCASTLE: How's this! [*Reads.*] Dear Squire, I'm now waiting for Miss Neville, with a post-chaise and pair, at the bottom of the garden, but I find my horses yet unable to perform the journey. I expect you'll assist us with a pair of fresh horses, as you promised. Dispatch is necessary, as the *hag* (ay the hag) your mother, will otherwise suspect us. Yours, Hastings. Grant me patience. I shall run distracted. My rage choaks me.

MISS NEVILLE: I hope, Madam, you'll suspend your resentment for a few moments, and not impute to me any impertinence, or sinister design that belongs to another.

MRS. HARDCASTLE: [*Curtesying very low.*] Fine spoken, Madam, you are most miraculously polite and engaging, and quite the very pink of curtesy and circumspection, Madam. [*Changing her tone.*] And you, you great ill-fashioned oaf, with scarce sense enough to keep your mouth shut. Were

1. Feeder and hence trainer of fighting cocks.
2. The reference is to two fighting cocks. A shake-bag was a large fighting cock, whereas goose [turd] green refers to the colour of the other cock.

you too join'd against me? But I'll defeat all your plots in a moment. As for you, Madam, since you have got a pair of fresh horses ready, it would be cruel to disappoint them. So, if you please, instead of running away with your spark, prepare, this very moment, to run off with *me*. Your old aunt Pedigree will keep you secure, I'll warrant me. You too, Sir, may mount your horse, and guard us upon the way. Here, Thomas, Roger, Diggory, I'll shew you that I wish you better than you do yourselves. [*Exit.*]

MISS NEVILLE: So now I'm completely ruined.

TONY: Ay, that's a sure thing.

MISS NEVILLE: What better could be expected from being connected with such a stupid fool, and after all the nods and signs I made him.

TONY: By the laws, Miss, it was your own cleverness, and not my stupidity, that did your business. You were so nice[1] and so busy with your Shake-bags and Goose-greens, that I thought you could never be making believe.

[*Enter* HASTINGS.]

HASTINGS: So, Sir, I find by my servant, that you have shewn my letter, and betray'd us. Was this well done, young gentleman?

TONY: Here's another. Ask Miss there who betray'd you. Ecod, it was her doing, not mine.

[*Enter* MARLOW.]

MARLOW: So I have been finely used here among you. Rendered contemptible, driven into ill manners, despised, insulted, laugh'd at.

TONY: Here's another. We shall have old Bedlam broke loose presently.

MISS NEVILLE: And there, Sir, is the gentleman to whom we all owe every obligation.

MARLOW: What can I say to him, a mere boy, an ideot, whose ignorance and age are a protection.

HASTINGS: A poor contemptible booby, that would but disgrace correction.[2]

MISS NEVILLE: Yet with cunning and malice enough to make himself merry with all our embarrassments.

HASTINGS: An insensible cub.

MARLOW: Replete with tricks and mischief.

TONY: Baw! damme, but I'll fight you both one after the other, – with baskets.[3]

MARLOW: As for him, he's below resentment. But your conduct, Mr.

1. Precise.
2. Because of Tony's age, it would be impossible to challenge him to a duel.
3. Swords with basket hilts.

Hastings, requires an explanation. You knew of my mistakes, yet would not undeceive me.

HASTINGS: Tortured as I am with my own disappointments, is this a time for explanations! It is not friendly, Mr. Marlow.

MARLOW: But, Sir –

MISS NEVILLE: Mr. Marlow, we never kept on your mistake, till it was too late to undeceive you. Be pacified.

[*Enter* SERVANT.]

SERVANT: My mistress desires you'll get ready immediately, Madam. The horses are putting to. Your hat and things are in the next room. We are to go thirty miles before morning. [*Exit* SERVANT.]

MISS NEVILLE: Well, well; I'll come presently.[1]

MARLOW: [*To* HASTINGS.] Was it well done, Sir, to assist in rendering me ridiculous? To hang me out for the scorn of all my acquaintance. Depend upon it, Sir, I shall expect an explanation.

HASTINGS: Was it well done, Sir, if you're upon that subject, to deliver what I entrusted to yourself, to the care of another, Sir?

MISS NEVILLE: Mr. Hastings. Mr. Marlow. Why will you increase my distress by this groundless dispute? I implore, I intreat you –

[*Enter* SERVANT.]

SERVANT: Your cloak, Madam. My mistress is impatient.

MISS NEVILLE: I come. Pray be pacified. If I leave you thus, I shall die with apprehension.

SERVANT: Your fan, muff, and gloves, Madam. The horses are waiting.

MISS NEVILLE: O, Mr. Marlow! if you knew what a scene of constraint and ill-nature lies before me, I'm sure it would convert your resentment into pity.

MARLOW: I'm so distracted with a variety of passions, that I don't know what I do. Forgive me, Madam. George, forgive me. You know my hasty temper, and should not exasperate it.

HASTINGS: The torture of my situation is my only excuse.

MISS NEVILLE: Well, my dear Hastings, if you have that esteem for me that I think, that I am sure you have, your constancy for three years will but encrease the happiness of our future connexion. If –

MRS. HARDCASTLE: [*Within.*] Miss Neville. Constance, why Constance, I say.

MISS NEVILLE: I'm coming. Well, constancy. Remember, constancy is the word. [*Exit.*]

HASTINGS: My heart! How can I support this. To be so near happiness, and such happiness.

1. Immediately.

MARLOW: [*To* TONY.] You see now, young gentleman, the effects of your folly. What might be amusement to you, is here disappointment, and even distress.

TONY: [*From a reverie.*] Ecod, I have hit it. Its here. Your hands. Yours and yours, my poor Sulky. My boots there, ho. Meet me two hours hence at the bottom of the garden; and if you don't find Tony Lumpkin a more good-natur'd fellow than you thought for, I'll give you leave to take my best horse, and Bet Bouncer into the bargain. Come along. My boots, ho. [*Exeunt.*]

Act V, [Scene I]

[SCENE *continues.*
Enter HASTINGS *and* SERVANT.]

HASTINGS: You saw the Old Lady and Miss Neville drive off, you say.

SERVANT: Yes, your honour. They went off in a post coach, and the young 'Squire went on horseback. They're thirty miles off by this time.

HASTINGS: Then all my hopes are over.

SERVANT: Yes, Sir. Old Sir Charles is arrived. He and the Old Gentleman of the house have been laughing at Mr. Marlow's mistake this half hour. They are coming this way.

HASTINGS: Then I must not be seen. So now to my fruitless appointment at the bottom of the garden. This is about the time. [*Exit.*]

[*Enter* SIR CHARLES *and* HARDCASTLE.]

HARDCASTLE: Ha, ha, ha. The peremptory tone in which he sent forth his sublime commands.

SIR CHARLES: And the reserve with which I suppose he treated all your advances.

HARDCASTLE: And yet he might have seen something in me above a common inn-keeper, too.

SIR CHARLES: Yes, Dick, but he mistook you for an uncommon inn-keeper, ha, ha, ha.

HARDCASTLE: Well, I'm in too good spirits to think of any thing but joy. Yes, my dear friend, this union of our families will make our personal friendship hereditary; and tho' my daughter's fortune is but small –

SIR CHARLES: Why, Dick, will you talk of fortune to *me*. My son is possessed of more than a competence already, and can want nothing but a good and virtuous girl to share his happiness and encrease it. If they like each other, as you say they do –

HARDCASTLE: *If*, man. I tell you they *do* like each other. My daughter as good as told me so.

SIR CHARLES: But girls are apt to flatter themselves, you know.

HARDCASTLE: I saw him grasp her hand in the warmest manner myself; and here he comes to put you out of your *iffs*, I warrant him.

[*Enter* MARLOW.]

MARLOW: I come, Sir, once more, to ask pardon for my strange conduct. I can scarce reflect on my insolence without confusion.

HARDCASTLE: Tut, boy, a trifle. You take it too gravely. An hour or two's laughing with my daughter will set all to rights again. She'll never like you the worse for it.

MARLOW: Sir, I shall be always proud of her approbation.

HARDCASTLE: Approbation is but a cold word, Mr. Marlow; if I am not deceived, you have something more than approbation thereabouts. You take me.

MARLOW: Really, Sir, I have not that happiness.

HARDCASTLE: Come, boy, I'm an old fellow, and know what's what, as well as you that are younger. I know what has past between you; but mum.

MARLOW: Sure, Sir, nothing has past between us but the most profound respect on my side, and the most distant reserve on hers. You don't think, Sir, that my impudence has been past upon all the rest of the family.

HARDCASTLE: Impudence! No, I don't say that – Not quite impudence – Though girls like to be play'd with, and rumpled a little too sometimes. But she has told no tales, I assure you.

MARLOW: I never gave her the slightest cause.

HARDCASTLE: Well, well, I like modesty in its place well enough. But this is over-acting, young gentleman. You *may* be open. Your father and I will like you the better for it.

MARLOW: May I die, Sir, if I ever –

HARDCASTLE: I tell you, she don't dislike you; and as I'm sure you like her –

MARLOW: Dear Sir – I protest, Sir –

HARDCASTLE: I see no reason why you should not be joined as fast as the parson can tie you.

MARLOW: But hear me, Sir –

HARDCASTLE: Your father approves the match, I admire it, every moment's delay will be doing mischief, so –

MARLOW: But why won't you hear me? By all that's just and true, I never gave miss Hardcastle the slightest mark of my attachment, or even the most distant hint to suspect me of affection. We had but one interview, and that was formal, modest and uninteresting.

HARDCASTLE: [*Aside.*] This fellow's formal modest impudence is beyond bearing.

SIR CHARLES: And you never grasp'd her hand, or made any protestations!

MARLOW: As heaven is my witness, I came down in obedience to your commands. I saw the lady without emotion, and parted without reluctance. I hope you'll exact no further proofs of my duty, nor prevent me from leaving a house in which I suffer so many mortifications. [*Exit.*]

SIR CHARLES: I'm astonish'd at the air of sincerity with which he parted.

HARDCASTLE: And I'm astonish'd at the deliberate intrepidity of his assurance.

SIR CHARLES: I dare pledge my life and honour upon his truth.

HARDCASTLE: Here comes my daughter, and I would stake my happiness upon her veracity.

[*Enter* MISS HARDCASTLE.]

HARDCASTLE: Kate, come hither, child. Answer us sincerely, and without reserve; has Mr. Marlow made you any professions of love and affection?

MISS HARDCASTLE: The question is very abrupt, Sir! But since you require unreserved sincerity, I think he has.

HARDCASTLE: [*To* SIR CHARLES.] You see.

SIR CHARLES: And pray, madam, have you and my son had more than one interview?

MISS HARDCASTLE: Yes, Sir, several.

HARDCASTLE: [*To* SIR CHARLES.] You see.

SIR CHARLES: But did he profess any attachment?

MISS HARDCASTLE: A lasting one.

SIR CHARLES: Did he talk of love?

MISS HARDCASTLE: Much, Sir.

SIR CHARLES: Amazing! And all this formally?

MISS HARDCASTLE: Formally.

HARDCASTLE: Now, my friend, I hope you are satisfied.

SIR CHARLES: And how did he behave, madam?

MISS HARDCASTLE: As most profest admirers do. Said some civil things of my face, talked much of his want of merit, and the greatness of mine; mentioned his heart, gave a short tragedy speech, and ended with pretended rapture.

SIR CHARLES: Now I'm perfectly convinced, indeed. I know his conversation among women to be modest and submissive. This forward canting ranting manner by no means describes him, and I am confident, he never sate for the picture.

MISS HARDCASTLE: Then what, Sir, if I should convince you to your face of my sincerity? If you and my papa, in about half an hour, will place yourselves behind that screen, you shall hear him declare his passion to me in person.

SIR CHARLES: Agreed. And if I find him what you describe, all my happiness in him must have an end. [*Exit.*]

MISS HARDCASTLE: And if you don't find him what I describe – I fear my happiness must never have a beginning. [*Exeunt.*]

[Act V, Scene II]

[SCENE *changes to the Back of the Garden.*
Enter HASTINGS.]

HASTINGS: What an ideot am I, to wait here for a fellow, who probably takes a delight in mortifying me. He never intended to be punctual, and I'll wait no longer. What do I see. It is he, and perhaps with news of my Constance.

[*Enter* TONY, *booted and spattered.*]

HASTINGS: My honest 'Squire! I now find you a man of your word. This looks like friendship.

TONY: Ay, I'm your friend, and the best friend you have in the world, if you knew but all. This riding by night, by the bye, is cursedly tiresome. It has shook me worse than the basket of a stage-coach.

HASTINGS: But how? Where did you leave your fellow travellers? Are they in safety? Are they housed?

TONY: Five and twenty miles in two hours and a half is no such bad driving. The poor beasts have smoaked[1] for it: Rabbet me, but I'd rather ride forty miles after a fox, than ten with such *varment*.[2]

HASTINGS: Well, but where have you left the ladies? I die with impatience.

TONY: Left them. Why where should I leave them, but where I found them.

HASTINGS: This is a riddle.

TONY: Riddle me this then. What's that goes round the house, and round the house, and never touches the house?

HASTINGS: I'm still astray.

TONY: Why that's it, mon. I have led them astray. By jingo, there's not a pond or slough within five miles of the place but they can tell the taste of.

HASTINGS: Ha, ha, ha, I understand; you took them in a round, while they supposed themselves going forward. And so you have at last brought them home again.

TONY: You shall hear. I first took them down Feather-bed-lane, where we stuck fast in the mud. I then rattled them crack over the stones of Up-and-down Hill – I then introduc'd them to the gibbet on Heavy-tree Heath, and from that, with a circumbendibus,[3] I fairly lodged them in the horse-pond at the bottom of the garden

HASTINGS: But no accident, I hope.

TONY: No, no. Only mother is confoundedly frightened. She thinks herself

1. Galloped.
2. Vermin. A not very flattering reference to his mother and cousin.
3. A roundabout route.

forty miles off. She's sick of the journey, and the cattle[1] can scarce crawl. So if your own horses be ready, you may whip off with cousin, and I'll be bound that no soul here can budge a foot to follow you.

HASTINGS: My dear friend, how can I be grateful?

TONY: Ay, now its dear friend, noble 'Squire. Just now, it was all ideot, cub, and run me through the guts. Damn *your* way of fighting, I say. After we take a knock in this part of the country, we kiss and be friends. But if you had run me through the guts, then I should be dead, and you might go kiss the hangman.

HASTINGS: The rebuke is just. But I must hasten to relieve miss Neville; if you keep the old lady employed, I promise to take care of the young one.

[*Exit* HASTINGS.]

TONY: Never fear me. Here she comes. Vanish. She's got from the pond, and draggled[2] up to the waist like a mermaid.

[*Enter* MRS. HARDCASTLE.]

MRS. HARDCASTLE: Oh, Tony, I'm killed. Shook. Battered to death. I shall never survive it. That last jolt that laid us against the quickset hedge has done my business.

TONY: Alack, mama, it was all your own fault. You would be for running away by night, without knowing one inch of the way.

MRS. HARDCASTLE: I wish we were at home again. I never met so many accidents in so short a journey. Drench'd in the mud, overturn'd in a ditch, stuck fast in a slough, jolted to a jelly, and at last to lose our way. Whereabouts do you think we are, Tony?

TONY: By my guess we should be upon Crackskull common, about forty miles from home.

MRS. HARDCASTLE: O lud! O lud! the most notorious spot in all the country. We only want a robbery to make a complete night on't.

TONY: Don't be afraid, mama, don't be afraid. Two of the five that kept here are hanged, and the other three may not find us. Don't be afraid. Is that a man that's galloping behind us? No; its only a tree. Don't be afraid.

MRS. HARDCASTLE: The fright will certainly kill me.

TONY: Do you see any thing like a black hat moving behind the thicket?

MRS. HARDCASTLE: O death!

TONY: No, it's only a cow. Don't be afraid, mama; don't be afraid.

MRS. HARDCASTLE: As I'm alive, Tony, I see a man coming towards us. Ah! I'm sure on't. If he perceives us we are undone.

TONY: [*Aside.*] Father-in-law, by all that's unlucky, come to take one of his night walks. [*To her.*] Ah, it's a highwayman, with pistils as long as my arm. A damn'd ill-looking fellow.

MRS. HARDCASTLE: Good heaven defend us! He approaches.

1. A reference to his horses.
2. Bedraggled.

TONY: Do you hide yourself in that thicket, and leave me to manage him. If there be any danger I'll cough and cry hem. When I cough be sure to keep close.[1]

[MRS. HARDCASTLE *hides behind a tree in the back scene.* *Enter* HARDCASTLE.]

HARDCASTLE: I'm mistaken, or I beard voices of people in want of help. Oh, Tony, is that you. I did not expect you so soon back. Are your mother and her charge in safety?

TONY: Very safe, Sir, at my aunt Pedigree's. Hem.

MRS. HARDCASTLE: [*From behind.*] Ah death! I find there's danger.

HARDCASTLE: Forty miles in three hours; sure, that's too much, my youngster.

TONY: Stout horses and willing minds make short journies, as they say. Hem.

MRS. HARDCASTLE: [*From behind.*] Sure he'll do the dear boy no harm.

HARDCASTLE: But I heard a voice here; I should be glad to know from whence it came?

TONY: It was I, Sir, talking to myself, Sir. I was Saying that forty miles in four hours was very good going. Hem. As to be sure it was. Hem. I have got a sort of cold by being out in the air. We'll go in, if you please. Hem.

HARDCASTLE: But if you talk'd to yourself, you did not answer yourself. I am certain I heard two voices, and am resolved [*Raising his voice.*] to find the other out.

MRS. HARDCASTLE: [*From behind.*] Oh! he's coming to find me out. Oh!

TONY: What need you go, Sir, if I tell you. Hem. I'll lay down my life for the truth – hem – I'll tell you all, Sir. [*Detaining him.*]

HARDCASTLE: I tell you, I will not be detained. I insist on seeing. It's in vain to expect I'll believe you.

MRS. HARDCASTLE: [*Running forward from behind.*] O lud, he'll murder my poor boy, my darling. Here, good gentleman, whet your rage upon me. Take my money, my life, but spare that young gentleman, spare my child, if you have any mercy.

HARDCASTLE: My wife! as I'm a Christian. From whence can she come, or what does she mean!

MRS. HARDCASTLE: [*Kneeling.*] Take compassion on us, good Mr. Highwayman. Take our money, our watches, all we have, but spare our lives. We will never bring you to justice, indeed we won't, good Mr. Highwayman.

HARDCASTLE: I believe the woman's out of her senses. What, Dorothy, don't you know *me*?

MRS. HARDCASTLE: Mr. Hardcastle, as I'm alive. My fears blinded me. But who, my dear, would have expected to meet you here, in this frightful place, so far from home? What has brought you to follow us?

1. Stay hidden.

HARDCASTLE: Sure, Dorothy, you have not lost your wits? So far from home, when you are within forty yards of your own door. [*To him.*] This is one of your old tricks, you graceless rogue you. [*To her.*] Don't you know the gate, and the mulberry-tree; and don't you remember the horsepond, my dear?

MRS. HARDCASTLE: Yes, I shall remember the horsepond as long as I live; I have caught my death in it. [*To* TONY] And is it to you, you graceless varlet, I owe all this. I'll teach you to abuse your mother, I will.

TONY: Ecod, mother, all the parish says you have spoil'd me, and so you may take the fruits on't.

MRS. HARDCASTLE: I'll spoil you, I will. [*Follows him off the stage. Exit.*]

HARDCASTLE: There's morality, however, in his reply. [*Exit.*]

[*Enter* HASTINGS *and* MISS NEVILLE.]

HASTINGS: My dear Constance, why will you deliberate thus? If we delay a moment, all is lost for ever. Pluck up a little resolution, and we shall soon be out of the reach of her malignity.

MISS NEVILLE: I find it impossible. My spirits are so sunk with the agitations I have suffered, that I am unable to face any new danger. Two or three years patience will at last crown us with happiness.

HASTINGS: Such a tedious delay is worse than inconstancy. Let us fly, my charmer. Let us date our happiness from this very moment. Perish fortune. Love and content will encrease what we possess beyond a monarch's revenue. Let me prevail.

MISS NEVILLE: No, Mr. Hastings; no. Prudence once more comes to my relief, and I will obey its dictates. In the moment of passion, fortune may be despised, but it ever produces a lasting repentance. I'm resolved to apply to Mr. Hardcastle's compassion and justice for redress.

HASTINGS: But tho' he had the will, he has not the power to relieve you.

MISS NEVILLE: But he has influence, and upon that I am resolved to rely.

HASTINGS: I have no hopes. But since you persist, I must reluctantly obey you. [*Exeunt.*]

[Act V, Scene III]

[SCENE *Changes.*
Enter SIR CHARLES *and* MISS HARDCASTLE.]

SIR CHARLES: What a situation am I in. If what you say appears, I shall then find a guilty son. If what he says be true, I shall then lose one that, of all others, I most wish'd for a daughter.

MISS HARDCASTLE: I am proud of your approbation, and to shew I merit it, if you place yourselves as I directed, you shall hear his explicit declaration. But he comes.

SIR CHARLES: I'll to your father, and keep him to the appointment.

[*Exit* SIR CHARLES.]

[*Enter* MARLOW.]

MARLOW: Tho' prepar'd for setting out, I come once more to take leave, nor did I, till this moment, know the pain I feel in the separation.

MISS HARDCASTLE: [*In her own natural manner.*] I believe those sufferings cannot be very great, Sir, which you can easily remove. A day or two longer, perhaps, might lessen your uneasiness, by shewing the little value of what you now think proper to regret.

MARLOW: [*Aside.*] This girl every moment improves upon me. [*To her.*] It must not be, Madam. I have already trifled too long with my heart. My very pride begins to submit to my passion. The disparity of education and fortune, the anger of a parent, and the contempt of my equals, begin to lose their weight; and nothing can restore me to myself, but this painful effort of resolution.

MISS HARDCASTLE: Then go, Sir. I'll urge nothing more to detain you. Tho' my family be as good as hers you came down to visit, and my education, I hope, not inferior, what are these advantages without equal affluence? I must remain contented with the slight approbation of imputed merit; I must have only the mockery of your addresses, while all your serious aims are fix'd on fortune.

[*Enter* HARDCASTLE *and* SIR CHARLES *from behind.*]

SIR CHARLES: Here, behind this screen.

HARDCASTLE: Ay, Ay, make no noise. I'll engage my Kate covers him with confusion at last.

MARLOW: By heavens, Madam, fortune was ever my smallest consideration. Your beauty at first caught my eye; for who could see that without emotion. But every moment that I converse with you, steals in some new grace, heightens the picture, and gives it stronger expression. What at first seem'd rustic plainness, now appears refin'd simplicity. What seem'd forward assurance, now strikes me as the result of courageous innocence, and conscious virtue.

SIR CHARLES: What can it mean! He amazes me!

HARDCASTLE: I told you how it would be. Hush!

MARLOW: I am now determined to stay, Madam, and I have too good an opinion of my father's discernment, when he sees you, to doubt his approbation.

MISS HARDCASTLE: No, Mr. Marlow, I will not, cannot detain you. Do you think I could suffer a connexion, in which there is the smallest room for repentance? Do you think I would take the mean advantage of a transient passion, to load you with confusion? Do you think I could ever relish that happiness, which was acquired by lessening yours?

MARLOW: By all that's good, I can have no happiness but what's in your power to grant me. Nor shall I ever feel repentance, but in not having seen your merits before. I will stay, even contrary to your wishes; and tho' you should persist to shun me, I will make my respectful assiduities atone for the levity of my past conduct.

MISS HARDCASTLE: Sir, I must entreat you'll desist. As our acquaintance began, so let it end, in indifference. I might have given an hour or two to levity; but seriously, Mr. Marlow, do you think I could ever submit to a connexion, where *I* must appear mercenary, and *you* imprudent? Do you think I could ever catch at the confident addresses of a secure admirer?

MARLOW: [*Kneeling.*] Does this look like security. Does this look like confidence. No, Madam, every moment that shews me your merit, only serves to encrease my diffidence and confusion. Here let me continue –

SIR CHARLES: I can hold it no longer. Charles, Charles, how hast thou deceived me! Is this your indifference, your uninteresting conversation!

HARDCASTLE: Your cold contempt; your formal interview. What have you to say now?

MARLOW: That I'm all amazement! What can it mean!

HARDCASTLE: It means that you can say and unsay things at pleasure. That you can address a lady in private, and deny it in public; that you have one story for us, and another for my daughter.

MARLOW: Daughter! – this lady your daughter!

HARDCASTLE: Yes, Sir, my only daughter. My Kate, whose else should she be.

MARLOW: Oh, the devil.

MISS HARDCASTLE: Yes, Sir, that very identical tall squinting lady you were pleased to take me for. [*Curtesying.*] She that you addressed as the mild, modest, sentimental man of gravity, and the bold forward agreeable rattle of the ladies club; ha, ha, ha.

MARLOW: Zounds, there's no bearing this; it's worse than death.

MISS HARDCASTLE: In which of your characters, Sir, will you give us leave to address you. As the faultering gentleman, with looks on the ground, that speaks just to be heard, and hates hypocrisy; or the loud confident creature, that keeps it up with Mrs. Mantrap, and old Miss Biddy Buckskin, till three in the morning; ha, ha, ha.

MARLOW: O, curse on my noisy head. I never attempted to be impudent yet, that I was not taken down. I must be gone.

HARDCASTLE: By the hand of my body, but you shall not. I see it was all a mistake, and I am rejoiced to find it. You shall not stir, I tell you. I know she'll forgive you. Won't you forgive him, Kate. We'll all forgive you. Take courage, man. [*They retire, she tormenting him to the back Scene.*]

[*Enter* MRS. HARDCASTLE, TONY.]

MRS. HARDCASTLE: So, so, they're gone off. Let them go, I care not.

HARDCASTLE: Who gone?

MRS. HARDCASTLE: My dutiful niece and her gentleman, Mr. Hastings, from Town. He who came down with our modest visitor here.

SIR CHARLES: Who, my honest George Hastings? As worthy a fellow as lives, and the girl could not have made a more prudent choice.

HARDCASTLE: Then, by the hand of my body, I'm proud of the connexion.

MRS. HARDCASTLE: Well, if he has taken away the lady, he has not taken her fortune, that remains in this family to console us for her loss.

HARDCASTLE: Sure Dorothy you would not be so mercenary?

MRS. HARDCASTLE: Ay, that's my affair, not yours.

HARDCASTLE: But you know if your son, when of age, refuses to marry his cousin, her whole fortune is then at her own disposal

MRS. HARDCASTLE: Ay, but he's not of age, and she has not thought proper to wait for his refusal. [*Enter* HASTINGS *and* MISS NEVILLE.]

MRS. HARDCASTLE: [*Aside.*] What returned so soon, I begin not to like it.

HASTINGS: [*To* HARDCASTLE.] For my late attempt to fly off with your niece, let my present confusion be my punishment. We are now come back, to appeal from your justice to your humanity. By her father's consent, I first paid her my addresses, and our passions were first founded in duty.

MISS NEVILLE: Since his death, I have been obliged to stoop to dissimulation to avoid oppression. In an hour of levity, I was ready even to give up my fortune to secure my choice. But I'm now recover'd from the delusion, and hope from your tenderness what is denied me from a nearer connexion.

MRS. HARDCASTLE: Pshaw, pshaw, this is all but the whining end of a modern novel.

HARDCASTLE: Be it what it will, I'm glad they're come back to reclaim their due. Come hither, Tony boy. Do you refuse this lady's hand whom I now offer you?

TONY: What signifies my refusing. You know I can't refuse her till I'm of age, father.

HARDCASTLE: While I thought concealing your age boy was likely to conduce to your improvement, I concurred with your mother's desire to keep it secret. But since I find she turns it to a wrong use, I must now declare, you have been of age these three months.

TONY: Of age! Am I of age, father?

HARDCASTLE: Above three months.

TONY: Then you'll see the first use I'll make of my liberty. [*Taking* MISS NEVILLE*'s hand.*] Witness all men by these presents, that I, Anthony Lumpkin, Esquire, of BLANK place, refuse you, Constantia Neville, spinster, of no place at all, for my true and lawful wife. So Constance

Neville may marry whom she pleases, and Tony Lumpkin is his own man again.

SIR CHARLES: O brave 'Squire.

HASTINGS: My worthy friend.

MRS. HARDCASTLE: My undutiful offspring.

MARLOW: Joy, my dear George, I give you joy sincerely. And could I prevail upon my little tyrant here to be less arbitrary, I should be the happiest man alive, if you would return me the favour.

HASTINGS: [*To Miss Hardcastle.*] Come, madam, you are now driven to the very last scene of all your contrivances. I know you like him, I'm sure he loves you, and you must and shall have him.

HARDCASTLE: [*Joining their hands.*] And I say so too. And Mr. Marlow, if she makes as good a wife as she has a daughter, I don't believe you'll ever repent your bargain. So now to supper, to-morrow we shall gather all the poor of the parish about us, and the Mistakes of the Night shall be crowned with a merry morning; so boy take her; and as you have been mistaken in the mistress, my wish is, that you may never be mistaken in the wife.

Epilogue[1]

By DR. GOLDSMITH

WELL, having stoop'd to conquer with success,
And gain'd a husband without aid from dress,
Still as a Bar-maid, I could wish it too,
As I have conquer'd him to conquer you:
And let me say, for all your resolution,
That pretty Bar-maids have done execution.
Our life is all a play, compos'd to please,
"We have our exits and our entrances."[2]
The first act shews the simple country maid,
Harmless and young, of ev'ry thing afraid;
Blushes when hir'd, and with unmeaning action,
I hopes as how to give you satisfaction.
Her second act displays a livelier scene, –
Th' unblushing Bar-maid of a country inn,
Who whisks about the house, at market caters,
Talks loud, coquets the guests, and scolds the waiters.

1. In the first editions of the play, the Epilogue was printed immediately after the Prologue.
2. *As You Like It*, Act II, scene iv. The remainder of the epilogue is a parody of Jaques's 'seven ages of man' speech.

Next the scene shifts to town, and there she soars,
The chophouse toast of ogling connoisseurs.
On 'Squires and Cits she there displays her arts,
And on the gridiron broils her lover's hearts –
And as she smiles, her triumphs to compleat,
Even Common Councilmen forget to eat.
The fourth act shews her wedded to the 'Squire,
And Madam now begins to hold it higher;
Pretends to taste, at Operas cries caro,
And quits her Nancy Dawson, for Che Faro.[1]
Doats upon dancing, and in all her pride,
Swims round the room, the Heinel *of Cheapside:*[2]
Ogles and leers with artificial skill,
Till having lost in age the power to kill,
She sits all night at cards, and ogles at spadille.[3]
Such, thro' our lives, the eventful history –
The fifth and last act still remains for me.
The Bar-maid now for your protection prays,
Turns Female Barrister, and pleads for Bayes.[4]

Epilogue*

To be spoken in the Character of TONY LUMPKIN
By J. CRADDOCK, Esq.

WELL – *now all's ended – and my comrades gone,*
Pray what becomes of mother's nonly son?
A hopeful blade! – in town I'll fix my station,
And try to make a bluster in the nation.
As for my cousin Neville, I renounce her,
Off – in a crack – I'll carry big Bett Bouncer.
Why should not I in the great world appear?
I soon shall have a thousand pounds a year;
No matter what a man may here inherit,
In London – 'gad, they've some regard to spirit.
I see the horses prancing up the streets,
And big Bett Bouncer, bobs to all she meets;
Then hoikes to jiggs and pastimes ev'ry night –

1. Nancy Dawson was a famous hornpipe dancer. *Que faro* is the opening line of the best-known aria from Gluck's opera *Orfeo ed Eurydice*.
2. Mlle Heinel was a leading dancer at the Haymarket.
3. The name for the ace of spaces in the card game ombre.
4. The laurel wreath of success. There is also a punning reference to the character Bayes, a parody of all would-be dramatists, in Buckingham's play *The Rehearsal*.

Not to the plays – they say it a'n't polite,
To Sadler's-Wells perhaps, or Operas go,
And once by chance, to the roratorio.[1]
Thus here and there, for ever up and down,
We'll set the fashions too, to half the town;
And then at auctions – money ne'er regard,
Buy pictures like the great, ten pounds a yard;
Zounds, we shall make these London gentry say,
We know what's damn'd genteel, as well as they.

*This came too late to be be Spoken.

1. Oratorios were a popular form of entertainment during Lent.

The Marriage of Figaro

Pierre Augustin Caron de Beaumarchais

INTRODUCTION

The story of Beaumarchais's life reads like the plot of an improbable picaresque novel.[1] From humble beginnings as the son of a watchmaker in Paris, Beaumarchais used his wits and his artistic talents to advance himself in the glittering but ruthless court world of the Bourbon kings. Having elbowed his way into the nobility, Beaumarchais made and lost a fortune as a speculator, pursued a successful career as a man of letters, fought numerous protracted legal battles, worked as a secret agent for the king, spent several short spells in prison, almost lost his life during the reign of terror, but finally was permitted to die in peace in his own home in Paris in 1799.

Born in 1732, Pierre Augustin was the son of a master watchmaker named Caron. His father was an educated and thoughtful man who had experienced life as a soldier as well as a craftsman and who had left his physical roots in the provinces and spiritual roots in Calvinism to settle in Paris and embrace Roman Catholicism. Pierre Augustin had little formal education, but he lived in a lively and educated household and read widely in his father's extensive collection of books. As the only surviving son, he was apprenticed to his father and expected to make his career in the family business. After a brief period of youthful rebellion, he applied himself with considerable flair to the watchmaker's craft so that by the age of twenty-two he had become a master watchmaker and had even

1. A lively account of a ten-year period (1775–85) in Beaumarchais's life is given in the film *Beaumarchais l'insolent* (1996), directed by Edouard Molinaro.

designed a new form of regulator for watches. This led to a public dispute with the master watchmaker to the king, a man called Lepaute, who claimed the mechanism as his invention. Beaumarchais submitted a detailed protest to the Académie des Sciences. So meticulous was the documentation he provided that the members of the Academy were convinced by his appeal and found in his favour. As a result, he was appointed watchmaker to the king and to Mme de Pompadour. This was the first of many public disputes that were to advance his career.

In 1755 Beaumarchais purchased a minor office in the Royal Household, which gave him access to court society. He made good use of his entrée at court. Within a year, he had purchased a more substantial office as Comptroller-in-Ordinary of the Royal Household from a well-to-do courtier called Francquet. Even before the first instalment was paid, however, Francquet had died, leaving Beaumarchais free to pursue his growing interest in Francquet's widow. By 1756 Beaumarchais had married the wealthy Mme Francquet; he had made an auspicious start as a court official; and he had even changed his name from Caron to Caron de Beaumarchais, a name derived from one of his wife's properties. At this point, one of the many sudden changes of fortune occurred which were to typifiy his life. Within ten months of their wedding his wife died of a fatal illness and left him, not a fortune, but a tangled web of litigation.

Despite this setback, Beaumarchais used his growing network of friends and supporters at court to advance his career in a completely new direction. In addition to his skills as a watchmaker, he was also a gifted musician and composer. By 1759 his friends helped him to the post of music teacher to the unmarried sisters of Louis XV, who greatly enjoyed both his music-making and his company. This new role in turn brought him into contact with a rich financier called Pâris-Duverney, who enlisted the young man's support in furthering one of his largest projects. Pâris-Duverney desperately needed the king's patronage for the École Militaire, which he had built at great expense in Paris. Beaumarchais, through his regular music-making with the princesses, was able to persuade them to visit the academy with him and subsequently to obtain the favour of a visit by the king. Having thus gained the royal patronage he needed, Pâris-Duverney repaid his debt to Beaumarchais by involving him as a partner in future ventures and by teaching him the skills involved in becoming a successful entrepreneur. Within a mere two years, Beaumarchais had begun to accumulate a significant fortune.

By 1763, Beaumarchais's wealth, with additional backing from his mentor, was sufficient to permit him to purchase one of the higher court offices. This brought with it admission to the ranks of the nobility. Initially, there was vigorous opposition to this move on the part of other nobles, and Beaumarchais's efforts to purchase the office of Grand Maître des Eaux et Forêts were thwarted. However, the king was persuaded to sign his nomination as Keeper of the Royal Warren and Hunting Grounds before other nobles could mount a protest. Beaumarchais's new office brought with it certain responsibilities as a magistrate; this involved trying cases of those accused of poaching or other minor offences within the royal hunting grounds. Beaumarchais exercised the role of magistrate for over twenty years, which may have provided some of the inspiration for the rustic court scene in *Le Mariage de Figaro*.

In 1764, Beaumarchais travelled to Madrid, ostensibly to defend the honour of one of his sisters, Marie-Louise, known as Lisette, who had been jilted by a Spanish fiancé named José Clavijo. Beaumarchais's colourful account of his journey to Spain and of his dealings with Clavijo were published some ten years later in his *Mémoires contre Goëzman*. His vivid prose inspired the young Goethe in 1774 to base one of his early plays, *Clavigo*, on Beaumarchais's narrative. In reality, however, Beaumarchais was more successful in pursuing commercial and political contacts during the two years he spent in Madrid than in defending his sister's honour.

After his return to Paris in 1767, Beaumarchais wrote his first major play for public performance. This was a sentimental piece called *Eugénie* which, when published, was accompanied by an essay on the *genre dramatique sérieux*. Both the play and the essay show Beaumarchais's debt to the example of Diderot. In the late 1750s Diderot had advocated a sentimental approach to playwriting in his theories and had attempted to put his ideas into practice in two less than successful plays, *Le Fils Naturel* and *Le Père de Famille*. Beaumarchais's attempt at writing a sentimental play was not much more successful. The play was roundly condemned by the critics, although some deft rewriting after the opening night at the Comédie-Française helped the play to achieve some degree of popular success. Beaumarchais attempted a second play in a sentimental vein, *Les Deux Amis ou le négociant de Lyon*, in 1770. It was duly performed by the Comédie-Française, but was a complete failure.

After this experience, Beaumarchais turned away from the sentimental genre and experimented with a diametrically opposed approach. In 1772 he completed the first version of his sparkling comedy *Le Barbier de Séville*. Initially Beaumarchais had conceived the piece as a comic opera. But when his libretto was rejected by the Opéra Comique, he wrote the work as a comedy in five acts and submitted it to the Comédie-Française. Although the play was accepted for performance by the actors of the Comédie-Française in 1773, plans for an immediate production had to be shelved as Beaumarchais had just lost an important legal battle and found himself stripped of his civil rights. It was not until 1775 that permission was given for the play to be performed. As happened with his earlier play *Eugénie*, the opening night was a disaster. Beaumarchais spent two frantic days rewriting and reshaping the comedy (changing the five-act structure to four acts); the result was an unqualified success that has remained on the repertoire of the Comédie-Française ever since.

The early 1770s brought a period of great turbulence in Beaumarchais's life. A second marriage to a wealthy widow ended with the death of his new wife in 1770 after only two years of marriage. That same year saw the death of his mentor and benefactor, Pâris-Duverney. Beaumarchais was owed a modest sum of money from his benefactor's estate. Instead of releasing this sum, the executor, Count de la Blache, disputed the validity of Pâris-Duverney's signature and sued Beaumarchais for debt. This began a protracted legal process that was to drag on throughout the 1770s. Confronted by a seemingly unassailable combination of a corrupt judiciary and a mendacious aristocracy (la Blache spread the most appalling rumours at court about Beaumarchais's conduct), Beaumarchais did his best to turn his tribulations to his own advantage.

The trial judge, Goëzman, was particularly corrupt. This inspired Beaumarchais to write a series of trenchantly witty *Mémoires contre Goëzman* (three were published in 1773 and a fourth in 1774), which were read and admired as models of satiric writing all over Europe. Initially things went disastrously for Beaumarchais. In 1773 he lost his case on appeal and found his house and goods impounded, while he was deprived of his civil rights. A personal quarrel with the Duc de Chaulnes, a peer of the realm, saw him briefly imprisoned at the very point when his appeal was being heard. By 1774 his forthright accusation of corruption levelled against Goëzman led to a judicial enquiry, which found against the judge but still censured

Beaumarchais for publishing his various memoires and left him deprived of his civil rights. It was not until 1779, after further court hearings and a judgment delivered by the *parlement* of Aix-en-Provence that Beaumarchais was finally vindicated and had his civil rights and court office restored to him.

Such an ordeal might have broken the spirit of a lesser man, but Beaumarchais somehow found the time and the energy at the height of his battle with Count de la Blache to write his sparkling comedy, *Le Barbier de Séville*. Throughout the mid-1770s he also spent considerable time and energy ingratiating himself, first with Louis XV and then, after the latter's death in 1774, with Louis XVI by undertaking secret and delicate missions on their behalf in London. Initially his tasks bordered on the trivial: he was to suppress a scurrilous tract describing the colourful early life of the king's mistress Mme du Barry; he was to recover sensitive state papers from another, distinctly unreliable spy, the Chevalier d'Éon, who specialised in cross-dressing; he was to suppress yet another offensive work attacking Marie Antoinette. Soon, however, Beaumarchais found a more significant issue to grapple with. He became fascinated with the rebellion of the American colonies against their English masters. With his usual entrepreneurial flair, he had spotted an opportunity to combine personal commercial advantage with the interests of France. In 1775 he sent a series of cogently argued papers to the king, making the case for France to support the American rebels. Beaumarchais took action even before he had won the support of the king. He set up a holding company, organised a substantial loan, and was soon sending fleets of ships carrying arms and amunition to the rebels. The American Congress would be slow to repay their debt to him, but without this aid it is doubtful if the American rebels could have won their decisive victory at Saratoga in 1777.

Back in France in the late 1770s, Beaumarchais found himself involved in new projects and new struggles. In 1777, following the continued success of *Le Barbier de Séville*, Beaumarchais joined forces with other writers to protest at the shabby way playwrights were treated by the actors of the Comédie-Française. The fees received by playwrights were not particularly generous: at best one-ninth of the net takings, after deducting all the ordinary and daily expenses of the house (expenses that were easily inflated by the actors). In addition, the actors insisted that if the takings on any one night fell below 1200 livres in winter or 800 livres in summer, then the play thereafter would 'become the property of the actors'.[1] By arranging performances on unsuitable evenings, it was quite easy for the actors to ensure that takings fell below the specified figure. When Beaumarchais was subjected to this procedure, he demanded to see the full accounts of the theatre, organised a public protest, and formed an association of authors to fight the actors. It was some years before the issue was finally resolved, but in 1791 the Freedom of the Theatres Act gave dramatists the right to retain control of their own 'intellectual property' which would pass to their heirs for five years after their death.[2]

The year after he began his struggle with the actors of the Comédie-Française, Beaumarchais embarked on yet another major project. Voltaire had died in 1778 and Beaumarchais was determined to mark this occasion by publishing a full edition of Voltaire's work. With his usual energy and commitment, he bought up Voltaire's existing manuscripts and purchased a publishing house in the German town of Kehl, just across the river from Strasbourg. (This was to avoid the heavy hand of the French police censor.) Although the take-up of subscriptions for the edition was disappointing, Beaumarchais spared no expense in completing the publication of his definitive and complete edition of Voltaire's work in seventy volumes. The first volumes of the edition were published in 1783, the last were sent to subscribers in 1790. Given the political instability of the period, as well as opposition from the church and the censor, this was a remarkable achievement.

Le Mariage de Figaro/The Marriage of Figaro

It was during this same period of time that Beaumarchais wrote his most ambitious play yet, *Le Mariage de Figaro*. Using the same main characters who had made their first appearance in *Le Barbier de Séville* (Count Almaviva, Rosine – now his Countess, and the barber Figaro – now his serving-man), Beaumarchais traced out in his new play the fortunes of Figaro and his bride-to-be, Suzanne, on the day of their wedding. The plot of this new comedy shows the bridal couple combining with the Countess to fight off the Count's predatory designs on Suzanne. Beaumarchais began work on the play in the mid-1770s. A first version was completed by 1778, and

1. William D. Howarth, *Beaumarchais and the Theatre* (Routledge: London & New York, 1995) p. 37.
2. Ibid., p. 41.

was accepted for performance by the Comédie-Française in 1781. Although this version was approved (with minor amendments) by the censors, rumours had reached the court that its content was sufficiently provocative to warrant more careful consideration. Beaumarchais arranged a private reading for the king and queen late in 1781, in the hope that this would help to gain their approval of the play. His hopes were dashed when Louis is reported to have said: 'This is detestable: it will never be played. It would be necessary to destroy the Bastille for a performance of this play not to be thoroughly irresponsible. This fellow mocks everything that should be respected in a government.'[1] What particularly shocked the king was Figaro's long soliloquy, which, in this early version of the play, included specific references to the Bastille, censorship and economics. After this abortive reading, Beaumarchais duly edited his text, pruning the most offensive sections of Figaro's monologue and transferring the setting of the play from France to Spain. The revised text was submitted to the censors, but on this occasion approval for performance was refused.

Meanwhile, the king's reported response to the play ensured that other members of the court were keen to have private readings organised for them, and Beaumarchais was more than willing to oblige. A command performance with actors from the Comédie-Française was arranged for the king's brother at the Menus-Plaisirs theatre but the performance was banned in the king's name at the very last moment on 13 June 1783. A third censor's report was favourable. This opened the way to the play being performed by actors from the Comédie-Française in September 1783 at the home of the Duc de Fronsac, in honour of the king's brother. On this occasion, the king gave his approval. Two further censors reported positively. A final and sixth censor called Bret, who was himself a playwright, reported entirely positively on the play. Beaumarchais mounted a successful publicity campaign, calling for an independent tribunal to judge his work, in an open letter to the king. This persuaded Louis, much against his better judgement, to give permission for the play to be performed in public. It was a momentous decision, which led to one of the most popular and successful productions ever seen on the stage of the Comédie-Française. The play ran for some sixty-eight continuous performances. Despite its predominantly light-hearted tone, the response of audiences during

1. The comment is reported in Mme Campan's biography of Marie-Antoinette, published in 1822. Quoted from Howarth, *Beaumarchais and the Theatre*, p. 177.

its run suggests that, much as Louis had feared, the play helped to fan the flames of political dissent in the years leading up to the French Revolution of 1789.

Le Mariage de Figaro opened at the Comédie-Française on 27 April 1784. Hours before the performance was due to begin at 5.30 p.m., the auditorium was packed. Members of the court, the aristocracy and even the royal family jostled with the citizens of Paris for the privilege of seeing and listening to a play that expressed at its very heart a nation's growing disenchantment with its corrupt, aristocratic form of government. The amazement this caused was reflected in some of the published reviews of the production, as in the following by La Harpe:

> I shall never forget my astonishment at the fifth-act soliloquy, which lasted at least a quarter of an hour. But the focus of my astonishment soon changed, for this speech was astounding in more than one sense. A good half of it was nothing more than a satirical attack on the government; I knew it already, since I had heard it before. But I was far from expecting that a government could possibly agree to such attacks being uttered on a public stage. The more they applauded, the more I was amazed and perplexed.[1]

Whether deliberately or intuitively, Beaumarchais had put his finger on the pulse of a new age. He was not an obvious revolutionary, and when the revolution came, its leaders were slow to acknowledge him as one of them. Nevertheless, in *Le Mariage de Figaro*, Beaumarchais wrote one of Europe's greatest ever revolutionary plays.

Comparing the major characters from *Le Barbier de Séville* with their counterparts in *Le Mariage de Figaro* provides a very clear indication of how far Beaumarchais had moved in the few years that separated the two plays. There are topical references in the earlier play, in particular to the way Beaumarchais had been made the victim of smears and calumny during his legal battle with Count de la Blache. But the characters in the earlier play are closer to *commedia dell'arte* stereotypes than to real individuals. The Count is the traditional young lover determined to wed the innocent young Columbine figure, Rosine. In order to achieve this aim, he has to enlist the help of Figaro, a Harlequin figure, to outwit an older

1. Quoted from Howarth, *Beaumarchais and the Theatre*, p. 187.

Pantelone figure, Dr Bartholo, who is Rosine's predatory guardian. The politics of the plot are both harmless and timeless; there are no significant social or political issues involved. The style of writing is sharp and witty, but the author leaves ample scope for the actors to fill out their stereotypical roles with their presence.

In *Le Mariage de Figaro*, these various stereotypical figures have matured into fully rounded individuals, who have both a past history and a distinctive, socially determined role in their present environment. Count Almaviva, for instance, is no longer the ardent and committed young lover we saw in the earlier play. He is the ruler of a large estate at Aguas Frescas, near Seville, and exhibits all the worst attributes of the Bourbon aristocracy: he is utterly self-centred and expects to enjoy his privileges without matching obligations; he believes in his own absolute, God-given authority, which he sees as extending into every corner of his subjects' experience, including their sexual experience; and, like the Bourbon courtiers, he forgets nothing and learns nothing. Rosine has changed even more radically. She is no longer an innocent young Columbine figure, but a mature married woman who suffers the daily indignity of watching her husband abusing his authority by attempting to seduce a succession of young women on his estate. The neglect and humiliation she has suffered make her susceptible to the spontaneous but fervent devotion shown her by her godchild, the page Chérubin. Rosine is a complex and attractive figure, whose behaviour is motivated by an often conflicting set of emotions: loyalty to her wayward husband, fear of his temper, sadness at the repeated humiliations he inflicts on her, a real warmth towards her chambermaid Suzanne, and surprise at her own emotional response to Chérubin.

Figaro has developed from a scheming Harlequin figure, from a singing barber, with quick wits and a lively tongue, into a politically alert manservant who has every intention of defending his own interests despite the arbitrary and absolute authority wielded by his master. Figaro has also acquired a past. Much to own amazement, he discovers that the Dr Bartholo, whom he helped to outwit in the previous play, is in fact his father. His mother is the scheming Marceline, who is mentioned but not seen in the previous play. In her youth she was seduced and then deserted by Dr Bartholo. Figaro, as a child, was stolen by gypsies and bandits. Brought up in their ways, he yearned for a more honest life. As a young man he embarked on a series of picaresque adventures that quite closely reflect Beaumarchais's own kaleidoscopic experiences. Having at last found himself working as a manservant to Count Almaviva, he is outraged at his master's blatant and repeated attempts to seduce his fiancée, Suzanne, before they have even had the chance to marry. When he suspects, quite wrongly, that his bride-to-be is about to give into the Count's remorseless pressure, Figaro expresses a critique of aristocratic behaviour that must have been electrifying when uttered on a public stage in Paris a mere five years before the French Revolution, and there is every indication that his contemporaries understood exactly what he meant:

> No, my very worthy Lord and Master, you have not got her yet – What! Because you are a great Man, you fancy yourself a great Genius. – Which way? – How came you to be the rich and mighty Count Almaviva! Why truly, you gave yourself the Trouble to be born! While the obscurity in which I have been cast demanded more Abilities to gain a mere Subsistence than are requisite to govern Empires. And what, most noble Count, are your Claims to Distinction, to pompous Titles, and immense Wealth, of which you are so proud, and which, by Accident, you possess?

Much of the play is very light-hearted in tone. Figaro and Suzanne are a delightful young couple, who laugh and banter with each other, while they bustle through their world. Their determination to marry each other, whatever obstacles the Count and others may place in their way, keeps the action of the play moving along at a sparkling pace. Chérubin is an equally attractive character, offering a light-hearted study of the emotional world of a young adolescent. Prepared to swoon at the feet of anyone in a skirt, Chérubin is a harmless and innocent version of the Count. Unlike the Count, whose intentions are distinctly phallic, there is little immediate threat in Chérubin's erotic fantasies. This is why the part is always played by a young woman. Nevertheless, the Count recognises in Chérubin a rival in the making and is immensely irritated at invariably finding him with the young women who have caught his eye, notably Suzanne and Fanchette, and is even prepared to see Chérubin as competing for his own wife's affections.

The secondary characters are presented in an equally light-hearted manner. They range from the stuttering judge Don Guzman (who is clearly intended as a cartoon image of the corrupt judge Goëzman) to the drunken gardner Antonio, and his attractive young daughter, Fanchette, who is just discovering the first stirrings of erotic desire. They are drawn with a sure touch and add brief but distinctive moments of comic experience to the overall fabric of the play. Marceline and Dr Bartholo are more complex figures who provide a bridge between the light-hearted and the more serious sections of the play. To begin with, they appear as figures of fun. Marceline is well past her prime, but is still intent on capturing a husband for herself. She has her eyes on Figaro who has borrowed money from her, with a written proviso that he will marry her if he fails to repay the loan. Bartholo is a curmudgeonly figure who has consistently refused to marry Marceline since making her pregnant in her youth. But he is quite willing to help her to gain Figaro as a husband by representing her interests at law. The behaviour of these two in the early sections of the play provides the basis for scenes of almost farcical quality. Marceline has a slanging match with Suzanne, which leaves her spluttering with rage. Figaro hands out similarly rough treatment to his old adversary, Dr Bartholo, both before and during the court scene. However, when the two discover that Figaro is their long-lost son, they undergo a distinct change of character. Marceline turns into a warm and supportive mother, helping both Figaro and Suzanne in their plots to outwit the Count. (More improbably in a passage in the French text which was omitted in performance and therefore omitted from Holcroft's translation, Marceline becomes a serious spokeswoman for all women wronged by men.) Even Dr Bartholo is gradually persuaded to accept the role of both husband and father, which he has so long resisted.

The light-hearted tone of much of the play is very deceptive. Underneath all the good-humoured laughter, the play offers a serious and thought-provoking study of how the behaviour of different social classes is informed by diametrically opposed values. Diderot, who had inspired Beaumarchais's early attempts at playwriting, had suggested in the third of his *Entretiens sur le Fils Naturel* (1757) that the behaviour of characters in plays should be determined by their social class and condition. Furthermore clashes and conflicts engendered by social class and condition would provide a fruitful source of inspiration for dramatists. It was essentially this idea that Beaumarchais took up and exploited so brilliantly in his play. The Count represents all the worst attributes of the aristocracy in pre-revolutionary France. He assumes that he has a natural right to impose his authority on all his creatures, an authority that reaches into the most intimate parts of their lives.

Although he has abolished the ancient (but probably mythical) custom of the *droit de seigneur*, he has no intention of giving up his privilege in reality. His attempt to impose his sexuality on Suzanne, by sleeping with her before her husband does, is a clear expression of his political absolutism. For him, sex and politics are inextricably intertwined. Political power brings with it sexual power, which explains why he is so incensed at the thought that his wife (who is no more than his creature) should deceive him with another. This would undermine the very basis of patriarchal control. When the Count suspects that there is another man in his wife's bed-chamber, his rage is such that he would be quite capable of murder. In contrast, it seems to him perfectly natural that his political authority should give him unlimited sexual authority. During the course of the action, we learn that he has already been on secret visits to the young, barely pubescent Fanchette, to prepare her for future sexual experiences with kisses and promises of suitable rewards. Suzanne needs no such preparation. She is a mature young lady, about to be married. The Count wants her and is determined to have her. If she refuses to sleep with him, he intends to use every method to delay or prevent her marriage to Figaro. After her marriage, he has laid careful plans which will guarantee him access to her whenever he pleases.

The Count's designs are eventually thwarted by a close alliance between his wife, Rosine, and the two servants who are to be married, Suzanne and Figaro. These three share the same values, despite the class boundaries which separate them. All three believe in commitment, honesty and relationships based on affection not coercion. Theirs is a protective but also a subversive alliance, which is designed to thwart and ultimately to undo the authority of their ruler, the Count. In the final act of the play, the Countess dresses up as Suzanne, so that the Count unwittingly finds himself attempting to seduce his own wife. Worse still, he falls into a rage when he sees his patriarchal authority not so much threatened but mocked by Figaro apparently attempting to seduce his wife. This is of course Suzanne dressed up as the Countess. When the deception practised by the two women is revealed, the Count's humiliation is embarrassingly public. As he kneels to beg the Countess's forgiveness, he represents a graphic image of a whole social class, namely the French aristocracy, that was soon to be equally publicly humiliated during the reign of terror in 1792 but with none of the benign forgiveness shown by the Countess. This visually striking final scene of the play, in which the Count has lost both his credibility and his authority, pointed to the end of an era. Louis was astute enough to realise this; his advisers were not. He did, however, enjoy a brief moment of revenge. A year after Beaumarchais's play had opened at the Comédie-Française, the author wrote in the *Journal de Paris* in the spring of 1785 that he had had to fight with 'lions and tigers' to get the play performed. Quite correctly, Louis interpreted this as a mocking reference to his own opposition to the play, and had Beaumarchais thrown into prison. Within five days Beaumarchais was released: he was too popular a figure to keep incarcerated, and all too soon was pressing the king with some success for public signs of esteem. Like Figaro, Beaumarchais used his wits to break through the brittle façade of Bourbon absolutism to defend his interests and to advance his own career. His play continued its successful run until well after the outbreak of revolution in 1789.

The remaining years of Beaumarchais's life were full of yet more breathtaking reversals of fortune. But at least he enjoyed for the first time in his life a stable domestic base. In 1786 he married a young woman called Thérèse Willermaulaz, by whom he had already had a daughter Eugénie in 1777. She was to prove a loyal and devoted companion during the troubled years of the revolution. In the late 1780s Beaumarchais enjoyed further artistic success with the production of his musical drama *Tarare* at the opera in 1787. Gluck's pupil Salieri wrote the music for the piece, which was not only acclaimed when first performed, but continued to figure in the repertoire of the opera until well into the nineteenth century.

As the political mood of the country darkened, life became more difficult for Beaumarchais. He made unnecessary enemies of men who were to become powerful figures in the revolutionary movement. In particular, his quarrel with the lawyer Bergasse, with whom he became embroiled in a much-publicised lawsuit, lost him a lot of public sympathy. In addition, he had acquired two acres of land in the Marais, not far from the Bastille, where he proceeded to build a palatial house for himself, set in beautiful landscaped gardens. At a time of seething political instability, this was an unwise move. Beaumarchais made matters worse by organising a sumptuous feast in his house, with leading stars from the opera performing music by Gluck, Salieri and himself, on the very eve of the revolution. Inevitably, these actions were seen as deliberate provocations. When the revolution came, Beaumarchais took good care to become chairman of his electoral district, but this did not prevent accusations being made against him of profiteering and hoarding. On several occasions, his property was invaded as mobs searched in vain for supposedly hidden stocks of wheat.

By openly declaring his support for much of what the revolutionaries believed in, Beaumarchais somehow managed to survive the early years of the revolution without undue threats of violence. He even managed to complete the third play in the trilogy of plays involving the characters of the Count, the Countess, Figaro and Suzanne: *La Mère coupable* was a distinctly dark and bitter piece which was performed initially at the new Théâtre du Marais in June 1792. It was at this point that things really began to go wrong for Beaumarchais. In March 1792 he was informed that a stock of 60,000 rifles, seized from rebels by the Austrians, was being held on the Dutch coast. These weapons could be of use to the French government, as France was at war with other European nations. Once again, Beaumarchais saw the opportunity of combining personal advantage with service to his country. But he underestimated the scale of the difficulties involved in obtaining the necessary loans, and clear government support (at a time of administrative chaos and instability); he also underestimated the scale of personal abuse he would suffer because of the affair and had great difficulty in rebutting the continuous slanders made by his many enemies. The sad upshot of all this was that Beaumarchais found himself in prison in Paris just before the September massacres of the aristocrats began in 1792. He was released just in time to save his life, and fled to London where he wrote his account of the 'most painful nine months of his life'. In 1793–4, he was permitted to pursue further negotiations in respect of the arms deal, but the whole project collapsed in 1794 when the English seized the rifles. Although he was acting on behalf of the French government, Beaumarchais was now branded as an *émigré*. This meant that he was unable to return to France and his wife was obliged to divorce him. He spent the next two years in poverty, living in Hamburg.

Beaumarchais pursued the reinstatement of his civic rights with the same energy as he had shown during the *ancien régime*. Eventually, his efforts were rewarded with success. He was allowed to return to Paris in July 1796 in time to attend the wedding of his daughter Eugénie. He and Thérèse remarried shortly after. He had the pleasure of seeing his final play *La Mère coupable* performed in a new production at the Comédie-Française in May 1797, at which he was called onto the stage by an enthusiastic audience. He spent the remaining years of his life living quietly in his much-loved house and garden in the Marais. Beaumarchais died peacefully in his sleep in May 1799, aged 67, following a convivial evening spent with his family and friends. After a lifetime of instability and sudden changes of fortune, the concluding years of his life were uncharacteristically calm and serene. Perhaps this may explain why, in a letter written to Madame Staël at this point in his life, Beaumarchais claimed that he had been 'one of the happiest men in my country and in my age'.[1]

1. Quoted from R. Greaves, *Beaumarchais: The Man who was Figaro* (New York: Crowell, 1977) p. 293.

Deſsiné par Sᵗ Quentin ancien pensionaire du Roy.
Malapeau Sculp.
Il vous rend chaſte et pure aux mains de votre époux

A scene from Act IV of *Le Mariage de Figaro*, drawn by St Quentin, reproduced from Beaumarchais, *Le Mariage de Figaro* (Paris, 1785).

The Follies of a Day

OR, THE

MARRIAGE OF FIGARO.

A COMEDY,

AS IT IS NOW PERFORMING AT THE
THEATRE-ROYAL,
COVENT-GARDEN.

FROM THE
FRENCH OF M. DE BEAUMARCHAIS.
BY THOMAS HOLCROFT.

AUTHOR OF DUPLICITY, A COMEDY , THE NOBLE
PEASANT, AN OPERA, & c.

LONDON:
Printed for G. G. J. and J. ROBINSON,
PATER-NOSTER ROW,
M DCC LXXXV.

Advertisement

Though to thank the Public is to thank nobody, since no particular Person takes this Sort of Compliments to himself, yet were I not to feel that Gratitude, which individually I know not where to pay, I were unworthy of past, of present, or of future Favours.

An Author's Thanks to the World at large may be seen under two very different Aspects: For, to thank the Public is to tell the Public he is successful; which, supposing it true, would be strange if they did not already know; it appears therefore only to be taking an Opportunity of indulging his Vanity: And yet to thank them seems his Duty, since his Silence might not only be construed a want of Respect, but an arrogant Self-confidence that, when they applauded or approved his Work, they only did him justice. The Reader must determine which of these Faces he will please to view.

I am so well convinced that the best Writer stands in need of Indulgence, and that he only does well by Comparison, and might do much better, that I shall find little Mortification in subscribing to the Opinions of those who shall tell me I am in this latter Predicament.

Readers are divided into two Classes; the one will allow an Author much more than he merits, and the other much less; but the principal Excellencies of *The Follies of a Day* are so known to be another's Right, that for me to claim them would be ridiculous. Some, however, have affirmed that it is a mere Translation, who have never seen, read, or heard the Original; if they had, indeed, they would have been still more culpable. Few will trouble themselves to examine the precise Extent of my Claims; nor, if they did, would they have an Opportunity 'till M. *de Beaumarchais* shall think proper to publish LA FOLLE JOURNÉE. The Public in general are so willing to overlook Defects, and applaud wherever they can, that to complain of, or be angry at the Few who seek for, and wish to find, Errors only, can proceed alone from the Self-love which is so inherent and irritable in all bosoms, and so difficult to subdue.

To enumerate all the Obstacles encountered and overcome in bringing this Comedy on the English Stage, would be to indulge this Vanity; which it is every wise Man's Pride, and every prudent Man's Interest to resist. It may, however, afford some Pleasure to be informed, that, finding it impossible to procure a Copy of the original French, though a Journey to Paris was undertaken expressly for that Purpose, the Copy made use of in the composing *The Follies of a Day*, was taken by Memory, only, during eight or nine Representations; that I furnished the Plot, Incidents, Entrances, and Exits, and gave some other occasional Hints; that the remainder was the Work of a young Frenchman, whose Talents and whose Heart are an Ornament and an Honour to his Country; and that, after it was brought to *England* and received by Mr. *Harris*, it was translated, cast, copied, recopied, studied, and, in one of its longest Parts, re-studied, and played in little more than a Month. The Attention and Care of Mr. *Harris*, and the Merits of the respective Performers in playing, as they did, under such Circumstances, need not my Encomiums. Had the Town known the peculiar Exertions, of those especially who performed the longest and most essential Parts, the applause would have been endless. From me they are justly entitled to my warmest and sincerest Thanks.

UPPER MARY-LE-BONE STREET.
FEB. 21, 1785.

Prologue

Spoken by MR. DAVIES.

To-night, a Child of Chance is hither brought,
Who could be neither *borrow'd, begg'd,* nor *bought;*
Nay, so alert was said to be the Droll,
'Twas well affirm'd he was not to be *stole;*
But hence dispatch'd, back'd by Appollo's warrant,
A messenger has *kidnapp'd* this Wag-errant;
Poetic Fugitive, has hither dragg'd him,
And, safely here arriv'd, has now ungagg'd him,
To plead before this Court, his whole amenance;
Where, should you sentence him to public Penance,
Oh, sad reverse! how would he foam and fret,
And sigh for Paris and his sweet *Soubrette*!
Where twice ten thousand tongues are proud to greet him,
And wing'd Applause, on tip-toe, stands to meet him;
Where the grim Guard, in nightly rapture, stands,
And grounds his musquet to get at his hands;
Where the retentive Pitt, all prone t'adore him,
Repeat his *Bon mots* half a bar before him;
While every *Bel-Esprit*, at every hit,
Grows fifty-fold more conscious of his Wit.

If *far fetch'd and dear bought* give Trifles worth,
Sure you'll applaud our FIGARO's second birth.
Nought of his present merit must we say;
Bear but in mind, OUR Day's a SPANISH Day.
Cupid, in warmer Climes, urg'd by the Grape,
Calls not each petty violence a Rape!
But oft his Votaries leaves intoxicate,
Hence FIGARO himself is illegitimate.

Sanction'd by you, howe'er, this little Blot,
so much in fashion, will be soon forgot;

That Signature which each kind hand bestows,
Shall make him well receiv'd where'er he goes!

Dramatis Personae[1]

COUNT ALMAVIVA,	*Mr. Lewis.*
DON GUZMAN, [Don Gusman Brid'oison]	*Mr. Quick.*
DOCTOR BARTHOLO,	*Mr. Wilson.*
FIGARO,	*Mr. Bonnor.*
ANTONIO,	*Mr. Edwin.*
BASIL, [Basile]	*Mr. Wewitzer.*
DOUBLE FEE, [Double-Main]	*Mr. Thompson.*
BOUNCE, [Grippe-Soleil]	*Mr. Stevens.*
COURIER,	*Mr. Jones.*
CRIER OF THE COURT,	*Mr. Bates.*
SERVANT,	*Mr. Newton.*
PAGE,	*Mrs. Martyr.*
COUNTESS,	*Mrs. Bates.*
MARCELINA, [Marceline]	*Mrs. Webb.*
AGNES, [Fanchette]	*Miss Wewitzer.*
SUSAN, [Suzanne]	*Miss Younge.*

Counsellors, Guards, Vassals.

Act I

[SCENE, the Castle of Count ALMAVIVA.
FIGARO *and* SUSAN:
FIGARO *measuring the chamber with a wand.*]

FIGARO: Eighteen feet by twenty-six, good.

SUSAN: What art thou so busy about?

FIGARO: Measuring, to try if the bed our noble Lord intends to give us will stand well here.

1. Holcroft has made a number of alterations to the original French names. Some are minor: for instance, Suzanne becomes Susan, Basile becomes Basil, and Marceline becomes Marcelina. Others are more significant: Double-Main becomes Doublefee; Grippe-Soleil becomes Bounce; Fanchette becomes Agnes; and Chérubin becomes Hannibal. For the purposes of this edition, the name Hannibal has been discarded in favour of Cherubin. Otherwise Holcroft's anglicised names have been retained. The original French names are given in square brackets in the dramatis personæ.

SUSAN: In this chamber!

FIGARO: Yes.

SUSAN: I won't lie in this chamber.

FIGARO: Why so?

SUSAN: I tell you I won't lie in this chamber.

FIGARO: Well but –

SUSAN: I don't like it.

FIGARO: Your reason.

SUSAN: What if I have no reason? – What if I don't chuse to give my reason?

FIGARO: Ah, ah! – Thus it is when once they think they have us fast.

SUSAN: Are you, or are you not my most obedient very humble servant?

FIGARO: Your slave – [*Bows very low.*]

SUSAN: Oh!

FIGARO: But wherefore take exception to the most convenient room in the whole house?

SUSAN: Yes, yes! – The most convenient! – [*Satirically.*]

FIGARO: If during the night my Lady should be taken ill, she rings her bell, and crack! – in two steps thou art standing at her side. – In the morning when the Lord wakes, he calls, I start, and pop – three skips and I am there.

SUSAN: Very true – And in the morning when my Lord has sent thee on some fine errand of an hour long, he starts from his bed as soon as Mr. Figaro's back is turn'd, and crack! – in three skips – he – [*significantly.*]

FIGARO: He?

SUSAN: Yes – he –

FIGARO: [*Keeps rubbing his forehead and looking at Susan.*] He!

SUSAN: He! – Dost thou feel any thing?

FIGARO: [*Presses his finger and thumb against his forehead.*] Buttons! – In pairs! – Mushrooms sprout not so suddenly – Yes, yes, – it's a fruitful spot.

SUSAN: Thou knowest how our *generous* Count when he by thy help obtained Rosina's hand, and made her Countess of Almaviva, during the first transports of love abolished a certain gothic right –

FIGARO: Of sleeping the first night with every Bride.

SUSAN: Which as Lord of the Manor he could claim.

FIGARO: Know it! – To be sure I do, or I would not have married even my charming Susan in his Domain.

SUSAN: Tired of prowling among the rustic beauties of the neighbourhood he returned to the Castle –

FIGARO: And his wife.

SUSAN: And *thy* wife – [*Figaro stares.*] – Dost thou understand me?

FIGARO: Perfectly!

SUSAN: And endeavours, once more, secretly to purchase from her, a right which he now most sincerely repents he ever parted with.

FIGARO: Most gracious Penitent!

SUSAN: This is what he hints to me every instant, and this the faithful Basil, honest agent of his pleasures, and my most noble music master, every day repeats with my lesson.

FIGARO: Basil!

SUSAN: Basil.

FIGARO: Indeed! But if tough ashen plant or supple-jack twine not round thy lazy sides, Rascal –

SUSAN: Ha, ha, ha! Why wert thou ever wise enough to imagine the portion the Count intends to give us was meant as a reward for thy services?

FIGARO: I think I had some reason to hope as much.

SUSAN: Lord, lord! What great fools are you men of wit!

FIGARO: I believe so.

SUSAN: I am sure so.

FIGARO: Oh that it were possible to deceive this arch Deceiver, this Lord of mine! To lead him into some excellent snare, pocket his gold and –

SUSAN: Hah! Now thou art in thy element – Gold and intrigue – Plots and purses – But let him that diggeth a pit beware he –

FIGARO: I'll try – The Lover's jealousy and the Husband's shame shall not deter me – Your trick, most noble Count, is common place – A thousand blundering Boobies have had art enough to filch a Wife from the side of her sleeping, simple, unsuspecting Spouse, and if he complained, to redress his injuries with a cudgel – But to turn the tables on this Poacher, make him pay for a delicious morsel he shall never taste, infect him with fears for his own honor, to –

SUSAN: [*The bell rings.*] Hark! My Lady is awake – I must run, for she has several times strictly charged me to be the first at her bedside the morning of my marriage.

FIGARO: Why the first?

SUSAN: The old saying tells us, that to meet a young Bride the first on the morning of her wedding-day is lucky to a neglected wife. [*Going.*]

FIGARO: Prithee, my Susan, give me a kiss before thou goest – It will quicken my wits, and lend imagination a new impulse.

SUSAN: To be sure! – But if I kiss my Lover today what will my Husband say to me to morrow? [*Seems to refuse, Figaro kisses her.*] Pshaw Figaro! when wilt thou cease to trifle thus from morning till night. [*Playfully.*]

FIGARO: When I may trifle from night to morning. [*In the same tone.*]

SUSAN: There, there – There's all the kisses I shall give. [*Kisses her hand at him and runs, he pursues to the side.*]

FIGARO: Stop, stop, you cheating little knave; that was not the way you received them. [*Returns.*] A sweet Girl! An Angel! Such wit! Such grace! and so much prudence and modesty too! – I am a happy fellow! – So Mr. Basil! Is it me, Rascal, you mean to practice the tricks of your trade upon? – I'll teach you to put your spoon in my milk – But hold – Dissemble is the word – Feign we ignorance and endeavour to catch them in their own traps – I wondered why the Count, who had made me Steward and Inspector-general of the Castle, should change his mind so suddenly, and want to take me with him on his embassy to Paris, there to institute me his Messenger in ordinary – A cunning contrivance that – He, Plenipotentiary in chief, I, a break-neck Politician, and Susan, Lady of the back-stairs, Ambassadress of the bed-chamber – I dashing through thick and thin and wearing my self to a skeleton, for the good of my most gracious Lord's family, and he labouring, night and day, for the increase of mine – Really, most honorable Count, you are too kind – What to represent his Majesty and me both at once – It's too much, too much by half – A moment's reflection friend Figaro on the events of the day – First, thou must promote the Sports and Feasting already projected, that appearances may not cool, but that thy Marriage may proceed with greater certainty; next, keep off one madam Marcelina, whose liquorish mouth waters at thee, and to whom thou hast given a Promise of Marriage, in default of the repayment of certain borrowed Sums which it would be very convenient to thy affairs never more to mention – Talk of the Devil and –

[*Enter Doctor* BARTHOLO *and* MARCELINA.]

MARCELINA: Good-morrow to Mr. Bridegroom.

FIGARO: Good-morrow to madam Marcelina – What! My old fat friend the Doctor! Are you there?

DOCTOR: Yes, Knave's face.

FIGARO: As witty, I perceive, and no doubt as wise as ever – And have you been complaisant enough to come thus far to see me married?

DOCTOR: To see thee hang'd.

FIGARO: Most kind Doctor – But who takes care of your Mule? I know you have as much mercy on your Beast as you have on your Patient.

DOCTOR: Do you hear him?

FIGARO: And you, gentle Marcelina, do you still wish to marry me – What, because I cannot fall in love with you, would you drive me to hate you? [*Exit* FIGARO.]

DOCTOR: The Rascal will never mend.

MARCELINA: 'Tis you, Doctor, will never mend – You are so eternally wise, dull and slow, that when a Patient has need of your assistance he may die before you get to him, like as formerly your Mistress got married in spite of your precautions.

DOCTOR: Was it to entertain me thus agreeably that you sent for me in such haste from Seville?

MARCELINA: Not entirely for that.

DOCTOR: What then – Is any body ill? Is the Count indisposed?

MARCELINA: No, it is the Countess who is indisposed.

DOCTOR: What the artful, deceitful Rosina? What's her disorder?

MARCELINA: A faithless Husband.

DOCTOR: A very common complaint indeed.

MARCELINA: The Count forsakes her, and falls in love with every fresh face.

DOCTOR: I am glad of it – I am glad of it – I foresaw it – I thought Count Almaviva would revenge the wrongs of Doctor Bartholo.

MARCELINA: After toying with a thousand neighbouring Beauties, he now returns to the castle to terminate the marriage of Susan and Figaro.

DOCTOR: Which he himself has made necessary.

MARCELINA: Oh no – But at which he wishes to act rather as a Principal than an Agent.

DOCTOR: In private with the Bride.

MARCELINA: Even so.

DOCTOR: She I suppose has no great objection.

MARCELINA: Charitable Doctor – Basil, however, her music master, who takes great pains to instruct her, says to the contrary.

DOCTOR: Basil! What is that other Rascal here too? – Why the house is a den of Thieves – What does he do here?

MARCELINA: All the mischief he can – He persecutes me with his odious love unceasingly; I cannot get rid of him.

DOCTOR: Marry him – I'll answer for his cure.

MARCELINA: That's what he wants – But pray Doctor, why will not you get rid of me by the same means? The claims of Justice and oaths out of number should –

DOCTOR: So so so so – What is the matrimonial furor come upon you again?

MARCELINA: Our long lost son, Fernando! the dear pledge of my virgin love! were he but found, perhaps –

DOCTOR: And so you sent for me to hear this stale rhodomontade?

MARCELINA: And are you, now you have lost your Rosina, as inflexible and unjust as ever?

DOCTOR: Pshaw!

MARCELINA: Well – Since you are determined never to marry me yourself, will you have the complaisance to aid me in marrying another?

DOCTOR: With all my heart! – With all my heart! –

MARCELINA: Ah! [*Curtsies.*]

DOCTOR: But who? – What miserable Mortal, abandoned of Heaven and Women –

MARCELINA: Who but the amiable, the gay, the ever sprightly Figaro?

DOCTOR: Figaro! That Rascal!

MARCELINA: Youthful and generous!

DOCTOR: As a Highwayman.

MARCELINA: As a Nobleman –

DOCTOR: Pshaw, impossible! what on the very day he is going to marry another?

MARCELINA: Things more improbable have come to pass.

DOCTOR: But your motive?

MARCELINA: For you, Doctor, I have no secrets.

DOCTOR: Women seldom have for Doctors.

MARCELINA: I own our sex, though timid, is ardent in the pursuit of pleasure. There is, in all our bosoms, a small still voice which unceasing cries – Woman, be as beautiful as thou canst, as virtuous as thou wilt, but, at all events, be conspicuous, be talk'd about; for thy Wisdom, if thou hast it – if not for thy Folly.

DOCTOR: She utters Oracles – Well, well, accomplish this, and I will engage you shall be talk'd about.

MARCELINA: We must endeavour to work upon Susan by fear and shame, for the more obstinately she refuses the amorous offers of the Count, the more effectually she will serve our purpose; disappointment and revenge will lead him to support my cause, and as he is sovereign Judge in his own Lordship, his power may make Figaro's promise of marriage to me valid.

DOCTOR: Promise – Has he given you any such promise?

MARCELINA: A written one – You shall see it.

DOCTOR: By Galen, this is excellent! The rascal shall marry my old Housekeeper, and I shall be revenged for the tricks he lately played me, and the hundred pistoles he contrived to cheat me of.

MARCELINA: [*Transported.*] Yes, yes, Doctor! I shall have him! He shall marry me! He shall marry me!

[*Enter* SUSAN, *with a gown on her arm, and a cap and riband of the Countess, in her hand.*]

SUSAN: Marry you! Who is to marry you? Not my Figaro, I assure you, madam.

MARCELINA: Why not me, as soon as you, madam?

SUSAN: Indeed! your most obedient, madam.

DOCTOR: [*Aside.*] so now for a merry scolding match. – We were saying, handsome Susan, how happy Figaro must be in such a Bride –

[SUSAN *curtsies to the* DOCTOR.]

MARCELINA: Not to mention the secret satisfaction of my Lord the Count.

SUSAN: Dear madam, you are so abundantly kind.

MARCELINA: Not so abundant in kindness, as a liberal young Lord – But I own it is very natural, he should partake the pleasures he so freely bestows upon his Vassals.

SUSAN: [*Half angry.*] Partake – Happily madam, your Envy is as obvious, and your Slander as false, as your Claims on Figaro are weak and ill founded.

MARCELINA: If they are weak, it is because I wanted the art to strengthen them, after the manner of madam.

SUSAN: Yet madam has ever been reckoned a mistress of her art.

MARCELINA: I hope, madam, I shall always have your good word, *madam.* [*Curtsies.*]

SUSAN: Oh, I can assure you, madam, you have nothing to regret on that score, *madam.* [*Curtsies mockingly.*]

MARCELINA: The young Lady is really a very pretty kind of Person – [*With a contemptuous side glance.*]

SUSAN: Oh yes. [*Mimicking.*] The young Lady is at least as pretty as the old Lady.

MARCELINA: And very respectable.

SUSAN: Respectable! Oh no, that is the characteristic of a Duenna.

MARCELINA: A Duenna! A Duenna!

DOCTOR: [*Coming between them.*] Come, come –

MARCELINA: I – I – You – your very humble servant, *madam.*

SUSAN: Your most devoted, *madam.*

MARCELINA: Farewell, *madam.*

[*Exeunt* DOCTOR *and* MARCELINA.]

SUSAN: Adieu, *madam* – this old Sibyl, because she formerly tormented the infancy of my Lady, thinks she has a right to domineer over every person in the Castle – I declare I have forgot what I came for.

[SUSAN *hangs the gown on a great arm chair that stands in the room, and keeps the cap and riband of the Countess in her hand.*]

[*Enter* CHERUBIN *the Page, running.*]

SUSAN: So, Youth! What do you do here?

PAGE: Good morrow, Susan – I have been watching these two hours to find you alone.

SUSAN: Well, what have you to say, now you have found me?

PAGE: [*Childishly amorous.*] How does your beauteous Lady do, Susan?

SUSAN: Very well.

PAGE: [*Poutingly.*] Do you know, Susan, my Lord is going to send me back to my Pappa and Mamma?

SUSAN: Poor Child!

PAGE: Child indeed! – Umph! – And if my charming God-mother, your dear Lady, cannot obtain my pardon, I shall soon be deprived of the pleasure of your company, Susan.

SUSAN: Upon my word! – He is toying all day long with Agnes, and is, moreover, in love with my Lady, and then comes to tell me he shall be deprived of my company. [*Aside.*]

PAGE: Agnes is good natured enough to listen to me, and that is more than you are, Susan, for all I love you so.

SUSAN: Love me! – Why you amorous little villain, you are in love with every Woman you meet.

PAGE: So I am, Susan, and I can't help it – if no-body is by, I swear it to the trees, the waters, and the winds, nay, to myself – yesterday I happened to meet Marcelina –

SUSAN: Marcelina! Ha! ha! ha! ha! ha!

PAGE: Why, she is a Woman, Susan.

SUSAN: Ha! ha! ha! ha! ha!

PAGE: And what's more, unmarried! Oh how sweet are the words Woman, Maiden, and Love, in my ear!

SUSAN: Ha! ha! ha! – He's bewitch'd! – And what is the Count going to send you from the Castle for?

PAGE: Last night, you must know, he caught me in the chamber with Agnes; begone, said he, thou little –

SUSAN: Little what?

PAGE: Lord, he called me such a name, I can't for shame repeat it before a woman.

SUSAN: And what were you doing in the chamber of Agnes?

PAGE: Teaching her her part.

SUSAN: Her part?

PAGE: Yes, the love scene, you know, she is to play in the Comedy this evening.

SUSAN: Which my Lord would chuse to teach her himself. [*Aside.*]

PAGE: Agnes is very kind, Susan.

SUSAN: Well, well, I'll tell the Countess what you say – But you are a little more circumspect in her presence.

PAGE: Ah Susan, she is a Divinity! How noble is her manner! Her very smiles are awful!

SUSAN: That is to say, you can take what liberties you please with such people as me.

PAGE: Oh how do I envy thy happiness, Susan! Always near her! Dressing her every morning! Undressing her every evening! Putting her to bed! Touching her! Looking at her! Speaking to – What is it thou has got there, Susan?

SUSAN: [*Counterfeiting the amorous air, and animated tone of the* PAGE.] It is the fortunate riband of the happy cap, which at night enfolds the auburn ringlets of the beauteous Countess.

PAGE: Give it me – Nay, give it me – I will have it.

SUSAN: But I say you shan't. [*The* PAGE *snatches it, and runs round the great chair, dodging* SUSAN.] Oh my riband!

PAGE: Be as angry as thou wilt, but thou shalt never have it again, thou shouldst have one of my eyes rather.

SUSAN: I can venture to predict, young gentleman, that three or four years hence, thou wilt be one of the most deceitful veriest Knaves –

PAGE: If thou dost not hold thy tongue, Susan, I'll kiss thee into the bargain.

SUSAN: Kiss me! – Do not come near me, if thou lov'st thy ears – I say, beg my Lord to forgive you, indeed! No I assure you – I shall say to him, you do very right, my Lord, to send this little Rascal packing, who is not only in love with my Lady, but wants to kiss other folks into the bargain.

PAGE: How can I help it, Susan!? Here, take this paper.

SUSAN: For what?

PAGE: It contains a Song I have written on thy beauteous Lady, my charming God-mother.

COUNT: [*Without.*] Jaquez.

PAGE: Ah! I'm undone! – 'Tis my Lord!

[*The* PAGE *crouches down, and hides himself behind* SUSAN*'s petticoats and the great chair.*]

[*Enter Count* ALMAVIVA. PAGE *remains hid behind the great chair.*]

COUNT: So, charming Susan, have I found thee at last? But thou seemest frightened my little Beauty.

SUSAN: Consider, my Lord, if any body should come and catch you here –

COUNT: That would be rather mal-a-propos; but there's no great danger.

[*The* COUNT *offers to kiss* SUSAN.]

SUSAN: Fie, my Lord! [*The* COUNT *seats himself in the great chair, and endeavours to pull Susan on his knee, who resists.*]

COUNT: Thou knowest, my charming Susan, the King has done me the honour to appoint me Ambassador to the court of Paris. I shall take Figaro with me, and give him a very – *excellent* post; and as it is the duty of a Wife to follow her Husband, we shall then have every opportunity we could wish.

SUSAN: I really don't understand you, my Lord. I thought your affection for my Lady, whom you took so much pains to steal from her old Guardian, Dr. Bartholo, and for love of whom you generously abolished a certain vile privilege. –

COUNT: For which all the young girls are very sorry; are they not?

SUSAN: No indeed, my Lord – I thought, my Lord, I say –

COUNT: Prithee say no more, my sweet Susan, but promise thou wilt meet me this evening, at twilight, by the Pavilion in the garden; and be certain, that if thou wilt but grant me this small favour, nothing thou canst ask shall –

BASIL: [*Without.*] He is not in his own room.

COUNT: Heavens! Here's somebody coming! Where can I hide! Is there no place here?

[*The* COUNT *runs to get behind the great chair,* SUSAN *keeps between him and the* PAGE, *who steals away as the* COUNT *advances, leaps into the great chair, with his legs doubled under him, and is covered over with the Countess's gown, by* SUSAN.]

[*Enter* BASIL.]

BASIL: Ah, Susan, Good morrow – Is my lord the Count here?

SUSAN: Here! What should he be here for?

BASIL: Nay, there would be no miracle in it if he were; would there, hey gentle Susan? [*Smiles and leers at her.*]

SUSAN: It would be a greater miracle to see you honest.

BASIL: Figaro is in search of him.

SUSAN: Then he is in search of the man who wishes most to injure him – yourself excepted.

BASIL: It is strange, that a man should injure the Husband by obliging the Wife. [*The* COUNT *peeps from behind the great chair.*]

COUNT: I shall hear, now, how well he pleads my cause.

BASIL: For my part, Marriage being, of all serious things, the greatest Farce, I imagined –

SUSAN: All manner of wickedness.

BASIL: That though you are obliged to fast to-day, you might be glad to feed to-morrow, grace being first duly said.

SUSAN: Be gone, and do not shock my ears with your vile principles.

BASIL: Yes, my Susan, but you must not suppose I am the dupe of these fine appearances. I know it isn't Figaro who is the great obstacle to my Lord's happiness, but a certain beardless Page, whom I surprised here, this morning, looking for you as I entered.

SUSAN: I wish you would be gone, you wicked – Devil.

BASIL: Wicked Devil! Ah, one is a wicked Devil for not shutting one's eyes.

SUSAN: I wish you would be gone, I tell you.

BASIL: Was it not for you that he wrote the Song, which he goes chanting up and down the house, at every instant?

SUSAN: O yes! For me, to be sure!

BASIL: At least it was either for you, or your Lady.

SUSAN: What next?

BASIL: Why really, when he sits at table, he does cast certain very significant glances towards a beauteous Countess, who shall be nameless – But let him beware! If my Lord catches him at his tricks, he'll make him dance without music.

SUSAN: Nobody, but such a wicked creature as you, could ever invent such scandalous tales, to the ruin of a poor Youth, who has unhappily fallen into his Lord's disgrace.

BASIL: I invent! Why it is in every body's mouth.

[*The* COUNT *discovers himself, and comes forward.*]

COUNT: How! In every body's mouth!

BASIL: Zounds.

COUNT: Run, Basil, let him have fifty pistoles and a horse given him, and sent back to his friends instantly.

BASIL: I'm very sorry, my Lord, I happened to speak –

SUSAN: I'm quite suffocated.

[SUSAN *seems almost ready to faint, the* COUNT *supports her, and* BASIL *assists.*]

COUNT: Let us seat her in this great chair, Basil.

SUSAN: [*Frightened, and exclaims*] No! – I won't sit down! – [*After a pause.*] – This wicked fellow has ruined the poor boy.

BASIL: I assure you, my Lord, what I said, was only meant to sound Susan.

COUNT: No matter, he shall depart! A little, wanton, impudent Rascal, that I meet at every turning – No longer ago than yesterday I surprised him with the Gardiner's daughter.

BASIL: Agnes?

COUNT: In her very bed chamber.

SUSAN: Where my Lord happened to have business himself.

COUNT: Hem! – I was going there to seek your uncle Antonio, Susan, my drunken Gardiner; I knock'd at the door, and waited some time; at last Agnes came, with confusion in her countenance – I entered, cast a look round, and perceiving a kind of long cloak, or Curtain, or some such thing, approach'd, and without seeming to take the least notice, drew it gently aside, thus – Hey!

BASIL: Zounds! [*The* COUNT, *during his speech, approaches the arm chair, and acting his description draws aside the gown that hides the* PAGE. *They all stand motionless with surprise, for some time.*]

COUNT: Why, this is a better trick than t'other!

BASIL: No! – I won't sit down! [*Mimicking* SUSAN.]

COUNT: [*To Susan.*] And so it was to receive this pretty Youth, that you were so desirous of being alone – And you, you little Villain, what you don't intend to mend your manners then? But forgetting all respect for your friend Figaro, and for the Countess your Godmother, likewise, you are endeavouring here to seduce her favourite woman! I, however [*Turning towards* BASIL.] shall not suffer Figaro, a man – whom – I *esteem – sincerely* – to fall the Victim of such deceit – Did he enter with you, Basil?

BASIL: No, my Lord.

SUSAN: There is neither Victim nor deceit in the case, my Lord. He was here when you entered.

COUNT: I hope that's false: his greatest Enemy could not wish him so much mischief.

SUSAN: Knowing that you were angry with him, the poor Boy came running to me, begging me to solicit my Lady in his favour, in hopes she might engage you to forgive him; but was so terrified, as soon as he heard you coming, that he hid himself in the great Chair.

COUNT: A likely story – I sat down in it, as soon as I came in.

PAGE: Yes, my Lord, but I was then trembling behind it.

COUNT: That's false, again, for I hid myself behind it, when Basil entered.

PAGE: [*Timidly.*] Pardon me, my Lord, but as you approach'd, I retired, and crouched down as you now see me.

COUNT: [*Angrily.*] It's a little Serpent that glides into every crevice – And he has been listening too to our discourse!

PAGE: Indeed, my Lord, I did all I could not to hear a word.

COUNT: [*To* SUSAN.] There is no Figaro, no Husband for you, however.

BASIL: Somebody is coming; get down.

[*Enter the* COUNTESS, FIGARO, AGNES, and VASSALS, *in their holiday cloaths.*

FIGARO *carrying the nuptial cap – The* COUNT *runs and plucks the* PAGE *from the great chair, just as they enter.*]

COUNT: What! Would you continue crouching there before the whole world? [*The* COUNT *and* COUNTESS *salute.*]

FIGARO: We are come, my Lord, to beg a favour, which we hope, for my Lady's sake, you will grant. [*Aside to* SUSAN.] Be sure to second what I say.

SUSAN: It will end in nothing. [*Aside.*]

FIGARO: No matter: let us try, at least. [*Aside.*]

COUNTESS: You see, my Lord, I am supposed to have a much greater degree of influence over you than I really possess.

COUNT: Oh no, my Lady; not an atom, I assure you.

FIGARO: [*Presenting the cap to the* COUNT.] Our petition is, that the Bride may have the honor of receiving from our worthy Lord's hand, this Nuptial-Cap; ornamented with half-blown roses, and white ribands, Symbols of the purity of his intentions.

COUNT: Do they mean to laugh at me? [*Aside.*]

FIGARO: And as you have been kindly pleased to abolish that abominable right, which, as Lord of the Manor, you might have claimed, permit us, your Vassals, to celebrate your praise, in a rustic Chorus I have prepared for this occasion. The Virtues of so good a master should not remain unsung.

COUNT: A Lover, a Poet, and a Musician! – These titles, Figaro, might perhaps merit our indulgence, if –

COUNTESS: Let me beg, my Lord, you will not deny their request: in the name of that love you once had for me.

COUNT: And have still, Madam.

FIGARO: Join with me, my friends.

OMNES: My Lord.

SUSAN: Why should your Lordship refuse Eulogiums which you merit so well?

COUNT: Oh the Traitress. [*Aside.*] Well, well, – I consent.

FIGARO: Look at her, my Lord: never could a more beauteous Bride better prove the greatness of the sacrifice you have made.

SUSAN: Oh do not speak of my Beauty, but of his Lordship's Virtues.

COUNT: My Virtues! – Yes, yes, – I see they understand each other. [*Aside.*] who can tell me where is Marcelina?

AGNES: I met her, my Lord, just now, in the close walk by the park wall, along with Doctor Bartholo. She seemed in a passion, and the Doctor tried to pacify her. I heard her mention my Cousin Figaro's name.

COUNT: [*Aside.*] No Cousin yet, my dear; and perhaps never may be.

AGNES: [*Pointing to the* PAGE.] Have you forgiven what happened yesterday, my Lord?

COUNT: [*Afraid lest the* COUNTESS *should hear, and chucking* AGNES *under the chin.*] Hush!

FIGARO: [*To the* PAGE.] What's the matter, young rogue? What makes you so silent?

SUSAN: He is sorrowful because my Lord is going to send him from the castle.

OMNES: Oh pray, my Lord!

COUNTESS: Let me beg you will forgive him.

COUNT: He does not deserve to be forgiven.

COUNTESS: Consider, he is so young.

COUNT: [*Half aside.*] Not so young, perhaps, as you suppose.

PAGE: My Lord certainly has not ceded away the right to pardon.

SUSAN: And if he had, that would certainly be the first he would *secretly* endeavour to reclaim. [*Looking significantly at the* COUNT *and* FIGARO *in turns.*]

COUNT: [*Understanding her.*] No doubt: no doubt.

PAGE: My conduct, my Lord, may have been indiscreet, but I can assure your Lordship, that never the least word shall pass my lips –

COUNT: [*Interrupting him.*] Enough, enough – Since every body begs for him, I must grant – I shall moreover give him a Company in my Regiment.

OMNES: Thanks noble Count.

COUNT: But on condition that he depart immediately for Catalonia to join the Corps.

OMNES: Oh my Lord?

FIGARO: To morrow my Lord.

COUNT: To day! It shall be so. [*To the* PAGE.] Take leave of your Godmother, and beg her protection. [*The* PAGE *kneels to the* COUNTESS *with a sorrowful air. As he approaches to kneel, he goes very slowly and* FIGARO *gently pushes him forward.*]

FIGARO: Go, go, Child; go.

COUNTESS: [*With great emotion.*] Since – it is not possible – to obtain leave – for you to remain here to day, depart, young man, and follow the noble career which lies before you – Forget not those with whom you have spent some of the first years of your life, and among whom you have friends who wish you every success – Go where Fortune and Glory call – Be obedient, polite, and brave, and be certain we shall take part in your Prosperity. [*Raises him.*]

COUNT: You seem agitated Madam.

COUNTESS: How can I help it, recollecting the perils to which his youth must be exposed? He has been bred in the same house with me, is of the same kindred, and is likewise my Godson.

COUNT: [*Aside.*] Basil I see was in the right. – [*Turns to the* PAGE.] Go; kiss Susan for the last time. [*The* PAGE *and* SUSAN *approach,* FIGARO *steps between them and intercepts the* PAGE.]

FIGARO: Oh! There's no occasion for kissing, my Lord: he'll return in the winter, and in the mean time he may kiss me. – The scene must now be changed my delicate Youth: you must not run up stairs and down, into the Women's Chambers, play at Hunt-the-slipper, steal Cream, suck Oranges, and live upon Sweetmeats. Instead of that, Zounds! You must look bluff! Tan your face! Handle your musket! Turn to the right! Wheel to the left! And march to Glory. – At least if you are not stopt short by a Bullet.

SUSAN: Fie, Figaro.

COUNTESS: [*Terrified.*] What a Prophecy!

FIGARO: Were I a Soldier I would make some of them scamper – But, come, come, my friends; let us prepare our feast against the evening. Marcelina I hear intends to disturb our Diversions.

COUNT: That she will I can assure you. [*Aside.*] I must go and send for her. [*Going.*]

COUNTESS: You will not leave us, my Lord?

COUNT: I am undrest, you see.

COUNTESS: We shall see nobody but our own servants.

COUNT: I must do what you please. Wait for me in the study, Basil.

[*Exeunt* COUNT, COUNTESS, *and* VASSALS. *Manent* FIGARO, BASIL, *and* PAGE.]

FIGARO: [*Retains the* PAGE.] Come, come; let us study our parts well for the Play in the evening: and do not let us resemble those Actors who never play so ill as on the first night of a Piece; when Criticism is most watchful to detect Errors, and when they ought to play the best – *We* shall not have an opportunity of playing better to-morrow.

BASIL: My part is more difficult than you imagine.

FIGARO: And you may be rewarded for it, in a manner your little expect. [*Aside.*]

PAGE: You forget, Figaro, that I am going.

FIGARO: And you wish to stay? [*In the same sorrowful tone.*]

PAGE: [*Sighs.*] Ah yes,

FIGARO: Follow my advice, and so thou shalt.

PAGE: How, how?

FIGARO: Make no murmuring, but clap on your boots, and seem to depart; gallop as far as the Farm, return to the Castle on foot, enter by the back way, and hide yourself till I can come to you.

PAGE: And who shall teach Agnes her part, then?

FIGARO: Oh oh!

BASIL: Why, what the devil have you been about, young Gentleman, for these eight days past, during which you have hardly left her? Take care, take care, or your Scholar will give her Tutor a bad character. – The Pitcher that goes often to the Well –

FIGARO: Listen to the Pedant and his Proverb. – Well, and what says the Wisdom of Nations – *The pitcher that goes often to the well* –

BASIL: Stands a chance, sometime, to return full.

FIGARO: Not so foolish as I thought.

Act II

[SCENE, *the* COUNTESS's *Bed-Chamber.*
A state-bed in the back ground under an Alcove: three doors; one the entrance into the room, another into Susan's room, and the third to the Countess's dressing-room: a large window that opens to the street.
The COUNTESS *seated,* SUSAN *waiting.*]

COUNTESS: Shut the door – And so the Page was hid behind the great chair?

SUSAN: Yes, Madam.

COUNTESS: But how did he happen to be in your room, Susan?

SUSAN: The poor Boy came to beg I would prevail on you to obtain his pardon of my Lord the Count.

COUNTESS: But why did he not come to me himself? I should not have refused him a favour of that kind.

SUSAN: Bashfulness, Madam. *Ah Susan*! said he, *she is a Divinity! How noble is her Manner! Her very smiles are awful.*

COUNTESS: [*Smiling.*] Is that true, Susan?

SUSAN: Can you doubt it, Madam?

COUNTESS: I have always afforded him my protection.

SUSAN: Had you, Madam, but seen him snatch the ribband from me!

COUNTESS: [*Rising.*] Pshaw! Enough of this nonsense – And so my Lord the Count endeavours to seduce you, Susan?

SUSAN: Oh, no indeed, Madam, he does not give himself the trouble to seduce; he endeavours to purchase me: and because I refuse him will certainly prevent my marriage with Figaro, and support the pretentions of Marcelina.

COUNTESS: Fear nothing – We shall have need, however, of a little artifice perhaps; in the execution of which Figaro's assistance may not be amiss.

SUSAN: He will be here, Madam, as soon as my Lord is gone a coursing.

COUNTESS: Your Lord is an ungrateful man, Susan! – An ungrateful man! [*The* COUNTESS *walks up and down the room with some emotion.*] Open the window; I am stifled for want of air – Vows, protestations and tenderness are all forgotten – My Love offends, my Caresses disgust – He thinks his own Infidelities must all be overlook'd, yet my Conduct must be irreproachable.

SUSAN: [*At the window looking into the street.*] Yonder goes my Lord with all his Grooms and Greyhounds.

COUNTESS: To *divert* himself, with hunting a poor timid harmless Hare to death – This, however, will give us time – Somebody knocks, Susan.

SUSAN: For Figaro's the lad, is the lad for me. [*Goes singing to the Door.*]

[*Enter* FIGARO.
He kisses SUSAN*'s hand, she makes signs to him to be more prudent, and points to the* COUNTESS.]

COUNTESS: Well, Figaro, you have heard of my Lord the Count's designs on your young Bride.

FIGARO: Oh yes, my Lady. There was nothing very surprising in the news. My Lord sees a sweet young, lovely – Angel! [SUSAN *curtsies.*] and wishes to have her for himself. Can any thing be more natural? I wish the very same –

COUNTESS: I don't find it so very pleasant, Figaro.

FIGARO: He endeavours to overturn the schemes of those who oppose his wishes: and in this he only follows the example of the rest of the world. I endeavour to do the very same.

SUSAN: But with less probability of success, Figaro.

FIGARO: Follow my advice, and I'll convince you of your mistake.

COUNTESS: Let me hear.

FIGARO: You, my lovely Susan, must appoint the Count to meet him, as he proposed, this evening, by the Pavillion in the Garden.

COUNTESS: How! Figaro! Can you consent?

FIGARO: And why not, Madam?

SUSAN: But if you can, sir, do you think I –

FIGARO: Nay, my Charmer, do not imagine I would wish thee to grant him any thing thou wishest to refuse – But first we must dress up the Page in your cloaths, my dear Susan; he is to be your Representative.

COUNTESS: The Page!

SUSAN: He is gone.

FIGARO: Is he? – Perhaps so. But a whistle from me will bring him back. [*The* COUNTESS *seems pleased.*]

SUSAN: So! Now Figaro's happy! – Plots and Contrivances –

FIGARO: Two! Three! Four at a time! Embarrass'd! Involv'd! Perplex'd! – Leave me to unravel them. I was born to thrive in Courts.

SUSAN: I have heard the Trade of a Courtier is not so difficult as some pretend.

FIGARO: Ask for every thing that falls, seize every thing in your power, and accept every thing that's offered – There is the whole art and mystery in three words.

COUNTESS: Well, but the Count, Figaro?

FIGARO: Permit me, Madam, to manage him – And first, the better to secure *my* property, I shall begin by making him dread the loss of *his own*. – Oh, what pleasure shall I have in cutting out Employment for him during the whole day! – To see him waste that time in jealously watching your conduct, Madam, which he meant to employ in amorous dalliance with my sweet Bride – To behold him running here and there and he does not know where, and hunting a monstrous Shadow, which he dreads to find, yet longs to grasp.

COUNTESS: Surely, Figaro, you are out of your wits.

FIGARO: Pardon, my dear Lady, but it is your good Lord who will soon be out of his wits.

COUNTESS: But as you know him to be so jealous, how will you dare? –

FIGARO: Oh, Madam! Were he not jealous, my scheme would not be worth a doit: but it will now serve a double purpose – The Jewel which Possession has made him neglect, will again become valuable, if once he can be brought to dread its loss.

COUNTESS: To confess the truth, Figaro, your project exactly corresponds with the one I meant to practise – An anonymous Letter must be sent, informing him, that a Gallant, meaning to profit by his neglect –

FIGARO: And absence – is at present with his beauteous Countess – The thing is already done, Madam.

COUNTESS: How! – Have you dared to trifle thus with a Woman of Honor?

FIGARO: Oh, Madam, it is only with a Woman of Honor I should presume to take a liberty like this; least my Joke should happen to prove a Reality.

COUNTESS: [*Smiles.*] You don't want an agreeable excuse, Figaro.

FIGARO: The hour of performing the marriage Ceremony will arrive post haste – he will be disconcerted, and having no good excuse ready, will never venture in your presence, Madam, to oppose our union.

SUSAN: But if he will not, Marcelina will; and thou wilt be condemned to pay –

FIGARO: Poh! Thou hast forgot the Count is our Judge! – And, after being entrapp'd at the rendezvous, will he condemn us, thinkest thou? – But come, come, we must be quick – I'll send the Page hither to be dress'd – We must not lose a moment. [*Exit* FIGARO.]

COUNTESS: [*Examining her head dress in a pocket looking-glass.*] What a hideous cap this is, Susan; its quite awry – This Youth who is coming –

SUSAN: Ah, Madam! Your Beauty needs not the addition of Art in his eyes.

COUNTESS: And my hair too – I assure you, Susan, I shall be very severe with him.

SUSAN: [*Smoothing the* COUNTESS's *hair.*] Let me spread this Curl a little, Madam – Oh, pray Madam, make him sing the song he has written.

[SUSAN *throws the song into the* COUNTESS's *lap, which the* PAGE *had given her.*]

COUNTESS: I shall tell him of all the complaints I hear against him.

SUSAN: Oh Yes Madam; I can see you will scold him, heartily.

COUNTESS: [*Seriously.*] What do you say, Susan?

SUSAN: [*Goes to the door.*] Come; come in Mr. Soldier.

[*Enter* PAGE.
SUSAN *pretends to threaten him by signs.*]

PAGE: Um – [*Pouts aside.*]

COUNTESS: Well, young gentleman, [*With assumed severity.*] – How innocent he looks, Susan! [*Aside to* SUSAN.]

SUSAN: And how bashful, Madam!

COUNTESS: [*Resuming her serious air.*] Have you reflected on the duties of your new Profession?

[*The* PAGE *imagines the* COUNTESS *is angry, and timidly draws back.*]

SUSAN: [*Aside to the* PAGE.] Ay, ay, young Rake, I'll tell all I know. – [*Returns to the* COUNTESS.] Observe his downcast eyes, Madam, and long eyelashes. – [*Aside to the* PAGE.] Yes, Hypocrite, I'll tell.

COUNTESS: [*Seeing the* PAGE *more and more fearful.*] Nay, – don't – be terrified – I – Come nearer.

SUSAN: [*Pushing him towards the* COUNTESS.] Advance, Modesty.

COUNTESS: Poor Youth, he is quite affected – I am not angry with you; I was only going to speak to you on the duties of a Soldier – Why do you seem so sorrowful?

PAGE: Alas, Madam, I may well be sorrowful! Being, as I am, obliged to leave a Lady so gentle and so kind –

SUSAN: And so beautiful – [*In the same tone and half aside.*]

PAGE: Ah, yes! [*Sighs.*]

SUSAN: [*Mimicking.*] Ah, yes! – Come, come, let me try on one of my Gowns upon you – Come here – Let us measure – I declare the little Villain is not so tall as I am.

PAGE: Um – [*Pouts.*]

SUSAN: Turn about – Let me untie your cloak. [SUSAN *takes off the* PAGE'S *cloak.*]

COUNTESS: But suppose somebody should come?

SUSAN: Dear, my Lady, we are not doing any harm – I'll lock the door, however, for fear – [*The* PAGE *casts a glance or two at the* COUNTESS, SUSAN *returns.*] Well! Have you nothing to say to my beauteous Lady, and your charming God-mother?

PAGE: [*Sighs.*] Oh, yes! That I am sure I shall love her as long as I live!

COUNTESS: Esteem, you mean.

PAGE: Ye – ye – yes – Es – teem! I should have said.

SUSAN: [*Laughs.*] Yes, yes, Esteem! The poor Youth overflows with Es – teem and Aff – ection – and-

PAGE: Um! [*Aside to* SUSAN.]

SUSAN: Nia, nia, nia, [*Mocking the* PAGE.] – Dear Madam, do make him sing those good-for-nothing Verses.

COUNTESS: [*Takes the verses* SUSAN *gave her, from her pocket.*] Pray who wrote them?

SUSAN: [*Pointing to the* PAGE.] Look, Madam, look! His sins rise in his face – Nobody but an Author could look so silly –

COUNTESS: Come, sing.

SUSAN: Ah, the bashful Scribbler!

SONG.

To the Winds, to the Waves, to the Woods I complain;
  Ah, well-a-day! My poor heart!
They hear not my Sighs, and they heed not my pain;
  Ah, well-a-day! My poor heart!

The name of my Goddess I 'grave on each Tree;
  Ah, well-a-day! My poor heart!
'Tis I wound the bark, but Love's arrows wound me;
  Ah, well-a-day! My poor heart!

The Heav'ns I view with their azure bright skies;
  Ah, well-a-day! My poor heart!
But Heaven to me are her still brighter eyes:
  Ah, well-a-day! My poor heart!

To the Sun's morning splendor the poor Indian bows;
  Ah, well-a-day! My poor heart!
But I dare not worship where I pay my vows:
  Ah, well-a-day! My poor heart!

His God each morn rises and he can adore;
  Ah, well-a-day! My poor heart!
But my Goddess to me must soon never rise more:
  Ah, well-a-day! My poor heart![1]

[*During the song the* COUNTESS *is evidently affected by the Passion with which the* PAGE *sings.*]

SUSAN: Now let us try whether one of my Caps –

COUNTESS: There is one of mine lies on my dressing-table. [*Exit* SUSAN *to the dressing room of the* COUNTESS.] – Is your Commission made out?

PAGE: Oh yes, Madam, and given me. Here it is.

[*Presents his commission to the* COUNTESS.]

COUNTESS: Already! They have made haste I see! They are not willing to lose a moment – Their hurry has made them even forget to affix the Seal.

SUSAN: [*Returns.*] The Seal! To what, Madam?

COUNTESS: His commission.

SUSAN: So soon!

COUNTESS: I was observing, there has been no time lost. [*Returns the* PAGE *his Commission; he sticks it in his girdle.*]

SUSAN: Come – [*Makes the* PAGE *kneel down, and puts him on the cap.*] what a pretty little Villain it is! I declare I am jealous: see if he is not handsomer than I am! Turn about – There – What's here? – The riband! – So, so, so! Now all is out! I'm glad of it – I told my young Gentleman I would let you know his thievish tricks, Madam.

COUNTESS: Fetch me some black patches Susan.

[*Exit* SUSAN *to her own chamber.*]

1. Holcroft appears to have 'borrowed' the opening verses of the song from Orpheus's Act I lament in Gluck's opera *Orfeo ed Euridice* (1762).

[*The* COUNTESS *and the* PAGE *remain mute for a considerable time during which the* PAGE *looks at the* COUNTESS *with great passion, though with the bashful side glances natural to his character – The* COUNTESS *pretends not to observe him, and visibly makes several efforts to overcome her own feelings.*]

COUNTESS: And – and – so – you – you are sorry – to leave us?

PAGE: Ye – yes – Madam.

COUNTESS: [*Observing the* PAGE*'s heart so full that he is ready to burst into tears.*] 'Tis that good-for-nothing Figaro who has frightened the child with his prognostics.

PAGE: [*Unable to contain himself any longer.*] N-o-o-o indee-ee-eed, Madam, I-I-am o-on-only-grieved to part from-so dear a-La-a-ady.

COUNTESS: [*Takes out her handkerchief and wipes his eyes.*] Nay, but don't weep, don't weep – Come, come, be comforted.

[*A knocking is heard at the* COUNTESS*'s chamber door.*]

Who's there? [*In an authoritative tone.*]

[*The* COUNT *speaks without.*]

COUNT: Open the door, my Lady.

COUNTESS: Heavens! It is the Count! – I am ruined! – if he finds the Page here after receiving Figaro's anonymous Letter I shall be for ever lost! – What imprudence!

COUNT: [*Without.*] Why don't you open the door?

COUNTESS: Because – I'm alone.

COUNT: Alone! Who are you talking to then!

COUNTESS: To you, to be sure – How could I be so thoughtless – This villainous Figaro.

PAGE: After the scene of the great chair this morning he will certainly murder me if he finds me here.

COUNTESS: Run into my dressing-room and lock the door on the inside.

[*The* COUNTESS *opens the door to the* COUNT.]

[*Enter the* COUNT.]

COUNT: You did not use to lock yourself in, when you were alone, Madam! Who were you speaking to?

COUNTESS: [*Endeavouring to conceal her agitation.*] To – To Susan, who is rumaging in her own room.

COUNT: But you seem agitated, Madam.

COUNTESS: That is not impossible [*Affecting to take a serious air.*] We were speaking of you.

COUNT: Of me!

COUNTESS: Your jealousy, your indifference, my Lord.

COUNT: I cannot say for indifference, my Lady, and as for jealousy, you know best whether I have any cause.

COUNTESS: My Lord!

COUNT: In short, my Lady, there are people in the world, who are malicious enough to wish to disturb either your repose or mine. I have received private advice that a certain Thing called a Lover –

COUNTESS: Lover!

COUNT: Ay, or Gallant, or any other title you like best, meant to take advantage of my absence, and introduce himself into the Castle.

COUNTESS: If there even were any one audicious enough to make such an attempt, he would find himself disappointed of meeting me; for I shall not stir out of my room to day.

COUNT: What, not to the Wedding?

COUNTESS: I am indisposed.

COUNT: Its lucky then that the Doctor is here.

[*The* PAGE *oversets a table in the* COUNTESS's *dressing-room.*]

COUNTESS: [*Terrified.*] What will become of me? [*Aside.*]

COUNT: What noise is that?

COUNTESS: I heard no noise.

COUNT: No? You must be most confoundedly absent, then.

COUNTESS: [*Affecting to return his irony.*] Oh, to be sure.

COUNT: But there is somebody in your dressing room, Madam.

COUNTESS: Who should there be?

COUNT: That's what I want to know.

COUNTESS: It is Susan, I suppose, putting the chairs and tables to rights.

COUNT: What! Your favourite woman turned house-maid! You told me just now she was in her own room.

COUNTESS: In *her* room, or *my* room it is all one.

COUNT: Really, my Lady, this Susan of yours is a very nimble, convenient kind of person.

COUNTESS: Really, my Lord, this Susan of mine disturbs your quiet very much.

COUNT: Very true, my Lady, so much that I am determined to see her.

COUNTESS: These suspicions are very much to your credit, my Lord.

COUNT: If they are not to your discredit, my Lady, it is very easy to remove them – But I see you mean to trifle with me [*He goes to the* COUNTESS's *dressing-room door, and calls.*] Susan! Susan! If Susan you are, come forth!

COUNTESS: Very well, my Lord! Very well! Would you have the girl come out half undressed? She is trying on one of my left off dresses – To disturb female privacy, in this manner, my Lord, is certainly very unprecedented.

[*During the warmth of this dispute,* SUSAN *comes from her own room, perceives what is passing, and after listening long enough to know how to act, slips, unseen by both, behind the curtains of the bed which stands in the Alcove.*]

COUNT: Well, if she can't come out, she can answer at least. [*Calls.*] Susan! – Answer me, Susan.

COUNTESS: I say, do not answer, Susan! I forbid you to speak a word! – We shall see who she'll obey.

COUNT: But if you are so innocent, Madam, what is the reason for that emotion and perplexity so very evident in your countenance?

COUNTESS: [*Affecting a laugh.*] Emotion and perplexity! Ha! ha! ha! Ridiculous!

COUNT: Well, Madam, be it as ridiculous as it may, I am determined to be satisfied, and I think present appearances give me a sufficient plea. [*Goes to the side of the Scenes and calls.*] Hollo! Who waits there?

COUNTESS: Do, do, my Lord! Expose your jealousy to your very servants! Make yourself and me the jest of the whole world.

COUNT: Why do you oblige me to it? – However, Madam, since you will not suffer that door to be opened, will you please to accompany me while I procure an instrument to force it?

COUNTESS: To be sure, my Lord! To be sure! If you please.

COUNT: And, in order that you may be fully justified, I will make this other door fast [*Goes to* SUSAN*'s chamber door, locks it, and takes the key.*] As to the Susan of the dressing-room, she must have the complaisance to wait my return.

COUNTESS: This behaviour is greatly to your honor, my Lord! [*This speech is heard as they are going through the door, which the* COUNT *locks after him.*]

[*Exeunt*]

[*Enter* SUSAN, *peeping as they go off, then runs to the dressing-room door and calls.*]

SUSAN: Cherubin! – Open the door! Quick! Quick! – It's I, Susan.

[*Enter* PAGE, *frightened.*]

PAGE: Oh Susan!

SUSAN: Oh my poor Mistress!

PAGE: What will become of her?

SUSAN: What will become of my marriage?

PAGE: What will become of me?

SUSAN: Don't stand babbling here, but fly.

PAGE: The doors are all fast, how can I fly?

SUSAN: Don't ask me! Fly!

PAGE: Here's a window open. [*Runs to the window.*] Underneath is a bed of flowers; I'll leap out.

SUSAN: [*Screams.*] You'll break your neck!

PAGE: Better that than ruin my dear Lady – Give me one kiss Susan.

SUSAN: Was there ever seen such a young – [PAGE *kisses her, runs and leaps out of the window, and* SUSAN *shrieks at seeing him.*] Ah! [SUSAN *sinks into a chair, overcome with fear – At last she takes courage, rises, goes with dread towards the window, and after looking out, turns round with her hand upon her heart, a sigh of relief, and a smile expressive of sudden ease and pleasure.*] He is safe! Yonder he runs! – As light and as swift as the winds! – If that Boy does not make some woman's heart ache I'm mistaken. [SUSAN *goes towards the dressing-room door, enters, and peeps out as she is going to shut it.*] And now, my good jealous Count, perhaps, I may teach you to break open doors another time. [*Locks herself in.*]

[*Enter* COUNT, *with a wrenching iron in one hand, and leading in the* COUNTESS *with the other. Goes and examines the door.*]

COUNT: Every thing is as I left it. We now shall come to an eclaircissement.

COUNTESS: But, my Lord! – He'll murder him! [*Aside.*]

COUNT: Now we shall know – Do you still persist in forcing me to break open this door? – I am determined to see who's within.

COUNTESS: Let me beg, my Lord, you'll have a moment's patience! – Hear me only and you shall satisfy your utmost curiosity! – Let me intreat you to be assured, that, however appearances may condemn me, no injury was intended to your honour.

COUNT: Then there is a man?

COUNTESS: No – none of whom you can reasonably entertain the least suspicion.

COUNT: How?

COUNTESS: A jest! – A meer innocent, harmless frolic, for our evening's diversion! Nothing more, upon my Honour! – On my soul!

COUNT: But who – who is it?

COUNTESS: A Child!

COUNT: Let us see your child! – What child?

COUNTESS: The Page.

COUNT: The Page! [*Turns away.*] This damnable Page again? – Thus then is the Letter! – thus are my suspicions realized at last! – I am now no longer astonished, Madam, at your emotion for your pretty Godson this morning! – The whole is unravelled! – Come forth, Viper! [*In great wrath.*]

COUNTESS: [*Terrified and trembling.*] Do not let the Disorder in which you will see him –

COUNT: The Disorder! – The Disorder!

COUNTESS: We were going to dress him in women's cloaths for our evening's diversion –

COUNT: I'll stab him! – I'll! – And this is your indisposition! – This is why you would keep your Chamber all day! False, unworthy Woman! You shall keep it longer than you expected. I'll make him a terrible example of an injured Husband's wrath!

COUNTESS: [*Falling on her knees between the* COUNT *and the door.*] Hold, my Lord, hold! Or let your anger light on me! – I, alone, am guilty! If there be any guilt – Have pity on his youth! His infancy!

COUNT: What! Intercede for him! – On your knees! – And to me! There wanted but this! – I'll rack him! – Rise! – I'll [*Furiously.*]

COUNTESS: Promise me to spare his life!

COUNT: Rise!

[*The* COUNTESS *rises terrified, and sinks into an arm chair ready to faint.*]

COUNTESS: He'll murder him!

COUNT: Come forth, I say, once more; or I'll drag –

[*While the* COUNT *is speaking,* SUSAN *unlocks the door and bolts out upon him.*]

SUSAN: I'll stab him! – I'll rack him!

[*The* COUNTESS, *at hearing* SUSAN's *voice, recovers sufficiently to collect herself, and turns back into her former position to conceal her surprise.*]

COUNT: [*After standing fixed some time, and first looking at* SUSAN *and then at the* COUNTESS.] What a blunder![1] – And can you act astonishment too, Madam? [*Observing the* COUNTESS, *who cannot totally hide her surprise.*]

COUNTESS: [*Attempting to speak.*] I – My Lord –

COUNT: [*Recollecting himself.*] But, perhaps, she was not alone. [*Enters the dressing-room,* COUNTESS *again alarmed,* SUSAN *runs to the* COUNTESS.]

SUSAN: Fear nothing – He is not there – He has jumped out of the window.

COUNTESS: And broke his neck! [*Her terror returns.*]

SUSAN: Hush! [SUSAN *claps herself bolt upright against her Lady, to hide her new disorder from the* COUNT.] Hem! Hem!

[*Re-enter* COUNT, *greatly abashed.*]

COUNT: Nobody there! – I have been to blame – [*Approaching the* COUNTESS.] Madam! – [*With great submission as if going to beg her pardon, but the confusion still visible in her countenance calls up the recollection of all that had just passed, and he bursts out into an exclamation.*] Upon my soul, Madam, you are a most excellent Actress!

SUSAN: And am not I too, my Lord!

COUNT: You see my Confusion, Madam – be generous.

SUSAN: As you have been.

COUNT: Hush! – [*Makes signs to* SUSAN *to take his part.*] My dear Rosina –

COUNTESS: No, no, my Lord! I am no longer that Rosina whom you formerly loved with such affection! – I am now nothing but the poor Countess of Almaviva! A neglected Wife, and not a beloved Mistress.

COUNT: Nay, do not make my humiliation too fevere – [*His suspicions again in part revive.*] But wherefore, my Lady, have you been thus mysterious on this occasion?

COUNTESS: That I might not betray that headlong thoughtless Figaro.

COUNT: What! He wrote the anonymous billet then?

1. Holcroft uses a literal translation ('Here's a seminary!') of the original, 'Quelle école!', a term borrowed from the game of trictrac, when a player forgets to mark his score.

COUNTESS: It was without my knowledge, my Lord.

COUNT: But you were afterwards informed of it?

COUNTESS: Certainly.

COUNT: Who did he give it to?

COUNTESS: Basil –

COUNT: Who sent it me by a Peasant – Indeed, Mr. Basil – Yes, vile Thrummer, thou shalt pay for all!

COUNTESS: But where is the justice of refusing that pardon to others we stand so much in need of ourselves? If ever I could be brought to forgive, it should only be on condition of passing a general amnesty.

COUNT: I acknowledge my guilt. [*The* COUNTESS *stands in the middle of the stage, the* COUNT *a little in the back ground, as if expressive of his timidity, but his countenance shews he is confident of obtaining his pardon –* SUSAN *stands forwarder than either, and her looks are significantly applicable to the circumstances of both parties.*]

SUSAN: To suspect a man in my Lady's dressing-room! –

COUNT: And to be thus severely punished for my suspicion! –

SUSAN: Not to believe my Lady when she *assured* you it was her Woman!

COUNT: Ah! – [*With affected confusion.*] Deign, Madam, once more, to repeat my pardon.

COUNTESS: Have I already pronounced it, Susan?

SUSAN: Not that I heard, Madam.

COUNT: Let the gentle sentence then escape.

COUNTESS: And do you merit it, ungrateful man? [*With tenderness.*]

COUNT: [*Looking at* SUSAN, *who returns his look.*] Certainly, my Lady.

COUNTESS: A fine example I set you, Susan! [*The* COUNT *takes her hand and kisses it.*] Who, hereafter, will dread a Woman's anger? [COUNTESS *turns her head towards* SUSAN, *and laughs as she says this.*]

SUSAN: [*In the same tone.*] Yes, yes, Madam – I observe – Men may well accuse us of frailty.

COUNT: And yet I cannot, for the soul of me, forget the agony, Rosina, in which you seemed to be just now! Your cries, your tears, your – How was it possible, this being a Fiction, you should so suddenly give it the tragic tone of a Reality? – Ha! ha! ha! – So astonishingly natural!

COUNTESS: You see your Page, and I dare say your Lordship was not sorry for the mistake – I'm sure the sight of Susan does not give you offence.

COUNT: Hem! – Offence! Oh! No, no, no – But what's the reason, you malicious little hussey, you did not come when I called?

SUSAN: What! Undress'd, my Lord?

COUNT: But why didn't you answer then?

SUSAN: My Lady forbad me: and good reason she had so to do.

COUNT: Such distraction in your countenance! [*To the* COUNTESS.] Nay, it's not calm even yet!

COUNTESS: Oh you – you fancy so my Lord.

COUNT: Men, I perceive, are poor Politicians – Women make Children of us – Were his Majesty wise, he would name you, and not me, for his Ambassador.

[*Enter* FIGARO, *chearfully: perceives the* COUNT, *who puts on a very serious air.*]

FIGARO: They told me my Lady was indisposed, I ran to enquire, and am very happy to find there was nothing in it.

COUNT: You are very attentive.

FIGARO: It is my duty so to be, my Lord. [*Turns to* SUSAN.] come, come, my Charmer! Prepare for the Ceremony! Go to your Bridesmaids.

COUNT: But who is to guard the Countess in the mean time?

FIGARO: [*Surprised.*] Guard her, my Lord! My Lady seems very well: she wants no guarding.

COUNT: From the Gallant, who was to profit by my absence?

[SUSAN *and the* COUNTESS *make signs to Figaro.*]

COUNTESS: Nay, nay, Figaro, the Count knows all.

SUSAN: Yes, yes, we have told my Lord every thing. – The jest is ended – Its all over.

FIGARO: The jest is ended! – And its all over!

COUNT: Yes – Ended, ended, ended! – And all over – What have you to say to that?

FIGARO: Say, my Lord!

[*The confusion of* FIGARO *arises from not supposing it possible the* COUNTESS *and* SUSAN *should have betrayed him, and when he understands something by their signs, from not knowing how much they have told.*]

COUNT: Ay, say.

FIGARO: I – I – I wish I could say as much of my Marriage.

COUNT: And who wrote the pretty Letter?

FIGARO: Not I, my Lord.

COUNT: If I did not know thou liest, I could read it in thy face.

FIGARO: Indeed, my Lord! – Then it is my face that lies; and not I.

COUNTESS: Pshaw, Figaro! Why should you endeavour to conceal any thing, when I tell you we have confess'd all?

SUSAN: [*Making signs to* FIGARO.] We have told my Lord of the Letter, which made him suspect that the Page, who is far enough off by this, was hid in my Lady's dressing-room, where I myself was lock'd in.

FIGARO: Well, well, since my Lord will have it so, and my Lady will have it so, and you all will have it so, why then so let it be.

COUNT: Still at his Wiles. –

COUNTESS: Why, my Lord, would you oblige him to speak truth, so much against his inclination? [COUNT *and* COUNTESS *walk familiarly up the stage.*]

SUSAN: Hast thou seen the Page?

FIGARO: Yes, yes: you have shook his young joints for him, among you.

[*Enter* ANTONIO, *the Gardiner, with a broken Flower-pot under his arm half drunk.*]

ANTONIO: My Lord – My good Lord – If so be as your Lordship will not have the goodness to have these Windows nailed up, I shall never have a Nosegay fit to give to my Lady – They break all my pots, and spoil my flowers; for they not only throw other Rubbish out of the windows, as they used to do, but they have just now tossed out a Man.

COUNT: A Man! – [*The* COUNT*'s suspicions all revive.*]

ANTONIO: In white stockings! [COUNTESS *and* SUSAN *discover their fears, and make signs to* FIGARO *to assist them if possible.*]

COUNT: Where is the Man? [*Eagerly.*]

ANTONIO: That's what I want to know, my Lord! – I wish I could find him, – I am your Lordship's Gardener; and, tho' I say it, a better Gardener is not to be found in all Spain; – but if Chambermaids are permitted to toss men out of the window to save their own Reputation, what is to become of mine? – It will wither with my flowers to be sure.

FIGARO: Oh fie! What sotting so soon in the morning?

ANTONIO: Why, can one begin one's day's work too early?

COUNT: Your day's work, Sir?

ANTONIO: Your Lordship knows my Niece, there she stands, is to be married to day; and I am sure she would never forgive me if –

COUNT: If you were not to get drunk an hour sooner than usual – But on with your story, Sir – What of the Man? – What followed?

ANTONIO: I followed him myself, my Lord, as fast as I could; but, somehow, I unluckily happened to make a false step, and came with such a confounded whirl against the Garden-gate – that I – I quite for – forgot my Errand.

COUNT: And should you know this man again?

ANTONIO: To be sure I should, my Lord! – if I had seen him, that is.

COUNT: Either speak more clearly, Rascal, or I'll send you packing to –

ANTONIO: Send me packing, my Lord? – Oh, no! If your Lordship has not enough – enough [*Points to his forehead.*] to know when you have a good Gardener, I warrant I know when I have a good Place.

FIGARO: There is no occasion, my Lord, for all this mystery! It was I who jump'd out of the window into the garden.

COUNT: You?

FIGARO: My own self, my Lord.

COUNT: Jump out of a one pair of stairs window and run the risk of breaking your Neck?

FIGARO: The ground was soft, my Lord.

ANTONIO: And his Neck is in no danger of being broken.

FIGARO: To be sure I hurt my right leg, a little, in the fall; just here at the ancle – I feel it still. [*Rubbing his ancle.*]

COUNT: But what reason had you to jump out of the window?

FIGARO: You had received my letter, my Lord, since I must own it, and was come, somewhat sooner than I expected, in a dreadful passion, in search of a man. –

ANTONIO: If it was you, you have grown plaguy fast within this half hour, to my thinking. The man that I saw did not seem so tall by the head and shoulders.

FIGARO: Pshaw! Does not one double one's self up when one takes a leap?

ANTONIO: It seem'd a great deal more like the Page.

COUNT: The Page!

FIGARO: Oh yes, to be sure, the Page has gallop'd back from Seville, Horse and all, to leap out of the window!

ANTONIO: No, no, my Lord! I saw no such thing! I'll take my oath I saw no horse leap out of the window.

FIGARO: Come, come, let us prepare for our sports.

ANTONIO: Well, since it was you, as I am an honest man, I ought to return you this Paper which drop'd out of your pocket as you fell.

COUNT: [*Snatches the paper. The* COUNTESS, FIGARO, *and* SUSAN *are all surprised and embarrassed.* FIGARO *shakes himself, and endeavours to recover his fortitude.*] Ay, since it was you, you doubtless can tell what this Paper contains [*Claps the paper behind his back as he faces* FIGARO.] and how it happened to come in your Pocket?

FIGARO: Oh, my Lord, I have such quantities of Papers. [*Searches his pockets, pulls out a great many.*] No, it is not this! – Hem! – This is a double Love letter from Marcelina, in seven pages – Hem! – Hem! – It would do a man's heart good to read it – Hem! – And this is a petition from the poor Poacher in prison. I never presented it to your Lordship, because I know you have affairs much more serious on your hands, the Complaints of such half-starved Rascals – Ah! – Hem! – this – this – no, this is an Inventory of your Lordship's Sword-knots, Ruffs, Ruffles, and Roses – must take care of this – [*Endeavours to gain time, and keeps glancing and hemming to* SUSAN *and the* COUNTESS, *to look at the paper and give him a hint.*]

COUNT: It is neither this, nor this, nor that, nor t'other, that you have in your hand, but what I hold here in mine, that I want to know the contents of. [*Holds out the paper in action as he speaks, the* COUNTESS *who stands next to him catches a sight of it.*]

COUNTESS: Tis the Commission. [*Aside to* SUSAN.]

SUSAN: The Page's Commission. [*Aside to* FIGARO.]

COUNT: Well, Sir! – so you know nothing of the matter?

ANTONIO: [*Reels round to* FIGARO.] My Lord says you – know nothing of the matter.

FIGARO: Keep off, and don't come to whisper me. [*Pretending to recollect himself.*] Oh Lord! Lord! What a stupid fool I am! – I declare it is the Commission of that poor youth, the Page – which I, like a Blockhead, forgot to return him – He will be quite unhappy about it, poor Boy.

COUNT: And how came you by it?

FIGARO: By it, my Lord?

COUNT: Why did he give it you?

FIGARO: To – to – to –

COUNT: To what?

FIGARO: To get –

COUNT: To get what? It wants nothing!

COUNTESS: [*To* SUSAN.] It wants the Seal.

SUSAN: [*To* FIGARO.] It wants the Seal.

FIGARO: Oh, my Lord, what it wants to be sure is a mere trifle.

COUNT: What trifle?

FIGARO: You know, my Lord, it's customary to –

COUNT: To what?

FIGARO: To affix your Lordship's Seal.

COUNT: [*Looks at the Commission, finds the Seal is wanting, and exclaims with vexation and disappointment*.] The Devil and his Imps! – It is written, Count, thou shalt be a Dupe! – Where is this Marcelina? [*Going*.]

FIGARO: Are you going, my Lord, without giving Orders for our Wedding?

[*Enter* MARCELINA, BASIL, BOUNCE, *and* VASSALS. *The* COUNT *returns*.]

MARCELINA: Forbear, my Lord, to give such Orders; in Justice forbear. I have a written promise under his hand, and I appeal to you, to redress my injuries! You are my lawful Judge.

FIGARO: Pshaw! A trifle, my Lord: a note of hand for money borrowed; nothing more.

COUNT: Let the Advocates and Officers of Justice be assembled in the great Hall; we will there determine on the justice of your claim. It becomes us not to suffer any Vassal of ours, however we may privately esteem him, to be guilty of public injury.

BASIL: Your Lordship is acquainted with my claims on Marcelina: I hope your Lordship will grant me your support.

COUNT: Oh, oh! Are you there, Prince of Knaves?

ANTONIO: Yes, that's his title, sure enough.

COUNT: Approach, honest Basil; faithful Agent of our Will and Pleasure. [BASIL *bows*.] Go order the Lawyers to assemble.

BASIL: My Lord! –

COUNT: And tell the Peasant, by whom you sent me the Letter this morning, I want to speak with him.

BASIL: Your Lordship is pleased to joke with your humble Servant. I know no such Peasant.

COUNT: You will be pleased to find him, notwithstanding.

BASIL: My Office, in this House, as your Lordship knows, is not to go of Errands! Think, my Lord, how that would degrade a man of my talents; who have the honour to teach my Lady the Harpsichord, the Mandoline to her Woman, and to entertain your Lordship, and your Lordship's good Company, with my Voice and my Guitar, whenever your Lordship pleases to honor me with your Commands.

BOUNCE: I will go, if your Lordship pleases to let me: I should be very glad to oblige your Lordship.

COUNT: What's thy Name?

BOUNCE: Pedro Bounce, my Lord, Fire-work maker to your Lordship.

COUNT: Thy zeal pleases me, thou shalt go.

BOUNCE: Thank your Lordship, thank your noble Lordship. [*Leaps.*]

COUNT: [*To* BASIL.] And do you be pleased, Sir, to entertain the Gentleman, on his Journey, with your Voice and your Guitar; he is part of my good Company.

BOUNCE: [*Leaps.*] I am part of my Lord's good Company! Who would have thought it!

BASIL: My Lord –

COUNT: Depart! Obey! Or, depart from my Service. [*Exit.*]

BASIL: 'Tis in vain to resist. Shall I wage war with a Lion, who am only –

FIGARO: A Calf – But come, you seem vex'd about it – I will open the Ball – Strike up, tis my Susan's Wedding-day.

BASIL: Come along, Mr Bounce. [BASIL *begins to play,* FIGARO *dances and sings off before him, and* BOUNCE *follows, dancing after.*]

[*Exeunt. Manent* COUNTESS *and* SUSAN.]

COUNTESS: You see, Susan, to what Danger I have been exposed by Figaro and his fine concerted Billet.

SUSAN: Dear Madam, if you had but seen yourself when I bounced out upon my Lord! So pale, such Terror in your Countenance! And then your suddenly assumed tranquility!

COUNTESS: Oh no, every Faculty was lost in my Fears.

SUSAN: I assure your Ladyship to the contrary; in a few Lessons you would learn to dissemble and fib with as good a Grace as any Lady in the Land.

COUNTESS: And so that poor Child jumped out of the Window?

SUSAN: Without the least hesitation – as light and as chearful as a Linnet.

COUNTESS: I wish however I could convict my false Count of his Infidelity.

SUSAN: The Page will never dare, after this, to make a second attempt.

COUNTESS: Ha! – A lucky project! I will meet him myself; and then nobody will be exposed.

SUSAN: But suppose, Madam –

COUNTESS: My success has emboldened me, and I am determined to try – [*Sees the Riband left on the chair.*] What's here? My Riband! I will keep it as a Memento of the danger to which that poor Youth – Ah my Lord – Yet let me have a care, let me look to myself, to my own Conduct, lest I should give occasion to say – Ah my Lady! [*The* COUNTESS *puts the Riband in her Pocket.*] You must not mention a Word of this, Susan, to any body.

SUSAN: Except Figaro.

COUNTESS: No exceptions, he must not be told; he will spoil it, by mixing some plot of his own with it – I have promised thee a Portion thou knowest – these men are liberal in their Pleasures – Perhaps I may double it for thee; it will be Susan's Right.

SUSAN: Your Project is a charming one, Madam, and I shall yet have my Figaro. [*Exit* SUSAN, *kissing the* COUNTESS's *Hand*.]

Act III

[SCENE, *the Great Hall.*
A Judge's Chair, four other Chairs, Benches with red Baize, a Table and a stool, with Pen, Ink and Paper.
Enter the COUNT, *dressed, and a* SERVANT, *booted.*]

COUNT: Ride to Seville with all speed; enquire if the Page has joined his Regiment, and at what o'clock precisely he arrived; give him this Commission, and return like lightening.

SERVANT: And if he is not there –

COUNT: Return still quicker. – Go; fly! – [*Exit* SERVANT.] – I was wrong to send Basil out of the way – He might have been very serviceable – But Anger was never wise – I scarcely know at present what I wish – When once the Passions have obtained the Mastery, there is no Mind, however consistent, but becomes as wild and incongruous as a Dream – If the Countess, Susan, and Figaro should understand each other and plot to betray me! – If the Page *was* shut up in her dressing-room – Oh! no! – The Respect she bears herself – my Honor! – My Honor? And in my Wife's keeping? – Honor in a Woman's possession, like Ice Cream in the mouth, melts away in a contest of Pleasure and Pain – I will sound Figaro, however.

[*Enter* FIGARO, *behind*.]

FIGARO: Here am I. [*Aside*.]

COUNT: And if I have reason to suppose them plotting against me, he shall marry Marcelina.

FIGARO: Perhaps not. [*Aside*.]

COUNT: But in that case, what must Susan be?

FIGARO: My Wife, if you please. – [FIGARO's *eagerness occasions him to speak aloud – The* COUNT *turns round astonished*.]

COUNT: My Wife, if you please! – To whom did you say my Wife, if you please?

FIGARO: To – to – to – That is – They were the last words of a sentence I was saying to one of the Servants – Go and tell so and so to – *my Wife, if you please.*

COUNT: Your Wife! – Zounds, you are very fond of your Wife.

FIGARO: I love to be singular.

COUNT: You have made me wait for you here a long while.

FIGARO: I have been changing my Stockings, which I dirtied in the fall.

COUNT: Servants, I think, are longer dressing than their Masters.

FIGARO: Well they may – They are obliged to dress themselves.

COUNT: If in sifting my Gentleman, I find him unwilling to go to France, I may conclude Susan has betrayed me. [*Aside.*]

FIGARO: He has mischief in his head, but I'll watch his motions. [*Aside.*]

COUNT: [*Approaches* FIGARO *with familiarity.*] – Thou knowest, Figaro, it was my intention to have taken thee with me on my Embassy to Paris, but I believe thou dost not understand French.

FIGARO: Perfectly.

COUNT: Indeed! – Let's hear. – [FIGARO *pulls out his purse and jingles it.*] – Is that all the French thou understandest?

FIGARO: All! – Is not that enough, think you, my Lord? – That's a language understood in every corner of the habitable Earth, and in no place better than in Paris. – Your Philosophers, who lament the loss of an universal Language, are Fools – They always carry one in their pockets. As for a knowledge of French, my Lord, I maintain, *s'il vous plait*, and a Purse are all that's necessary – Let but the sound of Silver jingle in a Frenchman's ears, and he will instantly understand your meaning, be it what it will. – If you have a Law-suit, and wish to gain your Cause, go to the Judge, pull off your Hat, and pull out your Purse; smile, shake it, and pronounce, *s'il vous plait, Monsieur* –

COUNT: And your Adversary is overthrown.

FIGARO: Undoubtedly – Unless he understands *French* still better than you – Do you wish the Friendship of a great Lord, or a great Lady, its still the same – Chink, chink, and *s'il vous plait, Monseigneur – S'il vous plait, Madame* – The French are a very witty People! – Amazingly quick of apprehension! – Therefore, my Lord, if you have no other reason than this for leaving me behind –

COUNT: But thou art no Politician.

FIGARO: Pardon me, my Lord, I am as great a master of Politics –

COUNT: As thou art of French.

FIGARO: Oh, my Lord, the thing is so easy – He must be a Fool indeed who would find his vanity flattered by his skill in Politics – To appear always deeply concerned for the good of the State, yet to have no other end but Self-interest; to assemble and say Nothing; to pretend vast Secrecy where there is nothing to conceal; to shut yourself up in your Chamber, and mend your Pen or pick your Teeth, while your Footmen inform the attending Croud you are too busy to be approach'd – this, with the art of intercepting Letters, imitating Hands, pensioning Traitors, and rewarding Flatterers, is the whole mystery of Politics, or I am an Idiot.

COUNT: This is the definition of a Partisan not a Politician.

FIGARO: Party and Politics are much the same, they are become synonimous terms.

COUNT: [*Aside.*] Since he is so willing to go to Paris, Susan has said nothing.

FIGARO: 'Tis now my turn to attack. [*Aside.*]

COUNT: And – I suppose thou wilt take thy Wife with thee – to Paris?

FIGARO: No – no – I should be obliged to quit her so frequently, that I am afraid the *Cares*, of the marriage state would lie too heavy on my head. [*Significantly.*]

COUNT: Susan has betrayed me. [*Aside.*]

FIGARO: [*Aside.*] He does not like the retort. [*The* COUNT *smiles, approaches* FIGARO *with great familiarity, and leans upon his shoulder – By-play between the* COUNT *and* FIGARO.]

COUNT: The time was, Figaro, when thou wert more open – Formerly thou wouldst tell me any thing.

FIGARO: And at present I conceal nothing.

COUNT: What can be the Countess's motives – [*The* COUNT *puts his arm round* FIGARO*'s neck – By-play again.*] – I – Thou seest I anticipate her wishes, load her with presents –

FIGARO: Will give her any thing but yourself – Of what worth are Trinkets when we are in want of Necessaries?

COUNT: Come, come; be sincere – Tell me – How much did the Countess give thee for this last plot?

FIGARO: As much as your Lordship gave me for helping you to steal her from her old jealous Guardian – A noble Lord should not endeavour to degrade an honest Servant, lest he should make him a Knave.

COUNT: But wherefore is there continually some Mystery in thy conduct?

FIGARO: Because the Conduct of others is mysterious.

COUNT: Appearances, my dear Figaro, really speak thee a great Knave.

FIGARO: [*Looking round at the* COUNT*'s hand upon his shoulders, and observing his familiarity.*] – *Appearances*, my dear Lord, are frequently false – I am much better than I appear to be – Can the Great in general say as much? – [*Aside.*] – Take that.

COUNT: Yes, yes; she has told him. [*Aside.*]

FIGARO: I shall content myself, my Lord, with the portion your Lordship has promised me on my Marriage, and the place of Steward of this Castle, with which you have honoured me, and willingly remain with my Wife here in Andalusia, far from troubles and intrigue.

COUNT: But thou hast Abilities, and might rise to Preferment.

FIGARO: Preferred by my Abilities my Lord! – Your Lordship is pleased to laugh at me.

COUNT: Yes, yes; Susan has betrayed me, and my Gentleman marries Marcelina. [*Aside.*]

FIGARO: He has been angling for Gudgeons, and what has he caught? [*Aside.*]

[*Enter a* SERVANT.]

SERVANT: Don Guzman and the Counsellors are without.

COUNT: Let them wait.

FIGARO: [*Ironically.*] Aye, let them wait. [*Exit* SERVANT.]

COUNT: And dost thou expect to gain thy Cause?

FIGARO: With, the assistance of Justice and my Lord's good wishes, who respects Youth too much himself to force others to wed with Age.

COUNT: A Judge knows no distinction of persons.

FIGARO: Well – Time, say the Italians, is a valiant Fellow, and tells Truth – But what was it your Lordship was pleased to send for me for?

COUNT: For – [*Somewhat embarrassed.*] To see these benches and chairs set in order.

FIGARO: That is already done, my Lord. Here is the great chair for your Lordship, a seat for the President, a table and stool for his Clerk, two benches for the Lawyers, the middle for the Beau monde, and the Mob in the back ground. [*Exit.*]

COUNT: He is too cunning; I can get nothing out of him; but they certainly understand each other. – They may toy and be as loving as they please, but as for wedding –

[*Enter* SUSAN.
She comes up to the COUNT*'s elbow while he is speaking, and is surprized to see him in such an ill humour.*]

SUSAN: My Lord!

COUNT: My Lady!

SUSAN: My Lady has sent me for your Lordship's smelling-bottle; she has got the vapours.

COUNT: Here; and when she has done with it, borrow it for yourself, – it may be useful.

SUSAN: I the vapours, my Lord! Oh no, that's too polite a disease for a Servant to pretend to!

COUNT: Fits may come; – Love so violent as yours cannot bear disappointment; and when Figaro marries Marcelina –

SUSAN: Oh, suppose the worst, my Lord, we can pay Marcelina with the Portion your Lordship has promised us!

COUNT: I promis'd you a portion?

SUSAN: If my ears did not deceive me, I understood as much.

COUNT: Yes, if you had pleas'd to *understand* me, but since you do not. –

SUSAN: [*Pretending bashfulness.*] It's always soon enough to own one's weakness, my Lord.

COUNT: [*With an instant change of countenance.*] What! Wilt thou take a walk this evening in the garden, by the Pavilion?

SUSAN: Don't I take Walks every evening, my Lord?

COUNT: Nay, nay, but let us understand each other – No Pavilion, no Marriage.

SUSAN: And no Marriage, no Pavilion, my Lord! [*Curtsying.*]

COUNT: What a witty little Devil! I wonder what she does to fascinate me so! – But prithee tell me why hast thou always, till now, refused with such obstinacy? This very Morning, thou knowest –

SUSAN: This Morning, my Lord! – What, and the Page behind the Great-chair!

COUNT: Oh, true! I had forgot! – But when Basil has spoken to thee in my behalf. –

SUSAN: Is it necessary, my Lord, such a knave as Basil should know every thing that passes?

COUNT: She is right again! – But – [*Suspicious.*] thou wilt go, now, and tell Figaro all.

SUSAN: To be sure, my Lord. I always tell him all – except what is necessary to conceal.

COUNT: Ah the Hussey! What a charming little Knave it is! Run, run to thy Mistress; she is waiting, and may suspect us.

SUSAN: [*Hesitating.*] So your Lordship can't perceive that I only wanted a pretext to speak to your Lordship.

[*The* COUNT *unable to conceal is transport, is going to kiss her, but hears somebody coming, and they separate.*]

COUNT: [*As he turns.*] She absolutely bewitches me! I had sworn to think no more of her, but she winds me just as she pleases!

[*The* COUNT *goes off, and* FIGARO *enters, but the* COUNT *hearing* FIGARO*'s Voice, returns and peeps.*]

FIGARO: Well, my Susan, what does he say?

SUSAN: Hush! Hush! He is just gone – Thou has gained thy Cause – Run, run, run. [*Exit* SUSAN, *running,* FIGARO *following.*]

FIGARO: Well, but how, how, my Charmer? [*Exeunt.*]

[*Re-enter* COUNT.]

COUNT: Thou hast gained thy Cause – Aha! And is it so, my pair of Knaves! – Am I your Dupe then? – A very pretty Net! But the Cuckoo is not caught – Come! – Proceed we to judgement! [*With passion.*] Be we just! – Cool! – Impartial! – Inflexible – [*Exit.*]

[*Enter* DON GUZMAN, MARCELINA, *and* DOCTOR.]

MARCELINA: I shall be happy, Mr. President, to explain the justice of my Cause.

DOCTOR: To shew you on what grounds this Lady proceeds.

GUZMAN: [*Stuttering.*] We-e-e-ell, le-et us exa-a-mine the matter ve-erbally.

MARCELINA: There is a promise of Marriage –

GUZMAN: I co-o-o-omprehend! Gi-i-iven by you-ou-ou – to –

MARCELINA: No, Mr. President, given *to* me.

GUZMAN: I co-o-o-omprehend! Gi-iven *to* you.

MARCELINA: And a sum of Money which I –

GUZMAN: I co-o-o-omprehend! Which you-ou ha-ave received.

MARCELINA: No, Mr. President, which I have lent.

GUZMAN: I co-o-o-omprehend! – It is re-e-paid.

MARCELINA: No, Mr. President, it is *not* repaid.

GUZMAN: I co-o-o-omprehend – The m-m-man would marry you to pay his de-de-de-bts.

MARCELINA: No, Mr. President, he would neither marry me, *nor* pay his debts.

GUZMAN: D-d—do you think I d-d-d-don't co-o-omprehend you?

DOCTOR: And are you, Mr. President, to judge this Cause?

GUZMAN: T-t-t-to be sure – Wha-at else did I purchase my Place for thi-ink you. [*Laughs stupidly at the supposed folly of the Question.*] And where is the De-fe-e-endant?

[*Enter* FIGARO.]

FIGARO: Here, at your service.

DOCTOR: Yes, that's the Knave.

FIGARO: Perhaps I interrupt you.

GUZMAN: Ha-ave not I see-een you before young Man?

FIGARO: Oh yes, Mr. President, I once served your Lady.

GUZMAN: How lo-ong since?

FIGARO: Nine months before the birth of her last Child – And a fine Boy it is, though I say it.

GUZMAN: Y-es – He's the F-flower of the Flock – And the cau-ause betwee-een –

FIGARO: A Bagatelle, Mr. President! A Bagatelle.

GUZMAN: [*Laughs.*] A Ba-ag-a-telle! A pro-o-mise of Ma-a-arriage a Ba-a-getelle! Ha! ha! ha! – And dost thou hope to ca-ast the Pla-aintiff?

FIGARO: To be sure, Mr. President! You being one of the Judges.

GUZMAN: [*With stupid dignity.*] Ye-e-es! I am one of the Judges! – Has thou see-een D-D-Doublefee, my Se-ecretary?

FIGARO: Yes, Mr. President! That's a duty not to be neglected.

GUZMAN: The young Fellow is not so si-i-imple I thought.

[*Enter* CRYER *of the Court*, GUARDS, COUNT, COUNSELLORS *and* VASSALS.]

CRYER: Make room there, for my Lord, the Count.

COUNT: Wherefore in your Robes, Don Guzman? It was unnecessary for a mere domestic matter like this.

GUZMAN: Pa-a-ardon me, my Lord! Those who would tre-e-emble at the Clerk of the Court in his Robes, would la-augh at the Judge without 'em. Forms! Forms! are sacred things.

[*The* COUNT *and the Court seat themselves.*]

COUNT: Call silence in the Court.

CRYER: Silence in the Court.

GUZMAN: Read over the Causes, D-D-Doublefee.

DOUBLEFEE: The Count de los Altos Montes di Aguas Frescas, Senor di Montes Fieros, y otros Montes, Plaintiff, against Alonzo Calderon, a Comic Poet. The question at present before the Court, is, to know the Author of a Comedy that has been damned; which they mutually disavow and attribute to each other.

COUNT: They are both very right in mutually disavowing it; and be it decreed, that if, hereafter, they should produce a successful Piece, its Fame shall appertain to the Count, and its Merit to the Poet – The next.

DOUBLEFEE: Diego Macho, Day-labourer, Plaintiff, against Gil-Perez-Borcado Tax-gatherer, and receiver of the Gabels,[1] for having violently dispossessed the said Diego Macho, Day-labourer, of his Cow.

COUNT: This Cause does not come within my Jurisdiction; but as it is probable the Day-labourer will never obtain Justice, do thou see, Figaro, that another Cow be sent him, lest his Family should be starved – The next.

DOUBLEFEE: Marcelina-Jane-Maria-Angelica-Mustacio, Spinster, Plaintiff, against – [*To* FIGARO.] Here's no surname.

FIGARO: Anonymous.

GUZMAN: Ano-o-onymous – I never heard the Name before!

DOUBLEFEE: Against Figaro Anonymous. What Profession?

FIGARO: Gentleman.

COUNT: Gentleman!

FIGARO: I might have been born a Prince, if Heaven had pleased.

DOUBLEFEE: Against Figaro Anonymous, Gentleman, Defendant. The Question before the Court relates to a promise of Marriage; the Parties have retained no Council, contrary to the ancient and established practice of Courts.

FIGARO: What occasion for Council? A race of Gentlemen who are always so very learned, they know every thing, except their Briefs! Who insolently interrogate Modesty and Timidity, and endeavour, by confusing, to make Honesty forswear itself; and, after having laboured for hours, with all legal prolixity, to perplex self-evident Propositions, and bewilder the understandings of the Judges, sit down as proud as if they have just pronounced a Phillipic of Demosthenes – [*Addressing himself to the Court.*] My Lord, and Gentlemen – The Question before the Court is –

DOUBLEFEE: [*Interrupting him.*] If is not you to speak, you are the Defendant – who pleads for the Plaintiff?

DOCTOR: I.

DOUBLEFEE: You! A Physician turn Lawyer? –

FIGARO: Oh yes, and equally skilful in both.

COUNT: Read the Promise of Marriage, Doctor.

1. Salt tax.

GUZMAN: Re-e-ead the Pro-o-omise of Mar-riage.

DOCTOR: [*Reads.*] I acknowledge to have received of Marcelina-Jane-Maria-Angelica-Mustachio, the sum of two thousand Piasters, in the Castle of Count Almaviva, which sum I promise to repay to the said Marcelina-Jane-Maria-Angelica-Mustachio, *and* to marry her. Signed, Figaro [*Addressing himself to the* COUNT.] My Lord, and Gentlemen! Hem! Never did cause more interesting, more intricate, or in which the Interest of Mankind, their Rights, Properties, Lives and Liberties were more materially involved, ever claim the profound Attention of this most learned, most honourable Court, and from the time of Alexander the Great, who promised to espouse the beauteous Thalestris –

COUNT: Stop, most formidable Orator; and ere you proceed, enquire whether the Defendant does not contest the validity of your Deed.

GUZMAN: [*To* FIGARO.] Do you co-ontest the va-va-va-va-lidity of the Dee-eed?

FIGARO: My Lord and Gentlemen! Hem! There is in this Case, either Fraud, Error, Malice, or mischievous Intention, for the Words of the Acknowledgement are, I promise to repay the said Marcelina-Jane-Maria-Angelica-Mustachio, the said sum of two thousand Piasters *or* to marry her, which is very different.

DOCTOR: I affirm it is AND.

FIGARO: I affirm it is OR.

DOCTOR: Well, suppose it.

FIGARO: No Supposition, I will have it granted.

COUNT: Clerk. Read you the Promise.

GUZMAN: Re-e-ead the P-P-P-Promise, D-D-D-Double-fee.

DOUBLEFEE: [*Reads.*] I acknowledge to have received of Marcelina-Jane-Maria-Angelica-Mustachio, the sum of two thousand Piasters, in the Castle of Count Almaviva, which sum I promise to repay to the said Marcelina-Jane-Maria-Angelica-Mustachio, *and – or – and – or – or* – The Word is blotted.

DOCTOR: No matter; the sense of the Phrase is equally clear. This learned Court is not now to be informed the word or particle, OR, hath various significations – It means *otherwise* and *either* – It likewise means *before* – For example, in the language of the Poet.

Or 'ere the Sun decline the western Sky,
'Tis Fate's decree the Victims all must die.

FIGARO: This was the language of Prophesy, and spoken of the Doctor's own Patients.

COUNT: Silence in the Court.

CRIER: Silence in the Court.

DOCTOR: Hence then, I clearly deduce (granting the word to be *Or*) the Defendant doth hereby promise, not only to pay the Plaintiff, but marry her *before* he pays her – Again, the word *Or* doth sometimes signify *Wherefore*, as another great and learned Poety hath it,

Or how could heav'nly Justice damn us all
Who ne'er consented to our Father's Fall?

That is *wherefore*? For what reason could heavenly Justice do such an unjust thing? Let us then substitute the adverb *Wherefore*, and the intent of the meaning of the Promise will be incontestable; for after reciting an acknowledgement of the debt, it concludes with the remarkable words, *Or* to marry her, that is, wherefore, for which reason, out of gratitude, for the Favour above done me, *I will marry her*.

FIGARO: Oh most celebrated Doctor! Most poetic Quibbler!

Hark with what florid Impotence he speaks,
And as his Malice prompts, the Puppet squeaks,
Or at the ear of Eve, familiar Toad,
Half froth, half venom, spits himself abroad
In legal Puns, *or* Quibbles, Quirks, *or* Lies,
Or Spite, *or* Taunts, *or* Rhymes, *or* Blasphemies.

What think you we know not Quotations, and Poets, and *Ands*, and *Ors*, and *Whys*, and *Wherefores*.

What Drop *or* Nostrum, can such Plagues remove,
Or which must end me, a Fool's Wrath – *Or* Love?

[*Pointing first to the* DOCTOR, *and then to* MARCELINA.]

We have neither forgot our Reading nor our Syntax, but can easily translate a dull Knave into a palpable Fool – My Lord, and Gentlemen, You hear his Sophisms, Poetical, and Conundrums, Grammatical.

COUNT: Yes, yes, we hear.

[COUNT *and the* COUNSELLORS *rise and consult together*.]

ANTONIO: I'm glad they have put an end to your prating.

MARCELINA: Their Whisperings and wise Grimaces forebode me no good. That Susan has corrupted the chief Judge, and he is corrupting all the others.

DOCTOR: It looks devilish like it.

[*The* COUNT *and* COUNSELLORS *resume their seats*.]

DOUBLEFEE: Silence in the Court.

CRIER: Silence in the Court.

COUNT: The judgement of the Court is, that since the validity of the promise of Marriage is not well established, Figaro is permitted to dispose of his Person.

FIGARO: The Day's my own.

MARCELINA: I thought how it would be.

COUNT: But as the Acknowledgement clearly expresses the words, *Which sum I promise to pay the said Marcelina-Jane-Maria-Angelica-Mustachio, or to marry her*, the said Figaro stands condemned to pay the two thousand Piasters to the Plaintiff, or to marry her in the course of the Day.

FIGARO: I'm undone!

MARCELINA: I am happy!

COUNT: And I am revenged!

ANTONIO: Thank your noble Lordship! Most humbly thank your noble Lordship! – Ah ha! I'm glad thou art not to marry my Niece! I'll go and tell her the good news! [*Exit.*]

CRIER: Clear the Court.

[*Exuent* GUARDS, COUNSELLORS, *and* VASSALS. *Manent* DON GUZMAN, FIGARO, MARCELINA *and* DR. BARTHOLO.]

FIGARO: 'Tis this Furze-ball, this Fungus of a President that has lost me my Cause.

GUZMAN: I a F-F-Furze-ball and a F-F-Fungus!

FIGARO: [*Sits down dejected.*] I will never marry her.

GUZMAN: Thou mu-ust ma-arry her.

FIGARO: What! Without the Consent of my noble Parents?

COUNT: [*Returning.*] Where are they? Who are they? – He will still complain of injustice – Name them.

FIGARO: Allow me time, my Lord – I must first know where to find them, and yet it ought not be long, for I have been seeking them these five Years.

DOCTOR: What! A Foundling?

FIGARO: No Foundling, but stolen from my Parents.

COUNT: Poh! This is too palpable. [*Exit* COUNT.]

FIGARO: Had I no other Proof of my Birth than the precious Stones, Ring, and Jewels found upon me, these would be sufficient – but I bear the Mark – [*He is going to shew his Arm.*]

MARCELINA: Of a Lobster on your left Arm.

FIGARO: How do you know that?

MARCELINA: 'Tis he himself!

FIGARO: Yes, its me myself.

MARCELINA: 'Tis Fernando!

DOCTOR: Thou wert stolen away by Gypsies.

FIGARO: By Gypsies – Oh Doctor, if thou can'st but restore me to my illustrious Parents, Mountains of Gold will not sufficiently speak their gratitude.

DOCTOR: Behold thy Mother. [*Pointing to* MARCELINA.]

FIGARO: Nurse, you mean!

DOCTOR: Thy own Mother!

FIGARO: Explain!

MARCELINA: And there behold they Father. [*Pointing to the* DOCTOR.]

FIGARO: He, my Father! Oh Lord! Oh Lord! Oh Lord! [*Stamps about.*]

GUZMAN: [*With great wisdom.*] It will be no m-m-maatch – that's evi-dent.

MARCELINA: Hast thou not felt Nature pleading within thee, at sight of me?

FIGARO: Never.

MARCELINA: This was the secret cause of all my Fondness for thee.

FIGARO: No doubt – And of my aversion – Instinct is very powerful.

MARCELINA: Come to my arms, my dear, my long lost Child.

[FIGARO *and* MARCELINA *embrace, the* DOCTOR *leans against the Benches.*]

[*Enter* ANTONIO *and* SUSAN
The Latter runs to find the COUNT.]

SUSAN: [*In great Agitation.*] Oh, where is my Lord? Here is the Money to pay Marcelina with! The Portion which my noble and generous Lady has given me!

ANTONIO: [*Pulling* SUSAN, *and pointing to* FIGARO, *who kisses* MARCELINA.] Here! here! Look this way! [SUSAN, *at seeing them embrace becomes furious, and is going away,* FIGARO *runs and brings her back.*]

FIGARO: Stop, stop, my Susan.

SUSAN: I have seen enough – Since you are so fond of her, pray marry her.

FIGARO: Thou art mistaken.

SUSAN: No, I am not mistaken. [*Gives him a slap in the face.*]

FIGARO: [*Rubbing his Cheek.*] This is Love – Pshaw! Prithee come hither, look at that Lady – How dost thou like her?

SUSAN: Not at all.

FIGARO: Well said Jealousy, she does not mince the Matter.

MARCELINA: Dear Susan, this, this is my Son!

FIGARO: Yes, they wanted me to marry my Mother.

ANTONIO: Your Mother! – It is not long since –

FIGARO: I have known it – True.

MARCELINA: Yes, my dearest Susan, embrace thy Mother – Thy Mother, who will love thee dearly.

SUSAN: And do you consent I shall have my Figaro?

MARCELINA: Willingly. [SUSAN *runs and kisses her.*] Here, my Son, here is the Promise. [*Gives him the Paper.*]

SUSAN: And here is the Portion. [*Gives him a Purse of Money.*]

FIGARO: My manly Pride would fain make me restrain my tears, but they flow in spite of me – Well, let 'em! Let 'em flow! Joys like these never come twice in one's Life! Oh, my Mother, Oh, my Susan!
[*They all three embrace, weeping.*]

GUZMAN: [*Weeping.*] What a Foo-oo-ool am I! L-L-Look, if I don't k-k-k-cry as well as the best of 'em.

FIGARO: [*To the* DOCTOR.] My Father.

DOCTOR: Keep off! I disclaim thee!

ANTONIO: Why then, if you are his Father, you are a Turkish Jew, and no Christian Father.

DOCTOR: A Knave that tricked me of my Ward, cheated me of my Money, and now has been turning my Wisdom into ridicule.

SUSAN: And are not you, being a wise Man, proud to have a Son wiser than yourself?

DOCTOR: No – I would have no one wiser than myself.

ANTONIO: Come, come, look you, I am a good Catholic, and an old Castilian, therefore, unless your Father and Mother become lawful Man and Wife, I will never consent to give you my Niece. No, no, she sha'n't marry a man who is the child of Nobody, neither.

GUZMAN: Here's an old Fool! – The Child of Nobody, Ha! ha! ha! [*Laughs stupidly, and then assumes great Wisdom.*] Hav'n't you lived long enough to know that every Child must have a Father?

MARCELINA: Consider, good Doctor, your Promise, if ever our Child was found.

DOCTOR: Pshaw!

MARCELINA: And here is a Son you surely need not be ashamed of.

SUSAN: Ah my dear Pappa!

FIGARO: My generous, worthy Father.

[SUSAN *strokes his Cheek,* FIGARO *kneels, and* MARCELINA *coaxes him.*]

SUSAN: You don't know how we will all love you.

MARCELINA: What care we will take of you.

FIGARO: How happy we will make you.

DOCTOR: Good Doctor, dear Pappa, generous Father! [*Bursts out a crying.*] See, if I am not even a greater Foo-oo-ool than Mr President! [GUZMAN *staggers back at the* DOCTOR's *Compliment.*] they mould me like Dough, lead me like a Child. [MARCELINA, SUSAN *and* FIGARO *testify their joy by their Actions.*] Nay, nay, but I hav'n't yet said yes.

SUSAN: But you have thought yes.

MARCELINA: And look'd yes.

FIGARO: Come, come, we must be quick; let us run and find the Count, otherwise he will invent some new pretext to break off the Match.

[*Exuent* DOCTOR, MARCELINA, FIGARO *and* SUSAN. *Manent Don* GUZMAN.]

GUZMAN: A greater Foo-oo-ool than Mr President! – The People of this House are truly very stupid and ill bred. [*Exit.*]

Act IV

[SCENE, *a large Saloon.*
FIGARO *and* SUSAN, *both joyous.*]

FIGARO: She has converted her Doctor at last – They are to be married, and these so late implacable Enemies are now become our dearest Friends.

SUSAN: What unexpected Happiness!

FIGARO: Chance, my Susan – All the effect of Chance – Yesterday, without a Relation in the World I could claim, to-day, behold me restored to my Parents – True it is, they are neither so rich nor so right honourable, so belaced nor betitled as my imagination had painted them – But that's all one, they are mine – I may truly be called both a Chance Child, and a Child of Chance – By Chance was I begot, by Chance brought into the World, by Chance was I stole, by Chance am I found, by Chance have I lived, and by Chance I shall die – Chance is Nature's Sovereign, and must be mine.

SUSAN: Yes, and by Chance thou mayst come to be hang'd. [*Laughs.*]

FIGARO: Or thou to be an Empress – Neither of them are impossible – He, the Conqueror, whose Ambition ravages the Earth, and whose Pride eats up Nations, is not less the sport of Chance than the blind Beggar who is conducted by his dog.

SUSAN: Ha, ha, ha! – Prithee leave thy Philosophy, and –

FIGARO: And think of that other blind beggar, Love – Most willingly, my Angel. [*Kisses her.*]

SUSAN: Pooh, Pooh! – That was not what I meant.

FIGARO: Rather say it was not half thy meaning, or thy meaning ill expressed. [*Kisses her again.*]

SUSAN: Ah, Figaro! Were this fondness, these days but durable –

FIGARO: Durable! – Iron and Adamant – No; may millions of imaginary Gallants wrack my heart and decorate my –

SUSAN: No rhodomantade, Figaro – Tell me the simple truth.

FIGARO: By the truest of all Truths I swear –

SUSAN: Truest of Truths – Are there various kinds of Truths then?

FIGARO: No doubt.

SUSAN: Fie!

FIGARO: There are Truths that may be spoken: such as the Peccadillos of a poor Rascal! Truths that may not be spoken: such as the Robberies of a rich Rascal – There are your Truths comprehensible: such as that two and two make four; and your Truths incomprehensible: such as that two and two make five – Then there are your Tradesman's Truths, which he retails to his Customers, your Lover's Truths, which he pours wholesale into his Mistress's ear – Your Courtier's Truths, on which he feeds his Dependants and Parasites – Your Court of Law, or Kiss-the-Book Truths, which are the daily support of a *vast* number of very honest people – There are also your physical and metaphysical Truths – Your old Truths and your new Truths – Your heterodox and orthodox Truths – Your Mahometan Truths, your Jewish Truths, and your – other kind of truths, concerning which there never was nor ever will be any doubt – Not to mention your Truths of fashion: such as that Idleness, Ignorance, Dissipation, Gaming and Seduction are the requisites of a Gentleman – And your Truths *out* of fashion: such as that Gentleness, Obedience, Œconomy, and connubial Love are the requisites of a *Gentlewoman*.

SUSAN: I find by your account of the matter, Figaro, that poor Truth, like a Lottery Ticket, is so divided and sub-divided, so halved, quartered, cut, carv'd, split and spliced, it is no where entire to be found.

FIGARO: No where.

SUSAN: And moreover, that what is Truth to-day may be a Lie to-morrow.

FIGARO: May be! Must be.

SUSAN: Consequently, that in less than twenty-four hours, my very tender submissive, ardent Lover may be metamorphosed into an arbitrary, cold, haughty *Husband*.

FIGARO: Impossible – Impossible, my Susan! As it is for thee, my gentle, kind, and beauteous Bride, to be transformed into an ill-tempered, extravagant slatternly *Wife*.

SUSAN: I understand thee – Well, Well – We will endeavour to convert the iron Bands of Matrimony into a flowery Wreath which Love shall teach us to bear lightly and joyously through Life.

FIGARO: Aye, and thus live a happy Exception to the established usage of a mad World.

SUSAN: But prithee, who is to go disguised and meet the count?

FIGARO: Who? Nobody – Let him wait and fret, and bite his Nails – I never meant thou shouldst go.

SUSAN: I assure thee I never had any inclination.

FIGARO: Is that the real Truth, Susan?

SUSAN: What! Thinkest thou I am as learned as thou art! And that I keep several sorts of Truths?

FIGARO: [*With fond Vivacity.*] And dost thou love me?

SUSAN: [*Tenderly.*] Too much, I doubt.

FIGARO: Ah! – That's but little.

SUSAN: How!

FIGARO: In Love's Creed, too much is not even enough.

SUSAN: I understand nothing of this over-refinement, but I feel I shall love my Husband most heartily.

FIGARO: Keep thy word, and put our modern Wives to the blush.

SUSAN: Afford them a subject to laugh and point at, thou mean'st.

[*Enter the* COUNTESS.]

COUNTESS: Wherever you meet One of them, be certain you shall find a Pair. [*They salute the* COUNTESS.] – The Bridesmen and Maids wait for you, Figaro.

FIGARO: I will take my excuse in my hand – [*Going to lead out* SUSAN.] – Few offenders can plead so charming a one.

COUNTESS: No, no: stop Susan: I want you – She shall come presently. [*Exit* FIGARO.] – Well, Susan, the time approaches, we must prepare for the Rendezvous.

SUSAN: I must not go, Madam, Figaro is unwilling.

COUNTESS: [*Angry.*] Figaro! – Figaro is not so scrupulous when a Marriage-portion is in question – That's a poor Pretence; you are sorry you have told the truth, and discovered the Intentions of the Count. – Go, go – I am not to be so deceived. [*Going.*]

SUSAN: [*Catching hold of her and kneeling.*] Ah, Madam! Let me conjure you to hear me, to pardon me. – How can you think me capable of deceiving so good, so liberal a Lady, whose bounties I have so often felt! – Oh, no; it is because I have promised Figaro.

COUNTESS: [*Mildly and Smiling.*] Rise – Hast thou forgot, silly Girl, that it is I who am to go and not thee – [*Kisses her forehead.*] – But – I was too hasty.

SUSAN: My dear, my generous Mistress.
COUNTESS: And what is the place of Rendezvous?
SUSAN: The Pavilion in the Garden.
COUNTESS: There are two.
SUSAN: But they are opposite.
COUNTESS: True – At what hour?
SUSAN: I don't know.
COUNTESS: That must be fixed – Sit down, take the pen and write –
[SUSAN *sits down, the* COUNTESS *dictates.*]

A NEW SONG,
To the Tune of,
The Twilight past, the Bell had toll'd.

SUSAN: [*Writes.*] New song – Tune of – Bell had toll'd – What next, Madam?
COUNTESS: Dost think he will not understand thee?
SUSAN: [*Looking archly at the* COUNTESS.] Very true – [*Folding up the Letter.*] – But here is neither Wax nor Wafer.
COUNTESS: Fasten it with a Pin, and write on the direction, *Return the Seal.* [*Smiling.*]
SUSAN: [*Laughs.*] The Seal! – [*Gets up.*] – This is not quite so serious as the Commission just now was.
COUNTESS: [*Sighs.*] Ah, Susan.
SUSAN: I have never a Pin.
COUNTESS: Take this.
[*Gives her one which fastened the* PAGE*'s riband to her breast; it falls.*]
SUSAN: [*Picking up the riband.*] This is the Page's riband, Madam.
COUNTESS: Wouldst thou have me let him wear it? It will do for Agnes: I will give it her the first Bouquet she presents me. [*Just as the* COUNTESS *has said this,* AGNES *and a troop of young Maidens, among them the* PAGE, *in girl's cloaths, enter with nosegays for the* COUNTESS, *who instantly puts the riband in her pocket, with an evident wish, by her looks and action, to preserve it.*]
COUNTESS: [*Looking at the* PAGE.] What pretty maiden is this?
AGNES: A Cousin of mine, Madam, that we have invited to the Wedding.
COUNTESS: Well, then, as we can wear but one nosegay, let us do honour to the Stranger [*Takes the Nosegay from the* PAGE, *and kisses his forehead. – Aside to* SUSAN.] Don't you think, Susan, she resembles amazingly – [*Stops short, and looks at* SUSAN.]
SUSAN: Amazingly, indeed, Madam!
PAGE: [*Aside.*] What a precious kiss! I feel it here. [*Putting his hand on his heart.*]

[*Enter the* COUNT, *and* ANTONIO *with a hat in his hand.*]

ANTONIO: [*As he enters.*] Yes, yes, my Lord, I'm certain it was him. The rakish little Rascal is disguised among the Girls. I found his new hat and cockade here – hid in a basket. [*The* COUNTESS *and* SUSAN *surprised, look at the* PAGE, *and then at each other. The girls surround and endeavour to hide the* PAGE; ANTONIO *seeks among them.*] Ay, ay, here he is – here he is. [ANTONIO *takes off his cap, and puts on his hat.*] There, my Lord! There's a pretty, modest Virgin for you!

COUNT: Well, my Lady!

COUNTESS: Well, my Lord! – I am as much surpized as you can be; and, I assure you, not less vex'd. – At present, however, it is time to tell you the whole Truth. This young gentleman [*Pointing to the* PAGE.] was hid in my Dressing-room. – We attempted a Joke, which these Girls have put in practice.

COUNT: But wherefore hide him from me?

COUNTESS: Because, my Lord, when your Passions are predominant, you are incapable of either listening to or believing the Truth.

COUNT: [*Aside.*] Must I for ever be disturbed, haunted, and bewitch'd thus by this beardless Boy? [*Turning with great wrath towards the* PAGE.] What is the reason, Sir, you have not obeyed my Commands?

PAGE: [*Draws back frightened, and takes off his hat.*] My-my-my Lord, I staid to teach Agnes the Love scene she is to play in the Comedy this evening.

AGNES: [*Steps forward.*] Ah, my Lord, when you come to my room, you know, and want to kiss me –

COUNT: I! [*The* COUNTESS *remarks his embarrassment,* SUSAN *laughs silently, and makes signs to the* COUNTESS.]

AGNES: Yes, my Lord! You say to me, My pretty Agnes, if you will but love me, I will give you any thing you wish to have; now, my Lord, if you will give me Cherubin for a husband, I will love you with all my heart.

COUNTESS: You hear, my Lord! – Has not the simplicity of this Child's confession, as artless as the one I have this moment made, sufficiently justified my Conduct? And do not circumstances prove, how injurious your Suspicions have been, and how well founded mine?

[COUNT *bows to the* COUNTESS.]

ANTONIO: You see, my Lord, what a giddy young thing it is.

COUNT: And very loving too,

ANTONIO: Her mother, as every body knows, was just such another.

[*Enter* FIGARO.]

FIGARO: Come, my pretty Maidens, come. [*Turns to the* COUNT.] While you keep the Lasses here, my Lord, we can neither begin our Procession nor our Dances.

COUNT: [*Gravely putting on his hat.*] Why surely, Sir, you don't intend to dance.

FIGARO: Why not, my Lord?

COUNT: What! With a hurt in your ancle?

FIGARO: Oh! Is that all? – It pains me a little, to be sure; but that's a trifle – Come Girls.

COUNT: [*Turning him back.*] You were very lucky to light upon such soft ground.

FIGARO: Exceedingly, my Lord: – Come Lasses.

ANTONIO: [*Turning him back on the other side.*] And then you double yourself up, when you take a leap? Yet, like a Cat, you fall on your feet.

FIGARO: What then? – Come Gir –

COUNT: But how unhappy the poor Youth will be about his Commission.

FIGARO: What is the meaning of all this, my Lord?

ANTONIO: [*Bringing the* PAGE *forward.*] Do you know this bashful young Lady?

FIGARO: The Devil! Cherubin! – [*Aside.*] Well, and what Riddle has he to propound?

COUNT: No Riddle, Sir, but a simple matter of fact: – he affirms, it was he who jump'd out of the window.

FIGARO: Does he? – Well, if he say so, I suppose it is so.

COUNT: How! What two at a time?

FIGARO: Two? Twenty! Why not, my Lord? One sheep begins, the rest naturally follow: [*Flourish of Music without.*] Come, come, my merry Maidens, don't you hear the music? Quick, quick, run, run, run.

[*Exuent* SUSAN *and* FIGARO, *with the Girls.*]

COUNT: [*To the* PAGE.] Harkee, little Rascal, begone, instantly; put off your Petticoats, and don't stir out of your room the rest of the day. – Take care, Sir, I don't meet you again.

PAGE: [*Putting on his hat.*] No matter – I bare away that upon my forehead, which would compensate for an age of imprisonment. [*Exit joyously.*]

COUNT: [*Looks at the* COUNTESS, *who recollects the kiss she had just given the* PAGE.] His forehead! What is it he bears away so triumphantly upon his forehead?

COUNTESS: [*Embarrassed.*] A – His Officer's hat, I suppose. Every new Bauble pleases a Child. [*Going.*]

COUNT: The Procession is coming, will not your Ladyship stay and be a witness of your Favourite's happiness.

COUNTESS: As your Lordship pleases.

[*Enter the Procession of the two Weddings. A March is played;* DOCTOR BARTHOLO *and* MARCELINA *are preceded by* CRYER *of the Court, Guards,* DOUBLE-FEE, *Counsellors,* DON GUZMAN; *after them come* ANTONIO, FIGARO, *and* SUSAN, *followed by the Bridesmen and Maids, and a troop of Dancers. They all salute the* COUNT *and* COUNTESS *as they pass; and after making the tour of the stage,* ANTONIO *presents his Niece to the* COUNT; SUSAN *kneels, one of the Bridesmaids gives the* COUNT *the nuptial Cap; and* SUSAN, *while the* COUNT *is placing it on her head, plucks him by the cloak, and shews him the Note she had just before written. He pretends to keep adjusting the Cap, and slily reaches to take the Note, which he instantly claps to his bosom, having previously unbuttoned himself for that purpose. While this is transacting a Castanent-Dance is performed. As soon as* SUSAN *rises, she purposely places herself before the* COUNTESS, *to encourage the* COUNT *to read the Note, who accordingly steps forward, is going to open it, and pricks his finger with the Pin, which he plucks out and throws angrily on the floor.*]

COUNT: These Women and their curst Pins.

FIGARO: [*Aside to his Mother laughing.*] The Count has received a Billet-doux from some pretty Girl, sealed with a Pin! This is a new fashion, which he does not seem to admire. [*The* COUNT *reads the Note, is exceedingly pleased, folds it up again, and reads on the outside, "Return the Seal", he pretends to walk carelessly about the stage, but is all the while looking earnestly for the pin he had thrown away, which he at last finds, picks up sticks upon his Sleeve.*]

FIGARO: [*To his Mother.*] Every thing is precious that appertains to a beloved object. – He picks up the very Pin, you see. [*All this while* SUSAN *and the* COUNTESS *remark what is passing with laughter, and private looks and gestures.*]

COUNTESS: [*Rising.*] Come with me, Susan. We shall soon be back, my Lord, [*Aside to* SUSAN.] Let us make haste and exchange dresses.

[*Exeunt* COUNTESS *and* SUSAN.]

CRIER: Guards! Guards! – This way, Guards! [*Places the Guards at the door, runs up to the* COUNT.] My Lord, here's Mr. Basil coming, my Lord, with the whole Village at his heels, because he has been singing all the way he went.

FIGARO: Orpheus and the Brutes. But I'll make him change his Tune.

[*Enter* BASIL *singing, followed by* BOUNCE.]

COUNT: So, Mr. Basil, what is your will and pleasure?

BASIL: After having fulfilled your Lordship's commands, by amusing this honest Gentleman –

BOUNCE: Me, my Lord? I assure your Lordship he has not amused me in the least.

BASIL: I now return to enforce my claims on Marcelina.

FIGARO: Look you, Sir – Should you venture but to cast one look, or approach on step nearer that Lady –

DOCTOR: Let him speak, Figaro, let him speak.

GUZMAN: Oh f-f-fie! – What f-f-friends! –

FIGARO: I dislaim such friendship.

BASIL: And I – Error in Judgement, Mr. President.

FIGARO: He! – A Street-corner Ballad-Bawler!

BASIL: As good, at least, as a Barber-Surgeon!

FIGARO: Who hashes up a dinner out of Horse-hair and Catgut!

BASIL: Who has hungrily devoured Razors and Hones, and fed half his life upon Froth! [*Imitates beating up a Lather.*]

FIGARO: The high Priest of Pimps!
BASIL: The vile Drudge of Intrigue!
FIGARO: Execrated by those he serves!
BASIL: Gulled by his own Cunning!
FIGARO: So great a Fool, Knavery itself cannot make him thrive!
BASIL: So stupid, he never yet could invent a probable Lie!
DOCTOR: } Hold, hold.
GUZMAN: } Hold, hold.
FIGARO: A Pedantic!
BASIL: Pert!
FIGARO: Preposterous!
BASIL: Pragmatical!
FIGARO: Braying!
BASIL: Lop-eared!
FIGARO: Ass!
COUNT: How now! – Is this all the Respect you shew? –
BASIL: You hear, my Lord, how he insults me! When, it is well known, there is not, in all Andalusia, a more eminent! –
FIGARO: Empty!
BASIL: Able!
FIGARO: Abject!
BASIL: Musician!
FIGARO: Miscreant!
BASIL: Is this to be borne?
FIGARO: Whose countenance prophecies of Pillories, Scaffolds, and the stretching of Hemp; and whose whole appearance is a continual Memento of public Calamity, Plague, Pestilence, and Famine; – A Misericordia, Sackcloth-and-ashes Knave; – A Scape Goat, that looks like a Jew in the yellow Jaundice. [DOCTOR BARTHOLO *and* DON GUZMAN *prevent* BASIL *from falling upon* FIGARO.]
COUNT: Do you think this proper, Mr.Figaro?
FIGARO: Why not, my Lord? – Let him listen to Truth, since he is too Poor to pay Parasites and Liars.
COUNT: Silence, Sir! – Let us hear, Mr. Basil, what you have to say.
BASIL: [*Composing himself.*] I demand the hand of Marcelina, my Lord, who promised to marry me.
MARCELINA: On what condition was this promise made?
BASIL: That I should adopt your lost Son, if ever you should be happy enough to find him.
MARCELINA: Well.
DOCTOR: He is found.
BASIL: Where is he?
GUZMAN: The-e-e-ere he stands.
BASIL: He! – Oh, my curst Stars!
GUZMAN: Do you re-e-nounce your pre-e-tentions to his de-e-ear Mother?

BASIL: Renounce! – As I would renounce the Devil and all his Works.

FIGARO: What! Renounce your best Friend? – But that's like your Rogue's tricks.

BASIL: I will not live under the same roof as him – I would rather even quit the service of my Lord.

FIGARO: Don't be uneasy, I shan't trouble you long – Restored to my Parents, and married to my Susan, I shall retire and live in Peace.

COUNT: [*Aside.*] And I shall retire to meet my Mistress.

GUZMAN: So every body is sa-a-tisfied.

COUNT: Let the marriage Contracts be prepared, and I will sign them.

FIGARO: Thanks, gracious Lord.

BOUNCE: And I will go and prepare the Fireworks in the Garden, near the Pavilion.

COUNT: [*Returning.*] Who, pray Sir, gave you those Orders? – The Countess is too much indisposed to come out; let them, therefore, be played off in front of the Castle, facing her Windows – [*Aside.*] – The Rascal was going to set fire to my Place of Rendezvous! [*Exeunt.*]

[*Manent* FIGARO *and* MARCELINA.]

FIGARO: How attentive he is to his Wife.

MARCELINA: It is necessary – My dear Figaro, I should undeceive thee respecting my former false accusations of Susan – Basil has always told me she obstinately refused to listen to the Count's Overtures, and I am both sorry and ashamed to have excited thy Jealousy.

FIGARO: Oh, be under no apprehensions, my dear Mother; Jealousy is the foolish Child of Pride, the Disease of a Madman – My Philosophy is invulnerable to its poisonous Arrows.

[FIGARO *turns and sees* AGNES *just behind him, coming down the Stage.*]

– So! What you have been listening, my little inquisitive Cousin?

AGNES: Oh, no; they tell me that is not polite.

FIGARO: Then what's your errand? – He is not here.

AGNES: Who?

FIGARO: Cherubin.

AGNES: Oh, I know that very well – I know where he is – I want my Cousin Susan.

FIGARO: Aye! – And what do you want with her?

AGNES: Not much; only to give her a Pin.

FIGARO: [*Starts.*] A Pin! [*Striding about in great anger.*] A Pin! – And how dare you, you little Hussey, undertake such Messages? – What! Have you learnt your trade already? – [MARCELINA *makes a sign to* FIGARO, *who recollects himself, and endeavours to disguise his feelings.*] – Come, come, my pretty Cousin, don't be frighten'd, I was but in joke – I – I – I know all about it; its a Pin that my Lord has sent by you to Susan.

AGNES: Since you know so well, why need you ask me then?

FIGARO: [*Coaxing*.] Only to hear what my Lord said when he sent thee on this errand.

AGNES: Here, said he, here, my pretty little Agnes, take this Pin to thy Cousin Susan, and tell her it is the Seal of the new Song about the Twilight and the Pavilion.

FIGARO: And the –

AGNES: The Pavilion – And take great care, said he, that nobody sees thee.

FIGARO: Well, well, I was but joking; go and execute thy Message faithfully, exactly as my Lord bade thee.

AGNES: Law! My Cousin takes me for a Ninny, I believe. [*Exit skipping*.]

FIGARO: So, my Mother!

MARCELINA: So, my son!

FIGARO: Here's a sweet Daughter! – A delightful Bride! – And will be a most virtuous Wife! – [*Walking up and down with great agitation*.] – A false – Deceitful – I'm happy, however, I have found her own – I will detect, expose and abandon her!

MARCELINA: Nay, but gently, my son, gently; recollect that Jealousy is the disease of a Madman, and that your Philosophy is invulnerable. – Fie! fie! – All this passion about a Pin!

FIGARO: A Pin that has wounded me to the heart! – Didn't we see the Count pick it up?

MARCELINA: We did so; but how can we tell whether she means to deceive thee or him? – Art thou sure she will go to the Rendezvous; and wilt thou condemn her without hearing her?

FIGARO: I am sorry – I am a Fool – And yet! – If she should be false!

MARCELINA: Nay, but my dear Figaro –

FIGARO: Well, well; I will be calm – Yes, my amorous Count, you will at least meet with somebody you don't expect – If you do not make haste we shall be at the Pavilion as soon as your Lordship! [*Exeunt*.]

Act V

[SCENE, *the Garden,*
with walks of cut trees in the back ground, and two
Pavilions, one on each side of the stage.
Enter AGNES. *A lanthorn in one hand, and two cakes and an orange in the other*.]

AGNES: The Pavilion to the left? Ay, that's it. – But if he should not come soon! – He has not half learnt me my part yet – Poor thing, he hasn't eat any thing all day; and the cross, good-for-nothing Cook would not give me a morsel for him; so I was obliged to ask the Butler for these Cakes and this Orange: – it cost me a good kiss on the cheek, but I know who'll repay – Oh dear, here's somebody coming! –

[*Enter* FIGARO, *disguised in a red Rocquelaure;* DOCTOR BARTHOLO, DON GUZMAN, BASIL, ANTONIO. FIGARO *imagines at first* AGNES *to be* SUSAN; *and, as it is too dark to see, endeavours to follow the sound of her voice, having entered while she was speaking.* AGNES *enters the Pavilion on the left.*]

FIGARO: I was mistaken, 'tis Agnes! [*They all grope down the stage till they get round* FIGARO.] What o'clock is it?

ANTONIO: Almost near the moon's rising.

BASIL: What a gloomy night.

DOCTOR: We look like so many Conspirators.

FIGARO: You understand, Gentlemen, why you are come hither – It is to be Witnesses of the Conduct of the virtuous Bride I am soon to espouse, and the honourable Lord who has graciously bestowed her upon me.

BASIL: [*Aside.*] This will be a precious Revenge.

DOCTOR: Remember, Figaro, a wise Man has never any Contest with the Great; it is the Battle of Don Quixote with the Windmills; they whirl and dash you to a Distance, without once altering or retarding their Course.

FIGARO: Rather remember they have not courage to oppress any but Cowards.

DOCTOR: He's mad.

GUZMAN: Ye-e-es, he is ma-a-ad.

ANTONIO: But what about?

BASIL: A certain Rendezvous; – Come this way, and I'll tell you the whole.

FIGARO: Hide yourselves hereabouts, and come running the Moment you hear me call.

DOCTOR: He is turning Fool.

GUZMAN: Ye-e-es, he's turning foo-oo-ool – Stay and take ca-are of him. [*Exuent.*]

[*Manent* FIGARO *and* DOCTOR.]

FIGARO: Oh Woman, Woman, Woman! Inconstant, weak, deceitful Woman! – But each Animal is obliged to follow the instinct of its Nature; and it is thine to betray! – What, after swearing this very Morning to remain for ever Faithful; and on the identical Day! The bridal Day! –

DOCTOR: Patience.

FIGARO: I even saw her laugh with Delight, while he read her Billet! – They think themselves secure, but perhaps they yet may be deceived. – No, my very worthy Lord and Master, you have not got her yet – What! Because you are a great Man, you fancy yourself a great Genius. – Which way? – How came you to be the rich and mighty Count Almaviva! Why truly, you gave yourself the Trouble to be born! While the obscurity in which I have been cast demanded more Abilities to gain a mere Subsistence than are requisite to govern Empires. And what, most noble Count, are your Claims to Distinction, to pompous Titles, and immense Wealth, of which you are so proud, and which, by Accident, you possess?[1] For which of your Virtues? Your Wisdom? Your Generosity? Your Justice? – The Wisdom you have acquired consists in vile Arts, to gratify vile Passions; your Generosity is lavished on your hireling Instruments, but whose Necessities make them far less Contemptible than yourself; and your Justice is the inveterate Persecution of those who have the Will and Wit to resist your Depredations. But this has ever been the Practice of the *little* Great; those they cannot degrade, the endeavour to crush.

DOCTOR: Be advised, Figaro – be calm – there has ever been a Respect paid –

FIGARO: To Vice – where it is not due. – Shame light on them that pay it.

DOCTOR: Consider, he is –

FIGARO: A Lord – and I am – a Man! – Yes, I am a Man, but the nocturnal Spells of that enchantress Woman, soon shall make me a Monster. Why, what an Ass am I! – Acting here the idiot part of a [*Strikes his forehead.*] – a – *Husband* – Altho' I am but half finished.

[AGNES *peeps out of the Pavilion, and approaches a little way to listen.*]

AGNES: Is that Cherubin?

DOCTOR: I hear somebody! [AGNES *hears the voice of the* DOCTOR, *and runs in again.*] I will retire, but if you are wise, you will wait the Event patiently; your suspicions may be unjust, – should they prove real, then shake her from you, as her Ingratitude deserves. [*Exit.*]

FIGARO: Oh, how easy it is for the prayer mumbling Priest to bid the Wretch on the Rack suffer patiently. [FIGARO *listens.*] I hear nothing – all is silent – and dark as their designs. [FIGARO *pulls off his Roquelaure, and throws it on a Garden-bench.*] Why, what a Destiny is mine – Am I for ever doom'd to be the foot-ball of Fortune? – Son of I knew not who, stol'n I knew not how, and brought up to I knew not what, lying and thieving excepted, I had the sense, tho' young, to despise a life so base, and fled such infernal Tutors. My Genius, tho' cramp'd, could not be totally subdued, and I spent what little time and money I could spare in Books and Study. Alas! it was but time and money thrown away. Desolate in the world, unfriended, unprotected, my poor stock of knowledge not being whip'd into me by the masculine hic haec hoc hand of a School-master, I could not get Bread, much less Preferment. – Disheartened by the failure of all my projects, I yet had the audacity to attempt a Comedy, but as I had the still greater audacity to attack the favorite Vice of the favorite Mistress, of the favorite Footman of the Favorite Minister, I could not get it licensed. – It happened about that time, that the fashionable Question of the day was an enquiry into the real and imaginary Wealth of Nations; and, as it is not necessary to possess the thing you write about, I, with lank Cheeks, pennyless Purse, and all the simplicity of a Boy, or a

1. The remainder of this speech was omitted in the officially approved edition of the play published by Beaumarchais in April 1785. Some of the references to censorship and economic issues in Figaro's monologue are also omitted.

Philosopher, freely described the true causes of national Poverty: when suddenly I was awaken'd in my bed at Mid-night, and entrusted to the tender care of his Catholic Majesty's Mirmidons, whose Magic-power caused the heavy gates of an old Castle to fly open at my approach, where I was graciously received, lodged, and ornamented, according to the fashion of the place, and provided with Straw, and Bread, and Water gratis. My ardor for Liberty sufficiently cool'd. I was once more turned adrift into the wide World, with leave to provide Straw and Bread and Water for myself. – On this my second birth, I found all Madrid in Raptures, concerning a most generous Royal Edict, lately published, in favour of the Liberty of the Press: and I soon learnt, that, provided I neither spoke of the Wealth of Nations in my writings, nor of the Government, nor of Religion, nor of any Corporate-Companies, nor offended the favorite Mistress of the Minister's favorite Footman, nor said any one thing which could be twisted into a reference, or hint, derogatory to any one Individual, who had more powerful friends than I had, I was at liberty to write, freely, all, and whatever I pleased, under the inspection of some two or three Censors! – soon after this, a Place happened to be vacant, which required a person well acquainted with Calculation; I offered my Services; my Abilities were not questioned; I waited, in anxious expectation of the Event, and, in three days, learnt it had been bestowed, two days before, upon a Dancing-master. – Persecuted by Creditors, tired of starving, and unable, through the feebleness of Youth to sustain so unequal a Struggle, I had the weakness, at last, to sink before Temptation, and set up a Pharaoh Bank.[1] And now, for once, behold the Scene changed! See me equally familiar with Lords as with their Lacquies! Every door was open to me! Every hand held out! But, notwithstanding my desire to be Something in this world, my detestation of the brazen Effrontery, profound Ignorance, and insupportable Insolence of these fashionable Friends of Nobility was so innate that I found I could better endure all the Miseries of Poverty than the Disgrace and Disgust of such Society. – Quitting, therefore, with contempt this new Trade, and leaving false shame behind me, as a burthen too heavy for a Foot-passenger, I once more took up my strap and hone, and travelled for employment from Town to Town. – At Seville I found a Lord mad to marry his Mistress; my Wit procured him what his could not, a Wife; and, in return, he gratefully endeavours to Seduce mine – Strange concatenation of circumstance! My Parents all at once claim me! – 'Tis he, 'tis she, 'tis me, 'tis – I don't know who! – I came into the world without my Knowledge, and I shall go out on't without my Will; and thus do I continue to torment myself about what this Being is,

1. A gaming house for the wealthy. Pharaoh or Faro was a card game at which fortunes could be won and lost. It was fashionable throughout the eighteenth century and remained a popular gambling game in casinos until the end of the nineteenth century.

what it was, what it shall be, whence it came, where it is, or whither it shall go. – I only know it to be a compound of Contradictions! A little, wise, foolish Animal, ardent in pursuit of Pleasure, capricious through Vanity, laborious from Necessity, but indolent by Choice. After having exhausted every Art for enjoyment, and every Profession for a livelihood, I found myself intoxicated by a heavenly Illusion, that has vanish'd at my approach! – Vanished! – And is it vanish'd? – Oh Susan! Susan! [FIGARO *sinks melancholy upon the garden-seat; but being suddenly roused by a noise, wraps himself up in his Roquelaure.*]

[*Enter softly, in each other's dress, the* COUNTESS *and* SUSAN, *followed by* MARCELINA.]

SUSAN: So Figaro is to be here. [*In an under voice.*]
MARCELINA: He is here.
SUSAN: Thus one is come to lay the Springe, and the other to seize the Game.
MARCELINA: I will go and hide myself in this Pavilion, where I shall hear all. [*Exit into the Pavilion on the left.*]
SUSAN: We may begin. [*Speaks louder.*] If my Lady does not want me, I will walk and enjoy the fresh air.
FIGARO: Oh, the Cocatrice.
COUNTESS: It may give thee cold.
SUSAN: Oh no, my Lady.
FIGARO: Oh no! She'll not take cold to-night. [*Aside.*]
[SUSAN *retires a little towards the Pavilion on the left;* CHERUBIN *is heard singing, and, as he enters, perceives the* COUNTESS, *in* SUSAN'*s dress.*]
PAGE: Is that Agnes, yonder? [*He approaches.*] By her long Lappets and white Feathers, it must be Susan. [*Comes up and takes hold of the* COUNTESS'*s hand.*] Ah, my dear Susan!
COUNTESS: Let me go. [*In a feigned voice.*]
PAGE: Come, Come; don't be so coy. I know it is not Figaro you are waiting for, it is my Lord the Count – what! Did not I hear, this Morning, when I was behind the great Chair?
SUSAN: [*Aside.*] The babbling little villain.

[*Enter the* COUNT *behind, and hears the* PAGE.]

COUNT: Is not that somebody with Susan? – [*Advances close up to them, and draws back in fury.*] – 'Tis that infernal Page again. [SUSAN *keeps out of the way and silently laughing.*]
PAGE: 'Tis in vain to say no: – Since thou art going to be the Representative of the Countess, I am determined to give the one kiss for thyself, and a hundred for thy beauteous Lady.
SUSAN: [*Aside.*] As impudent as a Page, says the Proverb.
[*The* COUNTESS *draws back to avoid being kissed by the* PAGE, *and the*

COUNT *advances and presents himself in her place: the* PAGE *feels the rough beard of the* COUNT, *and suddenly retreats, crying in an under voice.*]

– Oh, the Devil! – The Count again!

[*Exit* PAGE *into the Pavilion on the left.*]

[*While this passes,* FIGARO *likewise advances to drive the* PAGE *from* SUSAN; *meanwhile the* COUNT, *on the* PAGE'*s supposed next approach, prepares to give him a proper reception.*]

COUNT: [*Thinking he speaks to the* PAGE.] Since you are so fond of kissing, take that. [*Gives* FIGARO *a severe box on the ear.*]

FIGARO: I have paid for listening. [SUSAN *cannot contain herself, but bursts out a laughing.*]

COUNT: [*Hears her laugh.*] Why this is inconceiveable! – Do such Salutations make the impudent Rascal laugh?

FIGARO: It would be strange if he should cry this time. [*Aside.*]

[COUNT *and* COUNTESS *approach.*]

COUNT: But let us not lose the precious moments, my charming Susan! – Let these Kisses speak my ardour! [*Kisses the* COUNTESS *several times with rapture.*]

FIGARO: [*Aside, and beating his forehead.*] Oh! Oh! Oh!

COUNT: Why dost thou tremble?

COUNTESS: [*Continuing her feigned voice.*] Because I am afraid.

COUNT: Thou seemest to have got a cold. [*Takes the* COUNTESS'*s hand between his own, and amorously strokes and kisses her fingers.*] What a sweet, delicate, Angel's hand! – How smooth and soft! – How long and small the fingers! – What pleasure in the touch! – Ah! how different is this from the Countess's hand! –

COUNTESS: [*Sighing.*] And yet you loved her once.

COUNT: Yes – Yes – I did so – But three Years of better Acquaintance has made the Marriage-state so respectable – And then Wives are so loving – when they *do* love, that is – that one is surprised when in search of Pleasure, to find Satiety.

COUNTESS: Pleasure? – Love!

COUNT: Oh, no; Love is but the Romance of the Heart; Pleasure is its History – As for thee, my dear Susan, add but one grain more of Caprice to thy Composition and thou wilt make one of the most enticing, teazing, agreeable Mistresses.

COUNTESS: 'Tis my Duty to oblige my Lord.

FIGARO: Her Duty! –

COUNT: Yes – Women's Duties are unlimited – They owe all – Men nothing.

COUNTESS: Nothing?

COUNT: It is not our Faults; 'tis the law of Nature – And then Wives think to ensure our fidelity by being always Wives – Whereas they should sometimes become –

COUNTESS: What?

COUNT: Our Mistresses – I hope thou wilt not forget this Lesson.

COUNTESS: Oh no, indeed, not I.

SUSAN: [*Aloud.*] Nor I.

FIGARO: [*Aloud.*] Nor I.

COUNT: [*Astonished.*] Are there Echoes here?

COUNTESS: Oh, yes.

COUNT: And now, my sweet Susan, receive the Portion I promised thee. [*Gives a purse and puts a ring upon her finger.*] – And continue likewise to wear this Ring for my sake.

COUNTESS: Susan accepts your Favours.

FIGARO: [*Aside.*] Was there ever so faithless a Hussey?

SUSAN: [*Aside.*] These riches are all for us! [*Still keeps chuckling very heartily at what is going forwards.*]

COUNTESS: I perceive Torches.

COUNT: They are preparatory to thy Nuptials. [*The* COUNTESS *pretends to be afraid.*] Come, come, let us retire for a moment into the Pavilion.

COUNTESS: What! In the dark?

COUNT: Why not? There are not Spirits.

FIGARO: [*Aside.*] Yes, but there are; and evil ones too. [COUNTESS *follows the* COUNT.] She is going! – Hem! [FIGARO *hem's in a great passion.*]

COUNT: [*Raising his voice majesterially.*] Who goes there!

FIGARO: A man.

COUNT: [*Aside to the* COUNTESS.] It's Figaro! [*The* COUNTESS *enters the Pavilion on the right hand and the Count retires.*]

FIGARO: [*Desperate.*] They are gone in. [*Walks about.*] Let her go – Let her go!

SUSAN: [*Aside.*] Thou shalt pay presently for these fine Suspicions. [SUSAN *advances and mimics the voice of the* COUNTESS.] Who is that?

FIGARO: 'Tis the Countess [*Aside.*] – What lucky Chance conducted you hither, Madam – You know not what Scenes are this moment transacting.

SUSAN: Oh yes, but I do, Figaro.

FIGARO: What! That the Count and my very virtuous Bride are this moment in yonder Pavilion Madam!

SUSAN: [*Aside.*] Very well, my Gentleman! — I know more than thou dost.

FIGARO: And will you not be revenged?

SUSAN: Oh yes, we always have our Revenge in our own power.

FIGARO: [*Aside.*] What does she mean? – Perhaps what I suspect – Why that would be a glorious Retaliation. – [*To* SUSAN] There is no Means but one, Madam, of revenging such Wrongs; that now presents itself.

SUSAN: [*Jealous.*] What does the good-for-nothing Fellow mean? [*Speaks in a tone of compliance to* FIGARO.] Does it Figaro?

FIGARO: Pardon my Presumption, Madam! On any other occasion, the Respect I bear your Ladyship would keep me silent, but on the present I dare encounter all! [*Falls on his knees.*] Oh, excuse, forgive me, Madam; but let not the precious moments slip! – Grant me your hand.

SUSAN: [*Unable any longer to contain herself gives him a slap on the face.*] Take it.

FIGARO: I have it, I think! — The Devil! This is the Day of Stripes!

SUSAN: Susan gives it thee [*As soon as* FIGARO *hears it is* SUSAN, *his satisfaction is so extreme, he laughs very heartily, and keeps laughing all the while she keeps beating him.*] and that, and that, and that, and that for thy Insolence – And that for thy Jealousy – And that for thy Infidelity. [SUSAN *out of breath,* FIGARO *still laughing.*]

FIGARO: Oh happy Figaro – Take thy Revenge, my dear, kind, good Angel; Never did Man or Martyr suffer with such Extacy!

SUSAN: Don't tell me of your Extacy! How durst you, you good for nothing, base, false-hearted Man, make love to me, supposing me the Countess.

FIGARO: I must bring myself off. [*Aside.*] – Dost think I could mistake the music of my Susan's Voice?

SUSAN: What, you pretend you knew me then?

FIGARO: Pretend! Canst thou doubt it?

SUSAN: And this was a Trick upon me! – But I'll be revenged.

FIGARO: Talk not of Revenge, my Love, but tell me what blest Angel sent thee hither, and how thou camest by this Disguise, which so fully proves thy Innocence!

SUSAN: I could find in my Heart not to tell thee; but know, to thy Confusion, it is my Lady's; and that, coming to catch one Fox, we have entrapped two!

FIGARO: But who has taken the other?

SUSAN: His Wife.

FIGARO: His Wife! – Go and hang thyself, Figaro – Go and hang thyself, for wanting the Wit to divine this Plot! – And has all this intriguing been about his Wife?

SUSAN: Yes, about his Wife.

FIGARO: But who did the Page kiss?

SUSAN: The Count.

FIGARO: The Count! Ha! ha! ha! that is excellent. [*Resuming his gravity.*] But who did the Count kiss?

SUSAN: The Countess.

FIGARO: Ay, but who did he kiss this Morning – behind the Great Chair?

SUSAN: [*Gravely.*] Nobody.

FIGARO: Art thou – quite sure?

SUSAN: [*Holding out her Hand.*] Dost thou want another Proof?

FIGARO: Ah! Thine are but proofs of Love – That the Count, indeed, was not so gentle.

[*Enter* COUNT *behind.*]

COUNT: 'St – 'st! Susan! – Susan!

FIGARO: [*Aside to* SUSAN.] A lucky thought strikes me; prithee second me, Susan, [*Speaks in a feigned Voice, falls on his knees and kisses* SUSAN's *Hand.*] – Ah Madam! Let us not longer converse of Love, but enjoy its Treasures.

COUNT: What's here! A Man on his knees to the Countess! – [*Feels for his Sword, they keep silently laughing.*] And I unarm'd!

FIGARO: [*Acting the Petit Maitre.*] Upon my Honour Madam, I could not have supposed Timidity should make you hesitate a moment.

COUNT: [*Furiously.*] So this is our Dressing-room Gentleman, at last! I shall know all at least, now – [FIGARO *kisses her hand again.*] Oh Rage! Oh Hell!

SUSAN: How delightfully he swears.

FIGARO: [FIGARO *and* SUSAN *still inwardly laughing.*] Quickly then, Madam, let us repair the wrong which Love this Morning suffered at the impertinent intrusion of your Lord.

COUNT: This is not be borne [*Darts between them, seizes* FIGARO *by the Collar, while* SUSAN *escapes into the Pavilion on the left.*]

FIGARO: [*Pretends amazement.*] My Lord!

COUNT: How! Rascal! And is it you! – Hollo – Hollo – Who hears?

[*Enter blundering in the dark, and in a great hurry, the* COURIER, *who had been to Seville after the* PAGE.]

COURIER: Here! – Here! – Here am I, my Lord! Just arrived from Seville! But he is not there! I might as well have sought for this Page in my pocket! Here is the Packet again.

COUNT: Stand out of the way, Rascal – Hollo! – Where are my People, Lights! Lights!

COURIER: What's my Lord afraid of? Is there not Mr Figaro and I?

[*Enter Flambeaux,* DON GUZMAN, DR. BARTHOLO, ANTONIO, BASIL, *and* SERVANTS.]

COUNT: [*To the* SERVANTS.] Guard that Door and some of you seize this Fellow.

FIGARO: You command, with absolute Authority, over all present, my Lord, except yourself.

COUNT: The Villain's impenetrable, cool Impudence is intolerable.

FIGARO: We are not Soldiers, that we should kill one another without Malice: for my part, I like to know why I am angry.

COUNT: Be pleased, Sir, to declare, before this Company, who the – the – Woman is that just now ran into that Pavilion.

FIGARO: Into that – [*Going to cross to the Pavilion on the right.*]

COUNT: [*Stopping him.*] No, prevaricating Fiend; into that. [*Pointing to the other.*]

FIGARO: Ah! That alters the Case.

COUNT: Answer, or –

FIGARO: The Lady that escaped into that Pavilion?

COUNT: Ay, Demon, the Lady.

FIGARO: The Lady that escaped into that Pavilion, is a young Lady to whom my Lord once paid his Addresses, but who, happening to love me more than my Betters, has this day yielded me the Preference.

COUNT: The Preference! – The Preference! – he does not lie at least. – Yes, Gentlemen, what he confesses, I pledge my Honour I just have heard from the very mouth of his Accomplice!

GUZMAN: His Accomplice!

COUNT: Come forth, Madam! [*Enters the Pavilion.*]

BASIL: Which of these two has made a – Gentleman of the other.

FIGARO: Perhaps neither.

COUNT: [*In the Pavilion.*] Come forth, I say shew yourself. [*Enter, dragging out the* PAGE, *still speaking, and not looking at him till he gets on a line with the rest of the Company.*] Happily, Madam, there is no Pledge of a Union, now so justly detested. –

OMNES: The Page!

GUZMAN: [*After all the rest.*] The Pa-a-age!

COUNT: Again! And again! And everlastingly this damn'd, diabolical page. [PAGE *flies to the other side of the stage.*] You shall find, however, he was not alone.

PAGE: Ah, no! My lot would have been hard indeed then.

COUNT: Enter Antonio, and drag the guilty Thing before her Judge.

ANTONIO: [*In the Pavilion.*] Come, Madam, you must come out; I must not let you go since my Lord knows you are here.

[*Enter with his Daughter,* AGNES.]

OMNES: Agnes!

GUZMAN: A-A-Agnes!

ANTONIO: Odzooks, my Lord, its a pleasant Trick, enough, to send me in, before these good Folks, for my Daughter.

COUNT: I'll find her, I warrant. [*Going.*]

DOCTOR: [*Stopping the* COUNT.] Pardon me, my Lord, but you are too angry at present; let me go. [*Exit* DOCTOR *to the Pavilion.*]

GUZMAN: This Cause is very perplex'd.

DOCTOR: [*Entering with* MARCELINA.] Fear nothing, Madam, fear nothing.

OMNES: Marcelina!

FIGARO: My Mother too! Ha! ha! ha! ha! ha!

COUNT: Where then is this Daughter of Infamy who thus evades my just Fury?

[*Enter* SUSAN, *with her Fan before her face.*]

Here she comes, at last; bearing her own Shame and my Dishonour. [SUSAN *kneels to him, still hiding her Face.*]

OMNES: Pardon, pardon, gracious Lord!

COUNT: No! No! No! [*They all fall on their knees.*] No! No! Were the World to kneel I would be deaf.

[*Enter the* COUNTESS *from the Pavilion on the right, and kneels to the* COUNT, *whose back is turned to her.*]

COUNTESS: At least I will make one of the Number. [SUSAN *drops her fan, the* COUNT *hears the voice of the* COUNTESS, *looks round, and suddenly conceives the whole Trick they have been playing him. All the company burst into a laugh: the* COUNT*'s shame, confusion, &c.*]

GUZMAN: [*Laughing stupidly.*] Ha! ha! ha! ha! 'Tis the Countess!

COUNT: [*With great humility.*] And – is it you my Lady?

COUNTESS: [*Inclines her body in token of Affirmation.*]

COUNT: [*Returning her bow with great confusion.*]
Ah! – Yes! – Yes! A generous pardon – tho' unmerited. –

COUNTESS: Were you in my place, you would exclaim, No! No! No! But I grant it without a single Stipulation.

SUSAN: And I.

FIGARO: And I. – There are Echoes here.

COUNT: [*Surprised.*] I perceive – I perceive – I have been rightly served.

COUNTESS: Here, Susan, here is the Purse and Ring, which my Lord gave thee. He will remember thy sweet delicate Fingers, so long and so small.

SUSAN: Thank your Lordship – Here Figaro. [*Gives him the purse.*]

FIGARO: It was devilish hard to get at –

COUNT: [*To* SUSAN.] And the Letter you wrote –

SUSAN: Was dictated by my Lady.

COUNT: [*Smiling good naturedly.*] Well, well! I am an Answer in her Debt.

FIGARO: Thus every Man shall have his own.

BOUNCE: And shall we throw the Stocking?

COUNTESS: There is the Garter.

[*Throws down the Riband* CHERUBIN *had stolen in the Morning;* BOUNCE *is going to stoop for it, and the* PAGE *pushes him back.*]

PAGE: This is my Right, and if any one dare dispute it with me –

COUNT: Indeed! Mr. Officer – So bold a Champion already! – Pray how did your Valour like the Box on the Ear I gave you just now?

PAGE: [*With his Hand to his Sword.*] Me! My Colonel?

FIGARO: Which I kindly received.

COUNT: Thou!

FIGARO: I – And thus do the Great distribute Justice.

COUNT: [*Laughing.*] Well, Mr. President, [DON GUZMAN *instantly calls up all his Wisdom on finding himself addressed.*] what do you think of all these things?

GUZMAN: Thi-ink, my Lord? [*Considers.*] I-I-think that – I do-o-on't know what to think.

FIGARO: I think, a few such Days as this would form an excellent Ambassador – But lately I was a poor, deserted, solitary Being, in this wide World, and now I have Gold, Relations, and a handsome Wife –

DOCTOR: And Friends will flock in abundance.

FIGARO: Do you think so?

DOCTOR: Oh I know so.

FIGARO: Well, let them, they shall be welcome to all I have – My Wife and my Wealth excepted.

SUSAN: Our Errors past, and all our Follies done,
Oh! That 'twere possible you might be won
To pardon Faults, and Misdemeanours smother,
With the same ease we pardon One-another!
So should we rest, To-night, devoid of Sorrow,
And hope to meet you, joyously, To-morrow.

Emilia Galotti

Gotthold Ephraim Lessing

INTRODUCTION

Born on 23 January 1729, Gotthold Ephraim Lessing was the son of an impoverished Lutheran pastor whose living was in the town of Kamenz, north-east of Dresden. Despite initial opposition from his father, Lessing was to become Germany's first professional man of letters and first outstanding playwright. Between 1741 and 1746 he received a fine classical education as a scholar at a boarding school in Meissen. In September 1746 he matriculated at the University of Leipzig, with the intention of studying theology, but his good intentions did not last for long. Apart from discovering the pleasures of dancing, fencing and socialising, he became increasingly interested in literature and the theatre. The acting troupe led by Karoline Neuber was at the time based in Leipzig, and Lessing was soon an active admirer and literary collaborator. His very first comedy, *The Young Scholar*, was performed by Frau Neuber's troupe in January 1748. Lessing was already planning further playscripts when the precarious financial position of the troupe led them to leave Leipzig in some disarray. Somewhat quixotically, Lessing offered to act as a guarantor for the troupe, which meant that he too was soon obliged to leave Leipzig in some haste to escape a clutch of angry creditors. By February 1749 he had reached Berlin. He was still a young man of only twenty, but he now took the conscious decision to give up his studies and to dedicate himself to a literary career. He wrote a frank and detailed letter to his parents, explaining his decision. Although his father profoundly regretted this decision, Lessing managed to remain on good terms with him throughout his life. Lessing developed into a kind and generous individual, passionately committed to tolerance and understanding in an age that was so often dominated by intellectual and political zealots.

During the early 1750s, Lessing worked in Berlin as a journalist and writer of literary reviews. Gradually he built a solid reputation for himself as a critic, contributing to the best contemporary periodicals and mixing with a group of intellectuals who were to remain lifelong friends, in particular Nicolai and Mendelssohn. In 1755 he completed the first domestic tragedy to be written in German, *Miss Sarah Sampson,* which was performed to much acclaim in July. Heavily indebted to English sentimental novels, notably Richardson's *Clarissa,* this was a piece that was intended to induce pity and tears in its audiences.

After this success, Lessing left Berlin for Leipzig, where he continued his literary career, although further plans for travel were thwarted by the outbreak of the Seven Years War. In 1759 he was back in Berlin, publishing his influential *Literary Letters* in which he passionately advocated the cause of German literature and pleaded for it to be freed from the stifling control of French traditions and conventions. He viewed the robust and colourful traditions of English literature, and particularly the example of Shakespeare, as providing a more suitable model for German literary endeavour.

Despite his prolific output, Lessing was now faced by mounting debts. By the autumn of 1760 he found himself obliged to accept the well-paid post of Secretary to the Prussian General Tauentzien. This entailed a move to Breslau where his duties were light (mainly correspondence on administrative matters and on the exchange of prisoners captured during the Seven Years War), and the danger of boredom grew year by year. During this high-earning period, Lessing gambled a lot but managed to give large sums of money to his family, who had supported him in earlier times. He also worked on his comedy *Minna von Barnhelm* which traced the problematic courtship of a stubborn Prussian Major von Tellheim and his quick-witted Saxon fiancée Minna von Barnhelm. Completed in 1767, this sparkling piece was Germany's first comedy of distinction, and it still enjoys a popular place in the repertoire of the modern German theatre.

Having finally left the staff of General Tauentzien in 1765, Lessing had hopes of becoming the Royal Librarian in Berlin. In the spring of 1766 he completed and published his finely argued treatise on classical art called *Laokoon* and clearly expected this to add some weight to his application. However, the king of Prussia still valued French culture more highly than German, and deliberately chose to appoint a Frenchman to this prestigious post. Lessing's disappointment was short-lived. That same year he was invited to become house dramatist and literary adviser at the newly formed National Theatre in Hamburg. This ambitious undertaking, based in a theatre constructed in 1763, was designed to become a flagship model for German theatrical endeavour – hence its grandiose title. Lessing was excited at the prospect of involvement and took up his new post in April 1767. He published an ambitious prospectus for the *Hamburg Dramaturgy*, which was intended to be a collection of reviews and articles arising out of the work of the new National Theatre. In the event, through a disastrous combination of poor management and public indifference, the theatre foundered by the summer of 1768. Lessing struggled stubbornly to complete the run of issues he had planned for his *Hamburg Dramaturgy*; eventually the last twenty numbers appeared in the spring of 1769. The publication of the *Hamburg Dramaturgy* marked yet another first in German cultural history. It was the first significant contribution to dramatic theory and criticism written in German, an achievement that puts Lessing on a par with John Dryden in England and Pierre Corneille in France.

In his *Dramaturgy* Lessing analysed the function and the purpose of catharsis. Previously, he had felt that the object of tragedy was to arouse pity in an audience. It was this view that underpinned his work on *Miss Sarah Sampson*. Now he argued that the object of tragedy was to achieve catharsis by arousing pity *and* fear. The audience is to feel pity for the hero and fear for itself, and it is more likely to feel the necessary pity if the hero is of the same social class as the audience. Lessing argued that the theatre had a duty to contribute to the moral improvement of its audiences, but not by obvious moralising. Audiences would find it difficult to identify with completely good or completely evil figures. Pity would be most effectively aroused for figures whose normal human weaknesses contribute to their downfall. These ideas were soon to find dramatic expression in his own tragedy, *Emilia Galotti*, completed in March 1772.

The collapse of the National Theatre in Hamburg had left Lessing with an impossible burden of debt. He even had to sell his personal library to meet his most pressing creditors. It was therefore with some relief that he accepted an offer made by the Duke of Brunswick to become librarian at his country seat in Wolfenbüttel. Lessing took up his duties in May 1770. He appears to have enjoyed running a large library with a fine collection. But he felt lonely and isolated as the duke's court was centred around the town of Brunswick (Braunschweig) some eight miles distant from Wolfenbüttel. It was in this isolated setting that he took a renewed interest in a dramatic project, based on the classical story of Virginia, which he had first begun to explore as far back as 1758. The resulting play, *Emilia Galotti*, was first performed for the Duchess's birthday on 13 March 1772. It was widely praised in the contemporary press and was to exert a powerful influence on later German dramatists.

Emilia Galotti

The fate of Virginia is described by Livy in book III of his *History of Rome*. In his account, he tells of the way Appius Claudius, a fifth-century decemvir who had taken dictatorial powers, attempted to seduce Virginia, daughter of the Plebeian Virginius and fiancée of Icilius. Having failed in his attempts at seduction, Appius Claudius persuaded one of his henchmen to claim the girl as a slave. When the case came before the court over which Appius Claudius presided, he naturally found in favour of his henchman. At this point, Virginius realised that he would be quite unable to save his daughter's honour, so he seized a large knife and stabbed her to death. His drastic action prompted an uprising on the part of the Plebeians who overturned Appius Claudius's despotic government.

As early as 1754, Lessing had reviewed a play about Virginia by a contemporary Spanish dramatist for the periodical the *Theatrical Library*. Three years later, in 1757, he himself began work on a play based on the Virginia story when his friend Nicolai announced a competition for the best German tragedy by a contemporary writer. In a letter to Nicolai, written on 21 January 1758, Lessing indicated that his intention was to free the story from its political implications, and instead to stress the fate of the girl, a 'middle-class Virginia'.[1] It was essentially this same project that Lessing took up again when he began work on *Emilia Galotti* in the early 1770s.

The play is set, not in Germany, but in contemporary Italy in the

1. G. E. Lessing, *Werke*, vol. 1 (Berlin and Darmstadt: Tempel-Verlag, 1965) pp. 1074–5. The letter is also quoted by F. J. Lamport, *Lessing and the Drama* (Oxford: Clarendon Press, 1981) p. 160.

town of Guastalla, near Sabbioneta, and in a prince's palace at Dosalo, midway between the two towns. At this point in his career, Lessing had not yet visited Italy, and it is therefore hardly surprising that his use of an Italian setting lacks any sense of local colour. In reality, it is no more than a convenient fiction, which removes the action safely from the confines of a contemporary German court. Lessing may well have intended to play down the political implications of the story, but he was astute enough to realise that to set his play in contemporary Germany was to risk giving grave offence.

By comparison with the classical tale which inspired it, Lessing's play has more psychological than political depth. He carefully avoids drawing major characters who are quintessentially evil or virtuous. The prince, for instance, is not a corrupt despot of the kind one finds describes in Livy. He is young and irresponsible – a man who lives by and for the senses, who falls in and out of love with predictable regularity. Unfortunately he has the misfortune to occupy a social position that gives him absolute authority over his subjects. Because of his exalted status, he mistakenly assumes that he has a right to have whatever or whoever he wants. His misfortunes are compounded by the fact that his closest adviser, Marinelli, is keen to safeguard his own position by pandering to his master's every passing whim. Meanwhile, the realities of power bore him. He is quite prepared to sign a death warrant, without even considering the case. The elderly privy counsellor, Camilla Rota, who presents the warrant for signature, pretends to have forgotten it. He fully understands the implications of power over life and death, and is not willing to allow the prince to sign away a man's life in a moment of idle distraction. As Lessing has drawn him, the prince is not a fundamentally evil figure, merely young and irresponsible. Nevertheless, his thoughtless actions (and the more deliberate actions of his underlings) have fearful consequences.

The prince has grown tired of his mistress Countess Orsina and has fallen in love with a young middle-class girl, Emilia Galotti, whom he recently met at a reception in the house of his Chancellor Grimaldi. She has made a powerful impression on him, which is confirmed when the court portrait painter Conti brings paintings of both Orsina and Emilia to show him. The first painting was a commission, the second was an attempt by the artist to capture an image of outstanding natural beauty. The prince is no longer interested in the portrait of Countess Orsina; instead he is completely enthralled by Conti's artistic homage to Emilia's beauty. This only serves to heighten his distress when he discovers that Emilia is to marry Count Appiani that very same day. The awesome consequences of the action are unleashed when, in his distress, he gives his adviser Marinelli a free hand to deal with the situation as he best sees fit.

Initially Marinelli attempts the path of diplomacy. He attempts to offer Count Appiani a diplomatic mission to visit the Duke of Massa as an ambassador in order to make arrangements for the prince's marriage with the duke's daughter. The only proviso being that he must leave this very day and postpone his own wedding with Emilia Galotti. Appiani rejects the offer contemptuously and roundly insults Marinelli in the process, calling him a 'court-monkey'. This confirms Marinelli in his resolve to pursue his fall-back scheme, which is to have Appiani assassinated.

While Marinelli pursues the path of dispassionately planned strategies to prevent the marriage of Appiani and Emilia, the prince pursues his own impulsive course of action. Having observed Emilia attending daily mass at the Church of the Dominicans, he gambles on the fact that she will still do so even on her wedding day. He decides to sit behind her at mass and to whisper his own suit into her ear. When this happens, Emilia is deeply shocked and flees from the prince, hardly able to speak to him. When she arrives home, her mother Claudia persuades her to say nothing of this event either to her father Odoardo or to her fiancé. Claudia knows that Odoardo is quick to anger and Appiani, she suspects, may easily become jealous. Had she spoken out, the two men would at least have had some inkling of the danger that now faced them. As it is, Appiani rides unsuspecting into the trap set by Marinelli.

Odoardo leaves first to ride on to Sabbioneta. Appiani accompanies Emilia and her mother with only two servants. Not far from the prince's estate at Dosalo, they are attacked by brigands; these are professional killers hired by Marinelli. They do their work effectively. Appiani is shot and dies slowly. Emilia is 'rescued', and in the process is separated from her mother. She is brought to the prince by one of his loyal servants; throughout she is treated with due courtesy and decorum, but the prince loses no time in starting to impress Emilia with his particular blend of charm and authority.

Marinelli is at some pains to prevent mother and daughter and then father and daughter from seeing each other. His object is to give the prince as much time as possible to work on Emilia without interruption. Unfortunately for him, his plans are thwarted by the impulsiveness of all the characters surrounding him. He alone tries to operate as a calculating rationalist in a world that seems governed by emotional impulse.

Firstly, there is the behaviour of the prince himself. His rash attempt to seduce Emilia in the Church of the Dominicans naturally makes both her and above all her mother deeply suspicious of his behaviour now. Next, there is the impulsive passion of the wronged Countess Orsina, who arrives at Dosalo only to find herself thrust aside by Marinelli and the prince. In her jealous fury, she is determined to spoil Marinelli's strategy by informing Emilia's father Odoardo of all that has happened thus far, in the hope that he might be roused to take revenge on the prince. She even hands him a dagger to carry out the deed. Finally, there is Odoardo himself: an old soldier with a fiery temper and a profound sense of honour. Confronted by a situation where he learns of the prince's approach to his daughter in the church at Guastalla, where he assumes that Appiani has been assassinated at the prince's behest, and where he now discovers that his own daughter is to be kept under house arrest at the home of Grimaldi, the prince's chancellor: confronted by all of this, Odoardo might indeed be capable of murdering his ruler.

But there is yet another piece in this jigsaw of passion and impulse that is at odds with Marinelli's cool rationalism. This is Emilia's emotional response to the situation in which she now finds herself. Appiani is dead. The prince has already made clear his feelings for her. Instead of escaping to a convent, which is what her father wishes her to do, she is to be kept in Grimaldi's house: a house of sensual pleasure. The one hour she has already spent there, as she herself acknowledges, created a tumult in her soul. Emilia is honest enough with herself to recognise that she will not for ever resist the temptations that will face her there. Some writers, including Goethe, have concluded from this that Emilia was all the time secretly attracted to the prince. What is more likely is that Emilia recognises the power of the senses and is only too aware of how the prince will exploit both his authority and his attractiveness to break down her opposition. Confronted by the terror of what is likely to happen to her, Emilia first begs to be given a dagger with which to kill herself, and, when that fails, subsequently goads her father into stabbing her. With typical impulsiveness, Odoardo does so.

At the end of the play, Emilia, like 'a broken rose' is dead;

Odoardo is bereft; the prince is angry and confused; Marinelli is dismissed for being too assiduous a courtier. Politically, nothing has changed. The prince still wields absolute power and may well continue to do so with the same lethal combination of boredom and irresponsibility that he has shown so far. The world of rational strategies has been torn apart by passion and impulse. The gulf between the social classes has been shown to be a yawning chasm. Sexual attraction across this gulf means danger or social rejection. Even Count Appiani would have found himself rejected by his own social class after marrying the middle-class Emilia. That is why he plans to retire with her into the countryside. The prince could never marry Emilia. She could only be his mistress, a thing to be possessed, enjoyed and then discarded. She can in reality be no more to him than a beautiful picture. He can marvel at her beauty, but he could never share a life with her. That is the reality of sex and class in a world where birth brings either absolute privilege or complete subjection.

Lessing's intention in writing *Emilia Galotti* was to free the story of Virginia from its political connotations; even so, he managed to write a play with thought-provoking political implications. By concentrating on the psychological responses of the various characters, within a firm social and political framework, Lessing has indeed ensured that the main focus of his play is on the human destinies of the characters he has drawn. But the social and political framework is so clearly and pointedly drawn that it is quite impossible to avoid seeing certain fundamental political conclusions at the heart of the work. Regardless of whether this was the author's deliberate intention or not, the action of *Emilia Galotti* shows how all power corrupts and how absolute power corrupts absolutely. It is precisely because the prince is not an evil villain that the political implications of the action are so worrying. His position of absolute authority gives him the power to create havoc with the lives of his subjects. Strip him of his authority, and he would not have the power to intervene in the lives of Appiani and Emilia in the way that he does. If there is a real villain in the play it is the political system that gives a weak man like the prince an authority he does not merit. It is therefore hardly surprising that *Emilia Galotti* inspired so many of Germany's later, more revolutionary minded playwrights. And it is not fortuitous that this play has enjoyed particular popularity in Germany whenever basic political rights and freedoms have been threatened in that country. In eighteenth-century Germany, sexual attraction across the yawning chasm of class and caste boundaries brought to a head all the unresolved political conflicts engendered by the divergent aspirations of a prosperous middle class and the absolutist power structures holding together a fragmented nation. Without even intending to write a political play, Lessing in *Emilia Galotti* intuitively captured the irreconcilable tensions and conflicts built into contemporary German society.

After writing *Emilia Galotti* Lessing found himself facing a life of increasing loneliness and depression at Wolfenbüttel. He also disliked the way he had become dependent on the grace and favour of an aristocratic ruler, albeit a more benign and thoughtful ruler than the one depicted in his play. A short period of leave of absence, followed by an enforced journey to Italy as companion to the duke's son in 1775, did little to cheer him up. However, in 1776 his life, for an all too brief space of time, was transformed by marriage to Eva König, the widow of an old friend. Theirs was a happy marriage, but Eva died in childbirth in January 1778. Lessing was inconsolable. After a lifetime spent living as a lonely bachelor, he had found great happiness in marriage, only to see his wife die giving birth to a child who did not survive. His grief was exacerbated by a bitter theological controversy in which he became involved later that year. Worse was to follow, when the duke forbad him to reply to the attacks made on him. A year later, in 1779 he deliberately turned to playwriting again to take his mind off his own sorrows and tribulations. His play *Nathan the Wise* was written to be read rather than performed, but it is one of Europe's great pleas for religious and political understanding. It was to be a moving epitaph for a life dedicated to the pursuit of intellectual freedom and tolerance. Soon after completing this play, Lessing's health began to fail. In February 1781, he had a fatal stroke. He died completely exhausted from years of unremitting activity as Germany's first great man of letters.

Emilia Galotti

A Tragedy
IN FIVE ACTS

TRANSLATED FROM THE GERMAN OF
GOTTHOLD EPHRAIM LESSING
BY
Benjamin Thompson, Esq.

London:
Printed by J. Wright, Denmark Court
FOR VERNOR AND HOOD,
No 31, POULTRY
1800

Dramatis Personae

PRINCE *of Guastalla.*
MARQUIS MARINELLI, *his favourite.*
COUNT APPIANI.
CAMILLO ROTA, *a privy-counsellor.*
ODOARDO GALOTTI, *father of* EMILIA.
CONTI, *a painter.*
ANGELO, *an assassin.*
PIRRO, *servant of* GALOTTI.
BAPTIST, *servant of* MARINELLI.

COUNTESS ORSINA, *the* PRINCE'S *mistress.*
CLAUDIA GALOTTI, *mother of* EMILIA.
EMILIA GALOTTI.

Servants.

Act I

[SCENE, *the* PRINCE'*s cabinet*
The PRINCE *is discovered sitting at a desk, which is covered with papers.*]

PRINCE: [*Glancing over some of them.*] COMPLAINTS – nothing but complaints! Petitions – nothing but petitions! – What a distressing situation is mine! Yet princes are envied. – Yes. Could we relieve all who apply to us, we might with justice be envied – Emilia? [*Looking at the signature of a petition.*] But Emilia Bruneschi – not Galotti. What does this Emilia Bruneschi want? [*Reads.*] She requires much – but her name is Emilia. Her petition shall be granted. [*Signs the paper and rings.*]

[*Enter a* SERVANT.]

Are any of the council in the antechamber?
SERVANT: None, may it please your highness.
PRINCE: I have begun the day at too early an hour. The weather invites me abroad. Order the coach, and send for Marinelli. He shall accompany me. [*Exit* SERVANT.] I can attend to nothing more. I was composed – at least I fancied so – till this petition caught my eye – the petition of an Emilia. Farewel to all composure.

[*Re-enter* SERVANT.]

SERVANT: I have sent to the marquis. – A letter from the countess Orsina.
PRINCE: Orsina! Leave it on the table.

SERVANT: The messenger waits –

PRINCE: I will send an answer, if it be necessary. Where is she? In town, or at her villa?

SERVANT: She came to town yesterday.

PRINCE: So much the worse – better I mean! The messenger has so much the less occasion to wait. [*Exit* SERVANT.] My dear countess! [*With asperity, as he takes up the letter.*] What matters it whether I read it or not? [*Throwing it away again.*] Why yes – I once thought I loved her – perhaps too I really did – but the sensation has no longer any place in my breast.

[*Re-enter* SERVANT.]

SERVANT: Conti the painter request the honour –

PRINCE: Conti! 'Tis well. Admit him. His conversation will give another turn to my ideas.

[*Enter* CONTI.]

Good morning, Conti! How fare you? How do the arts thrive?

CONTI: They go a begging.

PRINCE: That they must not, and shall not, in my small territory, if the artist be willing to work.

CONTI: Work! I feel a pleasure in it. But an artist, who is obliged to work too much, will soon cease to deserve that title.

PRINCE: You misunderstand me. I do not mean that his works should be extensive, but that strict attention should be devoted to them. – Well, Conti, you have brought something with you?

CONTI: The portrait, which your highness ordered – as well as another, not ordered by your highness, but which, I think, deserves inspection.

PRINCE: The first is – I scarcely recollect –

CONTI: The countess Orsina.

PRINCE: True. – The order was given so long ago, that I had almost forgotten it.

CONTI: Our fine women are not every day at an artist's command. The countess has only been pleased to sit once during the last three months.

PRINCE: Where are the portraits?

CONTI: In the antechamber. I'll bring them to your highness. [*Exit.*]

PRINCE: Her picture may come – for her picture is not herself. Perhaps, too, I may again find in that what I no longer perceive in herself. But I wish not to find it again. Yet when I loved her, I was always jocund and happy. – Now I am exactly the reverse. – No, no, no. My ideas are more pleasant, though less extravagant.

[*Re-enter* CONTI, *with the pictures.*]

CONTI: [*Places one of them with the front towards a chair, and prepares the other for the* PRINCE'*s inspection.*] I must beg that your highness will confine yourself to the boundaries of our art. Stand here.

PRINCE: [*After having surveyed the picture for a few moments.*] Excellent, Conti – most excellent! – It does credit to your skill. But you have flattered her beyond all measure.

CONTI: The countess appeared to be of another opinion – and, in fact, I have flattered her no more than art must flatter. Art is obliged to paint as plastic nature designed the form, without the imperfections which the opposing materials cause – without the flaws occasioned by the ravages of time.[1]

PRINCE: A reflecting artist has a right to twofold credit. The original of this picture found, notwithstanding –

CONTI: I beg your highness not to mistake me. The original is a person who has a claim to my respect. I did not mean that any expression should escape my lips, which conveyed a contrary idea.

PRINCE: As many as you please. – Well! What said she?

CONTI: "I am satisfied," she said, "if I be not plainer."

PRINCE: Not plainer! – Exactly like her.

CONTI: And she said it with a look – of which I own this picture shews no trace.

PRINCE: That was my idea, when I told you how much you had flattered her. – Oh, I know that proud contemptuous look you mention. It would disguise the countenance of a Grace. I am willing to allow that a pretty mouth may, by a little satirical contraction, acquire additional beauty; but, observe me, this contraction must not extend to grimace, as it does in the countess. The eyes too ought to accompany this expression of satire – eyes, which the countess has not, either in reality or in this picture.

CONTI: Your highness's expressions quite astonish me.

PRINCE: Why so? All the beauty which art could bestow upon the bold, large, prominent Medusa's eyes of the countess, you have honestly bestowed. – Honestly, I say. But you might, in my opinion, have been more honest. For tell me yourself, Conti – does this picture express the character of the original? You have converted pride into dignity, disdain into a smile, and gloomy caprice into placid melancholy.

CONTI: [*Somewhat chagrined.*] Your highness must excuse me, if I say, that we painters expect the picture, when finished, to find the lover as warm as when he ordered it. We paint with the eyes of love, and the eyes of love alone must decide upon our works.

PRINCE: Well, well, Conti! you should have brought the picture a month since, then – Lay it aside. – What is the other?

CONTI: [*Taking it up, and still holding it turned from the* PRINCE.] Likewise the portrait of a female.

PRINCE: Then I had almost – rather not see it. For the image depicted here,

1. In his translation, Thompson uses the word 'deduction' instead of 'imperfections' and 'flaws'.

[*Placing his finger on his forehead.*] – or rather here [*Placing his finger on his heart.*] it cannot equal. I should like, Conti, to admire your art in other subjects.

CONTI: Other artists may certainly produce more admirable portraits; but a more admirable subject cannot exist.

PRINCE: Then I'll bet a trifling sum, Conti, that it is a portrait of your own mistress. [CONTI *turns the picture.*] What do I see? Is this your work, or do my eyes deceive me? – Emilia Galotti!

CONTI: How! Does your highness know this angel?

PRINCE: [*Endeavouring to compose himself, but unable to remove his eyes from the picture.*] A little – just enough to recognise her again. A few weeks since I saw her with her mother in a carriage – since that time only in sacred places – where I had not so good an opportunity of observing her. I know her father, too. He is not my friend. He it was, who most violently opposed my pretensions to Sabionetta. He is a proud, harsh, hasty old man, but in every other respect worthy of esteem.

CONTI: You speak of the father – but this is the daughter –

PRINCE: It is. By heavens, you must have stolen the resemblance from her mirror. [*With his eyes still riveted upon the picture.*] Oh, Conti! you know that the artist is best praised when his works make us forget to praise.

CONTI: Yet, I am extremely dissatisfied with this portrait – and am, notwithstanding, satisfied in being dissatisfied with myself. – What a pity is it that we cannot paint with our eyes! It is so long a journey from the eye, through the arm, to the pencil, that much, very much is lost. But as I have already said, though I know what is lost, though I know how it is lost, I am as proud, nay prouder of this loss, than of what I have retained. For by the former I perceive, more than by the latter, that I am a good painter, though my hand is not always so. Is not your highness convinced that Raphael would have had as great a genius as any painter ever possessed, had he unfortunately been born without hands.

PRINCE: [*Turning his eyes for a moment from the picture.*] What say you, Conti? What do you want to know?

CONTI: Oh nothing, nothing. – Your soul, I perceive, was quite in your eyes, I love such souls, and such eyes.

PRINCE: [*With affected coldness.*] You really then, Conti, think Emilia Galotti one of our first beauties.

CONTI: One of them! Yes. The very first. – Your highness is disposed to banter me – or you must, for some time, have seen as little as you have heard.

PRINCE: Dear Conti – [*Again riveting his eyes on the picture.*] No one but a painter can properly decide on beauty.

CONTI: And should every one's sensations, then, wait for the decision of a painter? – To a cloister let the torpid creature retire, who would learn of us what is beautiful. – But thus much I must, as a painter, own to your highness. I shall ever consider it one of the greatest delights which I have felt in this world, that Emilia Galotti has sat to me. This head, this countenance, this forehead, these eyes, this nose, this mouth, this chin, this neck, this bosom, this shape, this whole form, are from the present time my only model of female beauty. The picture itself, for which she sat, is in the possession of her father; but this copy –

PRINCE: [*Suddenly turning to him.*] Is not promised to any one, Conti.

CONTI: Is for your highness, if it be liked.

PRINCE: Liked! [*Smiling.*] Can I do better, Conti, than make your model of female beauty my own? Take back the other portrait – and procure a frame for it.

CONTI: I will.

PRINCE: As rich and magnificent as the carver can make it; for the picture is intended to be hung in the gallery. But this may remain here. As it is necessary that I should study the model of beauty, it must not be hung against a wall, but always at hand. I thank you, Conti, I thank you sincerely. – As I have already told you, the arts shall never beg their bread in my dominions – as long as I have any. – Send to my treasurer, Conti, and let him pay you for both the portraits – what you please – as much as you please.

CONTI: I am almost afraid that your highness means to reward me for something further than my skill.

PRINCE: How easily is the jealousy of an artist roused! – No, no. – Do you hear, Conti? – As much as you please. [*Exit* CONTI.]
Yes – as much as he pleases. [*Turning to the picture.*] Thou art bought too cheap at any price. Oh thou enchanting work of art, is it true that I possess thee? – Though enchanting master-piece of nature, would I could posses thee, too! Claim what you will, honest mother – claim what thou wilt, morose old father. Demand any price. – Yet, dear enchantress, I should be more happy, far more happy, could I buy thee of thyself: – This eye – how modest, how bewitching! This mouth – when it opens to address the adoring hearer – when it smiles. – Ha! Some one comes. I am as yet too envious of thee. [*Turns the picture to the wall.*] It is Marinelli. – I wish I had not sent for him. What a morning might I have had!

[*Enter* MARINELLI.]

MARINELLI: I hope your highness will pardon my delay. I was not prepared for so early a summons.

PRINCE: The morning was so fine, that I felt an inclination to take the air – but now it seems rather gloomy, and my inclination has subsided. [*After a short pause.*] Any news, Marinelli?

MARINELLI: I have heard nothing of consequence. – The countess Orsina arrived in town yesterday.

PRINCE: Yes – here lies her morning salutation, [*Pointing to the letter.*] or whatever else it may be. I feel no inclination to read it. – Have you seen her?

MARINELLI: Am I not unfortunately her confidant? – But if I again fill that situation with any lady, who may think proper to love your highness so sincerely, may I –

PRINCE: Make no rash vows, Marinelli.

MARINELLI: Indeed! Is it possible? – Then the countess is not so very wrong in her suspicions.

PRINCE: Very wrong, most certainly. My approaching union with the Princess of Massa, makes it necessary that I should for the present break off all connexions of such a nature.

MARINELLI: If this be the case, Orsina will certainly know as well how to submit to her fate as the prince to his.

PRINCE: Mine is undoubtedly more severe. My heart becomes a sacrifice to the welfare of the state, whereas she need but withdraw hers, without being obliged to bestow it on another against her inclination.

MARINELLI: Withdraw it – "Why withdraw it," says the countess, "for the sake of a wife, whom policy, not affection, unites to the prince?" – In such a case, if she be still beloved, she can retain her former situation. It is not therefore a wife, for whose sake she expects to be sacrificed, but –

PRINCE: Another object of affection. Well, Marinelli, should you think me criminal, if Orsina were right in her conjectures?

MARINELLI: I! – I hope your highness does not confound my sentiments with those of the silly woman, whose cause I assert – from compassion assert; for yesterday she affected me in a most singular manner. She wished to be perfectly silent on your present coldness. She affected to be quite composed. But in the midst of the most indifferent subjects, some expression, some reference escaped her, which betrayed the affliction of her heart. With an air of gaiety she said the most melancholy things, and, on the contrary, made the most ridiculous remarks with the mien of deep distress. She has taken recourse to books, which, I fear, will complete her malady.

PRINCE: Yes, for books at first deranged her shallow understanding – But that, which was the chief cause of our separation, you will scarcely use, Marinelli, for the purpose of renewing my attachment. – If love robbed her of her senses, it is certain she would have lost them, sooner or later, had she never felt the influence of love. – And now, enough of her! – Let us turn to some other subject. – Is nothing new, then, going forward in town?

MARINELLI: Nothing – or next to it – for that count Appiani is to be married to-day, is next to nothing.

PRINCE: Count Appiani! To whom? I never heard that it was talked of.

MARINELLI: It has been kept a profound secret – and, indeed, there was not much to talk of. – Your highness will laugh – but such is ever the fate of sentimental young men. Love always contrives to play them tricks of the worst kind. A girl without property or rank, has contrived to catch him in her snares, with very little trouble – merely a parade of virtue, sensibility, and so forth.

PRINCE: He who can, without hesitation, resign himself to the impressions which innocence and beauty make upon him, is, in my opinion, rather to be envied than derided. – What is the name of the happy fair one? – For, though I know, Marinelli, that you and Appiani dislike each other, he is, nevertheless, a very worthy young man, a handsome man, a rich man, an honourable man. I should be happy, if I could gain his good opinion – and shall think of the means.

MARINELLI: If it be not too late – for, as far as I can learn, it is not his intention to make his fortune at court. – He intends to retire with his sweet spouse, to his estate in Piedmont – that he may indulge himself in chasing goats upon the Alps, and training marmots. – What can he do better? Here his credit is destroyed by the base connexion he has formed. The first circles will, of course, no longer admit him.

PRINCE: The first circles! – Why mention them? Does not form, constraint, *ennui*, and often poverty appertain to them? – But let me hear the name of the fair damsel, who is the cause of all these wonderous sacrifices.

MARINELLI: One Emilia Galotti.

PRINCE: What, Marinelli? One –

MARINELLI: Emilia Galotti.

PRINCE: Emilia Galotti! Never!

MARINELLI: Most certainly. Your highness –

PRINCE: I tell you, *no*. It cannot be. – You have mistaken the name. – The family of Galotti is extensive. – It may be a Galotti – but not Emilia Galotti – not Emilia.

MARINELLI: Emilia – Emilia Galotti.

PRINCE: Then there must be another who bears both the same names. – You said *one* Emilia Galotti. You said it in a careless tone – one Emilia Galotti – in a tone, that if speaking of the Emilia I mean, none but a fool could use.

MARINELLI: You are incensed. Does your highness know this Emilia?

PRINCE: It is my place to ask, not yours. – Is she the daughter of Colonel Galotti, who resides at Sabionetta?

MARINELLI: The same.

PRINCE: Is it she who lives with her mother in Guastalla?

MARINELLI: The same.

PRINCE: Not far from the church of All-Saints.

MARINELLI: The same.

PRINCE: In a word – [*Seizes the portrait and gives it to* MARINELLI.] There! Is it this Emilia Galotti. Repeat thy two damning words "*the same*", and plunge a dagger in my heart.

MARINELLI: The same.

PRINCE: Hell and torments! – This – this Emilia Galotti will to-day become –

MARINELLI: The countess Appiani. [*The* PRINCE *snatches the picture from*

MARINELLI *and throws it aside.* MARINELLI *proceeds.*] The ceremony will be privately performed at the father's villa in Sabionetta. Towards noon, the mother and daughter, the count, and perhaps a friend or two, will leave town together.

PRINCE: [*Throws himself into a chair.*] Then I am lost, and will no longer live.

MARINELLI: What thus affects your highness?

PRINCE: [*Starting from his chair.*] Traitor! – What affects me thus! – Hear me. I love her – I adore her. Yes, you may know it – nay, doubtless, long have known it; but you and many more wish me to wear, for ever, the ignominious fetters of the proud Orsina. – That you, Marinelli, who have so often assured me how sincere was your friendship – but a prince has no friends – that you should act so treacherously, so deceitfully, as to conceal, till this moment, the dangers which threatened my attachment – Oh, if I ever forgive it, may my sins never be forgiven.

MARINELLI: Prince, I am thunderstruck. I cannot find words to express my astonishment. – You love Emilia Galotti? – Hear me, then. If I ever had the smallest knowledge, or suspicion of this attachment, may I be numbered with the damned! –

PRINCE: Pardon me, then, Marinelli – [*Throwing himself into his arms.*] and pity me.

MARINELLI: Well, yes, prince. Now see the consequence of your reserve. "A prince has no friends." And why? Because he will have none. To-day you honour us with your confidence, entrust to us your most secret wishes, open your whole soul to us, – and to-morrow we are as perfect strangers to you, as if you had never exchanged a word with us.

PRINCE: Alas, Marinelli, how could I entrust to you a secret which I would scarcely confess to myself?

MARINELLI: And have, therefore, of course, not confessed to the author of your uneasiness?

PRINCE: To her! – All my endeavours to obtain a second conversation have been fruitless.

MARINELLI: And the first –

PRINCE: Ask no more questions, unless you wish to drive me to distraction. You see me struggling in the waves. Why enquire how it happened? Save me if you can – then begin to ask questions.

MARINELLI: Save you! Is there any great difficulty in doing that? What your highness has not had an opportunity of confessing to Emilia Galotti must be confessed to the countess Appiani. Goods, which cannot be obtained in their primitive perfection, must be bought at second hand – and are often, on that account, bought at a cheaper rate.

PRINCE: Be serious, Marinelli, or –

MARINELLI: To be sure, such articles are generally so much worse –

PRINCE: You go too far, Marinelli.

MARINELLI: But the count intends to leave this country. – Well we must devise some scheme –

PRINCE: Dearest, best of friends – yes – devise a scheme for me. What would you do, were you in my situation?

MARINELLI: I would think a trifle no more than a trifle, and resolve to exercise the power which I possessed.

PRINCE: Mention not a power, of which I can, on this occasion, make no use. To-day, said you? – This very day?

MARINELLI: To-day, it is intended that the nuptials shall be solemnized – but, till that is absolutely the case, you may still cherish hope. [*After a short pause.*] Prince, will you let me act as I please? Will you approve all I do?

PRINCE: Any thing, Marinelli, which can avert this blow.

MARINELLI: Let us, then, lose no time. You must remain in town, but go to your palace at Dosalo. The party will pass it in their way to Sabionetta. Should I not succeed in eluding the count's vigilance, I think – yes, yes, he will be caught in that snare without doubt. You wish to send an ambassador to Massa respecting your marriage. Let the count be ambassador, and order him to depart this very day.

PRINCE: Excellent! – Bring him to my palace. – Haste, haste! – I will leave town instantly. [*Exit* MARINELLI.] Where is it? [*Turns to the portrait.*] On the earth! That was too bad. [*Takes it up.*] Yet still I will not look at thee. Why should I plunge the arrow deeper into my heart? [*Lays it on the table.*] I have sighed long enough – longer than I ought. – My inactivity had nearly ruined all. – And may not all be yet lost? May not Marinelli fail in his attempt? – Why should I rely on him alone? – It occurs to me that at this hour, [*Looks at his watch*] at this very hour, the pious girl constantly attends mass at the church of the Dominicans. – How, if I attempted to obtain a moment's conversation? – But to-day – the day of her marriage – her mind will be occupied with other things than mass. – Yet who knows? – I'll make the essay. [*Rings.*]

[*Enter* SERVANT.]

My carriage! – Are none of the council arrived?

SERVANT: Camillo Rota waits without.

PRINCE: Admit him. [*Exit* SERVANT.] But he must not attempt to detain me long. At another time, I will attend to his scrupulous investigations. – There was a petition of one Emilia Bruneschi – here it is – but good Bruneschi, if she who induced me to grant it –

[*Enter* CAMILLO ROTA.]

Come, Rota, come. – There lie the papers which I have examined this morning. You will know what is to be done.

ROTA: I will attend to them.

PRINCE: Here is a petition from one Emilia Galot – Bruneschi. I have already agreed to it, and signed it – but the request is not a trifle. – You may defer the matter – or not defer it, as you please.

ROTA: As your highness pleases.

PRINCE: Have you brought any thing?
ROTA: Sentence of death for your highness's signature.
PRINCE: With all my heart! – Where is it?
ROTA: [*Starts and gazes at the* PRINCE.] I said a death-warrant.
PRINCE: I understood you. Where is it? I am in haste.
ROTA: [*Looking at his papers.*] I really believe I have not brought it. I beg your highness's forgiveness. It can be signed to-morrow.
PRINCE: True. – To-morrow, more, Rota. [*Exit.*]
ROTA: [*Shaking his head, as he collects the papers.*] "With all my heart!" – So ready to sign the condemnation of a fellow-creature. I would not have been instrumental in procuring his signature at such a moment, had the criminal murdered my own son. – "With all my heart!" – The words have stunned me. [*Exit.*]

Act II

[SCENE, *a Room in* GALOTTI's *House.*
Enter CLAUDIA *and* PIRRO, *from opposite Sides.*]

CLAUDIA: Who arrived just now?
PIRRO: My master, madam.
CLAUDIA: My husband? Is it possible?
PIRRO: Here he comes.
CLAUDIA: So unexpectedly – [*Hastens towards him.*] My dearest lord!

[*Enter* ODOARDO.]

ODOARDO: Good-morning, my love. My arrival surprises you no doubt.
CLAUDIA: Most agreeably – if you bring no bad news.
ODOARDO: None whatever. The happiness, which awaited me to-day, would not allow me to sleep. The morning was so fine, and the ride so short – in a word, I am come to see how busy you are, and shall return immediately. Where is Emilia? Occupied by dress, I suppose?
CLAUDIA: No. She is much better employed; for she is gone to hear mass. She said she ought, to-day, to pray for heaven's blessing, more than on any other day – then took her veil, and went.
ODOARDO: Alone!
CLAUDIA: It is but a few steps –
ODOARDO: One step on the path of error is enough.
CLAUDIA: Be not angry – but come in and take some refreshment.
ODOARDO: Well, well, as you like. – But she ought not be have gone alone.
CLAUDIA: Stay here, Pirro, and if any one enquire for us, say we decline all visits to-day. [*Exeunt* ODOARDO *and* CLAUDIA.]

PIRRO: I shall have enough to do; for I have been plagued by fifty inquisitive people already. – Who comes this way?

[*Enter* ANGELO *in a short mantle, with which he conceals his face.*]

ANGELO: Pirro! Pirro!

PIRRO: An acquaintance, it seems. [ANGELO *throws back the mantle.*] Heavens! Angelo!

ANGELO: Yes, Angelo, as you perceive. – I have been wandering long enough round the house, in order to find some opportunity of speaking to you.

PIRRO: And dare you appear in public? Don't you know, that, in consequence of your last murder, a reward is offered for your head?

ANGELO: You don't intend to claim it, I presume?

PIRRO: What do you mean by coming hither?

ANGELO: [*Shews a purse.*] There! That belongs to you.

PIRRO: To me!

ANGELO: Have you forgotten the old gentleman – your last master? –

PIRRO: Don't mention him, I beseech you.

ANGELO: – Whom you led into our clutches on the road to Pisa.

PIRRO: Consider – if any one should overhear us –

ANGELO: You remember his diamond-ring. – It was so valuable, that we could not immediately convert it into money, without exciting suspicion. At length, however, I have succeeded. I received a hundred pistoles for it, and this is your share. Take it.

PIRRO: No – no – you may keep it.

ANGELO: Well, with all my heart! If you chuse to risk your life without any hope of recompence –

PIRRO: Give me the purse, then. [*Takes it.*] And now, what do you want? For, that you came in search of me merely to give me this money –

ANGELO: Seems to you not very natural. What do you mean? Do you think I would with-hold what is due to you? That may be customary among honest people, but we don't follow their fashions. – Farewel! – [*Affects to be going, but turns at the door.*] One question I must ask. Why did old Galotti come in such a hurry to town this morning?

PIRRO: For no reason in the world, but because the weather tempted him to ride. His daughter will be married at Sabionetta this evening, to count Appiani. He cannot stay here till the party leaves town –

ANGELO: Then he will return soon?

PIRRO: So soon, that if you remain any longer, he will discover you. – But you surely have not thoughts of attacking him. Beware, Angelo. He is a man –

ANGELO: Don't I know him? Have I not served under him in the army? – At what time do the younger people leave town?

PIRRO: Towards noon.

ANGELO: Will many friends accompany them?

PIRRO: None. A single carriage will contain the party, which consists of the mother, the daughter, and the count.

ANGELO: How many servants will attend them?

PIRRO: Only two. – I shall ride forward to apprize the old man –

ANGELO: Right, right. Another question. Is the carriage Galotti's or the count's ?

PIRRO: The count's. But surely you cannot think that the few ornaments which the bride may wear will reward you for –

ANGELO: Then the bride herself shall be my reward.

PIRRO: And you mean that I should be your accomplice in this crime, too?

ANGELO: Ride forward, and take no trouble about the matter.

PIRRO: Never!

ANGELO: What? – I believe the fellow means to play a conscientious part, – Pirro, you know me. If you utter a syllable – if every circumstance be not as you have described it –

PIRRO: But, Angelo, for heaven's sake –

ANGELO: Do what you cannot avoid. [*Exit.*]

PIRRO: Wretch that I am! – This villain – But my master comes.

[*Enter* ODOARDO *and* CLAUDIA.]

ODOARDO: She stays too long.

CLAUDIA: Be not in such great haste. It would distress her to learn that you had been here, without having seen your only child.

ODOARDO: I must wait upon the count, too. How eager am I to call this worthy man my son! His conduct enchants me, and, above every thing, his resolution to pass his days at a distance from the bustle of the world.

CLAUDIA: My heart almost breaks when I think of it. – Must we so entirely lose our only child?

ODOARDO: Can you think you have lost her, when you know she is in the arms of an affectionate husband? If she be happy, you ought to be fully satisfied. – You almost make me again suspect that your motive for remaining with her in town, far from an affectionate husband and father, was the dissipation of the world, and proximity of the court, rather than the necessity of giving her a proper education.

CLAUDIA: How unjust a suspicion! – But to-day, Odoardo, I may be allowed to speak somewhat in favour of town and court, though both are to you so hateful – for here alone could love have introduced to each other a couple formed for mutual comfort – here alone could the count have discovered our Emilia.

ODOARDO: That I allow. But were you right, good Claudia, because the event has been fortunate? – It is well that the plan has ended so happily. Let us not affect to be wise, when we have only been fortunate. It is well that the plan has ended so happily. They, who were destined for each other, have found each other. – Now, let them go where peace and innocence invite them. – Why should the count remain here? To cringe – to fawn – to flatter – to supplant the Marinellis – to make a fortune which he does not want – to obtain a dignity, which he does not value? Pirro!

PIRRO: Sir!

ODOARDO: Lead my horse to the count's door. I'll follow you anon, and mount it there. [*Exit* PIRRO.]

Why should the count serve here, when he may command elsewhere? – Besides, you do not consider, that, by marrying my daughter, he is sure to lose the prince's favour totally. The prince hates me –

CLAUDIA: Less, perhaps, than you fear.

ODOARDO: Fear! I fear his hate! Never!

CLAUDIA: For – did I tell you that he has seen our daughter?

ODOARDO: The prince! Where?

CLAUDIA: At the ball given by the chancellor Gramaldi, which he honoured with his presence. He conducted himself so graciously towards her –

ODOARDO: Graciously!

CLAUDIA: Yes. He conversed with her for some time.

ODOARDO: Conversed with her!

CLAUDIA: Appeared to be delighted with her cheerfulness and good sense.

ODOARDO: Delighted!

CLAUDIA: Spoke of her elegance and beauty, in terms of admiration.

ODOARDO: Admiration! And all this you relate to me in a tone of rapture!

CLAUDIA: Why should I not?

ODOARDO: Well, well. – This, too, has ended happily. – Ha! when I think – That were the place where a wound would be to me most mortal. – A libertine, who admires, instantly desires. – Claudia! Claudia! – The very thought rouses my fury. – You ought to have mentioned this to me at the very time it happened. – But to-day I would not willingly say any thing unpleasant to you. And I should, [*Taking her hand*] were I to stay longer. – Therefore, let me begone. God be with you, Claudia. [*Exit.*]

CLAUDIA: What a man! – What a rigid virtue – if virtue that should be called, to which every thing seems suspicious and wrong. – If this be a knowledge of mankind, who would not wish to remain in ignorance? – Why does Emilia stay so long? – He dislikes the father – consequently, if he admire the daughter, it is concluded that he means to bring disgrace into the family.

[EMILIA *rushes in, much alarmed.*]

EMILIA: Heaven be praised! I am now in safety. Or has he even followed me hither? [*Throwing back her veil and espying her mother.*] Has he, my mother, has he? – No, thank heaven.

CLAUDIA: What agitates you thus, dear girl?

EMILIA: Nothing – nothing.

CLAUDIA: Can nothing make you look thus fearfully around – and tremble thus?

EMILIA: What have I been obliged to hear? – And where have I been obliged to hear it?

CLAUDIA: I thought you were at church.

EMILIA: I was. But what are churches and altars to the vicious? – Oh, my mother! [*Throws herself into* CLAUDIA's *arms.*]

CLAUDIA: Speak, my daughter, and remove my fears. What evil can have happened to you in the sanctuary of the Lord?

EMILIA: Never should my devotion have been more fervent and sincere than on this day. Never was it less what it ought to have been.

CLAUDIA: Emilia, we are all human beings. The faculty of praying fervently is not always in our power, but even the wish to do so is considered as a prayer.

EMILIA: And our wish to sin as a sin.

CLAUDIA: That my Emilia never wished.

EMILIA: No, my mother. By Heaven's grace, I was spared from sinking so low.[1] But how hard it is that vice, while dwelling in another's bosom, should force us to become her accomplices.

CLAUDIA: Compose yourself. – Collect your ideas as well as you can. Tell me at once what has happened to you.

EMILIA: I had just sunk upon my knees, further from the altar than usual – for I arrived too late. – I had just begun to raise my thoughts towards heaven – when some person placed himself behind me – so close behind me, that willingly as I would have moved, I could not, lest the devotions of my neighbour might interrupt mine. Devotions! Mine failed completely.[2] But it was not long before I heard a sigh close to my ear, and not the name of a saint – no – the name – do not be angry, dear mother – the name of your daughter. – My own name! Oh, that a peal of thunder had at that moment made me deaf to the rest. The voice spoke of beauty and of love – complained that this day, which crowned my happiness (if such should eventually prove the case) made him, who spoke to me, the prey of misery for ever. He conjured me – all this I was obliged to hear, but I did not look round. I wished to seem as if I was not listening. – What more could I do? Nothing but pray that my guardian angel would strike me with deafness – even if for ever. This, too, I did. This was the only prayer, which I could utter. At length the service was at an end. I arose, trembling at the idea of beholding him, whose impiety had so much shocked me – and when I turned, when I beheld him –

CLAUDIA: Whom, my daughter?

EMILIA: Guess, dear mother, guess; I thought I should have sank into the earth. Himself.

CLAUDIA: Whom do you mean?

EMILIA: The prince.

1. In Thompson's version, this line is mistranslated.
2. Ibid.

CLAUDIA: The prince! Blest be the impatience of your father's disposition! He was here just now, and would not stay 'till you returned.

EMILIA: My father not stay 'till I returned!

CLAUDIA: If, in the midst of your confusion, you had told him what you have just related –

EMILIA: Well, dear mother – could he have found any thing in my conduct deserving censure?

CLAUDIA: No – as little as in mine. And yet, yet – you do not know your father. When enraged, he would have mistaken the innocent for the guilty – he would have fancied me the cause of what I neither could prevent nor foresee. But proceed, my daughter, proceed. When you recognized the prince, I trust you had sufficient command over yourself to convey, by your looks, the contempt which he deserved.

EMILIA: That I had not. After the look with which I recognized him, I had not courage to cast a second towards him. I fled.

CLAUDIA: And the prince followed you?

EMILIA: That I did not know till I had reached the porch, where I felt my hand seized – by him. Shame made me stop; for had I endeavoured to extricate myself, I should have attracted the attention of every one who was passing. This was the only idea which then occurred to me, or which I at present remember. He spoke, and I replied – but what he said, or what I replied, I know not. Should I recollect it, my dear mother, you shall know it. My senses had forsaken me – nor did they return till I found myself in the street. I heard his steps behind me – I heard him follow me into the house – I heard him run after me up stairs –

CLAUDIA: Fear has its peculiar faculty, my daughter. Never shall I forget the countenance with which you rushed into this room! – No. He dared not follow you so far. – Heavens! Had your father known this! – How angry was he when I merely told him that the prince had lately seen you, and spoken in your praise! – Be at ease, however, my dear girl. Fancy what has happened a mere dream. No serious consequences can arise from it. To-day you will become the wife of Appiani, and thereby escape every design which may be formed against you.

EMILIA: But at all events the count must know it. To him I must relate it.

CLAUDIA: By no means. Wherefore? Why? Do you wish to make him uneasy without a cause? And granting that he may not become so at present – know, my child, the poison, which does not operate immediately, is not on that account less dangerous. That which has no effect upon the lover, may have a serious one upon the husband. The lover might even be flattered with the idea of bearing away the prize of so great a rival; but when he has borne it away, – alas, my dear Emilia, the lover often becomes quite another being. Heaven forbid that you should ever know this by experience!

EMILIA: Dear mother, how willingly I always submit to your superior judgment. But should he learn from any other person that the prince spoke to me to-day, would not my silence increase his uneasiness? – I think it would be better not to conceal any thing from him.

CLAUDIA: Weakness – the weakness of a girl, who loves and is beloved. Let him, on no account, know what has happened.

EMILIA: I submit. I have no will when I hear yours – I feel, indeed, more easy. What a silly, fearful girl I am! I might have conducted myself otherwise, and should, perhaps, have as little cause to reproach myself.[1]

CLAUDIA: I would not say this, till your own good sense had said it, which I was sure would be the case as soon as your alarm was at an end. The prince is a gallant young man. You are not used to the unmeaning language of gallantry. In your mind a civility becomes a sensation – a compliment becomes a declaration – an idea, a wish – a wish, a design. Nothing, in this language, sounds like every thing, while every thing is in reality nothing.

EMILIA: Then must my terror have appeared to you ridiculous indeed. – Oh, you are right. My good Appiani shall never know what has happened. He might, perhaps, think me more vain than virtuous. – Ha! He comes. That is his step.

[*Enter* APPIANI, *in deep meditation. His eyes are cast down, and he approaches without observing* CLAUDIA *and* EMILIA, *till the latter runs towards him.*]

APPIANI: Ha! My dearest! I did not expect to find you in this room.

EMILIA: I wish you to be cheerful, though you may not expect to see me. Why so grave and solemn? Surely this day should inspire you with happy sensations?

APPIANI: This day is of greater value than my whole life; but it teems with so much bliss for me – perhaps it is this very bliss, which makes me so grave – so solemn, as you express it. [*Espies* CLAUDIA.] Ha! You too here, madam. This day I hope to address you by a more familiar name.

CLAUDIA: Which will be my greatest pride. – How happy you are, Emilia! Why would not your father share our delight?

APPIANI: But a few minutes have elapsed since I tore myself from his arms – or rather he from mine. – What a man is your father, my Emilia! A pattern of every manly virtue! With what sentiments does his presence inspire my soul? Never is my resolution to continue just and good, so firm as when I see or think of him. And by what, but by fulfilling this resolution, can I make myself worthy of the honour which is conferred upon me, when I become his son – when I become your husband, dear Emilia?

EMILIA: And he would not await my return home.

APPIANI: Because he would but have been distressed that his visit could be no more than momentary.

CLAUDIA: He expected to find you employed about your bridal ornaments, and heard –

1. In Thompson's version, this line is mistranslated.

APPIANI: What I heard again from him with every feeling of love and admiration. Right, my Emilia. I shall be blessed with a pious wife, and one who is not proud of her piety.

CLAUDIA: But let us not, by attending too much to one subject, entirely forget another. Now go, Emilia.

APPIANI: Go! Why?

CLAUDIA: Surely, my lord, you would not lead her to the altar in her present dress.

APPIANI: In truth, I was not, till you spoke, aware of that. Who can behold Emilia, and observe her dress? Yet why should I not lead her to the altar thus?

EMILIA: No, dear count, not exactly thus; yet in a dress not much more gay. In a moment I shall be ready. I do not mean to wear those costly jewels, which were the last present of your prodigal generosity. Oh, I could quarrel with those jewels were they not your present – for thrice I've dreamt, that while I wore them, every diamond changed suddenly to a pearl – and pearls, you know, dear mother, signify tears.

CLAUDIA: Child, the interpretation is more visionary than the dream. Were you not always more fond of pearls than diamonds?

EMILIA: I own that I –

APPIANI: [*Thoughtful and melancholy.*] Signify tears!

EMILIA: How! Does the idea strike you?

APPIANI: It does, though I ought to be ashamed that such is the case; yet when the fancy is disposed for sad impressions –

EMILIA: But why should yours be thus disposed? What did I wear, when I first attracted your attention? Do you remember?

APPIANI: Remember! I never see you in idea but in that dress.

EMILIA: I mean to wear one just the same – airy and free –

APPIANI: Excellent!

EMILIA: And my hair –

APPIANI: In natural ringlets as at that time.

EMILIA: Not forgetting the rose in it. Right! Have a little patience, and you shall see me thus. [*Exit.*]

APPIANI: [*Looks after her with a downcast mien.*] "Pearls signify tears!"

CLAUDIA: Emilia's remark was just, my lord. You are to-day more grave than usual. And why? You are now but a step from the point of your wishes. Can you repent that such is your situation?

APPIANI: How could such a suspicion find a place in your mind? But it is true. I am to-day uncommonly dejected. You say I am but a step from the point of my wishes. True. I therefore have not reached the point. All that I have seen, heard, or dreamt, has preached since yesterday this doctrine to me. To be one step from the goal, or not to have won the race, is in reality the same. This one idea incorporates itself with every other which occurs to me. What can it mean? I understand it not.

CLAUDIA: You make me uneasy, my lord.

APPIANI: I am angry at my friends – at myself too.

CLAUDIA: Why so?

APPIANI: My friends absolutely require, that, before I solemnize my marriage, I should acquaint the prince with my intentions. They allow I am not bound to do this, but still maintain that respect towards him demands it; and I have been weak enough to be prevailed upon. I have already ordered my carriage.

CLAUDIA: [*Starts.*] For the purpose of waiting on the prince!

[*Enter* PIRRO.]

PIRRO: My lady, the Marquis Marinelli is at the door, and enquired for the count.

APPIANI: For me!

PIRRO: Here his lordship comes. [*Opens the door and exit.*]

[*Enter* MARINELLI.]

MARINELLI: I beg pardon, madam. – My lord, I called at your house, and was informed that I should find you here. I have a matter of importance to communicate. Madam, I once more beg your pardon. My business will be adjusted in a few minutes.

CLAUDIA: I will not be any hinderance to it. [*Curtsies and exit.*]

APPIANI: Now, my lord?

MARINELLI: I come from his highness.

APPIANI: What are his commands?

MARINELLI: I am proud in being selected to convey his most distinguished preference towards your lordship – and if Count Appiani will do me the honour of believing me one of his most devoted friends –

APPIANI: No more ceremony, I beg.

MARINELLI: I obey. The prince is under the necessity of immediately sending an ambassador to make arrangements respecting his marriage with the daughter of the duke of Massa. He was long undetermined whom to appoint, till his choice, at last, fell upon you, my lord.

APPIANI: Upon me!

MARINELLI: Yes – and if friendship may be allowed to speak in its own favour, I was instrumental –

APPIANI: I must own you surprise me not a little. I have long concluded that the prince would never deign to employ me.

MARINELLI: I am sure he only waited for a proper opportunity, and if the present mission be not worthy of Count Appiani's consequence and talents, I own my friendship has been too precipitate.

APPIANI: You constantly mention this term friendship. With whom am I conversing? The Marquis Marinelli's friendship I never dreamt of gaining.

MARINELLI: I acknowledge my fault, Count Appiani, my unpardonable fault in wishing to be your friend without your permission. But this need not, at present, come under discussion. The favour of his highness, and the dignity he offers, remain the same. I am sure that they will be eagerly accepted.

APPIANI: [*After some consideration.*] Undoubtedly.

MARINELLI: Come, then, with me.

APPIANI: Wither?

MARINELLI: To the prince's palace at Dosalo. All is ready. You must depart to-day.

APPIANI: What say you? To-day!

MARINELLI: Yes. Rather now than in an hour hence. The affair requires the utmost dispatch.

APPIANI: Indeed! Then am I sorry that I must decline the honour which the prince intended to confer upon me.

MARINELLI: How!

APPIANI: I cannot depart to-day – nor to-morrow – nor the next day.

MARINELLI: You are joking, count.

APPIANI: With you!

MARINELLI: Inimitable! If with the prince, the joke is so much the merrier. – You cannot?

APPIANI: No, Sir, no – and I trust that the prince himself will think my excuse sufficient.

MARINELLI: I am eager to hear it.

APPIANI: Oh, it is a mere trifle. I mean to be married to-day.

MARINELLI: Well – and then?

APPIANI: And then? – A strange question, methinks.

MARINELLI: There are examples, count, of marriages having been deferred. I do not mean to infer that the delay was pleasant to the bride and bridegroom. To them it is natural enough that it should be unpleasant, yet the command of our sovereign –

APPIANI: Sovereign! A sovereign chosen by myself, I am not bound to obey as strictly as your lordship, who are by birth his subject. I came to his court a volunteer. I wished to have the honour of serving him, but not of being his slave. I am the vassal of a greater sovereign.

MARINELLI: Whether greater or smaller is immaterial. A monarch is monarch.

APPIANI: Idle controversy! Enough! Tell your prince what you have heard. Tell him I am sorry it is not in my power to accept the honour offered to me, as I to-day intend to solemnize an union, which will constitute my happiness.

MARINELLI: Will you not at the same time inform him with whom?

APPIANI: With Emilia Galotti.

MARINELLI: Of the family which resides in this house?

APPIANI: Yes.

MARINELLI: Humph!

APPIANI: What is your pleasure?

MARINELLI: I should think there would be on that account less difficulty in deferring the ceremony till your return.

APPIANI: The ceremony!

MARINELLI: Yes. The good honest parents will not think much about it.

APPIANI: The good honest parents!

MARINELLI: And the lady will remain faithful to you of course.

APPIANI: Of course! – But indeed these expressions are used of course by a court-monkey.

MARINELLI: This to me, count?

APPIANI: Why not?

MARINELLI: Heaven and hell! You shall hear from me.

APPIANI: Pshaw! The monkey is envious, but –

MARINELLI: Death and damnation! – Count, I demand satisfaction.

APPIANI: You shall have it.

MARINELLI: And would insist upon it instantly – did I not think it wrong to interrupt the bridegroom's joys.

APPIANI: Good-natured creature! – You shall not put yourself to any inconvenience. [*Seizes his arm.*] I own an embassy to Massa does not suit me, but I have time enough to take a walk with you. Come.

MARINELLI: [*Extricates himself from the Count's grasp.*] Patience, my lord, patience! [*Exit.*]

APPIANI: Go, worthless wretch. – I am obliged to him for having forced my blood into circulation. I feel better.

[*Enter* CLAUDIA, *hastily and alarmed.*]

CLAUDIA: Heavens! My lord – I overheard some warm expressions. Your cheeks glow with anger. What has happened?

APPIANI: Nothing, madam, nothing. The marquis has conferred a favour on me, by sparing me a visit to the prince.

CLAUDIA: Indeed!

APPIANI: We can therefore leave town at an earlier hour. I go to give orders respecting our departure, and shall return immediately. Emilia will, in the mean time, be ready.

CLAUDIA: May I be quite at ease, my lord?

APPIANI: Quite, I assure you. [*Exeunt severally.*]

Act III

[SCENE, *an apartment in the* PRINCE's *palace at* Dosalo.
Enter PRINCE *and* MARINELLI.]

MARINELLI: In vain. He refused the proffered honour with indescribable contempt.

PRINCE: Thus ends all hope then. Emilia will to-day be his.

MARINELLI: According to all appearances, she will.

PRINCE: I relied so firmly on your project – But who knows how ridiculously you acted? I ought to have recollected that though a blockhead's counsel may be good, an ingenious man must execute it.

MARINELLI: A pretty reward, this.

PRINCE: Why should you be rewarded?

MARINELLI: For having risked my life in your behalf. Finding that neither serious nor contemptuous remarks could prevail upon the count to accept the dignity of your ambassador, I tried to rouse his anger. I said things to him which made him forget himself. He used insulting expressions, and I demanded satisfaction – yes, satisfaction on the spot. One of us must fall, thought I. Should it be his lot, the field is ours – should it be mine – why, he must fly, and the prince will at least gain time.

PRINCE: Did you act thus, Marinelli?

MARINELLI: Yes – he, who is ready to sacrifice his life for princes, ought to be informed how grateful he will find them.

PRINCE: And how did the count act? Report says – that he is not the man, who would wait till satisfaction was a second time demanded.

MARINELLI: Circumstances alter cases. He said that he had something of greater consequence than a duel to occupy his attention at that time, and added, that he should be ready to meet me in a week after his marriage –

PRINCE: With Emilia Galotti. The idea drives me to distraction. – Thus, then the affair ended, and now you come hither to boast that you have risked your life in my behalf.

MARINELLI: What could I do more?

PRINCE: More! As if you had done any thing!

MARINELLI: May I be allowed to ask what your highness has done? – You were so fortunate as to see her at church – and spoke to her, of course.

PRINCE: [*With a sneer.*] You have curiosity enough – but I will satisfy it. All happened as I wished. You need take no further trouble, sir. She met my proposal more than half way. I ought to have taken her with me instantly. [*In a cold and commanding tone.*] Now you have had your answer, and may go.

MARINELLI: And may go! – Yes, yes. Thus the song ends, and thus it would end, were I to try impossibilities. – Impossibilities did I say? – No. Impossible it is not, but a bold attempt. Had we the girl in our power, I would answer for it that no marriage should take place.

PRINCE: Ay – you would answer for any thing. I suppose, for instance, you would like to take fifty of my guards, stop the coach on the high-way, and bear a shrieking girl in triumph to me.

MARINELLI: There are instances of girls having been obtained by force, though there has been no appearance of force in the transaction.

PRINCE: If you were able to do this, you would not talk so much about it.

MARINELLI: But I must not be answerable for the consequences. Unforeseen misfortunes may –

PRINCE: Is it my custom to require that people shall be answerable for what they cannot help?

MARINELLI: Therefore, your highness will – [*A pistol is fired at a distance.*] Ha! What was that? Did not my ears deceive me? Surely I heard a shot. – And hark! Another!.

PRINCE: What means this?

MARINELLI: How if I were more active than you thought me?

PRINCE: More active! Explain, then –

MARINELLI: In short, what I mentioned is now taking place.

PRINCE: Is it possible?

MARINELLI: But forget not, prince, what you just now promised. – You pledge your word that –

PRINCE: The preparations are surely arranged –

MARINELLI: As well as possible. The execution of my plan is entrusted to people on whom I can rely. The road, as you know, lies at the end of your garden. There the carriage will be attacked by a party, whose only intention will apparently be to rob the travellers. Another party (one of whom is my trusty servant) will leap from the garden as if between the two parties, my servant will seize Emilia, as if with the intention of rescuing her from the robbers, and bring her through the garden into the palace. This is the plan. What says your highness now?

PRINCE: You surprise me most extremely. – A fearful sensation overpowers me – [MARINELLI *walks to the window.*] For whom are you looking?

MARINELLI: That must be the scene of action – and see, some one approaches in a mask – doubtless to acquaint me with the issue of the attempt. Withdraw awhile, prince.

PRINCE: Alas, Marinelli –

MARINELLI: Well – now, doubtless, I have done too much – before too little.

PRINCE: Not so – not so – yet I cannot perceive –

MARINELLI: Perceive! – All will be clear to you at once. Instantly withdraw, I do beseech you. Let not this fellow find you here. [*Exit* PRINCE.]

MARINELLI: [*Goes again to the window.*] I see the carriage slowly returning to town, and two servants with it. I do not like this appearance. I fear the plot has but half succeeded. A wounded man they drive slowly – not a dead one. – The fellow in the mask comes nearer. 'Tis Angelo himself. – He beckons to me – he must be certain that he has succeeded. – Ha! Ha! Count Appiani. You refused an embassy to Massa, and have been obliged to go a longer journey. Who taught you so well to know a monkey? How do you like this monkey's trick? [*Walks towards the door.*] True – they are envious. – Well, Angelo?

[*Enter* ANGELO, *with his mask in his hand.*]

ANGELO: Be ready, my lord. She will be here directly.

MARINELLI: How did you succeed in other respects?

ANGELO: As you wished, I have no doubt.

MARINELLI: How is it with the count?

ANGELO: So, so. But he must have had some suspicions, for he was not quite unprepared.

MARINELLI: Quick tell me – is he dead?

ANGELO: I am sorry for him, poor man – yes.

MARINELLI: There! Take that for thy compassion. [*Gives him a purse.*]

ANGELO: And our poor Nicholas, he was dispatched too.

MARINELLI: What! Loss on both sides!

ANGELO: Yes. I could cry for the honest lad's fate; though I come in for another quarter of this purse by it; for I am his heir, because I revenged him. This is a law among us, and as good a law, methinks, as ever was made for the support of friendship and fidelity. This Nicholas, my lord –

MARINELLI: No more of your Nicholas! The count –

ANGELO: True. The count finished him, and I finished the count. He fell, and though he might be alive when they put him into the coach, I'll answer for it that he will never come alive out of it.

MARINELLI: Were you but sure of this, Angelo –

ANGELO: Never trust me again, if it be not true. – Have you any further commands? – For I must be on the other side of the borders before sun-set.

MARINELLI: Go, then.

ANGELO: Should any thing else occur in my way, you know where to hear of me, my lord. My terms will always be the most reasonable. [*Exit.*]

MARINELLI: 'Tis well – yet not so well as it might have been. Shame on thee, Angelo! Surely the count was worthy of a second shot. Now, the poor wretch must die in lingering agony. Shame on thee, Angelo! It was cruel not to dispatch him entirely. – The prince must not know what has happened. He himself must discover what advantages result to him from the count's death. – Death! – What would I give for certainty upon this subject!

[*Enter* PRINCE.]

PRINCE: She comes, she comes. She hastens hither even quicker than the servant. Fear seems to make her fly. She must not as yet suspect our design. Her present purpose is but to escape the robbers.

MARINELLI: We shall be in possession of her at all events.

PRINCE: But will not her mother come in search of her? Will not the count discover her retreat? What can we then do? How can I withhold her from them?

MARINELLI: To all this I own I can make no reply. But we must see. Compose yourself, prince. This first step was, at all events, necessary.

PRINCE: How so, if we be obliged to recede?

MARINELLI: That may, perhaps, not be the case. – There are a thousand arts which may be used. Have you forgotten the chief one?

PRINCE: Forgotten! How can I have forgotten that of which I never thought? What mean you?

MARINELLI: The art of pleasing and persuading – which in a prince who loves is never wanting.

PRINCE: Not wanting! – True, except when it is most necessary. I have already made a poor attempt in this art to-day. All my flattery, all my asseverations could not obtain one word from her. Mute, trembling, and abashed, she stood before me like a criminal, while listening to the judge's fatal sentence. Her alarms were infectious. I trembled also, and concluded by imploring her forgiveness. Scarcely dare I speak to her again – and at all events I dare not be present when she arrives. You, Marinelli, must receive her. I will listen to your conversation, and come when I feel more collected. [*Exit.*]

MARINELLI: If she did not see him fall – and of course she could not, as she fled so instantly. – I hear her, and will not meet her eye so suddenly. [*Withdraws to a corner of the apartment.*]

[*Enter* BAPTIST *and* EMILIA.]

BAPTIST: Into this room, dear lady.

EMILIA: [*Scarcely able to breathe.*] Oh! – I thank you, my friend – I thank you – But – Heavens! Where am I? – Quite alone too! – Where are my mother and the count? – They followed me I hope! They will soon be here?

BAPTIST: Most likely they will.

EMILIA: Are you not certain, then? Did you not see them? Were not pistols fired behind us?

BAPTIST: I did not hear them.

EMILIA: Surely, surely you did. Oh heavens! My mother or the count is murdered.

BAPTIST: I'll go in search of them instantly.

EMILIA: Not without me! I'll go with you – I must go with you. – Come friend.

MARINELLI: [*Approaches as if he had just entered.*] Ha! Fair lady! What misfortune, or rather what good fortune has procured me the honour –

EMILIA: How! – You here, my lord! – This, then, is, doubtless your house. Pardon my intrusion. We have been attacked by robbers. Some good people came to our assistance, one of whom was this honest man, who took me out of the carriage, and brought me hither. But I am alarmed to find that I alone am rescued. My mother is still in danger. Behind us I heard pistols fired. She is perhaps dead. Pardon me. I must away. I must return to the place, which I ought not to have quitted.

MARINELLI: Compose yourself, dear lady. All is well. The beloved persons, for whom you feel this tender anxiety, will soon be here. – Run, Baptist. They may perhaps not know where this lady is. See whether they have taken refuge in any house near the road and conduct them hither instantly. [*Exit* BAPTIST.]

EMILIA: Are you sure they are safe? Has nothing happened to them? – Oh what a day of terrors has this been to me! But I ought not to remain here. I ought to meet them.

MARINELLI: Why so, dear lady? You are even now almost breathless. – Rather compose yourself, and have the goodness to step into a room, where you will find less interruption than in this. I am sure the prince has already found your worthy mother, and is conducting her hither.

EMILIA: Who?

MARINELLI: Our gracious prince himself.

EMILIA: [*Extremely terrified.*] The prince!

MARINELLI: He flew to your assistance as soon as he was informed of your situation. He is highly incensed that such a crime should have been committed so close to himself – nay almost before his eyes. He has sent persons in search of the villains, and if they be seized, their punishment will be most severe.

EMILIA: The prince! – Where am I, then?

MARINELLI: At Dosalo, the prince's palace.

EMILIA: What an accident! – And you think he will soon be here? – But with my mother, surely.

MARINELLI: Here he is.

[*Enter* PRINCE.]

PRINCE: Where is she? Where is she? – We have been every where in search of you, dear lady. – You are well, I hope? – Now, all is well. The count and your mother –

EMILIA: Oh prince! Where are they? Where is my mother?

PRINCE: Not far from us – in the neighbourhood.

EMILIA: Heavens! In what a situation shall I find one or both of them! For your highness conceals from me – I perceive –

PRINCE: I conceal nothing, be assured. Lean on my arm, and accompany me to them.

EMILIA: [*Irresolute.*] But – if they be not wounded – if my presages be not true – why are they not already here?

PRINCE: Haste then, that all these sad presages may at once be banished.

EMILIA: What shall I do? [*Wrings her hands.*]

PRINCE: How! Can you harbour any suspicion against me?

EMILIA: [*Falls at his feet.*] On my knees I entreat you –

PRINCE: [*Raising her.*] I am quite ashamed. – Yes Emilia, I deserve this mute reproach. My conduct this morning cannot be justified. Pardon my weakness. I ought not to have made you uneasy by an avowal, from which I could expect no advantage. I was amply punished by the speechless agitation with which you listened to it. And though I may be allowed to think this accident the signal of more favourable fortune – this accident, which allows me to behold and speak to you again before my hopes for ever vanish – this accident, which gives me an opportunity of imploring your forgiveness – yet will I – do not tremble – yet will I rely entirely on your looks. Not a sigh, not a syllable shall offend you. All I beg is that you will not suspect me of any bad intention – that you will not for a moment doubt the unbounded influence which you possess over me – that you will never think you need the protection of another against me. And now come – come where transports, which you more approve, await you. [*Leads her away not without opposition.*] Follow us, Marinelli. [*Exeunt* PRINCE *and* EMILIA.]

MARINELLI: [*Alone.*] Follow us! That means of course – Follow us not. He will now find how far he can proceed with her, when no one witnesses their actions. All that I have to do is to prevent intrusion. On the part of the count I now do not expect it – but on that of her mother – Wonderful, indeed, would it be, were she to have quietly departed, leaving her daughter unprotected. – Well, Baptist, what now?

[*Enter* BAPTIST *in haste.*]

BAPTIST: The mother, my lord.

MARINELLI: As I suspected. Where is she?

BAPTIST: She will be here in a few moments, unless you prevent it. When you ordered me to look for her, I understood you, and felt little inclination for the employment. But by chance I heard her shricks. She is in search of her daughter, and will, I fear, discover our whole plot. All the people, who inhabit this retired country, have gathered round her, and each vies with his neighbour for the pleasure of shewing her the way. Whether she has been told that you are here, or that the prince is here, I know not. What is to be done?

MARINELLI: Let us consider. – Refuse her admittance when she knows that her daughter is here! – That must not be. Her eyes will roll with anger, to be sure, when she finds her lambkin in the clutches of the wolf. – Eyes! – They would be of little consequence, but heaven have mercy on our ears! Well, well. – A woman's lungs are not inexhaustible. She will be silent, when she can bawl no longer. – Besides, the mother it is whom we should gain over to our side – and if I be a judge of mothers – to be a sort of prince's stepmother would flatter most of them. – Let her come, Baptist, let her come.

BAPTIST: Hark, my lord!

CLAUDIA: [*Within.*] Emilia! Emilia! My child! Where are you?

MARINELLI: Go, Baptist, and use your endeavours to dismiss her inquisitive conductors.

[*As* BAPTIST *is going,* CLAUDIA *meets him.*]

CLAUDIA: Ha! – You took her out of the carriage. You led her away. I know you again. Where is she? Speak, wretch.

BAPTIST: Is this your way of returning thanks?

CLAUDIA: Oh, if you merit thanks – [*In a mild tone.*] forgive me, worthy man. – Where is she? Let me no longer be deprived of her. Where is she?

BAPTIST: She could not be more safe, were she protected by angels. – My master, here, will conduct you to her. [*Observes that some people are attempting to follow* CLAUDIA.] Back there! Begone.

[*Exit, driving them away.*]

CLAUDIA: Your master! [*Espies* MARINELLI, *and starts.*] Ha! – Is this your master? – You here, Sir – and my daughter here – and you – you will conduct me to her?

MARINELLI: With great pleasure, madam.

CLAUDIA: Hold! A circumstance just occurs to me. It was you, I think, with whom I this morning left Count Appiani at my house, and with whom he afterwards had a quarrel.

MARINELLI: Quarrel! That I did not know. We had a trifling dispute respecting affairs of state.

CLAUDIA: And Marinelli is your name.

MARINELLI: The Marquis Marinelli.

CLAUDIA: True. Hear then, Marquis Marinelli. Your name accompanied with a curse – but no – I will not wrong the noble youth – the curse was added by myself – your name was the last word uttered by the dying count.

MARINELLI: The dying count! Count Appiani! – You hear, madam, what most surprises me in this your strange address. – The dying count! – What else you mean to imply I know not.

CLAUDIA: [*With asperity, and in a deliberate tone.*] Marinelli was the last word uttered by the dying count. – Do you understand me now? I myself did not at first understand it, though it was spoken in a tone – a tone, which I still hear. Where were my senses that I could not understand it *instantly*?

MARINELLI: Well, madam, I was always the count's friend – his intimate friend. If, therefore, he mentioned my name at the hour of death –

CLAUDIA: Yes – and in what tone did he mention it? I cannot imitate – I cannot describe it – but it signified – everything – What! Were we attacked by robbers? No – by assassins – by hired assassins – and Marinelli was the last word uttered by the dying count, in such a tone –

MARINELLI: In such a tone! Did any one ever hear that the tone used by a man at the moment of alarm was made a ground of accusation against an upright man?

CLAUDIA: Oh that I could appear before a tribunal of justice, and imitate that tone! – Yet – wretch that I am! I forget my daughter. – Where is she? Dead too! Was it my daughter's fault that Appiani was thy enemy?

MARINELLI: I revere the mother's fears, and therefore pardon you. – Come, madam. – Your daughter is in one of the adjoining rooms, and I hope her alarms are by this time at an end. With the tenderest solicitude is the prince himself employed in comforting her.

CLAUDIA: Who?

MARINELLI: The prince.

CLAUDIA: The prince! – Wretched mother that I am! – And her father, her father! – He will curse the day of her birth. He will curse me.

MARINELLI: For heaven's sake, madam, what idea have you now adopted?

CLAUDIA: It is clear. – To-day – at church – before the eyes of the Redeemer – in the presence of the Eternal Judge, this act of villany began. Murderer! Mean cowardly murderer! Thou wert not bold enough to meet him face to face, but wert base enough to bribe assassins that another might be gratified. Thou scum of murderers! Why may I not spit my gall into thy face – thou *pander*?

MARINELLI: You rave, good woman. – Moderate your tone, and remember where you are.

CLAUDIA: Where I am! – What cares the lioness, when robbed of her young, in whose forest she roars?

EMILIA: [*Within.*] Ha! My mother! I hear my mother's voice.

CLAUDIA: 'Tis she. She has heard me. – Where are you my child? – I come, I come.

[*Rushes into the room, followed by* MARINELLI.]

Act IV

[SCENE, *as in the last act.*
Enter PRINCE *and* MARINELLI.]

PRINCE: Come, Marinelli, I must collect myself – I must have information from you.

MARINELLI: Ha! ha! ha! had you seen the frantic conduct of the mother, in this room! You heard how she raved and bawled – yet how tame she was as soon as she beheld you! Ha! ha! Yes – I never yet knew the mother who scratched a prince's eyes out, because he thought her daughter handsome.

PRINCE: You are not a correct observer. – Did not Emilia fall senseless into her mother's arms? This made the mother forget her rage. It was her daughter, not me, whom she spared, when, in a low voice, she uttered – what I myself had rather not have heard – had rather not have understood.

MARINELLI: What means your highness?

PRINCE: Why this dissimulation? – Answer me. – Is it true or false?

MARINELLI: And if it were true. –

PRINCE: If it were! – It is, then – He is dead. – [*In a threatening tone.*] Marinelli, Marinelli!

MARINELLI: Well?

PRINCE: By just Heaven I swear that I am innocent of the blood which has been shed. Had you previously told me that the count's life must be sacrificed – God is my witness, I would as soon have consented that my own should be sacrificed.

MARINELLI: Had I previously told you! As if the count's death was part of my plan! I charged Angelo that on his soul he should take care no harm was done; and this, too, would have been the case, had not the count irritated the assailants, by shooting one of them.

PRINCE: To be sure he ought to have understood the joke better.

MARINELLI: That Angelo was enraged, and instantly avenged his comrade's death –

PRINCE: Is certainly very natural.

MARINELLI: I have chided him not a little for it.

PRINCE: Indeed! How friendly! Advise him never to appear again in my dominions; for I might do something more than chide him.

MARINELLI: Very well. – I and Angelo. – Accident and premeditated murder seem to your highness the same. Remember, however, the promise claimed by me, that I was not to be answerable for any of the misfortunes which might arise.

PRINCE: Which might – or which should arise, did you say?

MARINELLI: Still better! But, before you tell me in plain terms what you think of me, I beg leave to make one remark. – The count's death is by no means a matter of indifference to me. I demanded satisfaction of him. He left the world without having granted it; and my honour, consequently, remains injured. Allowing, therefore, that in any other situation I might deserve the suspicion to which you have alluded, can I in this? [*With assumed anger*.] He who can have such an opinion of me –

PRINCE: [*Yielding*.] Well, well!

MARINELLI: Oh that he were still alive! I would give all that I possess; – [*With acrimony*.] even the favour of my prince – even that invaluable treasure would I give.

PRINCE: Well, well! I understand you. His death was accidental, merely accidental – you assure me that it was so, and I believe it. But will any one else believe it? Will Emilia – her mother – the world?

MARINELLI: [*Coldly*.] It is not probable.

PRINCE: What, then, will they believe? – You shrug your shoulders. They will suppose this Angelo an instrument employed by me.

MARINELLI: [*Still more coldly*.] That is very probable.

PRINCE: Me! me myself! – or from this hour I must renounce all hopes of ever possessing Emilia.

MARINELLI: [*In a tone of perfect indifference*.] Which you must also have done, had the count lived.

PRINCE: [*Violently*.] Marinelli! [*Checking his warmth*.] But you shall not rouse my anger. – Be it so. It is so. You mean to imply that the count's death is a favourable circumstance for me; – the most favourable which could have happened – the only circumstance which could assist my passion – and, since this is the case, no matter how it happened. A count more or less in the world is of little consequence. Do these sentiments suit you? – I am not alarmed at a petty crime; but of what avail is this? It has opened a passage only again to bar it. Such is the consequence of your wise deep-laid plan.

MARINELLI: My plan would have succeeded in every respect had not you interfered with it.

PRINCE: I!

MARINELLI: Allow me to say that the step which you took at church this morning was not likely to aid it.

PRINCE: How did that interfere with it?

MARINELLI: In a material point. When I undertook the business, Emilia and her mother were ignorant of the prince's attachment. How if I formed my foundation upon this circumstance, while the prince was undermining my building.

PRINCE: [*Striking his forehead.*] Damnation!

MARINELLI: How, if he himself betrayed his intentions?

PRINCE: Cursed idea!

MARINELLI: For had he not himself declared his passion, what part of my plan could now have raised the least suspicion in the mind of the mother or the daughter?

PRINCE: True! true!

MARINELLI: You will pardon me, therefore, if –

[*Enter* BAPTIST *hastily.*]

BAPTIST: The countess is arrived.

PRINCE: What countess?

BAPTIST: Orsina.

PRINCE: Orsina? – Marinelli! – Orsina? – Marinelli!

MARINELLI: I am as much astonished as yourself.

PRINCE: [*To* BAPTIST:] Go – run – fly. She must not alight. I am not here – not here to her. She must return. Go, go. [*Exit* BAPTIST.]
What does the silly woman want? How dares she take this liberty? By what means could she know that we were here? Is she come to be a spy upon my actions? Can she have heard of my new passion? – Oh, Marinelli, speak, answer me. Is the man offended, who so often has declared himself my friend – and offended by a mere paltry altercation? Shall I beg your pardon?

MARINELLI: Prince, as soon as you become yourself, I always instantly am yours again. – The arrival of Orsina is as enigmatical to me as to you. But she will hardly brook the dismissal you have sent. What will you do?

PRINCE: I will not speak to her. I will withdraw.

MARINELLI: Right! – Do so instantly, and let me receive her.

PRINCE: But merely for the purpose of telling her to go. Enter no further into conversation with her, for other things demand our attention.

MARINELLI: Not so, not so. These other things are done. Summon resolution. What is still wanting will follow of its own accord. – But do I not hear her? – Hasten prince. In that room [*Pointing to the adjoining apartment, to which the* PRINCE *retires*] you may, if you please, listen to our conversation. I fear it will not be very grateful to your ears.

[*Enter Countess* ORSINA.]

ORSINA: [*Without perceiving* MARINELLI.] What means this? No one comes to meet me, but a shameless servant, who endeavours to obstruct my entrance. Surely I am at Dosalo, where, on former occasions, an army of attendants rushed to receive me – where love and ecstasy awaited me. – Yes. The place is the same, but – Ha! you here, Marinelli. I am glad the prince has brought you with him. – Yet, no. My business with his highness must be transacted with his highness only. Where is he?

MARINELLI: You suppose that he is here, then, – or know that he is here. He, however, does not expect a visit from your ladyship.

ORSINA: Indeed! Surely, then, he did not receive my letter this morning.

MARINELLI: Your letter! – But – yes. I remember he mentioned that he had received one.

ORSINA: Well? Did I not in that letter request he would meet me here to-day? I own he did not think proper to return a written answer; but I learnt that in an hour he actually drove from town to Dosalo. This I though a sufficient answer, and therefore came.

MARINELLI: An odd accident!

ORSINA: Accident! – It was an agreement – at least as good as an agreement. On my part the letter – on his the deed. – Why this appearance of surprise?

MARINELLI: You seemed yesterday resolved never to appear before the prince again.

ORSINA: Calm reflection has made me abandon that resolution. Where is he? Where is he? – Probably in the chamber where I heard a noise. I wanted to go in, but the impertinent servant would not let me pass.

MARINELLI: Dearest countess –

ORSINA: I heard a female shriek. – What means this, Marinelli? Tell me – if I be your dearest countess – tell me. You will not. Then I will see what it means. [*Going.*]

MARINELLI: Hold, countess! Whither go you?

ORSINA: Where I ought to have been long since. – Is it proper, think you, that I should waste my time in idle conversation with you, when the prince expects me?

MARINELLI: You are mistaken, countess. The prince does not expect you here. He cannot see you – will not see you.

ORSINA: And yet is here, in consequence of my letter.

MARINELLI: Not in consequence of your letter.

ORSINA: He received it, you say.

MARINELLI: Yes, but he did not read it.

ORSINA: [*Violently.*] Not read it! [*Less violently.*] Not read it! – [*Sorrowfully, and wiping away a tear.*] Not even read it!

MARINELLI: From absence, not contempt.

ORSINA: [*With pride.*] Contempt! Who thought of such a thing? To whom do you use the term? Marinelli, you are a frontless comforter. – Contempt! Contempt! To me! [*In a milder tone.*] It is true that he no longer loves me, and some other sensation must fill the place which love occupied in his mind. But why should this be contempt! May it not merely be indifference?

MARINELLI: Certainly, certainly.

ORSINA: [*With a scornful look.*] Certainly! – What a wise man art thou, who can be taught by others to say what they please! Indifference! Indifference in the place of love! – That means nothing in the place of something. For learn, thou mimical court-parrot, learn from a woman, that indifference is an empty word, a sound without meaning. The mind can only be indifferent to that of which it does not think. – Can you comprehend me, man?

MARINELLI: [*Aside.*] 'Tis as I feared.

ORSINA: Why do you mutter?

MARINELLI: I was admiring your remarks. Who does not know that the countess Orsina is a philosopher?

ORSINA: True. I am a philosopher. But have I now shewn it – or did I ever shew it? If so, no wonder were it if the prince despised me. How can man love a creature which in despite of him will *think*? A woman who thinks, is as disgusting as a man who uses paint. She ought to laugh – to do nothing but laugh, that the mighty lords of the creation may be kept in good humour – Ha! Ha! Ha! – What makes me laugh now, Marinelli? – Why the accidental circumstance that I should write requesting the prince to come hither – that he should not read my letter, and nevertheless come. Ha! Ha! Ha! 'Tis an odd accident, and really amusing. Why don't you laugh, Marinelli? The mighty lords of the creation may laugh, though we may not think. [*In a solemn and commanding tone.*] Laugh, marquis.

MARINELLI: Immediately, countess, immediately.

ORSINA: And while you speak the proper moment passes. No. Do not laugh – for, mark me, Marinelli, that which makes me laugh, has, like every thing in the world, its serious side. Accident! Could it be accidental that the prince, who little thought of seeing me, *must* see me? – Accident! Believe me, Marinelli, the word accident is blasphemy. Nothing under the sun is accidental, and least of all can this be so, of which the purpose is so evident. – Almighty and all-bounteous Providence, forgive that I with this weak sinner have given the name of accident to what so plainly is thy work – yes, thy immediate work. – [*In a hasty tone to* MARINELLI.] Dare not to lead me thus astray from truth again.

MARINELLI: But, countess –

ORSINA: Peace with your *but* – that term demands reflection, and – my head, my head! [*Puts her hand to her forehead.*] Contrive that I may speak to the prince immediately, or I fear I shall not be capable of doing it. You see, Marinelli, that I must speak to him – that I will speak to him.

[*Enter* PRINCE]

PRINCE: [*Aside as he advances.*] I must come to his assistance.

ORSINA: [*Espies him, but remains irresolute whether to approach him or not.*] Ha! There he is.

PRINCE: [*Walks straight across the room towards the other apartments.*] Ha! – the fair countess, as I live. How sorry I am that I cannot to-day enjoy the happiness which your society always affords me. I am engaged, and am not alone. Another time, dear countess, another time. – At present detain yourself no longer – no longer, I beg. – And you, Marinelli – I want you. [*Exit.*]

MARINELLI: Your ladyship has now heard from himself, what you would not believe when I mentioned it.

ORSINA: [*As if petrified.*] Have I? Have I indeed?

MARINELLI: Most certainly.

ORSINA: [*Deeply affected.*] "I am engaged, and am not alone." Is this the only excuse which I am worth? An excuse with which every petitioner, every importuning beggar is dismissed? Could he not even frame one little falshood for me? – Engaged! With what? – Not alone! Who is with him? – Marinelli, be compassionate – tell me a falsehood. What can a falsehood cost you? What has he to do? Who is with him? Tell me, tell me. Say any thing which first occurs to you, and I will go.

MARINELLI: [*Aside.*] On this condition I may tell her part of the truth.

ORSINA: Quick, Marinelli, and I will go. He said, "Another time, dear countess!" Did he not? – That he may keep his promise – that he may have no pretext to break it – quick, then, Marinelli – tell me a falsehood, and I will go.

MARINELLI: The prince, dear countess, is really not alone. There are persons with him, whom he cannot leave for a moment – persons, who have just escaped imminent danger. Count Appiani –

ORSINA: Is with him! – What a pity that I know this to be false! In an instant think of something else; for Count Appiani, if you do not know it, has been just assassinated by robbers. I met the carriage with his body in it as I came from town. Or did I not? Was it a dream?

MARINELLI: Alas, it was not a dream. But they, who accompanied the count were rescued, and are now in this palace; namely, a lady to whom he was betrothed, and whom, with her mother, he was conducting to Sabionetta, there to celebrate his nuptials.

ORSINA: A lady and her mother! Is the lady handsome.

MARINELLI: The prince is extremely sorry for her situation.

ORSINA: That he would be, I hope, even if she were hideous – for her fate is dreadful. Poor girl! At the moment he was to become thine for ever, he was torn for ever from thee. – Who is she? Do I know her? I have of late been so much out of town, that I am ignorant of every thing.

MARINELLI: Her name is Emilia Galotti.

ORSINA: What? – Emilia Galotti! Oh Marinelli, let me not think thou speak'st truth.

MARINELLI: Why?

ORSINA: Emilia Galotti!

MARINELLI: Yes. it is improbable that you should know her.

ORSINA: I do know her – though I might not yesterday. Emilia Galotti! – Answer me seriously. Is Emilia Galotti the unfortunately lady, whom the prince is engaged in consoling?

MARINELLI: [*Aside.*] Can I have disclosed too much?

ORSINA: And was Count Appiani her destined bridegroom – the Count Appiani who was shot to-day?

MARINELLI: Exactly.

ORSINA: [*Clapping her hands.*] Bravo! Bravo! Bravo!

MARINELLI: What now?

ORSINA: I could kiss the demon that tempted him to do it.

MARINELLI: Whom? Tempted? To do what?

ORSINA: Yes, I could kiss him – even wert thou that demon, Marinelli.

MARINELLI: Countess!

ORSINA: Come hither. Look at me – stedfastly – eye to eye.

MARINELLI: Well?

ORSINA: Know you not my thoughts?

MARINELLI: How can I?

ORSINA: Have you no concern in it?

MARINELLI: In what?

ORSINA: Swear. – No, do not swear, for that might be another crime. – But yes – swear. One sin more or less is of no consequence to a man, who is already damned. – Have you no concern in it?

MARINELLI: You alarm me, countess.

ORSINA: Indeed! – Now, Marinelli – has your good heart no suspicion?

MARINELLI: Suspicion! Respecting what?

ORSINA: 'Tis well. – Then I will entrust you with a secret – a secret, which will make each hair upon your head bristle towards heaven. – But here, so close to the door some one might overhear us, and – [*Puts her finger to her mouth.*] mark me, it is a secret – a profound secret. [*Places her mouth to his ear, as if about to whisper and shouts as loudly as she is able.*] The prince is a murderer.

MARINELLI: Countess! Countess! have you lost your senses?

ORSINA: Senses! Ha! Ha! ha! I have very seldom, if every, been so satisfied with my understanding as I am at this moment. Depend upon it, Marinelli – but it must remain a secret between us – [*In a low voice.*] the prince is a murderer – the murderer of Count Appiani. The count was not assassinated by robbers, but by bravoes whom the prince employed.

MARINELLI: How can such a horrid suspicion fall from your lips, or enter your imagination?

ORSINA: How! – Very naturally. To this Emilia Galotti, who is now in the palace, and whose bridegroom was thus suddenly dispatched – to this Emilia Galotti did the prince to-day declare his passion in the church of the Dominicans. That I know, for my spies not only saw it, but heard what he said. – Now, Sir, have I lost my senses? Methinks I connect the circumstances which belong to each other very tolerably. – Or has all this happened, too, by accident? Marinelli, you no more comprehend the wickedness of man, than the ways of Providence.

MARINELLI: Countess, your life would be in danger –

ORSINA: Were I to mention this again? – So much the better! So much the better! To-morrow I will repeat it aloud in the market-place – and, if any one contradict me – if any one contradict me, he was the murderer's accomplice. – Farewel.

[*As she is going* ODOARDO *meets her.*]

ODOARDO: Pardon me, gracious lady –

ORSINA: I can grant no pardon here, for I have no command. You must apply to this gentleman. [*Pointing to* MARINELLI.]

MARINELLI: [*Aside.*] The father! This completes the matter.

ODOARDO: Pardon an anxious father, Sir, for entering unannounced.

ORSINA: Father! [*Aside.*] Of Emilia, no doubt! Ha! Thou are welcome.

ODOARDO: A servant came in haste to tell me that my family was in danger. I flew to the place he mentioned, and was there informed that Count Appiani is wounded – that he is carried back to town – and that my wife and daughter found refuge in this palace. Where are they, Sir, where are they?

MARINELLI: Be at ease, colonel. Your wife and daughter are as well as can be expected after the alarm. The prince is with them. I will immediately announce you.

ODOARDO: Why is it necessary to announce me?

MARINELLI: Why? – You know, Sir, that you are not upon the most friendly footing with the prince. Gracious as may be his conduct towards the ladies, will your unexpected appearance be welcome to him?

ODOARDO: You are right, Sir, you are right.

MARINELLI: But, countess, may I not first have the honour of handing you to your carriage?

ORSINA: By no means.

MARINELLI: [*Taking her hand not in the most gentle way.*] Allow me to do what civility requires.

ORSINA: Release me, Sir. There is no occasion. Why should civility precede duty? To announce this worthy man immediately is your duty.

MARINELLI: Have you forgotten what the prince himself commanded?

ORSINA: Let him come, and repeat his commands. I shall expect him.

MARINELLI: [*Draws* ODOARDO *aside.*] I am obliged to leave you, colonel, with a lady, whose wits – you understand me.[1] I mention this that you may know in what way to treat her remarks, which are sometimes of a very singular nature, It would be better were you not to enter into conversation with her.

ODOARDO: Very well, Sir. Hasten, I beseech you. [*Exit* MARINELLI.]

ORSINA: [*After a pause, during which she has surveyed* ODOARDO *with a look of compassion, while he has cast towards her a glance of curiosity.*] Alas! What has he said to you, unfortunate man?

ODOARDO: [*Half aside.*] Unfortunate!

ORSINA: Truth it certainly was not – at least not one of those mournful truths which await you.

ODOARDO: Which await me! – Do I, then, not know enough? Madam – but proceed, proceed.

ORSINA: You known nothing.

ODOARDO: Nothing!

ORSINA: Worthy father! – What would I give that you were my father. – Pardon me. The unfortunate so willingly bind themselves to each other. I would faithfully share your sorrows – and your rage.

ODOARDO: Sorrows and rage! Madam – but I forget – Go on.

ORSINA: Should she even be your only daughter – your only child – but it matters not. The unfortunate child is always the only one.

ODOARDO: Unfortunate! – Madam! – Why do I attend to her? Yet, by heaven, no lunatic speaks thus.

ORSINA: Lunatic! That, then, was the secret, which he took you aside to communicate. – Well, well. – It is perhaps not one of his greatest falsehoods. – I feel something like it – and believe me, Sir – they who, under certain circumstances, do not lose their wits, have none to lose.

ODOARDO: What shall I think?

ORSINA: Treat me not with contempt, old man. – You have sound wits. I know it by your resolute and venerable mien. Yet sound as they may be – I need to speak only one word – for you to lose them.

ODOARDO: Oh madam, I shall have none before you speak that word, unless you speak it soon. – Speak, I conjure you – or it is not true that you belong to the good class of lunatics, who claim our pity and respect – you are a common fool. You have not what you never had.

ORSINA: Mark my words, then. What do you know, who fancy that you know enough? – That Appiani is wounded? Wounded only? He is dead.

1. For 'wits' Thompson uses 'intellects'.

ODOARDO: Dead! Dead! – Woman, you abide not by your promise. You wish to rob me of my wits, when, alas you break my heart.

ORSINA: Thus much by the way. – Now, let me proceed – The bridegroom is dead – and the bride – your daughter – worse than dead.

ODOARDO: Worse! Worse than dead! – Confess she too is dead – for I know but one thing worse than death.

ORSINA: She is alive, and now will first enjoy the luxuries of life. – A life of joy, of bliss, of ecstasy – as long as it endures.

ODOARDO: The word, madam! Out with the single word, which will deprive me of my wits. Distil not thus your poison drop by drop. – The single word!

ORSINA: You yourself shall put the letters of it together. This morning the prince spoke to your daughter at church – this afternoon he has her at Dosalo – at his retired – his secret palace.

ODOARDO: The prince spoke to my daughter at church!

ORSINA: With familiarity and fervour. – What they had to agree upon was not a trifle – and if they did agree – if your daughter made this her voluntary asylum – why, then, the prince is not guilty of positive seduction, but merely of a *trifling* murder.

ODOARDO: Calumny! Infamous calumny! I know my daughter. If there be murder in the case, there is seduction also. [*Looks wildly around and stamps.*] Now, Claudia! Have we not lived to see a day of joy? – Oh the gracious prince! Oh the peculiar honour!

ORSINA: [*Aside.*] Have I roused thee, old man?

ODOARDO: Here I stand before the robber's cave. [*Throws his coat back on both sides, and perceives he has no fire-arms.*] I should not have been surprised had I, through haste, forgotten these my hands. [*Feeling in all his pockets.*] Nothing, nothing.

ORSINA: Ha! I understand, and can assist you. I have brought this [*Produces a dagger.*] There! Take it ere any one observes us. – I have something else too – poison – but that is fit for women, not for men. Take this, [*forcing the dagger upon him*] take it.

ODOARDO: I thank thee. If any one again assert thou art a lunatic, he shall not say it with impunity.

ORSINA: Conceal it instantly. [ODOARDO *hides the dagger.*] I have no opportunity of using it. Such will not be your case. – If you be a man, you will know when and how to use it. I am but a woman, yet I was resolute when I came hither – resolute and armed. In you I can confide – for you and I are by the same seducer injured. – Oh, if you knew how unutterably, how incomprehensibly I have been injured by him, you would almost forget his conduct towards yourself. – Do you know me? I am Orsina – the deluded forsaken Orsina – perhaps forsaken for your daughter. – But I do not mean to blame your daughter. – Soon she also will be forsaken – then another – another – and another. – Ha! [*As if in rapture.*] What a celestial thought! When all, who have been victims of his arts shall form a band – when we shall be converted into Demons – Furies – what transport will it be to tear him piecemeal, mangle his limbs, and wallowing through his entrails wrench from its seat the traitor's heart – that heart he promised to bestow on each of us, and gave to none. – What glorious revelry!

[*Enter* CLAUDIA.]

CLAUDIA: [*Looks round, and as soon as she espies her husband, flies to meet him.*] I was right. – Our protector, our deliverer! – Are you really here? Do I indeed behold you, Odoardo? Their whispers and their manner made me suppose it was the case. – What shall I say to you, if you as yet know nothing? – What shall I say to you if you know every thing? – But we are innocent. I am innocent. Your daughter is innocent.

ODOARDO: [*Who, on seeing his wife, has endeavoured to compose himself.*] 'Tis well. – Be calm, and answer me, [*To Orsina.*] – not that I doubt your information, madam – Is the count dead?

CLAUDIA: Alas, yes.

ODOARDO: Is it true that the prince spoke this morning to Emilia when at church?

CLAUDIA: It is; but if you knew how much she was alarmed – with what terror she rushed into the room where you had left me –

ORSINA: Now was my information false?

ODOARDO: [*With a revengeful smile.*] I would not that it were! For worlds I would not that it were!

ORSINA: Am I a lunatic?

ODOARDO: [*Wildly pacing the apartment.*] No – nor as yet am I.

CLAUDIA: You commanded me to be calm, and I obeyed – My dear husband, may I entreat –

ODOARDO: What do you mean? Am I not calm? – Who can be calmer than I am? [*Suppressing his fury.*] Does Emilia know that Appiani is no more?

CLAUDIA: She cannot know it, but I fear that she suspects it, because he does not appear.

ODOARDO: She weeps and shrieks, then –

CLAUDIA: No longer, You know her. She is the most timid, yet the most resolute of her sex – incapable of governing her first impressions; but after the least consideration calm and prepared for every thing. She keeps the prince at a distance – she speaks to him in a tone – Contrive, dear Odoardo, that we may depart immediately.

ODOARDO: I came on horseback hither. – What is to be done? – You, madam, will probably return to town?

ORSINA: Immediately.

ODOARDO: May I request you to take my wife with you?

ORSINA: That I will do with pleasure.

ODOARDO: Claudia, this is the Countess Orsina, my friend and benefactress.

Accompany her to town, and send our carriage hither instantly. Emilia must not return to Guastalla. She shall go with me.

CLAUDIA: But if – I am unwilling to leave her.

ODOARDO: Is not her father here? I shall be admitted at last. No objections! – Come, my lady. [*Apart to her.*] You shall hear from me. – Come, Claudia. [*Exeunt.*]

Act V

[SCENE *as before.*
Enter PRINCE *and* MARINELLI]

MARINELLI: From this window your highness may see him. – He is walking to and fro. Now he bends this way. He comes – No, he turns again. – He is still at variance with himself – but is much calmer than he was, or at least appears to be so. To us it is immaterial which is really the case. Baptist says that he desired his wife to send the carriage hither as soon as she reached town, for he came on horseback. Observe my words. When he appears before your highness, he will humbly return thanks for the gracious protection which you were pleased to afford his family, recommend himself and daughter to your further favour, quietly return to town, and with perfect submission await the further interest which your highness may think proper to take in the welfare of his child.

PRINCE: But should he not be so tame – and I know him too well to expect it – He may, perhaps, choke his suspicion, and suppress his indignation, but instead of taking Emilia to town, he may bury her in the country, or place her in some cloister beyond my dominions. – What can then be done?

MARINELLI: Love is ever fearful. – He will not –

PRINCE: But, if he were to do it, what would the death of the unfortunate count avail us?

MARINELLI: Why these side glances? The conqueror stalks forward, and heeds not whether friend or foe fall near him. – And should he even wish to proceed in the way that your fears predict – [*After some consideration.*] – I have it. Be assured the wish shall be the end of his success. I'll mar his plan. – But we must not lose sight of him. [*Walks again to the window.*] He had almost surprised us. – He comes. – Let us withdraw awhile, and you shall hear how I'll defeat the project which you fear.

PRINCE: [*In a threatening tone.*] But Marinelli –

MARINELLI: The most innocent thing in the world. [*Exeunt.*]

[*Enter* ODOARDO.]

ODOARDO: Still no one here! 'Tis well. They allow me time to become cool. Nothing is more contemptible than a hoary-headed man transported with a youth's ungovernable fury. I have often said this, yet I suffered myself to be hurried away – by whom? By a woman whom jealousy had driven to distraction. What has injured Virtue to do with the revenge of Vice? I have but to save the former. – And thy cause, my son – I could never weep – and will not learn it now. There is *another*, who will undertake thy cause. – Sufficient will it be for me that thy murderer does not enjoy the fruit of his transgression. – May this torment him more than even the crime itself, and when at length loathsome satiety shall drive him from one excess to another, may the recollection of having failed in this, poison the enjoyment of them all. In every dream may my Emilia appear to him, and at her side the murdered count – and when, in spite of this, he stretches forth his arms to seize the prize, may the derision and loud laughter of the damned sound in his ears, and wake him to be wretched.

[*Enter* MARINELLI.]

MARINELLI: We have been looking for you, Sir.

ODOARDO: Has my daughter been here?

MARINELLI: No – but the prince –

ODOARDO: I beg his pardon. I conducted the countess to her carriage.

MARINELLI: Well! And where is your lady?

ODOARDO: She accompanied the countess for the purpose of sending my carriage hither. I only request that the prince will have the goodness to let me stay with my daughter till it arrives.

MARINELLI: Why this ceremony? The prince would have conveyed both the ladies to town with the greatest pleasure.

ODOARDO: One of them would have been under the necessity of declining that honour.

MARINELLI: How so?

ODOARDO: My daughter shall not go to Guastalla again.

MARINELLI: Indeed! Why not?

ODOARDO: Count Appiani is dead.

MARINELLI: For that very reason –

ODOARDO: She shall go with me.

MARINELLI: With you!

ODOARDO: With me. – I tell you the count is dead. What therefore has she to do in Guastalla? She shall go with me.

MARINELLI: The future residence of the lady must certainly depend upon her father – but at present –

ODOARDO: Well? What?

MARINELLI: At present you must allow her to be conveyed to Guastalla.

ODOARDO: I must allow! and why?

MARINELLI: Why! Consider –

ODOARDO: [*Incensed.*] Consider! The matter needs no consideration. She must and shall go with me.

MARINELLI: We need have no contention on the subject, Sir. I may be mistaken. What I think necessary may not be so. – The prince is the best judge – he, therefore, will decide. I shall bring him to you. [*Exit.*]

ODOARDO: How! – Never! – Prescribe to me whither she shall go! – Withhold her from me! – Who will do this? – Who dares attempt it? – He, who dares here do any thing he pleases? – 'Tis well, 'tis well. – Then shall he see what I dare attempt, – Short-sighted voluptuary! I defy thee. He, who regards no law, is as independent as the prince, who is subject to no law. Come on, come on. – But what am I saying? My temper is again overpowering the dictates of my reason. What will not a courtier assert? Better would it have been, had I allowed him to proceed. He would have stated the pretext for conveying my daughter to Guastalla, and I could now have prepared myself to make a proper reply. – But can my reply be otherwise? – I hear footsteps. – I will be calm.

[*Enter* PRINCE *and* MARINELLI.]

PRINCE: My dear worthy Galotti, I hope you are well. Some accident must happen ere I can hope to see you – but I do not mean to reproach you.

ODOARDO: I have ever thought it wrong to force myself into the presence of my prince. He will send for those whom he wants. Even now I beg pardon –

PRINCE: Would that many, whom I know, possessed this modest pride! – But to the subject. You are, doubtless, eager to see your daughter. She is again alarmed on account of her mother's sudden departure. – And why should she have departed? I only waited till the terrors of your lovely daughter were removed, and then should have conveyed the ladies in triumph to Guastalla. Your arrival has diminished the pleasure of this triumph; but I will not entirely resign it.

ODOARDO: Your highness honours me too much. – Allow me to spare my unfortunate child the various mortifications, which friendship and enmity, compassion and malignity, prepare for her in town.

PRINCE: Of the sweet comforts, which the friendly and compassionate bestow, it would be cruelty to rob her; but against all the mortifications of enmity and malice, believe me, I will guard her, dear Galotti.

ODOARDO: Prince, the affection of a father makes him unwilling that others should participate his cares. I think I know what alone suits my daughter in her present situation. Retirement from the world – a cloister as soon as possible.

PRINCE: A cloister!

ODOARDO: Till then, let her weep under the protection of her father.

PRINCE: Shall so much beauty wither in a cloister? – Should one disappointment make us irreconcileable to the world? – But as you please. No one has a right to dictate to you. Take your daughter wherever you think proper, dear Galotti.

ODOARDO: [*To* MARINELLI.] Now, Sir?

MARINELLI: Nay, if you call upon me to speak –

ODOARDO: By no means, by no means.

PRINCE: What has happened between you two?

ODOARDO: Nothing whatever. We were only settling which of us had been deceived in your highness.

PRINCE: How so? – Speak, Marinelli.

MARINELLI: I am sorry to interfere with what your highness has adjusted, but friendship commands that I should make an appeal to you.

PRINCE: What friendship?

MARINELLI: Your highness knows how sincerely I was attached to Count Appiani – how our souls seemed to be interwoven –

ODOARDO: Does his highness know that? Then is he indeed the only one who knows it.

MARINELLI: Appointed his avenger by himself –

ODOARDO: You!

MARINELLI: Ask your lady. My name was the last word he uttered, and in such a tone – Oh may that dreadful tone sound in my ears for ever, if I do not exert every nerve to discover and to punish the offenders!

PRINCE: Rely upon my utmost aid.

ODOARDO: And upon my most fervent wishes. – All this is well. – But what further?

PRINCE: That I, too, want to know.

MARINELLI: It is suspected that the count was not attacked by robbers –

ODOARDO: [*With a sneer.*] Indeed!

MARINELLI: But that a rival hired assassins to dispatch him.

ODOARDO: [*With acrimony.*] Indeed! A rival!

MARINELLI: Exactly.

ODOARDO: Well then – Heaven's lightnings blast him!

MARINELLI: A rival – and a favoured rival too.

ODOARDO: How! Favoured! What say you?

MARINELLI: Nothing but what Fame reports.

ODOARDO: Favoured! Favoured by my daughter!

MARINELLI: That cannot be. Were you to say it I would contradict it. But, [*Turning to the* PRINCE.] though no prejudice, however well-grounded it may appear, can be of any weight in the scale of justice, yet it will, nevertheless, be absolutely necessary that the unfortunate lady should be examined.

PRINCE: True. – Undoubtedly.

MARINELLI: And where can this be done but in Guastalla?

PRINCE: There you are right, Marinelli, there you are right. – This alters the affair, dear Galotti. You yourself must perceive –

ODOARDO: Yes! I perceive – what I perceive. – Oh God! Oh God!

PRINCE: What now? What is the matter?

ODOARDO: I am only angry with myself for not having foreseen what I now perceive. – Well, then – she shall return to Guastalla. I will take her to her mother, and till she has been acquitted, after the most rigid examination, I myself will not leave Guastalla. – For who knows – [*With a smile of bitter irony.*] – who knows whether the court of justice may not think it necessary to examine me?

MARINELLI: It is very possible. In such cases justice rather does too much than too little. I therefore even fear –

PRINCE: What? What do you fear?

MARINELLI: That the mother and daughter will not at present be allowed access to each other!

ODOARDO: Not allowed access to each other!

MARINELLI: It will be necessary to keep them separate.

ODOARDO: To keep the mother and the daughter separate!

MARINELLI: The mother, the daughter, and the father. – The forms of the court absolutely enjoin this caution – and I assure your highness that it hurts me to be under the necessity of suggesting that Emilia ought, at all events, to be placed in proper custody.

ODOARDO: Proper custody! – Oh prince, prince! – But yes – of course, of course! – Right! In proper custody! – This is justice, no doubt. [*Hastily puts his hand into the pocket, in which he concealed the dagger.*]

PRINCE: [*In a soothing tone.*] Compose yourself, dear Galotti.

ODOARDO: [*Aside, drawing his hand, without the dagger, from his pocket.*] That was spoken by his guardian angel.

PRINCE: You are mistaken. You do not understand him. You think, perhaps, when you hear the word custody, of a prison and a dungeon.

ODOARDO: Let me think of them, and I shall be at ease.

PRINCE: Not a word respecting a prison, Marinelli. In this case the rigour of the law may easily be combined with the respect due to unblemished virtue. If Emilia must be placed in proper custody, I know the most proper situation for her – my chancellor's house. – No opposition, Marinelli. Thither I will myself convey her, and place her under the protection of a most worthy woman, who shall be answerable for her safety. – You go too far, Marinelli. you go too far, if you require more. – Of course, Galotti, you know my chancellor Grimaldi and his wife?

ODOARDO: Undoubtedly I do. I also know their amiable daughters. Who does not know them? [*To* MARINELLI.] No, Sir – do not consent to this. If my daughter must be confined, she ought to be confined in the deepest dungeon. Insist upon it, I beseech you. – Fool that I was to make any request. – Yes – the good Sibyl was right. "They, who, under certain circumstances, do not lose their intellects, have none to lose."

PRINCE: I do not understand you. Dear Galotti, what can I do more? Be satisfied, I beg. – Yes. She shall be conveyed to the chancellor's house – I myself will convey her thither, and if she be not there treated with the utmost respect, my word is of no value. You, Galotti, may act as you think proper with respect to yourself. You may follow us to Guastalla, or return to Sabionetta, as you please. – It would be ridiculous to dictate any conduct to you. – And now, farewel for the present, dear Galotti. – Come, Marinelli. It grows late.

ODOARDO: [*Who has been standing in deep meditation.*] How! May I not even see my daughter, then? – May I not even see her here? – I submit to everything – I approve of every thing. The chancellor's house is of course the sanctuary of virtue. Take her thither, I beseech your highness – no where but thither. – Yet I would willingly have some previous conversation with her. She is still ignorant of the count's death, and will be unable to discover why she is separated from her parents. That I may apprise her of the one, and prepare her for the other, in a proper manner – I must see her, prince, I must see her.

PRINCE: Come, then, with us.

ODOARDO: Surely the daughter can come to her father. Let us have a short conversation, without witnesses. – Send her hither, I beseech you.

PRINCE: That, too, shall be done. – Oh Galotti, if you would be my friend, my guide, my father – [*Exeunt* PRINCE *and* MARINELLI.]

ODOARDO: [*After a pause, during which his eyes follow the* PRINCE.] Why not? – Most willingly. – Ha! Ha! Ha! – [*Looks wildly round.*] Who laughed? – By the Almighty I believe it was myself. – Right! Right! – I will be merry. – The game is at an end. – Thus must it be, or thus. – But – [*Pauses*] how if she were in league with him? – How if this were the usual deception? – How if she were not worthy of that which I am about to do for her? – [*Pauses again.*] And what am I about to do for her? – Have I a heart to name it even to myself? – No. Scarcely dare I think of it. – Horrible! – I will go. I will not wait until she comes. [*Raises his eyes towards heaven.*] If she be innocent, let him who plunged her into this abyss, extricate her from it. He needs not my assistance. – I will away. [*As he is going he espies* EMILIA.] Ha! 'Tis too late. My assistance is required – demanded.

[*Enter* EMILIA.]

EMILIA: How! – You here, my father! – And you alone – without the count – without my mother! – So uneasy, too!

ODOARDO: And you so much at ease!

EMILIA: Why should I not be so, my father. Either all is lost, or nothing. The ability and the necessity to be at ease – are they not in reality the same?

ODOARDO: But what do you suppose to be the case?

EMILIA: That all is lost – therefore that we must be at ease, my father.

ODOARDO: And can you be at ease, because necessity requires it? – Who are you? – My daughter? – Then should your father be ashamed of you. – But let me hear. What mean you, when you say that all is lost? Is the death of Count Appiani all?

EMILIA: Ha! – Is it, then, true? – Alas! I read the horrid story in my mother's frantic looks. – Where is my mother?

ODOARDO: She is gone to town.

EMILIA: Oh, let us hasten after her – let us away. For if the count be dead – if he was doomed to die on that account – Ha! – Let us fly, let us fly, my father.

ODOARDO: Fly! – For what reason? – You are in the hands of the prince, and will remain in them.

EMILIA: Remain in them!

ODOARDO: And alone – without your mother – without me.

EMILIA: I remain alone in his hands! – Never, my father – or you are not my father. – I remain alone in his hands! – 'Tis well. Leave me, leave me. I will see who can detain me – who can compel me to remain. – What mortal dares attempt it?

ODOARDO: Is this your composure, Emilia?

EMILIA: What do you call composure? – To lay my hands in my lap, and patiently bear what I ought not to bear?

ODOARDO: Ha! – If such be thy sentiments, come to my arms, my daughter. I have ever said, that nature, when forming woman, wished to form her master-piece, and failed in only one respect. The clay she chose possessed too much tenuity. In every respect but this, man is inferior to woman. – Ha! – If this be thy composure, I recognize my daughter. Come into my arms. – Now mark me. Under the pretence of legal examination, the prince – the robber tears thee, – (Oh infernal villany!) tears thee from our arms, and places thee under the protection of Grimaldi.

EMILIA: Tears me from your arms! Grimaldi! – As if we ourselves had no will.

ODOARDO: So incensed was I that I was on the point of drawing forth this dagger, [*Produces it.*] and plunging it into the hearts of both the villains.

EMILIA: For heaven's sake, do not that, my father. This life is all that the bad can enjoy. – Give me, give me the dagger.

ODOARDO: Child, it is not a needle. – Recollect, Emilia, you too have but one life to lose.

EMILIA: And when I have once lost my innocence, is it not lost for ever?

ODOARDO: Your innocence is proof against all force.

EMILIA: But not against seduction. Force! What is that? Nothing. Seduction, my father, seduction is the only real force, by which my honour could be overcome. The blood that courses through my veins is warm. My mind is capable of feeling soft impressions. I cannot answer for myself, were I to be placed where you describe. Grimaldi's house is a house of revelry – I was there but for a single hour, under the protection of my mother – but that one hour created such a tumult in my soul, that all the rigid exercises of religion scarcely could quell it in whole weeks. Religion! And what religion? To avoid the snares which await me, thousands have sprung into the waves, and now are saints. – Give me the dagger.

ODOARDO: And didst thou know who armed me with this dagger? –

EMILIA: That matters not. An unknown friend is not the less a friend. Give me the dagger, I beseech you.

ODOARDO: And if I were – what then? There! [*He presents it – she seizes it with ardour, and is about to stab herself, when* ODOARDO *wrests it from her.*] Rash girl, forbear. This weapon ill befits thy hand.

EMILIA: As you will. – In former days there was a father, who, to save his daughter from disgrace and infamy, plunged the first deadly weapon which he saw into his daughter's heart – and thereby gave her life, a second time. – But all such deeds are past. – Such fathers are not to be found in these degenerate days.

ODOARDO: They are, they are, my daughter. [*Stabs her.*] – God of heaven! What have I done? [*Supports her in his arms.*]

EMILIA: Broken a rose before the storm had robbed it of its petals.[1] – Oh let me kiss this kind fatherly hand.

[*Enter* PRINCE *and* MARINELLI.]

PRINCE: Heavens! What means this? Is Emilia ill?

ODOARDO: No. Very well, very well.

PRINCE: [*Approaching her.*] Horror! What do I see?

MARINELLI: Damnation!

PRINCE: Cruel father, what have you done?

ODOARDO: 'Broken a rose, before the storm had robbed it of its petals.' – Said you not so, my daughter?

EMILIA: Not you, my father – I – I – myself –

ODOARDO: Emilia, quit not this world with a falshood on thy lips. 'Twas I, who gave the blow – I, thy unfortunate father.

EMILIA: My fa-ther – Oh! – [*Dies in his arms – he lays her gently on the floor.*]

ODOARDO: Farewel, sweet darling of my soul. – There, prince! – Does she still please you? Does she still rouse your appetite? – Look at her. There she lies weltering in her blood – that blood which cries for vengeance against you. [*After a pause.*] Doubtless you wait to see the end of this. You expect, perhaps, that I shall turn the steel against myself – but you are much mistaken. – There! [*Throws the dagger at his feet.*] There lies the blood-stained testimony of my crime. I go to deliver myself into the hands of justice. I go, and expect you to appear as my judge – then I shall expect you in another world, before the judge of all. [*Exit.*]

PRINCE: [*After a pause, during which he surveys the body with a look of horror and despair, turns to* MARINELLI.] Raise her from the earth. – How! – Dost thou hesitate? – Wretch! Villain! [*Tears the dagger from his grasp.*] No. Thy blood shall not be mixed with this. Go. Hide thyself for ever. – Begone, I say.

[*Exit* MARINELLI.]

Oh God! Oh God! – Is it not enough that monarchs are men? Must demons in disguise become their friends?

1. In the original the translator uses 'leaves'.

Bibliography

Eighteenth-century English Theatre

Avery, E. and Scouten, A. (eds), *The London Stage*, parts 2–4 (Carbondale: University of Illinois Press, 1960–2).

Leacroft, Richard, *The Development of the English Playhouse* (Ithaca, NY: Cornell University Press, 1973).

Leacroft, Richard and Leacroft, Helen, *Theatre and Playhouse* (London: Methuen, 1984).

Mullin, Donald C., *The Development of the Playhouse* (Berkeley: University of California Press, 1970).

Nicoll, A., *The Garrick Stage* (Manchester: Manchester University Press, 1980).

Price, Cecil, *Theatre in the Age of Garrick* (Oxford: Basil Blackwell, 1973).

Richards, Kenneth and Thomson, Peter (eds), *The Eighteenth-century English Stage* (London: Methuen, 1972).

Thomas, David (ed.), *Theatre in Europe: A Documentary History. Restoration and Georgian England, 1660–1788* (Cambridge: Cambridge University Press, 1989).

Sheridan and Goldsmith

Bingham, M., *Sheridan: The Track of a Comet* (London: Allen & Unwin, 1972).

Ginger, J., *The Notable Man: The Life and Times of Oliver Goldsmith* (London: Hamilton, 1977).

Loftis, J., *Sheridan and the Drama of Georgian England* (Oxford: Oxford University Press, 1976).

Morwood, J., *The Life and Works of Richard Brinsley Sheridan* (Edinburgh: Scottish Academic Press, 1985).

Morwood J., and Crane, D. (eds), *Sheridan Studies* (Cambridge: Cambridge University Press, 1995).

Nicoll, A., *A History of English Drama 1660–1900*, vol. III (Cambridge: Cambridge University Press, 1952).

Rousseau G. S. (ed.), *Goldsmith: The Critical Heritage* (London: Routledge & Kegan Paul, 1974).

Worth, Katharine, *Sheridan and Goldsmith* (London: Macmillan, 1992).

Eighteenth-century French Theatre

Arnott, Peter, *An Introduction to the French Theatre* (London: Macmillan, 1977).
Lancaster, H. C., *The Comédie Française, 1701–1774: Plays, Actors, Spectators, Finances* (Philadelphia: The American Philosophical Society, 1951).
Lough, John, *Paris Theatre Audiences in the Seventeenth and Eighteenth Centuries* (Oxford: Oxford University Press, 1957).

Beaumarchais

Cox, Cynthia, *The Real Figaro* (London: Longmans, 1962).
Greaves, R., *Beaumarchais: The Man who was Figaro* (New York: Crowell, 1977). A translation of F. Grendel, *Beaumarchais ou la Calomnie* (Paris: Flammarion, 1973).
Howarth, W. D., *Beaumarchais and the Theatre* (London: Routledge, 1995).

Eighteenth-century German Theatre

Bruford, W. H., *Theatre, Drama and Audience in Goethe's Germany* (London: Routledge & Kegan Paul, 1950).
Carlson, M., *Goethe and the Weimar Theatre* (Ithaca, NY: Cornell University Press, 1978).
Patterson, Michael, *The First German Theatre* (London: Routledge, 1990).
Prudhoe, John, *The Theatre of Goethe and Schiller* (Oxford: Basil Blackwell, 1973).

Lessing

Garland, H. B., *Lessing: The Founder of Modern German Literature* (Cambridge: Bowes & Bowes, 1949).
Lamport, F. J., *Lessing and the Drama* (Oxford: Clarendon Press, 1981).
Lamport, F. J., *German Classical Drama: Theatre, Humanity and Nation 1750–1870* (Cambridge: Cambridge University Press, 1990).
Robertson, J. G., *Lessing's Dramatic Theory* (Cambridge: Cambridge University Press, 1939).